RELIGIOUS EXPERIENCE and PROCESS THEOLOGY

PAULIST PRESS / New York, N.Y. / Paramus, N.J.

edited by
HARRY JAMES CARGAS
and BERNARD LEE

RELIGIOUS EXPERIENCE AND PROCESS THEOLOGY

the pastoral implications of a major modern movement

Cover Design: Tim McKeen

Library of Congress
Catalog Card Number: 75-46065

ISBN: 0-8091-1934-x

Published by Paulist Press
Editorial Office: 1865 Broadway, N.Y., N.Y. 10023
Business Office: 400 Sette Drive, Paramus, N.J. 07652

Printed and bound in the
United States of America.

Acknowledgments

"Beyond Enlightened Self-Interest" by Charles Hartshorne. Reprinted from *Ethics*, an
International Journal of Social, Political, and Legal Philosophy, Vol. 84, No. 3, April
1974. © 1974 by The University of Chicago. All rights reserved.

S-I-ZE by Bernard M. Loomer. Reprinted from *Criterion*, Spring, 1974, a publication
of the Divinity School of the University of Chicago, with permission of the University
of Chicago Press.

"Process Theology: A Pragmatic Version" by Eugene Fontinell from *Toward a Reconstruction of Religion* by Eugene Fontinell. Copyright © 1970 by Eugene Fontinell. Reprinted by permission of Doubleday & Company, Inc.

Oklahoma © 1943 by Williamson Music Inc. Copyright renewed. All rights reserved.
Used by permission of Williamson Music, Inc.

"Pisces" by R.S. Thomas from *Collected Poems* by R.S. Thomas, reprinted with permission of St. Martin's Press, Inc., Macmillan & Co., Ltd.

Excerpt from *Poems 1923-1954* by e. e. cummings, 1954. Reprinted with permission of
Harcourt Brace Javonovich, Inc.

Contents

PREFACE I.. ix

Bernard Lee

PREFACE II: COPERNICUS AND I.................................. xi

Harry James Cargas

PART ONE

PERSPECTIVES

1. PROCESS THEOLOGY: A WHITEHEADIAN VERSION.............. 3

Norman Pittenger

2. PROCESS THEOLOGY: A PRAGMATIC VERSION.................... 23

Eugene Fontinell

3. WHAT IS A CHRISTIAN THEOLOGY?................................. 41

Delwin Brown

4. WHAT WE NEED IS INDOOR PLUMBING *OR*, WHITEHEADIAN STYLE AND THE SEARCH FOR A NEW SCIENTIFIC ORDER..... 53

Richard H. Overman

5. S-I-Z-E IS THE MEASURE... 69

Bernard M. Loomer

PART TWO

THE CHRISTIAN GOD: HIS CHRIST AND HIS SPIRIT

6. THE POWER OF GOD AND THE CHRIST 79

Lewis S. Ford

7. THE CHRISTOLOGICAL SYMBOL OF GOD'S SUFFERING......... 93
  John Robert Baker

8. HOLY SPIRIT: COMPASSION AND REVERENCE FOR BEING 107
  David Griffin

9. THE HOLY GHOST IS DEAD—THE HOLY SPIRIT LIVES 121
  G. Palmer Pardington III

PART THREE
CHRISTIAN CONCERNS

THE CHURCH
10. TOWARD A PROCESS THEOLOGY OF THE CHURCH 137
  Joseph M. Hallman

11. MODES OF PRESENCE AND THE COMMUNION OF SAINTS...... 147
  J. Gerald Janzen

HOPE
12. SEX: BIOLOGICAL BASES OF HOPE 175
  William A. Beardslee

13. THE MEANING OF CHRISTIAN HOPE................................. 195
  Schubert M. Ogden

GRACE
14. GOD'S GIFT AND MAN'S RESPONSE: TOWARD A
  WHITEHEADIAN PERSPECTIVE..215
  David A. Fleming

FAITH AND BELIEF
15. RELIGIOUS TRUTH: A PRAGMATIC RECONSTRUCTION 231
  Eugene Fontinell

REVELATION AND ECUMENISM
16. CAN THE TRUE GOD BE THE GOD OF ONE BOOK?...............263

Jan Van der Veken

EUCHARIST
17. THE LORD'S SUPPER 283

Bernard Lee

ETHICS AND HUMAN EXPERIENCE
18. BEYOND ENLIGHTENED SELF-INTEREST 301

Charles Hartshorne

19. DIMENSIONS OF FREEDOM 323

Bernard M. Loomer

20. THE PRICE OF GREATNESS ("FORD TO NIXON")..................341

Bernard M. Loomer

SPIRITUALITY
21. SPIRITUAL DISCERNMENT IN A WHITEHEADIAN
PERSPECTIVE 349

John B. Cobb, Jr.

22. THE APPETITE OF GOD.......................................369

Bernard Lee

COMMITMENT
23. IDENTITY AND COMMITMENT 387

Robert E. Doud

DEATH AND DYING
24. A PASTORAL ON DEATH AND IMMORTALITY 399

Robert B. Mellert

PRAYER

25. GOD AS POET AND PERSONS AT PRAYER 411

Robert M. Cooper

26. OUR PRAYERS AS GOD'S PASSIONS 429

Lewis S. Ford

Preface I

Process theology is increasingly among the important contemporary attempts to present the New Testament claim to modern man. It strives to do this in a way that is faithful both to the heart and mind of the Jesus-event, and to the deepest instincts of contemporaneity. At this point, it seems to me that there are three kinds of homework necessary for carrying the movement further.

The first of these is the development of a biblical theology. Whiteheadian thought needs a Bultmann. There have been some significant explorations of such a theology. There has been excellent dialogue between the Society for Process Studies and the Society of Biblical Literature. But there is not yet a comprehensive, exegetical *process theology of the New Testament*.

The second need is also for a comprehensive statement; in this case a *systematic theology*. There has been a steady erosion of the "coherent story" that provided some form of cohesiveness in Western Christianity. Most recent attempts to construct a new story have been historical-existential. Process thought offers a cosmological story, and it is rooted in the scientific world that shapes modern consciousness so extensively. It is time for the large undertaking! Process theology, if faithful to basic process convictions, should be "the endeavor to frame a coherent, logical, necessary system of general ideas in terms of which every element of our experience can be interpreted" (Whitehead, *Process and Reality*, p. 4).

The third need is for much more attention to the pastoral implications of process theology. Hopefully, this volume contributes to that need. "The elucidation of immediate experience," says Whitehead, "is the sole justification for any thought" (*ibid.*, p. 6). Process thought *owes* that elucidation to human experience, and process theology *owes* that elucidation to Christian experience, or there is not that "sole justification." And just as earnestly, theology needs to check itself out with on-the-line experience.

The pastoral work affords both verification and new empirical data. Pastoral experience should keep theology on its toes (only too often they sit at opposite corners and stare).

A preface, I surmise, ought to say something about the whence and the wherefore of a book. The preceding reflections were a comment upon the "wherefore." I would also like to say something about the "whence."

That goes back to the Process Theology Institute in the summer of 1973, sponsored by Maryville College and the Marianist Apostolic Center in St. Louis. The professors during those six weeks were Eugene Fontinell, Charles Hartshorne, Bernard Lee, Bernard Loomer, Norman Pittenger, and Piet Schoonenberg. It was a rare experience in a community of inquiry, that is to say, both the quality of community and the quality of inquiry were exceptional. Originally Harry Cargas and I planned to edit and publish papers, lectures, and discussions from the Institute. But as we spoke about that project, and even began work on it, we felt more and more the need to add to the broader accessibility of process theology. We felt we wanted to do that through some less-technical presentations, and through materials more directly concerned with on-the-line issues. (The more technical discussions are being carried on adequately in scholarly meetings and journals, most notably in the journal *Process Studies*.)

We also felt that the project should be carried on by those who have been at work in the process theology enterprise. If the material was to be little encumbered (as little as possible) by technical language, it also had to be technically accurate. We wanted to highlight pastoral implications by treating issues and topics that are close to Christian experience (such as freedom, commitment, prayer, death), and close to symbols that are familiar to Christian thought (hope, God, Christ, the Spirit). Those were the guidelines that we indicated in extending invitations to many of those engaged in process theology, to address themselves to pastoral concerns.

The volume that has emerged is somewhat heterogeneous in both style and topic. That is probably to be expected in a volume that is a collection. But this great variety reflects a present characteristic of process theology, namely, that "process theology" does not have a univocal meaning. It has been greatly shaped by the several Christian historical traditions that have taken it up.

Somewhat artificially (but somewhat really), there are two trends in process theology: one that is highly empirical in its flavor, the other highly rationalistic. This contrast is very evident, for example, in the two chapters on ethical concerns, Bernard Loomer of the first bent and Charles Hartshorne of the latter bent. The contrast is equally evident in a Eugene Fontinell (empirical) and a Ian Van der Veken (rational), both represented in this volume.

In putting this collection together we had no explicit ecumenical intentions. But there is clearly an ecumenical bonus in process theology, for both Protestant and Catholic traditions are reflecting on Christian experience out of a same world view. Roman Catholic theology is more of a come-lately to process thought, whereas Protestant theologians have been at it some thirty years. The ecumenical possibilities look good.

As a last word of preface, for both myself and my friend and colleague, Harry Cargas (whom I asked to add an autobiographical prefatory statement), I want to offer some lively appreciation to those who have supported and encouraged this volume —and that means above all to those whose work and thought appear in these pages.

Bernard Lee
April 1975

Preface II
Copernicus and I

Ordinarily, the name of the junior high school one had attended is of minimal interest. But the fact that mine was called Copernicus has some bearing on my introduction to process theology. What follows, then, is not so much a theological approach but an autobiographical one: process theology has given my sense of commitment as a Christian the kind of grounding I intuitively felt was missing, but the absence of which I could not somehow explain to myself. What process thought has done for me, basically, is return to me a true sense of my own true worth.

Copernicus, after all, started me in the other direction. Actually it was probably Nicholas of Cusa who first substantially challenged Ptolemy's theory that the earth was the center of the universe. (I know *now* that Aristarchus in the third century B.C. believed in a heliocentric world, but that did little for *me* at 14!) Then Leonardo seems to have taught that the earth rotates on its axis, denying that the sun actually revolves around our planet. But it was the Polish priest Nicholas Copernicus, whose text *On the Revolutions of the Heavenly Spheres* was published in 1543, who really started to diminish my importance in my own eyes. Copernicus had the good fortune to die just as his work was published, so he never had to recant his truth via inquisitional investigations. Not so lucky was Galileo who provided the most convincing astronomical evidence for what has become known as the Copernican Revolution. My exalted position as the focus of creation suffered immensely. Nor was this the only abbreviation that I suffered. Darwin hurt me terrifically when he proved a certain kind of evolution. Giambattista Vico's cycle theory of history took its toll, as did Oswald Spengler's idea that the West was in decline. Einstein's insights into relativity were hardly of comfort value. Then there were two world wars, including a holocaust perpetrated by "Christians," and atomic bombs—particularly at Nagasaki; no matter how anyone tries to justify Hiroshima, no one has any rationale about the second bomb. These and the liberation needs had brought me to a terrible realization. Not only have I not been the center of the universe for some four centuries, I may be quite the opposite—the lowest form of human life. In some circles I suspect there is no person, hierarchically speaking, beneath a white, U.S., male, Christian. One has only to consider the crimes against humanity attributed to people of those four categories to comprehend my fears, my diminishment.

Frankly, a restoration has begun and, personally, process thought is responsible for the image of my self-rehabilitation. I can honestly agree with William Lynch who says in *Images of Faith* that "history is alive and growing. It needs me as much as I need it. There is a back and forth between me and history."[1]

I suppose the breakthrough came with my first reading of Teilhard de Chardin, particularly *The Phenomenon of Man*. Then, to select the major figures, came the writings of Leslie

Dewart[2] who dared to say that our notions of Christianity were tied up with our understanding of a culture. Next came Eugene Fontinell and his incredibly overlooked book, *Toward a Reconstruction of Religion*. He agrees with Dewart by noting how closely God in Christian history is bound up with Greek metaphysics.[3] Nikos Kazantzakis, that master portrayer of the process, the journey, the quest, in all of his works, particularly *The Odyssey: A Modern Sequel*, *Saviors of God*, and *Report to Greco*, showed me something of great value in the struggle to be more than Sisyphus, at the same time indicating the value of my place in history, of my duty to carry my fathers forward rather than to wallow in the self-indulgent pity of my lowliness. For this I bless Kazantzakis, a Greek like my own father. Karl Rahner who uses the term "self-creation" made an impression on me too. "Man is consciously and deliberately changing himself."[4] That really is only a step from the position I have now been able to formulate regarding my relationship with God. I do firmly believe in renewing the face of the earth,[5] in the value of my participating in the ongoing creation.

Perhaps the final, synthesizing element in my becoming process oriented was the result of a six-week process conference held at the Marianist Apostolic Center in Eureka, Missouri, during the summer of 1973. I was unable to attend most of the meetings, but my wife Millie went, and happily brought the meetings home with her each night. Father Ralph Dyer also gave me the tapes of the sessions and I became confirmed in process thought. In fact it was at this conference that I met Bernard Lee and where he suggested to me we work on this book.

The above has been autobiographical and is written at the risk of a "who cares" response. From a certain viewpoint, I hardly care myself. Yet Bernie Lee and I thought that it might be of some interest to have a rather personal statement in this book that would, possibly, exemplify the route a number of people may have taken, consciously or not, to arrive at process thought.

But, of course, process thought *is* a process and not a goal. And I wish to discuss this idea of the journey, briefly.

The person's ultimate goal cannot be known. Nevertheless *a goal* can be acknowledged without implying its strict definition. The woman or man who strives to reach that end, however mysterious it may be, as fully human as possible, is the courageous adventurer who is life oriented. I suspect this person would more closely identify with a Western tradition of mysticism, a tradition that recognizes the multiple and attempts to organize it into a unity. This is opposed to a more death-oriented view—an outlook that is basically Eastern; that says that the multiple, the material is evil and is to be shunned and somehow unity is to be arrived at that way. For these latter, the journey seems all, and here I think, we see the shortcomings in Kazantzakis, Camus, and the other existentialists. The Odysseus who travels his adventures *to get home* (whatever that goal symbolizes) is different from the Odysseus whose only purpose is to glory in the travel.

Indeed, the answers change; the questions are eternal. But questions do imply answers. And perhaps the concept of *parousia* is the concept of Answer. Maybe, then, all questions will be meaningless. Maybe.

Right now, however, I connect with Bernard Lee's sentence from another book of his, *The Becoming of the Church:* "God too must really change if his reality is to respect the nature of all reality as modern man tends to understand it. God too would become."[6] As Whitehead has written, "There is no entity, not even God, 'which requires nothing but itself in order to exist.' "[7] And for me Teilhard has canonized this position in *The Divine Milieu:* "Owing to the interrelation between matter, soul and Christ . . . with each one of our *works*, we labor—in individual separation, but no less really—to build the Pleroma; that is to say, we bring to Christ a little fulfillment."[8]

Christianity lives. It evolves. What we are involved in, I am convinced, is what Fontinell has urged and recognized: a reconstruction rather than a revolution. We may indeed envision a world that is being recreated, a personal-ness that is being recreated, and in fact we may speak of participating in the creation of God.

If that does not restore to me some sense of worth that Cusa, Copernicus, Darwin, the astronauts, *et al.*, seem to have stripped me of, clearly nothing can. Fontinell put it as succinctly as anyone: "In a very real sense God needs men, not to imitate or glorify him, but to join him and share with him in the undertaking traditionally called *creation* but more accurately described as *creating*." Jesuit author William Lynch sees it beautifully from another point of view: ". . . if the action of God in history produces no history in God, if all the sorrow of this world does not produce an affection within an all-perfect God, if nothing we do can add to the fullness of Being, then we are dealing with a God who satisfies the needs of a very distinctive rationality but cannot be said to satisfy the needs of biblical reality or human feeling."[9]

Satisfying as all of this tends to be, I cannot know where it is taking me. But that it is taking me *somewhere* I cannot doubt. Lynch insists that there is some intensely important way in which God remains the same.[10] My readings of Mircea Eliade and Joseph Campbell would support this.[11] How this is true I cannot now say.

What I can know, however, is that I have moved to a different point of appreciation regarding the honoree of Copernicus Junior High in Hamtramck, Michigan. It is true that the initial impact of his popularization of a non-earth-centered conception of my world caused significant diminishment in my perception of who I am. But now that I have had over four centuries to consider what Copernicus fully means to me, I consider his an important step in my freedom, in my release from a suffocating, claustrophobic, prison-like existence where true interaction was not considered—where I was as center, receiver only—to the responsible, duty-filled liberty that process thought epitomizes so well.

Indeed, no final doctrine of God can be formulated that will be forever valid. I agree with Gene Fontinell when he says further that in a culture "in which growth, creative novelty, development and process are viewed as the most significant traits of reality, it would seem that the symbol of a 'processive God' is more meaningful." But, to complete this autobiographical essay on a firmly autobiographical note, I would like to flip that coin to its reverse and say that there is mutual interaction even on that cultural level —that illumination from an understanding of a "processive God" should also help create a more meaningful, nonstagnating culture. Then, perhaps fully, I will be able to *know*, because others too will come to know, that white, male, U.S., Christian, Harry James Cargas is not the lowest of the low but instead, by virtue of my processive, I-Thou relationship with God, truly a significant creature of God. And I believe, ultimately, that is how the symbol of the Incarnation is meant to be understood.

Harry James Cargas

NOTES

1. P. 110.

2. See particularly *The Future of Belief* (New York, 1968) and *The Foundations of Belief* (New York, 1969).

3. P. 22.

4. *Theology Digest* (February, 1968), p. 58.

5. Cf. the book by that title on which I collaborated with the late Dr. Thomas P. Neill of St. Louis University (1968).

6. P. 15.

7. *Religion in the Making* (New York, 1960), p. 104.

8. P. 181.

9. *Images of Faith* (Notre Dame, 1973), p. 150.

10. *Ibid.*, p. 152.

11. Fontinell, p. 196.

PART ONE

PERSPECTIVES

Norman Pittenger
Eugene Fontinell
Delwin Brown
Richard H. Overman
Bernard M. Loomer

1 Process Theology: A Whiteheadian Version

NORMAN PITTENGER

Norman Pittenger surely belongs in a volume dedicated to bringing out the pastoral implications of process theology. Much of his long and productive career has been and is concerned with increasing the credibility, the intelligibility, and the desirability of process interpretations of Christian experience. In this chapter, he indicates five of the general characteristics of process modes of thought. And then he demonstrates what's at stake in process interpretations by briefly exploring four important areas of concern: the nature of human nature, human sexuality, Christian community, and eucharistic life. It is Professor Pittenger's concern to see to it that Love (not being, not process) operates as the *central* symbol in Christian theology and Christian life. But it is his strong conviction that process thought focuses strongly on God as the Cosmic Lover.

Norman Pittenger is senior resident at King's College, Cambridge University, England, and a member of the Faculty of Divinity in that University. Of American-Canadian descent, he was educated at Oxford and in New York, and for thirty-three years was on the faculty of the General Theological Seminary in New York. He is a former president of the American Theological Society and past chairman of the Theological Commission of the World Council of Churches. He is the author of some sixty books, many of which deal with the various aspects of process theology, including: The Word Incarnate, Process Thought and Christian Faith, God's Way with Men, The Christian Church as Social Process,

3

Christology Reconsidered, Making Sexuality Human, *and* The Holy Spirit. *Along with Bernard Meland, Daniel Day Williams, and Bernard Loomer, Norman Pittenger was one of the early theologians to employ a process conceptuality for Christian faith.*

To some readers well instructed in the technical details of the process conceptuality, what follows may well seem fragmentary—at best suggestive, at worst only sketchy. Yet I do not apologize, since what is being presented in this essay is a series of serious comments about what I have called "implications and applications of process theology"; and I might have added, "as this has relevance for significant aspects of Christian faith and practice."

Furthermore, I must assume that elsewhere in this book there is a detailed statement of the basic positions taken in the process conceptuality. But it will be well if I put down, very briefly, what I take to be its main emphases; and I shall do this under five heads.

First, everything—literally *everything*—about which we have experience or knowledge can be subsumed under the general description of event or energy-event. We have to do, not with substances or things, but with events, occasions, occurrences, happenings—what Whitehead called the "actual entities" that are (to use a very misleading, because a "thing," word) the "building-blocks" out of which everything is made. This is true of the natural order as studied by the physicist; it is equally true of those areas of creation investigated by the so-called "life-sciences" such as biology and its relations. But it is also true at the level of human experience, with its psychology and sociology as well as its physiology. And it is true of God, too, for in process thought God is not conceived to be an essence, not even *esse a se subsistens* (certainly in the first place, although there *may* be a sense in which the term can be used), *ens realissimum*, or "being itself." Rather, he is taken to be a dynamic event or series of events himself (since, as we shall see, we may use a personal pronoun for the divine event or series of events) as living and as much a "becoming" as anything else—indeed more so, since he is the "eminent case" of that which is taken to be the basic metaphysical principle in the entire cosmos.

Second, since all is seen as event or energy-event, all is at the same time in process. We have to do with no inert things, with no "*fixed* entities"; we have to do, rather, with a movement or direction or routing in which all is "coming to be" or "becoming," toward an end or goal that will be the realization of potentiality or (if the "wrong" decisions are taken at particular instants along the route) the denial of such actualization and hence a failure in realizing potentialities. Again this is as true of the physical world as it is of living matter (as we call it); it is true of man in his historical existence; and it is true of God who is "becoming," not more divine (since he is always the supreme and worshipful one), but in that he is more fully realizing his divine "reality" in relationship to the cosmos in which he is unfailingly at work and with which he identifies himself intimately and unceasingly.

Third, everything is related to everything else in the world as process thought understands it. By a process of mutual "prehension," in which entities grasp and are grasped by their fellows, a societal situation is established. The prehension is not simultaneous, since there is always a "time-lag" (however minimal, a matter of tenths of seconds, perhaps) between expression and apprehension or grasping of what is expressed; nonetheless, there is this constant movement of give-and-take, outgoing and receiving, participation, or interrelationship. Even of God this is true, and he is not simply the chief (although not the *only*) causative agency; he is also the chief recipient of all that happens in the created order. The whole world is knit together "in one bundle," as an Old Testament phrase puts it. Nowhere is this so obvious as in human existence, but it is true of anything and everything, divine and human.

Fourth, in such a world there is both freedom and responsibility. Whitehead is reported to have characterized "reality" in this way: "It matters and it has consequences." *It matters*: so everything is in one way or another *important* or has "value" or "meaning," not merely in its being what it is on the way to being, but also in its capacity for decision. In man this is some, but not all, of the time a business of consciously made choice among relevant possibilities; this or that given possibility is taken, negatively or positively, as a way to such fulfillment as will realize the aim initially given to each entity or series of entities. Such decision is not conscious at other levels (as, say, in a quantum of energy) but it is a genuine *decision* nevertheless—that is, a "cutting off" of some possibilities by the very fact of the opting for another or for others; and the word "decision" comes from the Latin *decidere*, which means "cutting off." Not only is there this freedom (within such limits as permit contrast but not irremediable conflict, cosmos but not chaos); there is also the significant point of consequences. *It has consequences*: by decisions that are taken and implemented, things are altered in the succeeding moments or the subsequent events in the creative advance. And this involves responsibility, certainly at the level of human experience but in appropriate fashion and with the necessary modifications in extent and content elsewhere as well.

Fifth and finally, the most powerful "thing" in the world is persuasion or love, tenderness or gracious concern. At the subpersonal levels this means growing-together in mutuality: it is the movement in "amorization" about which Teilhard de Chardin wrote. At the human level this means actual participation or relationship in mutuality, with the self-giving and the gracious willingness to receive which at its best is known when two persons can say sincerely and wholeheartedly, "We love each other." Obviously it *seems* that coercion or sheer force is the strong power in the world; but the insight of the race's great seers and prophets, saints and poets, coincides with the intuition expressed by Whitehead when he spoke of the inexhaustible, indefatigable, indefeasible, and utterly faithful activity of love. Man himself is becoming human through the decisions taken in response to lures offered; and to become human *is* to move "toward the image of God" who is Love—or better, "the Cosmic Lover" whose love "moves the sun and the other stars. The creation is nothing other than a great love story, in which the chief causative and receiving agency whom we name God is luring, attracting, enticing, inviting, soliciting, and (persuasively but not coercively) demanding a response of love from the creatures and more especially from the human creatures with whom, for whom, in whom, and by whom he works in the world—as well as working elsewhere, of course.

So much for a summary of the main points. We may now turn to some of the implications and applications of this position, so far as the chief emphases of Christian faith are concerned. I propose to consider the following: (1) the nature of human nature; (2) human sexuality; (3) the Christian community we know as the Church; (4) eucharistic life, both in respect to the central Christian sacrament and also in respect to the way in which "life in Christ" is everywhere and always eucharistic. If there were time and space, we might also see how process thinking illuminates the biblical picture of God himself as the living, loving, faithful one; the significance of the person and work of Jesus Christ in whom that Cosmic Lover is "enmanned" in focal and decisive fashion; the way in which Atonement or "at-one-ment" is established for, and shared with, men in their lovelessness (which is their "lostness" or alienation and estrangement); and the destiny of men to become genuine participants in the "consequent" nature of God (i.e., God as affected by the world) and hence sharers in what the Christian tradition calls the *communio sanctorum*. I have written of these other matters elsewhere, however, and I refer the reader to the following books, if he is interested in pursuing the subjects: *The Christian Church as Social Process* (Westminster, 1972); *Process-Thought and Christian Faith* (Macmillan, 1968); *The 'Last Things' in a Process Perspective* (Epworth Press, London, 1970), *God's Way with Men* (Judson Press, 1969); *God in Process* (SCM Press, London, 1967). And for a treatment of the "problem of evil" in connection with process theology, *Goodness Distorted* (Mowbrays, London, 1970); *Christology Reconsidered* (SCM Press, London, new edition, 1973).

I
THE NATURE OF HUMAN NATURE

We have already noted that man is a "becoming": to be human *is* to be "becoming" man. Despite the long tradition in which human nature has been defined in static (or at least, morphological) terms, such as "an individual substance of a rational nature," there is much more significance in our laying stress on man as a dynamic movement or a "routing" toward the fulfillment of potentiality such that his human possibilities, provided as he "comes into existence," are realized. After all, as we can easily see, most of the traditional definitions, like the one cited from St. Thomas (who derived it from Boethius), miss out on one very obvious fact—namely, that man is a living and dynamic creature, who cannot adequately be described simply in terms of some cross section of the process at a given moment along his routing.

Human nature is a strangely complex body-mind affair, in which the physiological aspect (itself grounded in the so-called "material" world, but in that world as "*living*" matter) is quite as important as the mental aspect. As Gabriel Marcel has taught us, man does not *have* a body: he *is* a body. Likewise, he does not have a mind: he is a mind, which is to say that he possesses the capacity for some measure of ratiocination, logical thought, intellectual activity. But he is also an emotional thrust or drive or desire, as well as a conational or striving creature. And he is all these in greater or less degree of integration. His fulfillment would be the achievement of such complete integration that all aspects or elements are held together in a rich but complex unity, with his dominant aim or purpose as human governing the totality.

But what *is* that "dominant aim or purpose," toward which he is moving if he is on the "right" line or development or away from which he is moving if he is on the "wrong" line? I should answer simply: man is purposed to become a lover, living in richest mutuality with others in and under and with the cosmic Love which is God himself. Thus the meaning of being human is to be in movement toward shared love, reflecting and expressing the divine Love but doing this in a finite and creaturely fashion.

Man is not only psychosomatic in nature; he is also societal. To speak of man *is* to speak of his belonging; and we might say that he is both a "becoming" *and* a "belonging." If he may be called personal or a self, as we shall indicate in a moment, he must at the same time be described as social; indeed, personality and sociality are two sides of the same coin. Even St. Thomas urged that a man is more than merely an individual, or one instance of the class *man*; he is also personal, which for the Angelic Doctor implied social relationships as also constitutive of what is meant by our manhood. Like everything else in the cosmos, but in a sense special to himself, man is in relationship with others of his species; he is also in relationship to the natural order from which he emerges and of which, in a very real sense, he is a part; and he is related to the divine Agency, toward whose image he is intended to move and by whom he is continually sustained and preserved.

It is precisely in this sociality of human nature that we find the "consequences" that attach to all human decisions, made in such freedom as radically marks him despite the limits which are set to that freedom by the necessary condition of order, not disorder, and contrast but not disastrous and destructive conflict. Yet in that freedom, man can and does make "wrong" choices: that is, he prefers to opt for what will *not* be widely shared and shareable and hence will damage both his own movement toward loving and the common good to which he is meant to contribute. This is his *sin*. Sin is not a violation of supposedly *ab extra* commandments; to think in that way would be a return to ideas that are pre-Christian, as well as a refusal to see that the whole point of moral decision is to bring man to move forward along the lines that will "make him and keep him human" (to use Paul Lehmann's splendid phrasing of "God's purpose for man," found in his *Ethics in a Christian Context*). By such decisions, made for falsely self-centered objectives and to secure satisfactions that do not contribute to the common good of the race and to the creative advance of the cosmos under God's love, man has put himself in a position of alienation or estrangement from his intended destiny. Hence his situation as "a sinner," from which the cosmic Lover "saves" him by establishing the conditions in which, in the future decisions man makes and in the circumstances that he may accept, genuine fulfillment (in accord with the purpose of his existence) may be given him.

Man, then, is a routing of events or occasions, in which past occurrences provide the material for present decisions toward future fulfillment. His identity as a man is given in this rich complexity of the past as remembered (both consciously and unconsciously, but also viscerally or in his very genes, as we may say, as well as in the racial inheritance into which he is born and in which he participates by virtue of his being a man at all); his present relationships enjoyed either negatively or positively as he makes his decisions for or against relevant possibilities as these are offered to him; and the future goal or "subjective aim" of realized manhood that lures him on and to which he may, or may not, respond. What is special about man is that this is a *consciously known* identity; man knows himself to be "a self." Somewhere along the evolutionary line, there emerged a kind of awareness in which past, present, and future could be held together with that sort of conscious apprehension that makes it possible to speak of an "I" and a "thou," as well as a "we."

In another place (my essay on "Selfhood in a Process Perspective," in the forthcoming *festschrift* for Peter Bertocci, to appear in due course), I have urged that such a view of selfhood delivers us from the impossible notion of a "substantial self" which is, so to say, intruded into the process from outside. This conception, reminiscent more of certain aspects of Greek thought than of biblical ideas, has wrought havoc in much Christian theology. It has enabled men to speak of "the soul" as if it were separable from the totality of human historical existence—which last is what the word *sarx* means in the Pauline writings, resting back upon the firm Hebrew insistence on man as indeed "made of the dust of the earth"; yet with God's "Spirit" having "breathed upon" that dust to make it a living entity, with awareness and with the capacity to live in conscious relationship with God and with other men. The notion of a substantial soul has also been responsible for the dubious notion that man has a "natural immortality" that belongs to him quite apart from his relationship both with God and with others; thus it tends to make the divine-human relationship an addendum to something otherwise guaranteed, and fails to recognize that it is in no "splendid isolation" by what Plotinus called "the flight of the alone to the Alone" that man's destiny is fulfilled, but rather in *communio sanctorum* or sharing with others in the richness of the ongoing divine life.

The realization of my selfhood is indeed mysterious; but it is not equivalent to the Cartesian "ghost in the machine" that Gilbert Ryle has so soundly criticized in his *The Concept of Mind*. On the contrary, even if we may wish to reject the quasi-behaviorism of much that Ryle says in his rebuttal of this view, the *point* of human selfhood is in man's being in fact *a man*—which is to say, a conscious or aware creature who knows himself as a complex identity in the bringing together of past, present, and future, with an aim that is to bring to completion the possibilities that are offered and to make responsible decisions in that direction.

But the very heart of human nature is its potentiality for loving, as we have seen. Thus man *is* a "becoming a lover"; at least this is the divine intention that is also his human characteristic and his defining quality, even if (as is so tragically the case) he is in most dreadful and disturbing defection from that intention. And if this "being made to become a lover" is true of man, then we must turn to the sexuality which is man's own, since that sexuality is the physiological-psychological ground for his capacity to love, to receive love, and to grow in love.

II
HUMAN SEXUALITY

Man is a sexual animal. But to say that, and leave it there, is to put him on the level of apes and apples, as a young student once remarked in the discussion following a lecture I gave on the subject. *Of course* man's sexuality is man's, not that of other species, whether in the animal realm or among other forms of living matter. And it is to the specifically *human* quality of sexuality that we must now give our attention.

In *Making Sexuality Human* (United Church Press, 1971) I made this point, attempting to show that with the emergence of the specifically human type of existence there necessarily emerged also the specifically human *sexual* quality. To speak about man's sexual nature as if it were simply identical with that of a dog or cat or horse would be to fail in perception about the genuine difference that is made as a new level or dimension or (best of all) type of integration appears in the cosmic process. Man has the same sort of sexual "equipment," so to say, as does a higher-level animal; but that is by no means the whole story. For man in his sexual nature, with the consequent activity which that nature enables, is not given to "rutting seasons," for example. The ordering of his sexual existence is in terms not only of his freedom for making conscious decisions, of greater or less importance; it is also in terms of kinds of attraction, desire for union with another, etc., that are much more than merely animal coupling. Doubtless there are glimmerings of love, not entirely remote from what we see in men, among certain of the animals, birds, and the like; at least, so it would seem to our observation and so some scientific observers have told us. But in its full sense, this capacity for love as giving and receiving, with the affective tones that are also present, is peculiarly intense and real at the human level.

Furthermore, with men the biological purpose of sexual activity—the continuance of the race by the production of offspring —is no longer the central point of sexual union. For a long time moral theologians have talked as if it were; unconsciously, they have thereby reduced human sexuality to the level of the barn-yard, where the end of sexual union is reproduction, accompanied by the excitement and pleasure given in the act of coupling. With such a notion in mind, it is easy enough to understand why con-traception was condemned and also why a St. Augustine, fol-lowed by the general tradition of Western moral theology, could think that part of the "sinfulness" in sex is to be found in that very excitement which makes physical union possible—it would be better, St. Augustine thought, if procreation could be had without such unruly emotional associations where rationality gives place to enormously strong and uncontrolled urges and de-sires. Indeed, he portrays such a mode for continuing the race when he writes in the *De Civitate Dei* about procreation before "the Fall"; his portrayal is unconsciously extremely funny, as my students used to find it when we were holding our seminar in Augustine's theology. But it was noticeable also that the humor-ous side veiled, for my students, their sense that the great African saint had quite failed (despite his own earlier experiences when he "came to Carthage, burning, burning," as T. S. Eliot puts it in *The Waste Land*) to grasp the specifically human side of man's sexual existence.

This brings me to suggest that what in physiology is known as the "reproductive system" *becomes* in the specifically human sexual existence more significantly what I believe might better be styled the "conjunctive system." For with man the point of his sexuality is not the merely biological possibility of continuing the species; rather, it is the way in which two human beings can give each of them himself to the other, in the fullest and most satisfy-ing, because both pleasurable and totally fulfilling, mode of union. And it is very important for us to notice that even in such documents as *Humanae Vitae* this particular aspect of sexuality is now given its due recognition, even if (as it seems) a little grudg-ingly and without adequate insistence on its utter centrality, to which the procreative side is secondary even if important—and important, I should wish to add, when and as the partners decide, in full freedom of decision and with willingness to assume full re-sponsibility for their choice, that a child can and should be con-ceived as a consequence of their physical union.

But my main point is that when we take seriously both the process insistence on movement or direction, with the emergence of genuinely new types of entities (such as the appearance of man), and also the process (and the Christian) recognition of *love* as the point of man's existence and the purpose of his life, we can see that the sexuality of man, in its broad sense of his total equipment for and his psychological drive toward union of life with life in as complete mutuality as his finite and creaturely existence can manage, does have its basis or grounding in precisely those aspects, parts, systems, or qualities that he shares with the animals; while at the same time, because he *is* a new emergent with his own peculiar kind of existence or structured dynamic, his sexuality is qualitatively different from that of the animals. It is a *human*, not an animal, quality for and in man.

I should be prepared to say that *all* human relationships, whether in marriage or friendship, in sharing of life whether heterosexual or homosexual and also in respect to the capacity of seeking urgently a union with the divine Lover toward whose image man is meant to tend, find their creaturely possibility in this pervasive and specific sexuality. Angels are supposed to be disembodied pure spirits; *their* way of loving must therefore be different from man's—that is, if angels exist at all. But man is not an angel; and we need constantly to be on our guard, as Jacques Maritain once warned, against the fallacy of "angelism" in respect to human nature, quite as much as against the fallacy of "animalism." For man, whatever may be true of angels or animals, the ability to love at all is both based upon and yet supervenient to the total sexual existence that is his. (And I might add that for me, with a conception of God's relation to the cosmos understood as more like self to body than like carpenter to table made by him, there is a certain attraction in the view that God too has a "body"—in this case, the created order or the world, in which he is present and active in every part in a fashion not entirely dissimilar from that in which my own self is present and active throughout my body.)

Perhaps I have said enough to indicate a way of understanding human sexuality that is indeed different from the traditional one but which to my mind is more profoundly biblical in content as well as in accordance with our newer grasp of the world, of nature, and of man. One point needs to be added, however. If some such portrayal be as near the truth as we can come, then it will follow that moral judgments about specific sexual acts (in the broad sense of thoughts, words, and deeds), as also about any and every decision made or action performed by men, must be in terms of directions or tendencies, rather than of discrete and particular things done. What is significant is not that this or that particular act has been done, but rather the way in which whatever *is* done indicates the general direction or movement of a human being's existence: toward, or away from, the fulfillment of his possibility as a lover, being made toward God's image; and thus moving toward, or away from, his own human realization of the purpose of his existence. Such a perspective, with such a way of dealing with "souls," can make a quite enormous difference in the hearing of confessions, for example, as well as in the business of giving counsel or advice to those who turn to the Church for help.[1]

III
THE CHRISTIAN COMMUNITY, THE CHURCH

In process thinking, as in Christian experience, the reality of human sociality is strongly emphasized. This is one aspect of the more general truth that (as we have seen) everything in the creative advance influences and is influenced by everything else: there is a process of mutual prehension, which at the human level involves relationships of a highly personalized order but which also includes the less personal but equally significant kind of relationship that might be styled "I-you" in contrast to those of the "I-thou" type.

Thus it is natural that in their response to the movement of God upon them and in them, men should have established social patterns of one sort or another. In the Christian understanding, this implies a recognition that the community which we call the Church is not only the consequence of the impact made upon men by the total event of Christ but is also an inevitable result of men's urgent desire to be associated together in their expression of faith as well as in their modes of worship and in their common life. Christians of course add to this their conviction that the emergence of the "new Israel" out of the older Jewish national-religious community is part of the divine purpose. God's children are called to be members of the Christian Church that is one, holy, catholic, and apostolic, because it is united in its responsive faith in God's creative and redemptive act in Jesus Christ; thus intimately at one with the divine action in history (hence it shares in God's "holiness"); continuous with and the implementation of that which was "determined, dared, and done" (in Christopher Smart's fine words) in the originating events to which the Apostles bore witness; and itself an organic (rather than merely organizational) society that is "for all men, everywhere, and at all times." Thus to be a Christian *is* to be a member of the Catholic Church of Christ (however we may wish to define the precise meaning of that phrase).

But like every other routing in history as in nature, the Church is itself a social process. It is neither an occasional gathering of men and women who happen to share common ideals and aims, nor a kind of mechanical organization that is incapable of growth, development, and change; rather, it is "the living Body of the living Lord" and as such is deeply ploughed into the historical movement as a whole, of which it is both a part and also a new emergent within the total creative advance. The Church, then, is best conceived after the analogy of a human body—and so St. Paul describes it in his correspondence.

As a "body" the Church has certain characteristic features, in this resembling any other routing of occasions. These may be described as (a) its dedication in commitment to the Lord whom it serves and whose representative it is meant to be; (b) its realization of its purpose and nature through a specific mode of worship, the Holy Eucharist, which links it with its own originating event and enables it "to become itself" as that event is made present, out of the past, in the immediacy of contemporary experience; and (c) its structured forward thrust, through appropriate agencies (ministry is significant here), which enable it to carry on its mission in a world that itself has such agencies as serve to make possible both continuity and advance. Furthermore, the Church is characterized (d) by its empowering of its members to be what St. Benedict (and Martin Luther too) called "other Christs" in the world, so that "every member of the same, in his vocation and ministry," as an old Anglican collect puts it, "may truly and godly serve" the divine purpose by giving himself in loving concern, care, and action for others, as well as participating in the God-man relationship that the event of Christ has established with peculiar intimacy and directness.

The ways in which these various characteristic features will be operative in the world will naturally be largely determined by the given situations in which they are present and active. Thus there is inevitably a development (of doctrine, worship, ministry, and modes of Christian living), but at the same time there is a continuity so that the Christian society remains identifiably itself —and this in the way in which any social process is identified, by its remembrance of its originating event and its own past, by its relationship with the world in which it is set, and by its striving towards its "subjective aim" that in the case of the Church is God's kingly rule in the world. Not that the Church is to pretend to *be* the Kingdom, although that Kingdom is properly said in one of the documents from Vatican Council II to "subsist in the Church"; neither is the Church to think that it will "bring in the Kingdom," as a facile liberalism used to say. Rather, the Church exists to "prepare and make ready the way," to employ another phrase from an Anglican collect in the Book of Common Prayer, so that *God* may give, or bring in, his Kingdom as and when he sees fit to do so. The Kingdom of God is his kingly rule, as we have seen; and with our stress on process and love we must say that such kingly rule is the sovereignty of love, first of all the cosmic Love that is God and then the human loving which is the creaturely reflection of that Love. This is always "coming into the world," but in divers manners and in varying degrees; it is both here and also always more than what we know to be here—hence it is both an immanent rule and also a transcendent and inexhaustible one. In fact it is nothing other than God himself in his relationship to his erring, finite, sinful, yet also beloved children, whom he would bring more and more to himself and to whom he would express his "good pleasure."

Now for the ordinary Christian this suggests above all that he is to become "a man in Christ," to use Pauline language. To be *in* Christ means to open oneself to his Spirit, to participate in his life, and to be an instrument of his love. Such life in Christ includes the whole of each man, his body (and his sexuality, to revert to our earlier point) as well as his mind and soul and spirit and will and desires. What is more, it means to be "in love," humanly shared, precisely because it is to be in Love, divinely given. Christ himself, as God's supreme and adequate expression in human history and experience, is best conceived as the embodiment, enfleshing, or en-manment of the Cosmic Lover; and therefore to be in *him* is to be "in love" both divine and human.

On the other hand, because men are frail and willful, and because their human situation has been affected by the millenia of wrong decisions made in the past, they are unable in and of themselves to live as befits men in Christ; that is, they are sinners. Here, then, the love of God imparted in Christ comes to them redeemingly as well as for their fulfillment and completion. By incorporation into him, a new situation is made possible, where "sanctification" (or life in love) is enabled for those who respond to God's outgoing and caring.

IV
EUCHARIST AND EUCHARISTIC LIFE

We have already noted that the Eucharist is one of the characteristic or identifying features of the social process we call the Catholic Church. And we have indicated that the Eucharist is the way in which the past event, from which Christian faith and life have their origin, is made a present reality for the members of the community, and also the enabling means by which they are given the possibility of realizing their fulfillment as men in Christ. It will now be in order to see how the use of a process conceptuality can illuminate this central action of Christian life and worship.

In traditional theology the eucharistic sacrament is seen as being a two-way affair: it has to do with what God does for men and with what men do toward God. In the former or God-for-men aspect it has been understood as incorporation into the *totus Christus* (as Aquinas put it), so that in receiving the consecrated species of bread (and wine) the faithful are in genuine communion with a Lord who is equally genuinely present. His present-ness (as I prefer to say, rather than his "presence") is made available through the thanking-over them which while in no sense negating their creaturely status as bread and wine gives them the abiding significance, within the eucharistic rite, of "the spiritual food of the body and blood of Christ." Thus we have God's granting a present-ness of the risen Lord Jesus Christ, with a consequent communion with him, and through him with the Father who sent him and who through him brought men newness of life—"eternal life" or "life in Christ."

In the man-toward-God aspect, there is both thankful remembrance and an offering or sacrifice. The Eucharist is the way in which the Christian community, following what it takes to be its Lord's own command on "the night in which he was betrayed," makes its "continual remembrance" of the total event of Jesus himself. Often, and especially in the Western Christian churches, this remembrance has so focused on passion and death that it has seemed to overlook or forget the previous life of filial obedience with all that Jesus both said and did, and also the subsequent triumph and vindication of this which is summed up when we speak of Resurrection and Ascension and Heavenly Session. But in the full-orbed understanding that is now increasingly being emphasized, it is indeed the total event of Christ—*tota vita Christi mysterium crucis*, or (in the words familiar from the new canons of the Mass) the complete *mysterium fidei* with its words about Christ as having died, as having risen, and as coming again.

Nor is the remembrance a merely mental one; it is more like the Jewish Passover remembrance, observed at the Seder, of the deliverance of the "chosen people" from the Egyptians, their crossing of the Sea of Reeds, and their entrance into the "promised land." When that Seder is celebrated during the Passover, no faithful Jew would think for a moment that this merely and only recalls a past event; he is certain that in doing what is done at the Seder, the past event is made into a present reality in the experience of the company gathered at table. So also, when the Christian Church "makes remembrance" of Christ, it rejoices in his very present-ness through such an act of remembrance. Thus the God-to-man movement is the completion and ratification of the man-to-God movement.

At the same time, in thus "making memorial" the Christian fellowship offers, to God the Father, the total Christ. A view of sacrifice which presumed to think that *we* offer anything to God, all on our own, is to rejected out of hand; it is both blasphemous and absurd. On the contrary, precisely because the Catholic Church *is* the Body of Christ, *he* (the incarnate, risen, and ascended Lord) who has incorporated men into his Body and made them participants in his very life offers the whole reality of himself— "Christ in and with his members," as the Epistle to the Ephesians would suggest—to the Father who sent him. This is why St. Augustine could rightly say that it is we ourselves who are present on or at the altar; for it is the Body of Christ the Church that offers the body of Christ in the sacramental action to the Father, so that the Lord who is the head of that Body may increasingly make actual in his members the perfection of his own self-giving in love, which is their whole purpose for existence and which in him finds its complete and adequate expression.

The twofold movement in the Eucharist, including remembrance and offering (or sacrifice) and also present-ness and communion, is not a static cultic rite but a living and dynamic *action*. Jesus is said to have told his disciples to *do* something, not to think something or say something. Faithfully through the centuries his people have *done this action*, however inadequate or deficient may have been their theoretical explanation of what they did and how they did it.

Now the process conceptuality, with its stress upon event or happening, helps us to see how we can conceive of a dynamic interchange in action between God and his human children. It also helps us to see how past and present can be brought together in a given moment of action, which at the same time has the eschatological or future emphasis that "looks for Christ's coming again." Once again, identity is made real and established for us in the Eucharist, for it is this one action that enables the faithful *to look back* in their commitment or faith to the originating events of their Christian existence, *to look forward* in hope or eager expectation for the vindication of all that those events intended and implied, and *in the present to live* in the love which is nothing other than "the love of God shed abroad in our hearts," as we unite in the remembrance (vitally understood, let us again insist) of him in whom the cosmic Love was enmanned and through whose human loving that cosmic Love was expressed in the human situation that he shared with us.

I hope that this discussion has been suggestive, however brief it must necessarily have been. One thing remains to be said. In the perspective that we have adopted, the key words are (as we have seen) process and love. Unhappily neither one of them has received from the majority of Christian theologians the emphasis that ought to have been given. The concept of process or movement, found indeed in the biblical record in its own mythological idiom, has been lost in a static philosophical insistence on talk about substance, sheer being, unmoved mover, and the like. This does not mean that any Christian theology can lack a metaphysical aspect; it means only that the particular metaphysic that has been taken for granted is inadequate to indicate the dynamic richness of the Christian (and generally biblical) way of seeing God, man, nature, and the relationships between and among them.

And the stress on love has been granted in theory but all too frequently not been given a very prominent place in the theological enterprise. Hence talk about "being itself," with its various correlatives, along with an abstract concern for what are indeed only "abstractions" (like the "absolute" and the "unchanging," or even like "aseity" as the supposedly formal definition of deity), has taken pride of place over talk about God as Love-in-action or as Cosmic Lover. I am convinced that until and unless these more abstract notions, insofar as they have any validity at all, are seen as adverbial in respect to the verbs (*not* the nouns, for that would once again get us into the more static substance mode of thinking) which are the final reality in the cosmos and in the very nature of God himself, we shall continue along lines of theologizing that fail to stake everything—literally *everything*—on the unmistakable Christian conviction that love is the ultimate clue and key. As the old Holy Thursday liturgy would have it, *ubi caritas et amor, Deus ibi est.* Courage to accept *that*, in a processive universe, is the point and meaning of Christian faith, Christian worship, and the Christian life in grace.

NOTE

1. If this perspective is adopted, the way in which "controls" or directives for "right" sexual expression, in the specifically genital sense, must be understood will obviously be different from the imposition of external regulations or "laws." It will be more like a modified version of "natural law," in that it will speak of "doing the good and avoiding the evil" in terms derived from the best possible human expressions of love, whose grounding or basis is in man's pervasive sexuality. I have argued the case in *Love and Control in Sexual Expression* (United Church Press, 1974), where I propose that "wrong" sexual acts are those that are totally self-centered, cruel, or harmful to one or both partners, impersonalizing rather than personalizing, irresponsible or unwilling to value the other's self-esteem and to take into account the consequences of an act, and "inordinate" or finding in such specific sexual acts the *only* aspect of a genuinely important human relationship.

SUGGESTED READINGS

Ogden, Schubert M. *The Reality of God and Other Essays.* New York: Harper and Row, 1963.

Pittenger, Norman. *God in Process.* London: SCM Press, 1968.

Williams, Daniel Day. *The Spirit and Forms of Love.* New York: Harper and Row, 1968.

2 Process Theology: A Pragmatic Version

EUGENE FONTINELL

By and large, the process school of theology has tended to locate its rootings in the thought of Alfred North Whitehead and Charles Hartshorne. More recently a Teilhardian approach to process has developed. Although American pragmatic philosophy is often thought of as an expression of process modes of thought, the thought of John Dewey and William James has not been sufficiently explored as a resource for theological reflection. Dewey and James have a far different "flavor" than Whitehead and Hartshorne. In this chapter, Professor Fontinell develops the character of a pragmatic process theology. In his book, *Towards a Reconstruction of Religion: A Philosophical Probe* (Doubleday, 1970), he explores the pragmatic theological sense of many of the central religious concerns.

Eugene Fontinell is currently Professor of Philosophy and was formerly Chairman of the Department of Philosophy at Queens College, City University of New York. His Ph.D. is from Fordham University, where he did his dissertation on Josiah Royce. He is an Associate Editor of Cross Currents, *and author of* Towards a Reconstruction of Religion: A Philosophical Probe *(Doubleday, 1970). He has written for a variety of journals and has contributed to a number of collections of essays in the area of moral philosophy and the philosophy of religion.*

Process theology is generally associated with Whiteheadian philosophy and quite properly, since it has been the followers of Whitehead who have explicitly and systematically begun to construct a theology that draws upon and develops the categories of Whitehead's philosophy. More recently, there has appeared a process theology built upon the thought of Teilhard de Chardin.[1] In addition to Whitehead and Teilhard, I believe that there are distinct resources for a process theology located in the American tradition of pragmatism, particularly in the thought of William James and John Dewey.[2] What I would like to do in this essay is indicate something of what would be involved in a pragmatic process theology.

WORLD VIEWS AND BASIC ASSUMPTIONS

It is now a commonplace that not only the way we think but our manner of living is profoundly influenced, if not determined, by a set of assumptions that constitute our world view. But while it is simple enough to assert that everyone is influenced by some world view, it is much more complicated to articulate a particular world view. Indeed, in most people, their world view acts unreflectively upon them, and it is this lack of consciousness that tempts people to believe that their world view is coextensive with reality (hence, objective), while that of others is shot through with prejudice and bias (hence, subjective). For this reason, I believe that a crucial step in any effort to resolve a human problem is to surface as explicitly as possible those assumptions that play a central and decisive role in whatever resolution is forthcoming. This is especially important as regards what are called "metaphysical assumptions," that is, those basic or fundamental assumptions that operate in all our thoughts and actions. More specifically, I mean the ways in which we view, understand, and experience reality, not in its particularized modes, but in its most pervasive characteristics.[3]

In a brief essay, one can do little more than assert those ideas, categories, or principles that are to be presupposed for the more specific analyses or speculations. Nevertheless, I would caution against two views concerning such assumptions. The first view is that which contends that one's metaphysical assumptions are capable of being established by rational arguments that produce absolute certainty of their truth. The effort to ground with rational definitude one's first principles has a long and distinguished history in Western philosophy. It is, however, a dream that the twentieth century has radically damaged, if not completely destroyed.[4]

The second view concerning basic assumptions is really a consequence of the virtual collapse of the first. Having become aware of the impossibility of grounding our first principles with absolute certainty, there is a great temptation to posit a relativism that despairs of making any evaluation whatsoever of competing assumptions. Pragmatism rejects both the absolutism of the first view and the nihilism of the second view. While conceding that ultimately one's world view is an option or a belief, it nevertheless insists that not all options or beliefs are of equal worth. Hence, a fundamental task of human thought is that of constructing and communicating arguments and evidence for or against the various world views that the human community has created.

A time-honored way of attempting to communicate a new or different idea or viewpoint is to contrast it with a more established one with which it is in conflict. The obvious if inevitable danger in this approach is that insofar as one favors the new idea, there will be a tendency to caricature or grossly oversimplify the idea that one is trying to replace. When one is considering competing world views this danger is immeasurably heightened. This is due to the fact that a world view is not merely a single idea; it involves a constellation of ideas, principles, categories and experiences that have grown together out of a variety of sources over an extended period of time. Further, any description of a world view is inescapably selective and partial and hence, in a very real sense, a distortion.[5] Nevertheless, I would maintain that this effort to sort out our world views must be undertaken. Nowhere is this effort more necessary than in the sphere of religion where a failure to exercise our critical faculty to the fullest cannot but contribute to perpetuating the worst and most destructive dimensions of religion while keeping us from making contact with, and developing, its liberating possibilities.

Few today seriously doubt that the Christian religion, for example, both at its inception and throughout its development, was formed in relation to the culture in which it was located. Even the most conservative Christian thinkers will concede that Christian doctrine and practice are historically conditioned. Nor will it be denied that the articulation of Christian faith (theology) has always utilized the philosophical concepts and categories that characterize the wider culture. Still, and this is particularly though not exclusively true of Roman Catholicism, most Christians believe that there is a core of truth, whether in the scriptures or in tradition, that remains essentially untouched by time, place, or circumstance. Thus the task of Christian theology is seen as having to distill the essential truths of Christianity from their accidental manifestations, thereby enabling the Christian community to pattern its life in accordance with these eternal and unchanging truths. I would argue that this attitude betrays a commitment to that dominant world view of Western culture which is being challenged by a variety of twentieth-century philosophies, among them pragmatism.

This dominant world view is variously labeled Hellenic, classical, or traditional and manifests itself in a variety of ways, conceptually and experientially. For the purposes of this essay, the most important feature of this view in all its forms is that it sees reality as divided into the essential and unchanging and the accidental and changing. Depending upon the distinctive orientation of a thinker or community, "essential reality" will be described as structured by God and/or atoms, essences, ideas, values, laws, and Nature or natures. The history of Western culture has brought forth a rich variety of metaphysical dualisms involving numerous basic differences. Nevertheless, they can be said to manifest a common world view insofar as they share the assumption of an eternally ordered world in which man's task is merely to discover and imitate this order. It would be foolish to dismiss lightly the fact that this world view has had and continues to have a hold on the minds and lives of many serious and sensitive people. In spite of this, I believe that as a result of radical changes in such realities as philosophical and scientific ideas, diverse human institutions and personal experience and consciousness, this older world view is no longer adequate. While I do not think that this judgment can be "proved," I do believe that there is much evidence to support it. The task of marshaling and evaluating this evidence is quite beyond the scope of this essay. I would simply like to describe, with a minimum of argument and nothing approaching "proof," a world view that I believe offers more possibilities for the development of human life.[6]

PRAGMATISM'S PROCESSIVE-RELATIONAL WORLD

Pragmatism is usually associated in both sophisticated and unsophisticated circles with a utilitarian or consequentialist theory of truth or value. This understanding of pragmatism is not erroneous in itself but it is inadequate and most misleading when, as is usually the case, the pragmatic method of evaluating in terms of consequences is considered in isolation from the metaphysics or world view that this method presupposes. If reality is already complete in its essential structure, as the classical view briefly described above maintains, then the pragmatic claims that "truth is made" or "values are created" are understandably rejected as irrational, subjectivistic slogans. If, however, we live in a radically dynamic world, a world that is "still in the making," then the suggestion that human activity has a creative role to play in bringing forth truths and values does not appear so patently absurd. Allow me, therefore, all too briefly, to describe the kind of world that a pragmatic process theology presupposes.

Pragmatism maintains that we inhabit a "world *in* process" rather than merely a "world *involving* process." This distinction succinctly expresses the rejection of all forms of metaphysical dualism that bifurcate reality into the eternal unchanging and the temporal changing. This does not mean that pragmatism asserts a world of sheer chaotic flux. If we endeavor to keep our philosophical language as faithful to human experience as possible, we should affirm a world involving order *and* disorder, regularity *and* chance, stability *and* precariousness. These are precisely the features of reality that have led so many thinkers to assign order, regularity, and stability to some transcendent world while attributing disorder, chance, and precariousness to the world of concrete experience. Pragmatism contends that these characteristics of reality are dialectically related to each other and hence, while functionally distinct, are not ontologically separate. The major implication of such a world view is that human activity is not relegated to some superficial role of simply imitating eternal essences or values or even an eternal God. In a processive world, human beings have the possibility and opportunity of transforming reality in its innermost depths. This "unfinished world" affirmed by pragmatism is radically open to the emergence of new ideas, values, events, and entities. Hence, the most significant mode of human activity is not discovery but creativity.

The world posited by pragmatism is not only a "world in process," it is also a thoroughly relational world. Negatively, this view rejects any form of atomistic individualism—there are no absolutely isolated and completely independent beings—neither eternally unchangeable atoms nor an eternally unchangeable God. Positively, pragmatism affirms that there are active centers of relational complexes, which centers can properly be called "individuals." Such individuals, however, have no reality in themselves, but are constituted through and through by a variety of relations. For this reason, pragmatism considers it fruitless to attempt to discover, analyze or describe any individual entity apart from its relations. In the case of the human individual, therefore, we must attend as fully as possible to a multiplicity of relations, including those we call physical, cognitive, personal, social, institutional, and religious.

In summation, pragmatism views reality as processive-relational, that is, as an ongoing relational-continuum or "field" embodying and bringing forth a plurality of subfields, each with a unique focus but interdependent with and shading-off into other fields. Such a world leaves open the possibility of believing that there is a total all-encompassing field with which the more limited fields are intimately related in accordance with their distinctive characteristics. It must be stressed, however, that in so describing reality, pragmatism is well aware that it is utilizing imaginative constructs. Hence, pragmatism acknowledges but rejects the great dream of Western metaphysics of being able to know reality as it is in itself, independently of the human knower, and in its totality or wholeness. There is no pretense, then, of having discovered a system of ideas that represents or corresponds to the essential structure of the world. This awareness of the profound inadequacy of even the most complex and sophisticated conceptual schemes keeps pragmatism open to that radical mystery which is at the center of so much of religious experience. Here I believe pragmatism is a corrective not only to classical rationalism but also to the rationalistic residue that seems to remain even in such process thinkers as Whitehead and Teilhard. At the same time, pragmatism does not fall prey to any pseudo-mystification or irrationalism. The construction of abstract ideas, theories, or metaphysical schemes are all recognized as important human activities. They are important because they make a unique contribution to the development, expansion, and enrichment of human life. On the other hand, ideas, theories, or conceptual systems are misleading and dangerous when we transform them into idols, that is, when we take them for reality itself rather than allow them to serve as channels of participation in the creative process.

PRAGMATIC METHOD

As with any philosophical expression, there is a superficial, almost caricature, portrayal of pragmatism and a more subtle and refined one. The description of the caricature is a simple task —pragmatism maintains that all problems are resolved solely on the basis of what works for or satisfies the individual. The very nature of a caricature is that it does present some characteristics of that which is being caricatured but it presents these in a highly exaggerated, isolated, and therefore grossly distorted fashion.

The presentation of a more subtle and refined pragmatism is, needless to say, not able to be accomplished with a few broad verbal strokes. Hence, the most I can hope to do here is to indicate the crucial presuppositions, the primary thrust, and the basic constituents of a pragmatic method.

The most important presupposition of a pragmatic method (or any other method for that matter) is the world view within which it operates. The pragmatic method that I am proposing presupposes a processive-relational world such as that briefly described above. Since it is a world without absolutes, there is no possibility of devising a method that will yield definitive, timeless solutions to human problems. It is this loss of absolutes, so characteristic of the twentieth century, that has given rise to so much despair—actual or potential. Pragmatism accepts this absence of absolutes while firmly denying that nihilism is the inevitable consequence of such absence. The impossibility of arriving at absolute truths, values, or solutions is not viewed by pragmatism as a defect in either the world or humanity. Rather, it is seen as evidence of the dynamic, ongoing, creative nature of these realities. The fact that we are in a radically changing world does not excuse us from affirming those truths, values, and solutions which we judge best at any particular moment. All such affirmations, however, involve a degree of tentativeness insofar as they must be open to modification, transformation, and even rejection in the light of new experience. This is not to suggest that every human value and institution has but a momentary duration subject to being whimsically or frivously discarded. Not at all. There are truths, values, and institutions that have been slowly and laboriously honed out of human experience and which give every indication of enduring indefinitely.[7] All that pragmatism insists upon is that any such claims be supported by showing their need for and fruits in human experience. They cannot be accepted on the basis of some acts of "reason" or "revelation" that allegedly transcend the experiential process and are verified outside human experience.

A simple, hopefully not simplistic, way of describing the pragmatic method is as follows: all human ideas, theories, values, practices, symbols and institutions are ultimately evaluated on the basis of their contribution to the development of the "quality of life." Quite obviously, such a method assigns a central and determining role to experience. As with such terms as "reason," "truth," "good," and "justice," "experience" is a term that is widely and commonly used but whose meaning is not self-evident nor universally agreed upon. Let me, therefore, merely assert how I think the term should be understood within the framework of a pragmatic philosophy. Experience is the transaction between an organism and its environment.[8] While I believe experience is a category more extensive than human experience, I will restrict myself to the transactions of human organisms. The term "transaction" is fundamental since it conveys the notion of a dialectical relation between organism and environment. Hence "organism" and "environment" are not two essentially independent realities that happen to interact; they are two interdependent "fields" that constitute and are constituted by virtue of this transactional relation. Consider, for example, an individual human organism: as an individual it is a center of activity constituted by a variety and diversity of relations involving such environments as the physical, the conceptual, the social, the personal, the institutional, and the like. A shorthand way of expressing this is to say that the human self engages in and is thereby constituted by a variety of experiences—physical, psychical, cognitive, affective, cultural, esthetic, and religious. While these are distinguishable, they are not ontologically separate and for this reason the concrete situation of any individual or group of individuals involves a richness of relations that can never be adequately expressed by an abstract conceptual scheme. Indeed, in keeping with the pragmatic method, the ultimate justification of any such conceptual scheme, whether in philosophy, science, or theology, is that it enriches human life.

Because of the emphasis that pragmatism places upon life and experience, it is often classified as a mode of irrationalism. This, I believe, is a gross misunderstanding of what pragmatism is attempting to do. Pragmatism's insistence that knowledge is for the sake of life rather than life for the sake of knowledge is in no way intended to diminish the importance of knowledge. The need to develop our cognitive possibilities to their fullest is well established—failure to do so results in an immeasurable impoverishment of the quality of human life. Insofar, therefore, as process theology is a mode of thought it must fulfill certain conditions that characterize any successful, that is, life-enhancing, mode of thought. There are at least four conditions that have been fulfilled by those cognitive efforts which have historically shown themselves of value to the human community.

The first condition is that of basic inner coherence, by which I mean that no worthwhile process theology can involve multiple fundamental contradictions and inconsistencies. For the more rationalistic philosophies or theologies, conceptual coherence is the central if not exclusive criterion of their truth or value. Pragmatism denies that absolute or complete coherence can ever be achieved in a world in which developing experience continually renders even our most sophisticated concepts inadequate.

Secondly, process theology must manifest a continuity with past thought and experience, for only by taking advantage of earlier human achievements can we hope to advance. This is a point that bears amplification since so often pragmatism is viewed as concerned solely with future consequences. What is not sufficiently recognized is that pragmatism strongly rejects any Cartesian-like mode of thought which pretends to reason from point-zero. All thinking—philosophical, scientific, or theological—proceeds from a concrete situation that is the result of a long historical development involving a variety and diversity of factors. Further, human experience is cumulative, that is, it embodies a score of relative achievements and failures. Pragmatism is firmly convinced that the best—perhaps the only—hope we have for bringing about a better future is by way of avoiding those paths that have led to destruction and pursuing more vigorously those that have already brought us to fruitful realizations. This is possible, of course, only if we are intimately acquainted with human history in all its dimensions.

The third condition that process theology must fulfill is to have a high degree of contemporary consistency, that is, it must show itself to be in touch with the best knowledge and experience of its time. This is in no way to suggest that it should strive for popularity by mindlessly running after the latest fads. Rather, it must be sensitive to and endeavor to assimilate that which is worthwhile in the sciences, philosophy, art, literature, politics, etc. This, of course, is an immensely difficult task that can never be more than partially accomplished. One thing, however, is quite clear—any theology that avoids intimate transactions with these other modes of human experience will inevitably become an irrelevant abstraction.

Finally, process theology must suggest new possibilities for the continuing development of human life. No theologian should rest content with being a kind of archivist. In addition to analyzing and describing, he must be willing to speculate. It is not enough merely to describe the way things are or have been; it is imperative that some thinkers have the courage to venture a guess as to the way things ought to be. Stated differently, and with apologies to Marx, it is not enough for a theologian to attempt to understand the religious life of his community, he must also attempt to change it.

PRAGMATIC JUSTIFICATION OF RELIGION

Up to this point I have been attempting to indicate the conditions, assumptions, and fundamental approach of a pragmatic process theology. In order to be a bit more concrete, I would like now to focus on religion as it might be justified by a pragmatist. Let me begin by posing the question in its sharpest form: Is religion something that is good for humanity and hence should be continued, or is it destructive of human life to such an extent that it should be done away with? The first point to be made in response to this question is that, strictly speaking, there does not exist some entity or essence called "religion" anymore than there exists something called "art" or "politics." What exists is a plurality of religions. Still, it is defensible to speak of the phenomenon of religion understood as a mode of human activity composed of ideas, symbols, doctrines, practices, beliefs, and institutions distinct but not separate from other such activities as science, art, or politics. Recall that, as mentioned above, in confronting any human problem, the pragmatist never pretends that we are at point-zero. He is acutely conscious of the fact that we are confronted with a concrete situation which has a lengthy history involving an indefinite number of factors only some of which are conceptual. Hence, before speculating about the future of religion, we must first try to grasp as fully as possible what it has been and is now. To do this we must draw upon the data and insights provided by the historian, anthropologist, psychologist, sociologist, artist, novelist, and poet.[9] But one wishing to render a judgment upon the worth of religion cannot wait until all the data are in from these various disciplines, since "all the data" will never be in. Hence, we must make a judgment as best we can at a particular moment without closing ourselves off from possible modification of this judgment as new data and experiences emerge. Further, no pragmatist could insist that there can only be one pragmatic evaluation or interpretation of the data. One need only recall that while following a pragmatic method, James and Dewey reached conflicting conclusions concerning the merits of religion. Still, James, who viewed religion positively, would have to concede that if religion could be shown to be essentially destructive of human life and an obstacle to the development of new possibilities (basically Dewey's judgment), then religion should be opposed. The reverse, of course, would hold for Dewey.

Whatever the situation may be at some time in the distant future, I believe that it is now so basically ambiguous that every reflective person must render his or her own judgment, fully conscious of the fact that it may be wrong. Personally, I believe that the only viable defense of religion is one made from some processive or developmental perspective. Looking at the record of religion, or more precisely, of religions, the very most that can be said in their favor is that they are a mix of good and bad features. The negative features of religion are more easily recognized and more widely acknowledged. Who would seriously deny that religions have involved destructive superstitions, prejudices, hatreds, and practices or that they have so often been allied with the more regressive if not repressive political and social forces? On the plus side, one would point out that some of the great human figures have emerged from religious communities and that their greatness was bound up with a vision and set of ethical ideals which have manifestly transformed human consciousness for the better.

The defender of religion, however, would be well advised to

avoid basing his defense upon an alleged favorable balance of positive over negative features of religion. First, because the negative features have persisted so long and remain so incontrovertibly evident. These include Hindus and Moslems or Irish Protestants and Catholics killing one another, the proliferation of magic and occult religions, widespread racial and religious bias on the part of so many practitioners of religion and opposition to new ideas that manifests itself in the book-burning of fundamentalist Christians or the Vatican's retention of arcane procedures to stifle dissent within the Roman Catholic community.

An even greater obstacle to a balanced-ledger defense of religion is that most of its positive ideals (value of human life, unity of mankind, sacredness of the individual, selfless dedication to others) are now quite capable of being affirmed by some form of secular humanism. Even, therefore, if it is conceded that most of our basic human values entered human consciousness by way of religion, it does not follow that religion is necessary for their continued development. Religion is defensible only if it can be shown that in spite of its destructive elements, it contains potentially liberating possibilities. In my view, only some kind of process theology will be adequate to the task of suggesting how a religious community can radically transform itself so as to move in the direction of an ever-fuller realization of its deepest vision and ideals. If the process theologian is a pragmatist, he will acknowledge that such suggestions will remain as bare and empty hypotheses unless they lead to the transformation of the life of the community. We are justified in suggesting, hoping, and striving for such a transformation only if human nature is not locked into and limited to the mode in which it is or has been. Unless there is the possibility for creating a humanity and a world that is profoundly different from what we now have, it is hard to see how we can ward off an ever-increasing despair and nihilism. It is in creating, sustaining, and developing faith and hope in the emergence of a better world that religion has a decisive role to play.

As already suggested, a pragmatist ultimately justifies any activity on the basis of its contribution to the development of human life. The contribution of some activities is so evident as to be beyond dispute. These would include the production of food and shelter and the means for maintaining good health. A bit less evident but still not seriously disputed (at least until quite recently in Western culture) are science, art, and politics. Religion, however, in spite of opinion polls, is an activity whose contribution to the enhancement of life is at best ambiguous. A primary task of any process theologian, therefore, is to attempt to show why religion should be affirmed rather than opposed. I can, of course, give only the barest hint here of how this might be done.

One way in which religion *cannot* be justified is by trying to prove that unless there is religion, humans will recede into barbaric immorality. Concerning the relation between religion and morality, I wish to make four brief points. First, there is no doubt that all religions have involved ethical ideals which have usually taken the form of a moral code. Secondly, there is no doubt that in contemporary society many individuals live moral lives completely independent of religion. Thirdly, there have emerged in the last several hundred years a number of thinkers who have argued most persuasively that whatever the merits of belief in God or participation in a particular religion, morality can rationally be defended in the absence of both. Finally, I think that there is a great need for some religionists to begin rethinking the relation between religion and morality, open to the possibility that this relation is not, nor should not, be what it has been in the past. Art, science, and politics were born out of a religious matrix but eventually had to become autonomous in order to pursue their distinct possibilities and make their unique contribution to the human community. Is it not possible that it is now the turn of morality to "come of age," and make its way without direct or formal dependence upon religion? This would not mean that morality would be absolutely separate from and untouched by religion anymore than are science, art, and politics. Rather, it means that we must devise a new relationship which hopefully will lead to the enrichment of both our religious and moral life.

The paradox I am presenting is that in surrendering its claims as a moral authority, religion may come to a greater awareness of its distinct and indispensible function. I would describe this function as follows: religion is that activity which by means of vision, symbols, and liturgical practices deepens man's awareness of being bound-up with a more encompassing reality, of being related to a transcendent-immanent Other, of being called to participate in a creative process that is the ultimate ground for hope. This not to suggest that only in formal religion do we achieve a sense of the whole or the encompassing or a process that engenders belief in the positive possibilities of reality. Indeed, such an awareness can emerge from any experience and often accompanies peak moments in personal, scientific, or artistic activity. Nevertheless, I still contend that there is need for an activity which explicitly focuses upon this mode of consciousness. In so doing religion would make two distinct contributions to the human community. Negatively, it would keep humans from demonic and Promethean self-deception whereby they view themselves as demigods and are led to transform their activities or artifacts into idols. Positively, it would energize human beings by heightening their belief that they live in a world of promise—a world of meaningful possibilities. It will thereby serve as a stimulus to struggle with our almost overwhelming problems through the hope that in so struggling we are cooperating with the creative and positive possibilities of reality (symbolized, perhaps, as God).

In brief, human beings will be energized by means of the belief that they are playing a role in radically transforming for the better both humanity and the world with which it is continuous. The pragmatist must concede that this belief *may* be an illusion. But then so may be the *belief* that we are alone in a purposeless and meaningless universe.[10] Needless to say, no process theology can "prove" which belief is the true one; the most that can be shown is that the first belief is not patently irrational and hence is worthy of the assent of a reflective person. Each individual, however, must make his or her act of faith that inevitably involves the risk of error and failure. But there is no way of completely avoiding the possibility of error and failure. The belief that we are active participants in a creative process at least allows us to hope that even our errors and failures count and that, in a way never to be completely comprehended, they make a contribution to the emergence of a fuller and richer life-reality.[11]

NOTES

1. See Eulalio R. Baltazar, *Teilhard and the Supernatural* (Baltimore: Helicon, 1966) and *God Within Process* (New York: Newman, 1970). Also Ewert H. Cousins, ed., *Process Theology* (New York: Newman, 1971). For a process theology that draws upon both Teilhard and Whitehead, see Bernard Lee, *The Becoming of the Church* (New York: Paulist Press, 1974).

2. For a more developed statement of my position, see *Toward A Reconstruction of Religion* (New York: Doubleday, 1970).

In using the terms "pragmatism" and "pragmatist" throughout this essay, I do not wish to give the impression that these are clearly definable terms that can be used unequivocally to identify a school of thinkers. For an introduction to a number of thinkers who can properly be called "pragmatists," see Amelie Rorty, ed., *Pragmatic Philosophy* (New York: Doubleday, Anchor Books, 1966). Rorty succinctly expresses the justification for labeling "pragmatic" philosophies that in some respects are radically different: "Pragmatism, like most philosophic 'isms,' is best thought of as a label for a range of views bearing a general family resemblance" (p.v.)

3. It should be noted that it is not only philosophers who acknowledge the presence of "metaphysical assumptions" in human reflection and activity. The distinguished sociologist Alvin W. Gouldner expresses such recognition when he states: "Background assumptions come in different sizes, they govern domains of different scope. They are arranged, one might say, like an inverted cone, standing on its point. At the top are background assumptions with the largest circumference, those that have no limited domain to which alone they apply. These are beliefs about the world that are so general that they may, in principle, be applied to any subject matter without restriction. They are, as Stephan Pepper calls them, 'world hypotheses.' . . . World hypotheses are the most pervasive and primitive beliefs about what is real. They may involve, for example, an inclination to believe that the world and the things in it are 'really' *one* or are 'truly' *many*. . . . World hypotheses—the cat may as well be let out of the bag —are what are sometimes called 'metaphysics.' " (*The Coming Crisis of Western Sociology*, New York: Basic Books, 1970, pp. 30-31.)

4. Actually the initial and in some ways the most devasting assault on "first principles" is to be found in the Humean-Kantian critique of classical metaphysics. But the persistence of the lure of absolute certainty was not to be quickly dissipated. Husserl's neo-Cartesian effort to ground philosophy-science on an absolutely certain rational foundation is perhaps the most significant twentieth-century piece of evidence of this persistence. John Dewey, though not responding directly to Husserl, has given us a powerful critique of that passionate "quest for certainty" which has been such a central concern of Western culture since the time of the Greeks. (See *The Quest For Certainty*, New York: Minton, Balch & Co., 1929.) But it is, ironically, in mathematics, long the paradigm of rational certainty in Western thought, which may contain the seeds for the final dissolution of this striving for certainty. William Barret, commenting on "the famous proof of the incompleteness of mathematics by Kurt Goedel in 1933," states: "For mathematics as an incomplete system now becomes the field of mathematical activity, open perpetually to mathematical creativity and construction, but also guaranteed by no rock-bottom proof of consistency, and hence in its very richness exposed to the hazards and risks of paradox." (*Philosophy in the Twentieth Century*, ed. by William Barret and Henry D. Aiken, New York: Random House, 1962, vol. 2, pp. 14-15.)

5. There is a double distortion involved in the attempt to describe the world view of any thinker. First, the thinker's own expression of his world view is a distortion in reference to the totality of the reality that he is endeavoring to

describe. Hegel notwithstanding, the "whole truth" or the "truth of the whole" is never able to be articulated in human language. This, I believe, is the fundamentally correct thrust of Whitehead's famous assertion that "Philosophy is an attempt to express the infinity of the universe in terms of the limitations of language."

There is another distortion that accompanies any effort to present the world view of another, regardless of whether one is sympathetic or antagonistic to this world view. This accounts, in part at least, for the continued efforts of commentators to discover just what a Plato, or an Aquinas or a Hegel "really meant." Thus, much of philosophical commentary is engaged in "correcting" earlier or other "distorted" interpretations of a particular thinker's thought.

6. I have called this world view "processive-relationalism" and while I will attempt to describe it in its pragmatic mode, it is most important to note that it has a variety of manifestations in the twentieth century. Indeed I believe that, while expressed in significantly different ways, it is now the dominant world view that permeates the thought and experience of most Western thinkers. A hypothesis that suggests the demise of one world view and the ascendancy of another is not subject to anything approaching mathematical proof. Its worth can be adjudicated only by an extensive survey of philosophical, scientific, artistic, and ordinary experience in order to see just what are the operative (though usually unexpressed) assumptions of these human activities.

7. Cf. John Dewey, *Theory of the Moral Life* (New York: Holt, Rinehart and Winston, 1960, c., 1908), p. 176. "The fundamental conceptions of morals are, therefore, neither arbitrary nor artificial. They are not imposed upon human nature from without but develop out of its own operations and needs. Particular aspects of morals are transient; they are often, in their actual manifestation, defective and perverted. But the framework of moral conceptions is as permanent as human life itself."

8. I am here basically following Dewey's "metaphysics of experience." For a description of the distinctive characteristics of "experience" in American thought, see his essay, "The Need for a Recovery of Philosophy," in *On Experience, Nature, and Freedom*, ed. by Richard J. Bernstein (New York: The Liberal Arts Press, 1960), in particular, p. 23.

9. Hence, whatever else it would be, a developed pragmatic method would not be easy to execute. What could be more demanding than a method that attempts to reach its conclusions only after having weighed and evaluated data and insights from such a range of human experiences? Further, since pragmatism is future-oriented, it must be alert to the multiple changes taking place in all aspects of human life. This means that its conclusions must be continuously reviewed and modified so as to remain relevant to the situation as it is rather than as it at one time was.

10. The understanding and role of belief or faith within a pragmatic world view is most important but can only be hinted at here. I have suggested elsewhere that "belief or faith is not merely a stopgap for ignorance, a resting place for the human subject until such time as reason catches up. Faith is actually an operative principle in the very making of man and the world. Along with knowl-

edge, art and other experiences, faith is a way of participating or sharing in the creating of man and the world. Again, in a static or finished reality, faith could have no other role but to anticipate the correspondence of mind to reality. But in a world in the making, the very kind of world that it will be depends at least in part upon the beliefs involved in the making of it." (*Reconstruction*, p. 70.)

11. It is important to note that a pragmatic process theology could not rest content with such a general conclusion, however crucial it is as a minimal affirmation. Since, as indicated above, it is not "religion" but "religions" that exist, it is incumbent upon the process theologian to reflect upon and render specific judgments on concrete historical religions. If the theologian is himself a member of a religious community, he must endeavor to evaluate and where necessary suggest ways of transforming the beliefs, symbols, practices, and institutions of that community. What I believe is excluded by pragmatic process theology is any claim that these realities are protected from change and hence from a critical scrutiny that might lead to their radical modification and possibly their dissolution.

SUGGESTED READINGS

James, William. *Essays in Pragmatism*. Edited by Alburey Castell. New York: Hafner Publishing Co., 1948.

McDermott, John J., editor. *The Philosophy of John Dewey* (2 vols). New York: Capricorn Books, G.P. Putnam's Sons, 1973.

Randall, John Herman, Jr. *The Role of Knowledge in Western Religion*. Boston: Starr King Press, 1958.

3 What Is a Christian Theology?

DELWIN BROWN

We are all aware that the structures of our behavior and the structures of our thought are intimately interrelated. Attitudes of behavior and attitudes of thought mutually inundate each other. In this chapter, Professor Brown explores the different possible attitudes toward the Jesus-event: how the Jesus-event is normative, and what that means; and how the Jesus-event is a source, and what that means. He then explores the implications of these different attitudes toward the Jesus-event for doing theology, relying at points on the philosophy of Whitehead. One of the noteworthy features of Professor Brown's work is his interest in "cultus" as a source of theological criticism, i.e., the stories, rituals, and symbols in any religious tradition.

Delwin Brown (B.D., Union Theological Seminary; Ph.D., Claremont School of Theology) wrote his divinity thesis under Reinhold Niebuhr on sin and grace, and his dissertation on the doctrine of God in process thought under John B. Cobb, Jr. He has published several articles in the areas of philosophy of religion, philosophical theology, and process theology. He coedited the book Process Philosophy and Christian Thought *(Bobbs-Merrill), and is the review editor for the journal* Process Studies. *Mr. Brown, a layperson in the Church of God (Anderson, Indiana), teaches in the Departments of Philosophy and Religious Studies at Anderson College. He has also been a visiting professor at Christian Theological Seminary and at Candler School of Theology.*

There is much ambiguity in the meaning of "theology," and much of the theologian's prefatory efforts are spent trying to meet this ambiguity. The

41

result is that another important methodological issue frequently gets scant attention. This issue is posed in the question, When is theology Christian?

Historically, the reflections of those who called themselves "Christian" have often occurred in relative isolation from the thinking of persons identified with alternative perspectives. In such isolation, the question, "What is a *Christian* theology?" can understandably remain dutifully in the background. But when—as is common today—what Christians say about the meaning and makeup of their lives seems little different from what might very well be affirmed by their non-Christian comrades, then the question of Christian identity becomes paramount. In this circumstance we are rightly pressed to say what, if anything, is distinctively Christian about our thinking and doing. The question of a Christian identity does not arise exclusively with respect to our thinking, to be sure; it is no less acute in the areas of ethical choosing and spiritual practice. I shall deal with the question in terms of theology, however, because I think it will become clear how an answer in this area implies also an answer in the others.

What, then, is a *Christian* theology? In order to deal with this question it will be helpful to consider the importantly different ways of attempting to do theology vis-à-vis that reality which is somehow central for Christianity, the "event of Jesus." Then we may ask which of these ways, if any, are possible, and which, if any, are properly called "Christian."

There are at least two different ways in which a theology may be said to be related to the event of Jesus (alternatively referred to as the "Jesus-event" or the "Christ-event" and sometimes as "Jesus" or "Christ"). The event of Jesus may be seen, first, as the source and, second, as the norm of theological thinking. A theology is said to have its *source* in the Jesus-event when it is thought to be in some decisive respect causally dependent upon that event for the form that it takes.[1] (Even theologies that negate traditional Christian teaching are, when viewed solely from the standpoint of their source, properly termed "Christian" if their negation is held to be derived in some decisive—and, as it is usually also claimed, "profound"—way from the Jesus-event.) The event of Jesus is said to be the *norm* of a theology when no statement is admitted into that theology which is not thought to be given in, implied by, or at least consistent with the Christ-event.

If we concentrate on these two types of relationships, and if we employ their denial as well as their affirmation, we see that theology may be done in four different ways with respect to the event of Jesus. These are:

(1) The event of Jesus *is* its (total, or primary[2]) source
" " " " *is* " " " " norm

(2) " " " " *is not* " " " " source
" " " " *is* " " " " norm

(3) " " " " *is* " " " " source
" " " " *is not* " " " " norm

(4) " " " " *is not* " " " " source
" " " " *is not* " " " " norm

Way Four—This alternative should be discussed first because it can immediately be rejected as a possibility for *Christian* theology If theology of this type is to be termed "Christian," then every theology is Christian and the term loses all significance. I am not claiming that a Way Four theology is impossible, or that it is false. I am only observing that a theology for which the event of Jesus is decisive neither as source nor as norm is irrelevant to our considerations.

Way One/Way Two—These two alternatives agree in viewing the event of Jesus as the norm for theological thinking. Inasmuch as this normative relationship seems to me to be the problematic one, I shall discuss Ways One and Two together, usually referring to them in the singular.

The claim here is that "Christ" is the sole or final norm of truth in all matters about which this event claims authority. This supposition gives to Way One/Two a decisiveness not characteristic of its competitors. Way One/Two has an objectively existing standard of truth. Its proponents may not agree on how to "go to" their authority or on what it "says" once it is properly approached. And because these hermeneutical and exegetical questions remain to be resolved by scholarly judgment, the not uncommon claim from "Evangelicals" that this alternative avoids the "slippery slopes of subjectivism" is quite indefensible. Theology done even in this manner cannot rightly be viewed as fixed or final. Nevertheless, proponents of Way One/Two do agree *that* a normative datum is objectively given and *where* it is. When they have a problem, theologians know where to go to seek its solution, and when they disagree with one another, they know what to argue from and about.

How is this kind of theology to be evaluated? First, one may reject any particular form of this approach by rejecting its datum. "I can only confess that the event of Jesus has no particular normative importance for me" is one perfectly rational way of preceding against a Way One/Two version of Christian theology. When the critic proceeds in this way, however, he or she is not necessarily judging the theology in question to be incoherent, impossible for other people, or patently foolish; the objector is simply acknowledging that, for good or ill, his or her starting point lies elsewhere. Moreover, the objector's confession does not entail a general rejection of Way One/Two theologies as such.

One may also reject Way One/Two at a more basic level. Here the complaint is not directed at the adequacy of the specific events or realities taken to be the normative ground of theology; the objection has to do with the view of language that seems to be implicit in *any* theology of this type, whatever its specific ground.

To avoid misunderstanding we should begin by acknowledging that Way One/Two need not be, and frequently is not, oriented primarily to that which is conceptual or doctrinal or verbal. The normative ground of theology need not in this case be construed as a set of doctrines or even as a less specific "vision or reality." Nor should that which must conform to the normative reality be thought of primarily as a set of beliefs or doctrines; it may be an experience (e.g., being "born again") or a style of life (e.g., "openness to the future"). The nonconceptual elements may be, and often are, the primary and prominent ones in this approach. Nevertheless, the conceptual element is utterly essential to this way of doing theology, because the conceptual dimension is required by its concern for normativeness. In order to speak of the conformation of the present experience or the present lifestyle to that which is implicit in the normative datum, the event of Jesus, one must be able, roughly at least, to identify that datum conceptually (linguistically, doctrinally) even though the datum is not itself conceptual. To allege "I feel what they felt on the Day of Pentecost," for example, assumes that one *knows* what or how "they" felt. The knowing is not the feeling, to be sure, but conceptualization is essential to any effort that speaks of normativeness.

As I see the matter, the more radical theories of language, such as those derived from the later Heidegger, are no less immune to the conceptual requirement. The issue being discussed is not that of the primacy or agency of language or of that reality "unveiled" in or by language. The issue is one of identification—is this the reality that appeared to men of old? I do not see how the question of identification can be addressed apart from the attempt to draw parallels that are conceptual in nature.

The difficulty of the Way One/Two approach to doing theology, I have said, is to be found in its implicit view of language. Any referential statement, I think we can agree, refers not only to the reality it seeks to witness to; it also refers to a dim horizon of complex meanings, feelings, and beliefs constituting the personal and cultural context of that statement. Of course we can translate with considerable precision New Testament terms, for example, into correlates in other language systems. In a sense, therefore, we can know what the words "say." But does this mean that we know what the speaker of these terms was saying in his or her use of them? My point is that language is always intoxicated with shadings of feeling and self-understanding unique to the moment of its speaking. Are not, then, the really important questions left open and elusive? What felt-difference did the utterance of such terms as "grace," "resurrection," "ascended," etc., make to the particular person who spoke them in that act of speaking and to his or her hearers (or readers)? And what verbal formulations would do the same job for the very different context today?

I am not concerned to ask whether words communicate or how they communicate. I am asking what is involved in determining *what* they communicate. I do not doubt that we can go a long way toward getting at the context-laden felt-meanings of ancient affirmations, and I am sure we can decide with fair assuredness that some contemporary formulations of those meanings are more adequate than others. But, I ask, can the felt-meanings of terms in the context of their original usage become available to us in our own uniquely different and highly variable world with sufficient clarity that we can use those terms as norms, or depend upon them to get us back to the normative reality behind them? I do not think so. Given the contextual nature of linguistic meaning, even if the fully adequate words of Truth had been spoken in that time and place, and even if we did have those words now, we could not with sufficient sureness grasp their original felt-intent, or enunciate their modern counterparts, to speak plausibly of their being normative for us today. One is reminded of the words of Faust:

> My friend, the times that antecede
> Our own are books safely protected
> By seven seals. What spirit of the time you call,
> Is but the scholars' spirit, after all,
> In which times past are now reflected.[3]

Way Three—We now seem to be left with an unsatisfactory choice: Either theology can no longer be Christian (Way Four), or it must be a Christian theology that claims no normative dependence upon the event of Jesus (Way Three). But in what *significant* sense can the latter be called "Christian"?

Way Three is that of a theology for which the Jesus-event is not intrinsically normative, but for which that first century event is viewed as being the decisive source. Questions concerning the adequacy of this account of Christian theology arise immediately: Is not the source-consequence relationship, basic to this alternative, too trivial to justify use of the term "Christian"? Are not our religious ideas and practices decisively dependent on a number of rather diverse sources? Is the matter of normativeness to be dispensed with altogether in a Christian theology that proceeds along this path? We shall consider these three questions in order.

(1) The suspicion of triviality arises in part, I think, because, as is well known, the validity of beliefs have nothing in particular to do with their source, but we must postpone the question of validity until later. The matter of triviality also comes up, however, because of the decline of the role of tradition in Western thinking. To some extent the facts to be cited here are those having to do with the Renaissance, the development of scientific method and, more recently, the secular sense of a world "come of age." These emphases, though—however valid and now indispensible to our Western self-understanding—may well have had a distorted impact upon us by virtue of their coalescence with what might be called the "trivialization of causal derivation." Here I have in

mind the Humean critique that rendered the cause-effect relationship to be merely that of "regular successiveness"—to call one event the cause of another is only to say that the former is regularly followed by the latter. What is lost in this account is the sense that the cause somehow *creates* the consequence, entering into it, sustaining it, becoming a part of it, giving it life and direction. Even the term "derivation" itself, as a consequence, has now lost the suggestion of physical power implicit in its etymology as "a 'drawing off from' and thus being sustained by a river or stream." Nowadays the term takes its primary meaning from the abstract and necessary deductions of logic, and apart from this its meaning seems largely metaphorical. Thus, Christian theology has come to be viewed either as the logical consequence of some normative "Christian" datum; or, rather implausibly, it is viewed as merely that kind of thinking which, perhaps with remarkable conformity, seems to succeed, to come after, the thinking of antecedent generations who also call themselves Christian. Unless it is also the norm, it would appear, the source of theology, as sheer source, can be elevated to significance only as it is perilously bouyed by metaphor and mystification. Way Three, interpreted in this manner, has little to commend it.

What is wrong with the foregoing account of Way Three, in my opinion, is the inadequate understanding of causal derivation embodied in it. The "regular succession" interpretation of causality is adequate neither to the cummulative character of natural processes nor to the factor of historical indebtedness ingredient in our human experience. A more defensible view of the matter, I believe, is offered by A.N. Whitehead. Whitehead's position, relative to this particular issue, is that the obvious and evident way in which we "take account of" the external world, i.e., through our sensory experience, is in fact the dependent, highly refined consequence of another more fundamental mode of our relatedness to things. Sense experience is the outcome of a rich yet chaotic and vague preconceptual mode of perception wherein the physical world enters into that organismic unity of chemical, visceral, and psychic processes called the human body. The sense of Whitehead's doctrine is conveyed in the following statements:

For the organic theory, the most primitive perception is "feeling the body as functioning." This is a feeling of the world in the past; it is the inheritance of the world as a complex of feeling; namely, it is the feeling of derived feelings. The later, more sophisticated perception is "feeling the contemporary world."[4]

The irresistible causal efficacy of nature presses itself upon us; in the vagueness of the low hum and insects in an August woodland, the inflow into ourselves of feelings from enveloping nature overwhelms us; in the dim consciousness of half-sleep, the presentations of sense fade away, and we are left with the vague feeling of influences from vague things around us.[5]

The perception of conformation to realities in the environment is the primitive element in our external experience. We conform to our bodily organs and to the vague world which lies beyond them. Our primitive perception is that of "conformation" vaguely, and of the yet vaguer relata "oneself" and "another" in the undiscriminated background. . . . One part of our experience is handy, and definite in our consciousness; also it is easy to reproduce at will. The other type of experience, however insistent, is vague, haunting, unmanageable. The former type, of all its decorative sense-experience, is barren. It displays a world concealed under an adventitious show, a show of our own bodily production. The latter type is heavy with the contact of the things gone by, which lay their grip on our immediate selves.[6]

Whitehead's view, if correct, affirms the significance of causal derivation in a manner that makes Way Three a viable way of doing Christian theology, it seems to me. Specifically, it gives to the sustaining force of the symbols, myths, and rituals within any cultic tradition a meaning not amenable to psychological reductionism. At a preconceptual level—at a level of felt-inheritance—these components of tradition body forth a "mythos," a "pattern of meaning and valuation" concerning the fundamental character of our lives.[7] As bearers of meaning, these cultic components—symbols, myths, and rituals[8]—give rise to a family of conceptualities that are related but by no means identical. As bearers of valuation, they nourish the intention to transform these conceptualities into action. The question of truth is important, as we shall see, but it is premature to ask whether the symbols, myths, and rituals are themselves true. Their purpose is sacramental, not veridical. Their function is to express, to call us to a mode of efficacy beyond themselves that is more than we can think and, nevertheless, is the source of our thinking.

Christian theology is that theology[9] which speaks from out of the preconceptual mode of efficacy whose chief point of historical identity is Jesus of Nazareth. This tradition is there as an objective reality. Its originative elements—those events of first-century Palestine centering in Jesus—are there in some form as objective realities. Even the symbols, myths, and rituals are in some sense objective—their affective power is not arbitrarily produced, nor may it arbitrarily be taken away. But a theology's aim is not to conform to these givens as its norm. It seeks instead to give conceptual witness to the power they are seen to convey at the level of felt-meaning. The role of the Christian cultus is formative, not normative. The theologian reflects, and calls those reflections "Christian" in order to acknowledge the historic sources and personal resources of his or her thinking and being. Theology is Christian if it occurs in felt-dependence upon the cultus that has its historic rootage in the event of Jesus.

(2) The second question raised with respect to the adequacy of Way Three has to do with our dependency upon a diversity of sources. When a theology is appropriately called "Christian," I have argued, it is so designated as a matter of confessional or descriptive accuracy. But such accuracy is not always the prime consideration. It is sometimes irrelevant, as when the theologian speaks on matters to which his or her cultic inheritance is only minimally or indistinctively related. It is sometimes impractical, as in those situations where use of the term "Christian" is so perverted that the Christian theologian elects to dispense with this designation in order the more fully to witness to the reality that he or she believes the term to denote. And certainly there may come a time in the life of anyone when the intrusion of other cultic traditions, or perhaps the seeming absence of all, is so marked that the term "Christian" now confuses more than it describes the identity of those resources out of which one thinks and is. All of this suggests, I believe, that rules for the use of the term "Christian" cannot be tightly drawn. In part, its use is to be pragmatically decided, depending upon contextual considerations like those mentioned.

(3) We come, finally, to the question of truth. I have argued that a theology is to be identified in terms of its source, not in

terms of norms. Does this mean that theology is without norms? Not at all. The theologian's norms are certainly not uninfluenced by cultic resources, as they are not uninfluenced by the character of contemporary existence, but formally—and almost certainly materially, too, in my view—the theologian's norms will not be identical to either of these. Formally, for example, the theologian might say that theological reflection must be adequate to the shared dimensions of our human experience, adequate to the sense of ones own unique tradition(s), internally coherent, and consistent with nontheological claims that are believed to be true. It is probable, moreover, that certain events or dimensions of experience will be thought to conform to, or to illustrate, the formal norm with such vividness that, tentatively at least, they will function as paradigms or material norms. It is not surprising, for example, that the event of Jesus, which has so decisively formed those of us who are Christians, should by and large operate as the predominating paradigm in our judgments of truth and value. Where this is the case, however, the identity of the Jesus-event and the Christian's material norm is a contingent one; logically, this identity neither entails nor is entailed by the fact that a theology is Christian.

For the finite mind in search of truth, however, the primary question in this area, and the most anguishing one, is that of authority. Who validates the claim that this or that formulation is the proper formal norm, and who identifies this or that reality as its most adequate expression? Who or what "authorizes" the claim that something is true (or is rightly believed to be true)? There is, it seems to me, but one answer to this question. The theologian—as responsible person—elucidates norms, identifies paradigms, and authorizes their alleged instantiations. To paraphrase an observation from Jean-Paul Sartre, even in the case of a visitation from the Angel of the Lord, it is still the theologian who must decide whether the angel is real or imagined and, if real, whether from God or from Satan. The theologian is the authority.

It is this critical dimension of reflection and questioning, of course, that counters the excesses of the cultus. The symbols, myths, and rituals are not the reality of the tradition; they are its bearers. Hence, in the name of the reality borne, and with appeal to alternative cultic elements, one can always ask about the adequacy of any of the elements of the mythos which seek to convey that reality. Yet, as I have also tried to show, it is from participation in the cultus that the power of the Christian's reflection emanates. Criticism without cultus is empty; cultus without criticism is blind.[10]

NOTES

1. All kinds of variations are possible in speaking of Christ as the source of theology, depending on the way the datum, "Christ," is viewed, the way the causal-dependency is conceived, etc. It will become clear, I think, that these distinctions are not germane to the present discussion.

2. This matter of "degree" introduces additional complexity into the typology. If "Christ" is the decisive norm of theology, however, then I should think "Christ" would in any controverted matters have the effect of being the only norm, so that any variation of degree with respect to the *norm* seems inconsequential to me. Variations of degree regarding the *source* factor will be discussed later.

3. Walter Kaufmann, trans., *Goethe's Faust* (Garden City, N.Y.: Doubleday, 1961), p. 109.

4. A.N. Whitehead, *Process and Reality* (New York: Macmillan, 1929), p. 125.

5. *Ibid.*, p. 267; cf. pp. 184 & 271.

6. A.N. Whitehead, *Symbolism: Its Meaning and Effect* (New York: Capricorn, 1959), p. 43f.; cf. pp. 39-49, 53-59. See, too, Whitehead, *Modes of Thought* (New York: Free Press, 1968), p. 71f.

7. The material in quotation marks is from Bernard E. Meland who, among Christian theologians attracted to Whiteheadian thought, has done the most to develop this point of view in terms of theological method. See, e.g., his *Faith and Culture* (New York: Oxford University Press, 1953), esp. Part II.

8. By "symbols, myths and rituals" I refer, respectively, to the objects, stories, and acts of a tradition *as affective realities*, as mediators of the fundamental preconceptual reality and power of that tradition. (A story, for example, may be a "myth" in this sense without regard to its historical accuracy, as is shown, for example, by both the passion narrative and by the stories of the virgin birth and the immaculate conception.) The "mythos" is the total complex of symbols, myths, and rituals, and the "cultus" is the historical reality associated with the mythos.

9. In order to ask, "what is *Christian* theology?" I have sidestepped the

logically prior questions, "what is theology?" Very briefly, my response to the latter question is that theology is the systematic effort to elucidate the meaning of belief in God. But since I also hold that belief in God is to be understood, most fundamentally, as a positive answer to the question of the ultimate significance of our lives, I can also say that theology is that form of reflection which seeks to unfold, in a reasoned and systematic way, what it means to affirm that our lives have an ultimate worth or significance. The Whiteheadian background of this position is discussed in my essay, "The World and God: A Process Perspective" (in Norbert O. Schedler, ed., *Philosophy of Religion: Contemporary Perspectives*, New York: Macmillan, 1974, 436ff.). This view of theology has been most fully developed by Schubert M. Ogden in *The Reality of God and Other Essays* (New York: Harper & Row, 1966), pp. 1-70. (I am not, however, persuaded by Ogden's claim that belief in life's ultimate worth, and hence faith in God, are "in the last analysis unavoidable," as I indicate in "God's Reality and Life's Meaning: A Critique of Schubert Ogden," *Encounter*, 28, 3 [Summer, 1967], 256-262.)

10. I am greatly indebted to several members of the faculty at Emory University for pressing the questions that stimulated this essay, and to Professor Hendrikus Boers in particular. It was enormously beneficial for me to be able to work for a semester in a community where an open, critical dialogue between colleagues is pursued and protected with such vigor.

SUGGESTED READINGS

Meland, Bernard E. *Faith and Culture*. New York: Macmillan, 1953.
——*The Realities of Faith*. New York: Oxford, 1962.

Whitehead, Alfred North. *Symbolism: Its Meaning and Effect*. New York: Macmillan, 1927.

4 What We Need Is Indoor Plumbing or, Whiteheadian Style and the Search for a New Scientific Order

RICHARD H. OVERMAN

It has been interesting in recent years to see story and biography and autobiography emerge as modes of theological discourse. If theology is to make much sense, it must stay solidly grounded in real experience—yet, by its nature, it generalizes the character of individual experiences in order to elucidate all experience. Not all storytelling does that—sometimes it does not depart from the mere particularity (albeit engrossing in its own right) of individual lives. But at a deep enough level each man's story is a historical inscape. In the "story" told in this chapter, Professor Overman talks about his own life and his romance with process thought as a way of discoursing about history: "And if you will not forget that I write with a real suspicion of my own villainy, I will say also that I have a sense that my own deep experience is not merely personal; I have to speak of it in ways suggestive of Jung's notion of a 'collective unconscious,' such that struggling to see what is happening in my depths is somehow the same as watching the whole of civilization groaning on to its next foothold."

Richard H. Overman has taught on the Faculty of Religion at the Methodist-related University of

Puget Sound since 1965, where he is now Professor and Department Chairman. After sampling geology and engineering, he took a premedical course at Stanford (B.S., 1950), where he was also graduated from the School of Medicine (M.D., 1954). He was in the general practice of medicine for four years. In 1958 he began theological studies at the University of Claremont. After ordination as a Methodist minister in 1962, he studied for a year at the University of Zurich, returning to Claremont to complete his Ph.D. in theology in the philosophy of religion. During these years he held Kent, Dempster, and Rockefeller fellowships. His publications include Evolution and the Christian Doctrine of Evolution: A Whiteheadian Interpretation *(Westminster, 1967), and a number of journal articles, including "A Christological View of Nature" in* Religious Education *(January-February, 1971); "Hat die Theologie die Natur Vergessen" in* Radius *(Stuttgart, September, 1973).*

Since American television-viewers are being required this year to feel nostalgic about the 1950's, let me steal ahead of the scriptwriters and let you hear a bit from 1943, the year the musical play *Oklahoma!* opened in New York:

Everythin's up to date in Kansas City—
   They've gone about as fur as they kin go!
They went 'n built a skyscraper seven stories high,
   'bout as high as a buildin' oughter grow!

Everythin's like a dream in Kansas City—
   It's better than a magic-lantern show!
Y' kin turn the radiator on whenever y' want some heat;
   With ev'ry kind of comfort ev'ry house is all complete;

   Y' kin walk to privies in the rain and never wet your feet!
They've gone about as fur as they kin go—yes sir!—
   They've gone about as fur as they kin go!

I can remember laughing and whistling my way through these lyrics thirty years ago, as a teen-ager. In those days my friends and I were tickled at the image of a country boy whose imagination was only seven stories high—yes sir!—wouldn't he be *paralyzed* if he could look down from the Empire State Building or glimpse the maze of metropolitan sewers beneath its concrete-and-steel feet! It was a real chuckle for us, hearing that simple musical version of where the "modrun world" was a-goin', for our own mental horizon seemed *so* much broader, *so* much more informed by the "big picture" of a world where human life expressed itself in scientific reason and leapfrogged ahead in a series of technical miracles. Most of us were Christians, which I am sure helped account for our confidence that the great war in Europe and Asia would turn out to be the temporary frenzy of a civilization destined for better things; after all, a high spiking fever seen on a big hospital chart need not mask the signs of gradual recovery. My real grounds for hope are the same now as they were then; but in those days our hope took the form of a picture of ourselves growing up to be engineers, helping to build the new world after the war—and many of us enrolled in courses for that future.

Looking back thirty years later, I notice that I actually did not finish the engineering course that I began; instead, I followed a medical course. But at a certain point I rather abruptly withdrew from a program leading to a specialty in eye surgery—and a few years later I left my medical practice entirely, to follow a theological course. I intended to become a minister of a congregation after ordination—but instead of that, I became a teacher of theology in a college. A few years after I began to teach, we bought an old house, and I have spent the last summers largely in rebuilding it, devouring books on carpentry, plumbing, and design. At the same time, I notice that I scrupulously avoid the meetings of the American Academy of Religion; I look on them from afar, almost as though they were meetings of the Flat Earth Society. And during these last years my mind and spirit have probed here and there, often in a mood of vague but profound dis-ease where I have no interest at all in the lists of new theological books that fall like a pot of hot tar on my head.

Without any prior conscious plan, I seem to have refused to specialize in first one thing and then another. Why? Is it because I am afraid of being exposed as a fraud? Because I am inclined to quit before things get tough? Over the years a series of such questions has occurred to me, and I can truthfully answer them any way you like. But the best thing to say is that as I reflect over this thirty years I have to confess that I don't understand what I'm doing. And since I have a great longing to understand things, including my own life, there are times when this ignorance causes me to "give free utterance to my complaint" and "speak in the bitterness of my soul" to God.

Sometimes I am quite sure that the proper text for this thirty years is Job 9:29, "I shall be condemned; why then do I labor in vain?" And that a statement Lewis Mumford once made to the Ribicoff Committee on governmental expenditures applies to my whole life: "In the course of doing this, you will bring about even more villainous conditions than those which you are trying to correct."[1] But all that suspicion of myself as a villain presents itself right along with another quite different feeling that has never been absent for any long period in my life and which, curiously, even grows stronger. It is a feeling of being the possessor of some inarticulate secret, of being close to some treasure, which others do not perceive. I recognize myself in C. G. Jung's description of himself in his old age: "Today as then I am a solitary, because I know things and must hint at things which other people do not know, and usually do not even want to know."[2]

Now in case it should turn out that I *do* know something, I will be puzzled as to why *I* know it and why it strikes me as a secret; and in case what I know turns out to be nothing at all, that will only confirm the suspicion of my villainy. Also, the only claim to *originality* I am obliged to feel is to the form of my villainy—and of that, the less the better—for I have no sense of inventing what I know, of being responsible for it. Responsible *to* it, yes, like any other gardener in such soil; but with such a secret one can hope for nothing more than to avoid chopping its fragile stem with some blunt hoe designed for other crops. It is there in the garden when I come upon it, it grows by itself, and it seems secret only because its roots are so nearly hidden from me and the other gardeners.

II

As it happens, I became acquainted with Whitehead's writings exactly halfway through the thirty years I have been describing—in 1959. Looking back now, I am struck by the fact that I never had to be persuaded against my will to take Whitehead's views seriously. On the contrary, from the first reading until now my usual response has been, "Yes, of course—." I simply recognized in Whitehead's work the fullest intellectual expression of what I knew in my depths to be so, but had not thought to say. During the past fifteen years I have written a couple of theses, a book, a few articles, and a large and apparently unending series of Whiteheadian "thought-probes" on sheets of paper that I pile up in my study—all expressing my confidence in the explanatory power of Whitehead's vision. For example, I believe that in the end the darkness of Hegel's language and the unfocused brilliance of Teilhard's poetic imagery can be brought together clearly in a Whiteheadian effort to describe what they saw—and that the great affirmations of Newton and Darwin and Marx merely call for similar restatement in order to find their own fuller places in our lives. (You see I am boasting like St. Paul that in my own way "I advanced . . . beyond many of my own age," so you will know I am an "insider" in the Whiteheadian enterprise, with a decoder pin and everything!)

Also by now I am aware that a good deal of my own unconscious "assembly plant" is working according to Whiteheadian principles—in recent years, I have several times waked in the morning after dreams of great colorful concrescent occasions in which the strangest paradoxes are overcome! Still, I know that my consciousness too easily tolerates ideas out of tune with what I know in my depths, ideas less expressive of what I know than are Whitehead's ideas; and I have learned by now that every rereading of Whitehead evokes in me a response not unlike that which grows from reading the New Testament—an awareness of "disclosure" from these depths, accompanied by an embarrassing recollection of my own guilty consciousness. When this happens, I am amused that a man named Overman reads Whitehead in order to discover what *Overman* thinks! But also it is quite clear that what I *do* finally think is the expression of some complex and unfathomable unconscious process in a deep and moving stream from which my thinking emerges at times, almost as the effluent used to emerge from our septic tank before the sewers came (If you are offended at that image, pray recall that my blackberry vines—older and wiser in the ways of fluids than we—found effluent to be quite nourishing!) And if you will not forget that I write with a real suspicion of my own possible villany, I will say also that I have a sense that my own deep experience is not merely personal; I have to speak of it in ways suggestive of Jung's notion of a "collective unconscious," such that struggling to see what is happening in my depths is somehow the same as watching the whole of civilization groaning on to its next foothold. More and more, it seems to me that there is some important connection between Whiteheadian ideas and my actual behavior during these years; and that the dual task of understanding myself and understanding the movement of history is a single adventure in what I might call "Whiteheadian auto-hermeneutics." So in what follows I will describe part of this adventure, hoping not to do harm where I intend good.

I remember quite clearly how it was that I came to be married to my wife. For several years I rather methodically refrained from marrying a succession of young women about whom I kept feeling, "No—something's wrong here—hold off," until at the right time I met my wife. Some of those ladies are still my good friends, and even now I would be hard put to say what *was* wrong, or in some cases whether the "wrongness" lay in them or in me or in the season of life. I am only describing the way it seemed: my task was to avoid doing something wrong, to back away when I felt a wrong move until the right move became clear. My expression of vocation seems to have followed a similar course. It is almost as though I were a giant amoeba, testing for wrong moves by slowly advancing part of myself and then withdrawing, advancing and withdrawing, groping uncertainly for the right opening, but in the meanwhile keeping most of myself in reserve. Again, the trick is to watch out for red flags so as to keep from getting trapped in one of those tentative "wrong" vocational explorations. During these years there have been many periods when things felt somehow "wrong" day after day, week after week, and when I have wished vainly for some sense of what *would* be the "right" move. Also, the things that have felt "wrong" to me have usually disclosed their "wrongness" only after I have made some kind of advance with them, so that I find myself triply embarrassed—by my own withdrawal, by my blundering inability to foresee the need to withdraw, and by my fumbling efforts to explain just *why* I am withdrawing. (There, I suppose an amoeba has an advantage on me in not being troubled by a guilty conscience!)

Such things have made it quite clear to me that my consciousness is far from autonomous. There is a deeper current of experience from which my conscious thought and behavior spring, and somewhere in this same deep current there is also an appellate court that continually approves or reverses the decisions of my consciousness. The sense of "wrongness" that so often lingers with me seems to occur when I have partially invested myself in some pattern of conscious order that proves to be out of tune with that deeper current—as though the various patterns of conscious order that I try on are probes at identifying the "narrow gate" (Matthew 7:14), and the deeper current that sifts those patterns is the "ax . . . laid to the root of the tree" (Matthew 3:10). In such matters, I feel quite comfortable explaining myself with Whitehead's ideas (especially when I recall certain Christian notions of original sin), for it does seem to me that the best description of my moment-by-moment and year-by-year adventures is one that stresses my difficulties in allowing a divinely given initial aim to become determinative of my whole conscious and unconscious experience.

III

In seeking to understand these matters I think first of Whitehead's observation that we inhabit a world stuck together in "layers of social order"[3]—cells are in organs, organs are in bodies, bodies are on the Earth. All of this social order can be discussed using the word "institution," since an "institution" is any planetary device for instituting some social characteristics into some other creatures down the line. From where I view things, then, there are some "institutions" that seem immediately important to me and some that play a smaller supporting role (often only incidentally, in the midst of having their own adventures). My family is an institution, and so is my own soul in its successive moments of experience; also there are a lot of tiny institutions that my soul lives with—"molecules" and "atoms" and "cells." These layers of social order together comprise the whole *kosmos* of my patterned consciousness, so that to ask after the source of "wrongness" in my conscious experience is at the same time to ask about my relationships with all these institutions, large and small.

Now, if my habit of interpreting myself with Whitehead's

ideas—my science of Whiteheadian auto-hermeneutics— has made any difference to me during the last fifteen years, the difference is that I have come to see that the "narrow gate" is narrower than I thought thirty years ago, and that the ax which is "laid to the root of the trees" chops where I never then dreamed it would. That is, the deeper currents of my experience have called into question some surprising parts of my conscious patterns of order, so that paths which I would once have taken to be rightly expressive of those divinely provided initial aims have come to be clothed in the sense of "wrongness" I have mentioned. It is not a feeling that some unseen *daimon* is destroying the entire *kosmos* of my conscious experience, leaving me before a *chaos*; for one thing, my marriage continues to be an almost embarrassing delight, compared with most others; and something does "ring true" when two boards match up in my workshop. But to be surprised by the appearance of "wrongness" where I did not expect it does cause me to reflect over all those patterns of my conscious order, seeking to prove their worth.

Regarding all the *tiny* institutions, the main report I have is a sense of getting on pretty well with them—they seem mainly to be all right. As it happens, I began to write these lines on Good Friday, a day when crosses are draped in black. But it was also the year's first really beautiful spring day where I live near Puget Sound. So if there is cause for gloom, I heard my daffodils say, it doesn't lie down here in the ground with us! Nor, I add, down here in my cells. When it comes to that world of tiny molecular and cellular institutions—what from my viewpoint can be called my support system—things are pretty good. Really, they are. I feed my liver cells delectable goodies and I keep away from carbon tetrachloride, so my liver cells probably feel as though all's right with the world. Of course there are a couple of things they don't much take into account: the fact that *I* am riding around up here, and the fact that *they* are going to suffer a surprising energy crisis one of these days! Meanwhile, though, we are all right together.

I am fascinated by the intricate cellular institutions of the human brain, all those fiber tracts, reserve depots, and inhibitory synapses—if we really understood the evolutionary development of all that, of how we came to have the strange ability to speak, wow!—but I know I am not a brain any more than I am a daf-

fodil. I can cause my daffodils to bloom on Good Friday by burying bulbs in October, and I can cause my speech to bloom by
burying myself in my brain in due season. But fundamentally,
brains and daffodil bulbs are "something else," and it is clear that
my disappointment at a stroke that might deprive me of the blos-
som of speech would be only a heightened version of the disappointment I would suffer if my daffodil bulbs failed to bloom. I
am leading up to reporting that neither the prospect of improvements in bulbs nor the prospect of improvements in brains seems
to relieve that sense of "wrongness" I have described. Brains and
bulbs belong to that world of tiny institutions where things are really mainly all right. Consequently, when Arthur Koestler specu-
lates about a chemical cure for what's wrong in the world,[4] I
think he has just made an error in diagnosis. I am not against
using chemicals any more than he is—we both enjoy our breakfast—but the "wrongness" I know just would not be helped by
applying any sort of chemical fertilizer, either to daffodils or to
brains. It does not spring from the tiny institutions in those layers
of social order.

I know there is cardiac "sudden death" and cancer and dia-
betes and Mongolism, and that they seem to occur when some of
these tiny institutions get to enjoying themselves in ways that happen to short out my circuits up the line. But physicians sometimes
approach these "social problems" with the fervor of Gnostic
priests, whose not-quite-explicit goal is to free the human soul entirely from its bothersome entanglements with liver cells and
heart-muscle fibers.[5] Such fascinated attention to the problems
caused for us by the innocent "misadventures" of our tiny bodily
institutions is impressive, but—after all—we will continue to live
and die *with* our tiny bodily institutions, so I would be glad to see
our enthusiasm for curing all diseases tempered just a bit by
remembering that all the people Jesus was reported to have
healed apparently died of something else later on! I am just reporting to you (and you may remember I am a physician, if you
like) that most of our cultural fascination with the "wrongness"
in Earth's tiny institutions seems to me a way of not paying attention to more important things. Each year, for example, about
120,000 Americans die and nearly 500,000 suffer permanent disa-
bilities from injuries—a "wrongness" that stems from Earth's
larger "institutions," the ones that employ guns, automobiles,

knives, and fire. Nevertheless, American research in healing the effects of trauma receives 50 cents per year per victim, compared with $238 for each victim of cancer.[6] It may sound odd, but there is a sense in which cancer research is the sand into which we stick our scientific ostrich's head.

IV

Delving among the cells and molecules, my Whiteheadian auto-hermenuetics seem to say, is somehow "wrong." I don't mean to say that such delving should be abandoned—that would be a revolutionary, even anarchic proposal. My point is really quite conservative, applauding all research that can protect daffodils, livers, and other anciently established planetary institutions. (I am never able to forget that a single species of fairy shrimp has endured without apparent change for 180 million years!) But still I do feel a "wrongness" associated with delving among cells and molecules these days; so there must be more involved than my sense of getting along all right with such tiny institutions.

I believe it is the fact that the sciences which delve in these institutions—physics, chemistry, biology—are in some sense drawing near the "end of the road." The deep currents of human life and their mental expressions move on, and the patterns of social order are forever giving way, so that old institutions gradually lose their importance. Now, ever since the beginning of civilization human beings have been fascinated by their intuitions of physical order.[7] And during the past several centuries the sciences that experiment with Earth's "tiny institutions" have themselves become the focussed institutional expression of that ancient and powerful stratum of human experience. *But it is this long chapter of man's history—the period of his fascination with objective patterns of physical order—that I feel drawing to a close.*

Sometimes institutions end because they have failed, but sometimes the reason is that they have been *successful*, reaching their goals and giving rise to something beyond themselves. It is in this sense of "end," then, that I feel much of modern science drawing to a close. In the gradual emergence, flowering, and fading of the modern mechanistic scientific vision I see a civilizational advance-and-withdrawal lasting far longer than any of my own adventures, yet present within them and recognizable there as a single amoeboid exploration by Western man. It has been an exploration to see whether the entire fabric of conscious order grows from roots that are merely physical, whether the whole world of human experience is "mechanical." And it has been marvelously successful, because it has helped us see for the first time what a "mechanism" *is*—and, in the end, that our world of experience *isn't* quite one of those.[8] It is as though the last few centuries of intensely focussed scientific work, and their final expression in technology, are merely the coda to a long symphony whose recurrent theme is never hidden by the solo instruments and that proclaims over and over, "That's an *order!* that's an *order!* that's an *order!*" The order of the day, or of the centuries, has been . . . order.

The symphony is nearly through; several thousand years of allowing consciousness to be filled with sensations and thoughts of every imaginable "routine," both in this world and in the next, draw toward their close—and with a gasp we stand on the brink of a holiday. When I try to understand that, there come to mind certain superficially paradoxical claims by Buddhists that a wholehearted plunge into the power-ridden world of earthly experience will demonstrate its impotence, that *nirvana* is the flip side of *samsara*. I am reminded also of Thomas Altizer's statement that the descent into hell will turn out to be the ascent into heaven,[9] of Marshall McLuhan's belief that the "linear age" is bringing about its own end,[10] even of the parable of the Prodigal Son.

Near the beginning of these remarks I said that as a teenager I felt World War II as the temporary frenzy of a civilization destined for better things. But now I see behind that image all the armies that ever were or are, looming up as the most familiar statement of that old symphonic theme that is now dying away and whose dying we can glimpse as modern science comes to its end. The fact is, however, that many people seem unable even to *imagine* a human world without armies! This strikes me as a kind of reverse twist on St. Anselm's claim that we are really unable to imagine the nonexistence of God; only muddleheaded people, he believed, would even *try* to imagine that.[11] And if he was correct, the odd thing will be why anyone ever *did* try to imagine it; but meanwhile there are people who do not seem to themselves at all perverse or foolish, and who persist in thinking you *can* imagine that. The currents moving in their depths fail to produce springs of thought like Anselm's. Similarly, there seem to be some deep currents (perhaps—the same ones?) moving in the human unconscious that still keep most people from recognizing armies as the temporary cultural extension of mankind during that period of a few thousand years when we have been fascinated by the patterns of objective physical order. It is possible that the dilemma of the atomic bomb will be more understandable in retrospect when we realize that producing an army of test-tube-equipped scientific researchers was very like producing an army of bazooka-equipped infantrymen, and that both kinds of armies can march to the same drummer.

V

There has been a recent upswing in the percentage of people who believe in the Devil; but Jung reminded us that the human unconscious and its *daimons* are "at least *neutral*,"[12] so we can look into those depths and wonder whether some refreshing currents have been flowing through the entire period of man's preoccupation with patterns of objective order. My thirty-year project has gotten to the point where the chief order of business seems to be a "plumbing" job, a job of "fishing" in a deep pool where "busy-ness" isn't an "order," but where I wait, wait, wait for the rippling of the pool. It is as though all the structures of civilized order, all the ways of building them into enduring symphonies and throwaway cities, all the ways of thinking them into conscious systems of thought (including especially my Whiteheadian way) point beyond themselves, down into those moving depths from which may emerge the form of a new order. The catchy tune from *Oklahoma!* now speaks to me not of seven-story buildings but of this new kind of "indoor plumbing" that may disclose that all my familiar forms of conscious order have "gone about as fur as they kin go!" Still, I am often aware that my Whiteheadian ideas do function as the abstracted history of civilization, a form of conscious order without which I might be either captured by some demonic novelty or carried off into some equally deadly routine—deadly not merely to me, but to that Creation that I feel groaning through me. And if I *do* manage to avoid being trapped in some advance, it will be partly the result of retaining that order. So, as I said, I am no revolutionary; neither am I a seeker after a "trip" or a romantic. But still: *when I am most "in tune" with that order is when I feel my world—with all its "routines"—to be on the brink of a holiday.*

In my university I have just begun my turn as chairman of a department, charged with glimpsing the way ahead, perceiving the outlines of an emerging order. I am sure Lewis Mumford was describing my task of learning to hear this refreshing stream in the depths when he wrote, "Such a reaction, one must honestly confess, has never yet occurred in history solely as a result of rational thinking and educational indoctrination: nor is it likely to occur in this way now."[13] And in such matters, Jung wrote, "Certainly the conscious mind seems unable to do anything useful."[14] But many of my colleagues are still preoccupied with that consciousness of the patterns of objective order which we call "reason," and so they say, "A university is dedicated to rational inquiry and conscious understanding." I hear them, and I know they are *almost* speaking the truth, that what they say *was* true all during that chapter of human history which is now drawing to its close. But now, and as far ahead as I can see, a university must be first of all a listening post, a sonar station ceaselessly tuning its ears to pick up the faint rushings of that deep water-spirit.

I do not know or much care what will happen to the word "science" in the midst of such listening. It may be that "science" will come to mean "routine" or even "nonsense." It may be that "science" will come to indicate a larger slice of human enterprise than it has during the past few centuries, a slice including, perhaps even *beginning* with, the subjective disciplines of "depth-charging" and stream-listening. This is, I believe, the best meaning of "a new scientific order." I do know that refreshing stream is running, even calling, and I suppose another thirty years of listening will let me speak of it more clearly than I can now. Meanwhile, if we feel any such stream moving, any calling toward vocations that are more than deadly routine or suicidal invention, I am sure the discovery of these callings will bring with it a recovery of a sense that we are provided for. My adventure of Whiteheadian auto-hermeneutics reminds me that, in a way which may even surprise the Woodsman, the ax laid to the root of the tree can slip off and lay open the soil for new grain.

NOTES

1. Lewis Mumford, "A Brief History of Urban Frustration," in *The Urban Prospect* (New York: Harcourt, Brace & World, Inc., 1968), p. 215.

2. C.G. Jung, *Memories, Dreams, Reflections*, recorded and ed. by Aniela Jaffé and trans. by Richard and Clara Winston (New York: Random House Vintage Books, 1963), p. 42.

3. Alfred North Whitehead, *Process and Reality* (New York: Macmillan, 1929), p. 138.

4. Arthur Koestler, *The Ghost in the Machine* (New York: Macmillan, 1967), especially ch. XVIII, "The Age of Climax."

5. I have even read of a surprising event called "surviving sudden death," written not by St. Mark but by a member of a cardiac-resuscitation team. See Randy Kobernick, "Heart Watch Up To 7000 Participants and Growing," *Health Science Review* (Spring, 1974), p. 2.

6. Dave Docter, "Texas Trauma and Burn Surgeon Comes to UW," *ibid.*, p. 1.

7. See Lewis Mumford's excellent comprehensive study in two volumes, *The Myth of the Machine: Technics and Human Development* and *The Myth of the Machine: The Pentagon of Power* (New York: Harcourt Brace Jovanovich, Inc., 1967 and 1970).

8. I am not implying that the mechanistic vision is *ineffective* in our world, since it is the formative vision in the lives of people whose fingers are hovering near dangerous push-buttons. It could be fatal to forget this. Nevertheless, that vision is like a rusty flywheel disengaged from its engine, running on mere momentum against increasing friction.

9. Thomas J.J. Altizer, *The Descent Into Hell: A Study of the Radical Reversal of the Christian Consciousness* (Philadelphia: Lippincott, 1970).

10. McLuhan's most focussed expression is in *The Gutenberg Galaxy: The Making of Typographic Man* (1962) and *Understanding Media* (1964), where he makes it quite clear that he is not an advocate of the "electronic immediacy" that destroys ordered conscious images.

11. See esp. Charles Hartshorne's discussion in *The Logic of Perfection* and *Anselm's Discovery* (Lasalle, Ill.: Open Court, 1962 and 1965).

12. C.G. Jung, "Approaching the Unconscious," in Jung *et al.*, *Man and His Symbols* (Garden City, New York: Doubleday, 1964), p. 103.

13. Mumford, *The Myth of the Machine: The Pentagon of Power*, p. 411.

14. Jung, "Approaching the Unconscious," p. 101.

SUGGESTED READINGS

Jung, C.G. *Memories, Dreams, Reflections.* New York: Random House, 1963.

Mumford, Lewis. *The Myth of the Machine: The Pentagon of Power.* New York: Harcourt Brace Jovanovich, 1970.

5 S-I-Z-E Is the Measure

BERNARD M. LOOMER

Systems of thought are, sooner or later, value stances. And usually sooner! But it is not all that easy to identify the value stances, for they are so intimately connected with the presuppositions upon which a system rests. If ethical systems are to emerge, they will "rise up" out of the presuppositions. Whitehead has said that beauty is the aim of existence, and perhaps some of the best clues to his value stances are to be found in his discussions of beauty, especially in the chapter on "Beauty" in *Adventures of Ideas*. His reflections there deal with minor forms of beauty and major forms of beauty. As accurate as beauty might be for the basic metaphor in Whitehead, beauty tends to be too tame a word to capture the stress and strain and satisfaction of process—especially in regard to "major forms of beauty." Dr. Loomer's discussion of size (spell it out in capitals, please: S-I-Z-E) is one of the best "translations" yet of the value stance that undergirds process/relational thought in the Whiteheadian mode. "Translation" must be in quotation marks, for it is only part of the picture—this essay on size is equally the product of Dr. Loomer's own significant contribution to process theology.

Bernard M. Loomer fully belongs in a volume on process theology, for it was he who baptized the "process" school of thought with the name that has stuck. He is presently Professor of Philosophical Theology at the Graduate Theological Union. He taught for many years at the University of Chicago, where he was Dean of the Divinity School. He received his training at Bates College (A.B.) and the University of Chicago (Ph.D.). His writings have appeared in previous collections of essays in process

69

theology, and in journals. He continues to be one of the important formative influences in the growth of process theology.

I suppose as one gets older, things sift through his total being as he moves along. Weights of emphasis alter and you find that the living of life requires simplification in order to make it manageable. The scientific method, as I would understand it, is the greatest illustration of the attempt to simplify life to manageable terms, with all the strengths and weaknesses and privileges apertaining thereto.

For myself, I find that I operate with fewer principles. I know much less than I used to. I have many more questions, and fewer answers. Sometimes I am not even sure that I am interested in the answers anymore. I get so interested in the questions that I do not have the patience to listen to someone who has gotten it all worked out in ways that I do not believe belong to life.

Finally, for me, the one basic principle that I operate with is the principle of *size.* That is the category of largeness or smallness. If it is small, I am not interested in whether it is true; I do not care; it really is not worth bothering with. If the idea is fertile, if the person has stature, I am interested.

I am first of all interested not in order to criticize, but rather simply to be with it for awhile. The criticism, if it comes, will come later. Moreover, the criticism, when it puts in an appearance, will arrive after I have lived with this largeness, this size, for a considerable amount of time.

By *size* I mean the stature of a person's soul, the range and depth of his love, his capacity for relationships. I mean the volume of life you can take into your being and still maintain your integrity and individuality, the intensity and variety of outlook you can entertain in the unity of your being without feeling defensive or insecure. I mean the strength of your spirit to encourage others to become freer in the development of their diversity and uniqueness. I mean the power to sustain more complex and enriching tensions. I mean the magnanimity of concern to provide conditions that enable others to increase in stature.

To me, this is the fundamental category, this is the essential principle. Everything else, I think, in my life is an abstraction from this or a commentary upon this. And I have concocted a few examples or dimensions of size to illustrate what I mean.

I believe that value is greater than truth. I am addicted to truth, but the problem with being addicted to truth is that it can throw you off from many of the deeper dimensions of life that I would include under the notion of value. Truth is a value. But truth is not the ground, not the source of value. If you want to put it differently, value is the genus and truth is the species.

I believe it is actually more important for someone to say something by which we can live, even if it is wrong, than it is to be preeminently concerned about the legitimacy or the validity of what can be said. I say this partly autobiographically because when I was in your position, I believed that no theologian should say anything until he got this question of truth straightened out. I thought that there ought to be a moratorium on theology until all the theologians, at least in this country, got together and settled the question of truth; and then on that basis, we might begin to make some assertions, hopefully. And I found that after a while I was eating out of my own stomach. But this really is a very meager diet and I decided to give up that way of life and try something else.

The difficulty is that scholars do not have to say anything by which people can live. They can in some legitimate way preoccupy themselves with whether or not what has been said should have been said or could be said with any validity. And sometimes I think biblical scholars are wholly dependent upon some damn fool theologian making some damn fool statement or another, and having the biblical scholar search throughout the Bible to find out whether it can be said in that way and on what, if any, biblical grounds. Otherwise they would have nothing to do.

I believe in reason; but I believe it is better to be right for the wrong reasons than to be wrong for the right reasons. Hopefully, it is desirable to be right for the right reasons, but it seems to me that this alternative all too seldom occurs in life. I would rather link myself with those who attempt to say something important, or even interesting, than to wait for the scholarly group to find out whether it is true. But fortunately, life moves ahead of scholarship, and we do not have to wait for the scholars to tell us whether we can actually live or even think or speak in the manners and styles that we have to use in order to live.

I believe it is of more size and therefore better to listen and to analyze than it is to argue or to counterthrust point by point. I believe that the greatest criticism of another can be given by one who is first of all content to understand the other, to hear the other out, to let the other be, to help the other become even greater than he is. To do this without fear, without being insecure, without feeling threatened; to let the other be, to provide the conditions and atmosphere by which that other person in his point of view can become more fully what he is to become. This is size. Later the criticism may come, but by that time the criticism will be quite different. It will take place in a different context and you will be addressing yourself to the largest possible other. On the other hand, where one is not careful, in argumentation one may address oneself to the worst possible other, or one may fail to provide the conditions whereby the other can be as strong and able as he could be.

I think this is the first obligation of the scholar: to let the other be as fully as he may become. Then later you may have a point or two to suggest to him. But, as I say, by that time you will be addressing quite a different individual, and you, yourself, doing the addressing will be quite a different individual, because you cannot, I think, deeply live with another without having that other become part of the very fiber of your being. At least, as I look around this room, I know from whence much of what I am came. It came from many, many hours listening to others, not always listening, I'm afraid, in ways that would help the others to become as great as they might become, but trying at least. And in this attempt finding myself being transformed by virtue of the relationship. Whether the others were being transformed by the relationship was their business, but it was my business to attempt to provide the conditions necessary.

I believe that an idea that can be generalized is greater in size than an idea that is simply a competent idea. I believe that the process of generalizing an idea or a meaning is a way of illustrating the size, the fertility, the creativity, of an idea. In this sense, generalization is an art lying beyond, presupposing but nonetheless transcending competence. I think if I had to do it over again and if we were still to keep the ranks of professors, I would attempt to preserve the title of full professor only for those who either have the capacity or concern to generalize the meaning of an important idea found in one field and to apply it to some other field beyond their competence. All other ranks would be reserved for those who are competent. Even if the person were the renowned expert, recognized world-wide in his field, and had neither the interest nor capacity to generalize, he would remain an associate professor.

Because until we generalize our ideas to apply beyond the source from whence we derive these ideas we contribute to the creation of the tower of Babel. We create the confusion because we cannot communicate with others in terms of our competencies. There are too many languages, too many niceties. Life is too short. Furthermore, as long as you are only competent, you have not paid the price in full of what it means to be human, the full price.

That full price has to do with size. This means you must generalize basic meanings in your field beyond their specialized meaning. In this respect I do not think the universities are justifiable in terms of the way they now operate.

I live in a state, California, where it is not that Mr. Reagan was right for the wrong reasons. He was wrong for all the right reasons, in many respects. But underneath it there is a germ in which he was right, although he does not have the wit to see it. One cannot justify what he was saying, but neither can one justify what the university professors are saying by their rebuttal. They still operate in terms of the self-justifying character and the self-sufficiency of the idea of competence and research and knowledge. I still think that it is possible to live very well without knowledge, important though knowledge is. We do not always live in terms of the manageabilities of life, and I wish that university professors would take this opportunity of great crisis and freely exercise the initiative to rethink what it is they are doing. Because the way things are going, I think it is quite possible (as this possibility has been explored in science fiction literature) that the public could end up by destroying all books and all scientific knowledge because the price of the knowledge has been too great and too dehumanizing with regard to the larger aspects of life itself.

I believe furthermore that the idea of the communal individual is larger than the idea of the noncommunal individual. I believe in the importance of the idea of the communal individual, although I would rather add the notion that the individual is an emergent from his communal relationships. And as one thinks of process thought, as I have tended to do for more than a little time now, the point of process thought is not simply the notion of a process as such. This is only one half of the story. The other half is the relationships of the process. The key, the punchline, the drive of process thought is not process in the abstract. It is the dynamic character of relations in process, relations leading to something emergent from the relationships. For this reason we need great communities in order to have great individuals, in order to have great relationships out of which concrete individuals can emerge with their power and with their strength. We need great communities, great academic communities, in order to produce more fully fulfilled students and faculty. I think the idea of a communal individual is a greater idea, has more size, more power than the notion of individuality that we have had before.

I believe that concrete individuality is greater than possibility. In certain respects we can say that there is a richness to potentiality that is never exhausted by actuality, but there is the other sense in which you do not have and cannot have a possible individual. The individual in his concreteness adds something, something indefinable, that possibility cannot include. I say this in order to emphasize the point that incarnation is not the embodiment of an idea. The idea is an abstraction from concrete individuality which has its own surdness, its own way of transcending all the forms and structures that have gone into its making.

This is one way of saying that the individual is an emergent from its relations. You do not write a book on how to play golf by sitting down and thinking about the idea of golf. You write a book about how to play golf from watching somebody actually hit a golf ball. (A little minor fact: the pros who write books about how to play golf themselves need to be the subject of criticism because certain scientific experiments indicate that they do not always in fact *do* what they say they do. But this is another reason why you should trust their actions much more fully than their statements about what they think they are doing.)

I believe, accordingly, in the principle of embodiment, the principle of incarnation, or, if you will, the principle of revelation. You start with the concreteness of history, with the people and persons doing things and saying things in their concreteness. Out of this comes the theology. But the theology is subject to what has been disclosed in the concreteness of individuality; and, therefore, the Christology itself is a matter of size.

What we mean by revelation refers to some person or societal situation or group of events of such size, of such compelling power, of such attractiveness that you are formed and shaped in relationship to it. This is not the case where you are talking about disclosure in any unimportant sense, it seems to me. Now in this respect no individual can claim his own messiahship, and if he does do so, the claim is really not important because that claim does not manifest the power that is involved. Somebody else has to contribute this truth, and I assume that George Herbert Mead of blessed memory of this institution would agree with this proposition, or he should.

I believe, by the same token, that every important revelation, every important incarnation, carries with itself the principle of self-transcendence. Every revelation exists to be surpassed and every revelation therefore contains within itself a pointing beyond itself. The tradition of Christian faith has tried to assure us of the size of Jesus Christ by talking about his unsurpassability. But for me the emphasis throughout Christianity upon the finality of Jesus Christ is ultimately treason to the human spirit, and treason I think, finally, to Jesus Christ himself, if that is important, and I think it is.

I believe there is a meaning to life, but I do not think it can be stated. I operate increasingly in ways that do bring something of a smile to Bernard Meland's face, once in a while. I do operate more in terms of what he wants to call the margins of intelligibility. (Actually I have always been that way all along, but he has just misunderstood me all these years.)

I do not know what ultimate sense it makes to speak of a God who needs man, anymore than it ever made sense to me to speak of a God who does not need man. This is just the way, I think, that we are today.

But the mystery has not been any more resolved by the movement from non-process modes of thought to existentialist and process modes of thought.

I believe that if war is too important to be left to the generals, then theology may be too important to be left to the theologians. Increasingly over the years, I find myself moving in the direction of stories, rather than explication of stories, that is, with the theologies and philosophies. In many respects, theology is the dullest or one of the dullest, of all human disciplines, and this is in part the product of those who produce it. I mean the theologians. I suppose the dullest subject of all for me is straight epistemology: how we know what we know. In this inquiry, you tend to end up not knowing anything about how you get on with the business of life. It seems, fortunately, that life or mother nature or whoever is running these things these days cannot wait for final returns.

I conclude with this little story from Elie Wiesel:

When the great Rabbi Israel Ball Shem-Tov saw misfortune threatening the Jews it was his custom to go into a certain part of the forest to meditate. There he would light a fire, say a special prayer and the miracle would be accomplished and the misfortune averted.

Later, when his disciple, the celebrated Mazid of Mezritch, had occasion for the same reason to intercede with heaven, he would go to the same place in the forest and say, "Master of the Universe, Listen. I do not know how to light the fire but I am still able to say the prayer!" And the miracle would again be accomplished.

Still later, Rabbi Moshe-Leib of Sasov, in order to save his people once more would go into the forest and say: "I do not know how to light the fire, I do not know the prayer, but I know the place and this must be sufficient." It was sufficient and the miracle was accomplished.

Then it fell to Rabbi Israel of Rizhyn to overcome misfortune. Sitting in his armchair, his head in his hands, he spoke to God: "I am unable to light the fire and I do not know the prayer; I cannot even find the place in the forest. All I can do is to tell the story, and this must be sufficient." And it was sufficient.

Wiesel's conclusion and mine: "God made man because he loves stories."

PART TWO

THE CHRISTIAN GOD:
His Christ and His Spirit

Lewis S. Ford
John Robert Baker
David Griffin
G. Palmer Pardington III

6 The Power of God and the Christ

LEWIS S. FORD

Not all the theology in the world can found a Faith or establish the content of a Faith. But theology has the task of making a faith credible by offering plausible interpretations for the claims of faith; preaching and teaching, in their turn and with the help of theology, are called upon to make plausible the manner of Christian living. Process theology, in its attempts to present an understanding of Jesus Christ, has tended to stress the continuity of God's presence in Jesus with God's action in all of the world, rather than stressing the discontinuity (i.e., the absolute uniqueness) of God's presence in Jesus. In this chapter, Professor Ford works with Whitehead's understanding of how God is at work in the world to explain how God acts in Jesus as the Christ.

Lewis S. Ford is a Professor of Philosophy at Old Dominion University. He received his B.A., M.A., and Ph.D. from Yale University. With John B. Cobb, Jr. he edits Process Studies. *He is editor and a contributor to* Two Process Philosophers: Hartshorne's Encounter with Whitehead, *and a contributor to the anthology,* Process Philosophy and Christian Thought, *and to* Hope and the Future of Man. *He plans to collect and reorganize his theological essays in a full-length study shortly, and is at work on a manuscript,* A Philosophical Theology for Whitehead's Metaphysics.

John Cobb, in particular, has the argument that persuasion is more powerful than force. In some ways this seems counter-intuitive; we think that anything that has coercion and force behind it is really more powerful. But

79

power is usually exercised in our culture through persuasive means. The power of rulers lies in the directions that they give and the obedience that they are able to command. In a way, coercion is a last resort measure, really an admission of failure, that one cannot get his way by persuasive means. Of course, we find ourselves always resorting to coercion. But in some sense, and particularly in the matter of disciplining children, we wish we could carry the day without going to that last resort which requires that we take coercive steps to get there.

There is a difference between a child controlling tin soldiers and a general commanding an army. The child who controls the tin soldiers exercises coercive power over things since the tin soldiers are just there and they are moved from place to place. There is a totally different exercise of power by which the general leads. If we adopt, as Whitehead does, the model that persuasion is the sole appropriate means for God's action, then this means that God relinquishes control over the course of the world. This has one large advantage in many ways: it resolves what is a persistent problem, namely, the entire issue of divine omnipotence and the presence of evil. If God is all powerful, and all good, then there ought not to be any evil in the world. The presence of evil in the world either means that God is not all good or that he is not all powerful. The position that we take, in company with Alfred North Whitehead and others, is that God does have the power appropriate to a divine being but this power is not to be understood as total control over the world.

There is another side to the issue, whether a world that is totally controllable is worth creating. In any world that God totally controls, he totally knows the outcome of things. It is no different from his standpoint than a world which he had simply imagined, for we assume that God has perfect powers of imagination. What is called for, the world worth creating, is a world which has its own powers, its own creativities, other than that of God. God, then, can experience and can derive something from the activity of the world. In many ways our traditional notions of God betray our basic insecurity. We feel that it would be better to be able to control things because we know if they are not controlled by us, they might overwhelm us. Also we think it better for God to know the future because then nothing can ever arise that could ever overwhelm God since he knows in advance what is happening. But from the standpoint of an absolutely secure being who has the resources to cope with any situation whatsoever that might arise, it is a very dull affair to know how the whole thing is going to eventuate. God might welcome a situation where there are surprises for him. Then there is a challenge, something to which he can respond, something he can interact with. Then life becomes an adventure, because an adventure involves an element of novelty and the one thing that a world can provide God with is novelty. Whitehead's argument is that the world and God are each the instruments of novelty for the other.

One reason why the view of God as persuasive is a fairly modern development is the whole question of the development of the world. Aristotle held the view of God as a persuasive being. Aristotle's God stands as a lure and an ideal of perfection toward which everything else moves, but Aristotle only uses God to explain why there is motion, why there is the circular movement of the planets. He does not explain how the world came to be the world which it is. Christian view of creation left them no alternative at the time except to argue that God created the world by the use of efficient causes. But Darwin's theory of evolution provided the opportunity whereby one could now consistently conceive of the world as having come into being by means of divine persuasion rather than by the use of coercive force or efficient causality.

The standard scientific theory of evolution is probably the best available theory on scientific ground that can be proposed. But as an account of the total story, it is highly improbable. We must consider the methodology operative within a scientific enterprise. That methodology tries to explain the present in terms of the past. For what one is doing in science is in effect establishing correlations between events according to laws and according to patterns of regularity. This works fine as long as we consider things that are regularly and established and have always been in existence. But what we confront in evolution is precisely the emergence of new structures, structures which had never existed in the world before.

Two basic principles are put forth to explain evolution, random mutation and natural selection. Now natural selection basically boils down to the thesis that those organisms which develop that are capable of surviving better than others will produce themselves and multiply and fill the earth. This, in a sense, is saying that there is a way of securing the gains achieved by the evolutionary process. The other principle, random mutation, focuses itself upon the place where change is most significant, namely, in genetic make-up, but it is really the absence of explanation! For it is based on chance, and chance is not a way of explaining things.

It seems to me that if this were all that were operating in the case, then the universe as we know it is a highly improbable affair. Given the chances and the probabilities, by and large, there should not be the emergence of more complicated structures. Rather the simpler structures would have the greater chance of coming into being and the greater chance of surviving. Whitehead suggests that God is operative within the evolutionary process in the form of providing the new possibilities towards which the creatures can move toward and develop. The evolutionary process is not merely chance, for the creatures decide how they appropriate their past, how they respond to lures directed toward greater and greater complexity.

Now, if God's activity in the world is a persuasive activity, then his activity always involves a creaturely response. That is to say, there is no action in the world which is purely a divine action because God is supplying the lure towards which the creature then is responding. In those cases where the response is totally atuned to the divine lure so that the intent which God had is realized in the action, then the action produced is equally divine and creaturely. In this action God's presence is most fully revealed to us in the world. Incarnation is not to be thought of as simply applying in one very unique case to one individual, Jesus of Nazareth, but it really pervades all of reality. Every action, to some degree or another, is the result both of a divine action and a creaturely action. The whole universe is incarnational in the sense that was used earlier to refer to the nature of Christ. Christology must be radically revised because the problem no longer is how one person can be both divine and human. Rather, the question becomes in what does the central significance of Jesus as the Christ lie if it is not that only in Jesus, God and man have been united. If this becomes a general feature of the universe, we must have another way of understanding Christ's role.

With respect to the whole incarnational issue, Whitehead argues that the Nicean fathers made one of the major advances in

Platonic theory. "These Christian theologians have the distinction of being the only thinkers who in the fundamental metaphysical doctrine have improved upon Plato."[1] The problem was that when Plato came to describe how the forms were operative in the world, he could only think in terms of dramatic imitation. You do not find on earth the presence of the forms themselves, you only find copies, imitations that are made. One of the results here is that Arianism was good Platonism. "On this topic, there can be no doubt that the Arian solution, involving a derivative image, is orthodox Platonism, though it be heterodox Christianity."[2] It is Platonic because Christ was understood there to be only a creature, in a sense an imitation of the presence of God but not God himself. The solution of Nicea is to argue that in Jesus as the Christ, God was immanent in the world directly. It was not simply a copy or an imitation of God that was present. "They pointed out the way in which Platonic metaphysics should develop if it was to give a rational account of the role of the persuasive agency of God. Unfortunately, these theologians never made this advance into general metaphysics. The reason for this check was another unfortunate presupposition. The nature of God was exempted from all of the metaphysical categories which applied to the individual things in this temporal world."[3] Thus in looking at God and Christ as exceptional, they did not then develop and capitalize on the insight they had had that God is immanent in the world in the form of the ideals and lures that he can provide the world with.

If it is the case that all action is a joint action involving both God and the creature, then we cannot isolate the divine activity and determine its character in and of itself except in very general contours. Whitehead's metaphysics is able to resolve what has always been a problem between philosophy and theology, namely, the problem of the relationship between reason and revelation. As long as God is understood to have totally unchanging characteristics which are necessary in all cases, then one ought to be able to know all there is to know about God by purely philosophical means. Yet every Christian theologian, with the possible exception of Anselm, has resisted this conclusion, aware that metaphysics has never really gotten at the heart of the Christian message. It lacks saving significance. Cardinal Newman was fond of saying, "It is not in dialectics or philosophy that God is pleased to save His people." Some additional dimension should be here; nevertheless Hegel was right, that if God's features are necessary, we should look upon religion as simply giving us a picture of God which is to be transcended when we know the truth we discover in philosophy. However, on a process view, God has both necessary metaphysical characteristics and contingent features, because he is involved in experiencing and responding to a world which is a contingent affair. If there is real contingency in the world, what happens in the world is not predetermined or pre-structured. God's experience of such a world cannot be pre-structured because it in turn is dependent upon what in fact happened. God's response to the world is thus contingent upon what happens in the world. Then the whole dimension of how God responds to his creation is something that philosophy cannot determine for us. This must be the domain in which we find revelation.

It is not necessary, in Whitehead's view, to make the usual argument that we must restrict reason in order to make room for revelation. One could argue that the Trinity is beyond knowledge by reason, and therefore, must be revealed. Or one could argue, in company with Calvin, that human reason is corrupt and therefore we must resort to revelation. But here we allow reason to go as far as it will, and let it pursue its attempt to understand fully. Through its own reasoning it discovers that there are things that it cannot possibly know about God's action. On analogy there are certain things we can know about man scientifically through biology and psychology, but all the biological and psychological knowledge will not give us knowledge of the particular life of a particular individual. We will not know his biography. Metaphysically we can know the necessary structure, the characteristics that God has at all times and in all places, but not how he has interacted with his people. For this we must look to historical testimony which speaks to how God has in certain situations responded. If one uses that as a criterion, then quite apart from claims that would be made by special communities as to its importance, simply looking at the records of man in terms of what testimony we can speak of God's historical action, then the biblical record must stand us in strong stead because its authors concentrated, particularly in the Old Testament, on the recital of how God acted on their behalf. This means that Christology should become a much more of a historical undertaking than it has ever been. It got off the track when it shifted to the abstract philosophical problem of reconciling how one and the same person could be both divine and human. The issue that should be faced is different. How is it and why is it that the Christ must come from Israel?

Given the classical model of God's omnipotence, one is always faced with the inexplicable datum: why did God choose Israel or why should God choose Jesus? A partial explanation, at least, can be given within a process view. We suggest that God calls every man, but men respond to the divine call in differing degrees. The particular response men have given to the call of God enables God to intensify that call and to develop it further. Taking, for the moment, an uncritical approach toward Israel's history, we can say that the possibility of Moses' responding to God's call to lead the people forth out of Egypt was dependent upon the response that Abraham had made in Ur of the Caldees when God called him forth on his journey to the Promised Land. The development of the whole prophetic movement was in turn dependent upon the fact that Moses was both a prince and a prophet. Therefore a prophet in Israel is on equal standing with kings. He is not a subordinate figure who must be a courtier with no independent status; he rather stands just as much in the tradition of Moses as does the king. In fact, in many senses, his status is even greater within Israel. The whole development of the prophetic movement and the prophet's response to the divine call then generates a context of meaning that makes it possible for Jesus to be the Christ. Without that context of meaning, dependent upon prior response, there is no way in which the people could have received or understood or been open to Jesus in the way in which they were.

I think the question must be put, why is it that Socrates could not have been the Christ? One can make the claim that Socrates was as sensitive to the divine call as Jesus. There is evidence, particularly in the *Apology*, of how Socrates allowed himself to be directed by what he calls his *daimon*, his inner spirit. I see no reason why we cannot think of this in terms of God's call to Socrates. But Socrates cannot be the Christ simply because he is not of the house of Israel and does not participate in that whole context of meanings which makes it possible for Jesus to fulfill a different role than is otherwise possible. I would define Israel, theologically, as the bearer of God's hopes and purposes for mankind. It is a question here of who in the tradition of Israel would actualize these hopes and purposes. It could be accomplished by the nation, it could be accomplished by the remnant, but it could also be accomplished by an individual functioning as the true Israel.

A good deal of contemporary Christological thinking, even within process circles, tends to see Jesus as revealing God because he fully actualizes the divine aim. This is basically true, because Jesus is the actualization of man's essence under the conditions of existence. But this is not enough. It does not distinguish Christ from the saints without making impossible dogmatic claims for Jesus' sinlessness. That is to say, we must make the assertion that Jesus is more fully responsive to the divine call than any other person that has ever lived. The evidence simply is not available. We do not know what Jesus' life was like for thirty years. There is one exception; Luke records that he apparently disobeyed his parents at the age of twelve. One is forced to make claims which we have no way of supporting.

The aims that God has for differing individuals will differ and only certain of these aims can also have more universal meaning. God has an aim for each situation, the best aim that is realizable under the circumstances and conditions. We can therefore designate certain aims which are capable of embodying a much broader aim, which we might designate as Christological aims. Here we can bring two factors to bear. There is not only the question of the quality of the response to the divine aim; there is also the character of the content that that aim will possess. Here we can appreciate in Jesus' life a deepening and intensifying of that aim comparable to the intensification of meaning and purpose that we find in the whole of Israel's history. As Jesus yields himself to the divine urging and responds to it, his response enables God to give a much more intensive meaning and aim for his life. Thus there is a real dynamism and growth of intensity that we find developing in Jesus' ministry.

In Jesus' life we see fulfilled God's aim as reaching beyond his own life into the lives of all of us. This might be understood in terms of his vision of reality of the presence of God's love and power, and I think that Jesus' message and teaching involves a radical breakthrough in terms of the apocalyptic world view he inherited. In the Old Testament the basic image used for God is that of a king. Then God's action is for the most part persuasive. God pleads with his people, he seeks to persuade them to act in a certain course of action and they are free to respond or not to respond. But his action is not understood as purely persuasive. As any king has at his disposal, there are also coercive measures to bring about obedience if the obedience is not freely forthcoming. Just as our earthly kings have their armies, their police powers, and their jails, so the Heavenly King has his messengers of destruction and his ways of coercing individuals. As long as we remain within the prophetic tradition this image of God as a king operating primarily persuasively, but in the last resort coercively, is the dominant image. As one moves from the prophetic picture into the more apocalyptic one, however, the insistence upon God's capacity to control events becomes more and more to the fore. There develops a determinism, that God knows the future because he controls it. This, however, always remains in tension and in logical contradiction with another theme that is always present, namely, that man is free and responsible. I think that we have inherited that particular problem of unifying God's omnipotence with man's freedom, both of these poles being affirmed in the tradition while they cannot in all consistency be held together.

Apocalyptic Judaism acknowledged God's lasting ever-present sovereignty in his lordship over Israel, but this was not where the action was. This sovereignty at best was a limited and hidden one as long as Israel was in slavery to Gentile nations who rejected the name of God. God's reign and the reign of Gentiles over Israel were an intolerable contradiction. Therefore, all hope and concern was directed toward God's future reign when Israel would be freed and the whole world would see and acknowledge God as king. I think Jesus shared this focus of concern toward God's coming future reign. As Joachim Jeremias reports, nowhere in the message of Jesus does the Basileia, the kingdom, denote a lasting reign of God over Israel in this age. But unlike Jewish apocalyptics before him and Christian apocalyptics after him, Jesus refused to speculate concerning the signs of the end which must first be fulfilled. He does not seek to explain why God's kingdom has been delayed so long, for he is grasped by its immediacy. Like John the Baptist, Jesus proclaims that the kingdom of God is at hand, it has come near. I think this means more than simply that it was expected to arrive at some time in the not too distant future. Its nearness is also a qualitative measure of its power in affecting the present, a power which has already come to be felt. This future reality exerts its own power more or less felt in varying degrees of nearness or distance. As this nearness was experienced in all of its power and poignancy, it was natural to assume, given the apocalyptic expectations of the day, that the long-awaited kingdom of God was also chronologically near as well. But the experienced nearness of the kingdom may be independent of its chronological date since it applies directly only to the power which the future exerts on the present. This proclamation is also coupled with the summons to repentance and faith. The power of this nearness does not affect us indifferently shunting us to and fro in the matter of physical force acting in terms of efficient causation. This power addresses our freedom eliciting a response of acceptance or hostility. Its power lies precisely in its capacity to call forth our freedom for it stirs us to our very depths. The possibility of repentance and faith requires the fullest exercise of freedom as they involve the transformation of our own selfhood.

This power of the future (or, to use Pannenberg's phrase that God is the power of the future in the present) expresses the way in which Whitehead conceives God's power operating. We may conceive of three powers: the power of the past is the way efficient causes are operative upon us, the power of the present is our own present freedom of decision, and the power of the future is the way lures, possibilities, ideals can direct our actions. If God is the ultimate source for these values and aims, then he is the ultimate power of the future that confronts us.

The power of the future does not reside in some future actuality. In the first place this is a contradiction in terms, if in our freedom we face a genuinely open future such that nothing is actual until it has been actualized in the present. Secondly, it is not as if this awaited actuality first exerts its power when it becomes actual. For any power it exerted then would be the power of the past or the present and not the power of the future. To understand the power of God, then, we must focus our attention on how the future can be effective in the present. It is precisely on this point that Jesus' teaching is liberating, for it portrays this future kingdom as it impinges upon the present. Both dimensions are crucial. If the kingdom is simply a present reality, then it is just one more actuality among others in our present world although mysteriously hidden from view. If the kingdom is simply future, then it exerts no power to which the present must respond, but remains merely an inert possibility we hope someday might be realized. It is the energizing of possibilities by the divine luring, the divine appetition, that constitutes the power of the future in the present which is the nearness of God's reign.

If the kingdom of God were to become a present reality it would no longer be future. God, however, exercises the power of an absolutely inexhaustible future. Thus the reigning of God is forever future, never capable of surrendering its futurity to present realization. This emphatically does not mean that the kingdom is infinitely distant and therefore unrealizable. It means, rather, that it is precisely as future that God's reign exerts its power affording the opportunity for its realization here and now however fragmentarily. We can confess, therefore, that God's sovereign majesty did draw nigh unto man in the person of Jesus Christ. Through Jesus' faithful response to the Father, his human activity became the vehicle for divine activity, for Jesus' own power of the present allowed the divine power of the future to become fully effective. It is our contention then that Jesus' response to the present power of the coming kingdom implicitly undermined the apocalyptic expectation for an unambiguous display of divine majesty in this world though he himself continued to share that hope. Therefore, in a programmatic way I am calling for a form of demythologizing. We must demythologize the deterministic apocalyptic world view within which most of the New Testament is framed. I am urging this on the basis of Jesus' own teaching and message, for tragically the apocalyptic view in its way of understanding God's power as controlling lost sight of the way in which the kingdom was a purely persuasive activity.

The vision of reality that Jesus proclaims in the nearness of the kingdom may be articulated in Whitehead's description of religion. Whitehead's topic is religion, but I think what he says applies most appropriately to the kingdom of God as found in Jesus' proclamation. "Religion is the vision of something which stands beyond, behind, and within, the passing flux of immediate things; something which is real, and yet waiting to be realized; something which is a remote possibility and yet the greatest of present facts; something that gives meaning to all that passes, and yet eludes apprehension; something whose possession is the final good, and yet is beyond all reach; something which is the ultimate ideal, and the hopeless quest."[4]

Much of this is consonant with claims made by David Griffin. "The aims given to Jesus and actualized by him during his active ministry were such that the basic vision of reality contained in his message of word and deed was the supreme expression of God's eternal character and purpose."[5] I agree with Griffin as far as his argument goes. He has supported it with a great deal of evidence and he is particularly good on showing that much of what has been done thus far in developing a Christology along Whiteheadian lines does not make full uses of its resources. He particularly criticizes those who see the specialness of Jesus to lie in the fact that he fully responds to the divine aim. This makes one's Christology very Pelagian, because everything hinges on the character of the response and nothing is given to the character of the divine initiative that introduced it.

But in our conviction Griffin does not himself utilize all the resources that are available for process Christology because he limits himself to a revelational Christology. What is important is what Jesus reveals rather than what he accomplishes or does. Secondly, what Jesus reveals is described as God's eternal character and purpose. It seems to me that God's eternal character and purpose ought to be recognizable on purely metaphysical ground. Though perhaps we have not achieved it, it is the ideal of the metaphysical quest and metaphysics is ordinarily understood as not to require revelation. At best we could say that revelation is the source from which the metaphysical vision is put forth, but it does not then serve a function of verifying it. The verification of metaphysics must proceed on other canons, canons of consistency, of necessity, of adequacy to experience, and of applicability. Therefore, there would be no reason to appeal to Christ other than to say as a historical footnote that this metaphysics was first brought to our attention, if you will, through Jesus.

Divine action reveals to us God's contingent aspects as well as his necessary aspects. This contingent dimension is omitted in Griffin's Christology. What the revelation in Jesus concerns is not so much God's nature (though that is included too), but God's address to the human situation. This address is contingent because the human situation is contingent. In Whitehead's view, there is no necessity that man must have existed. Man is the result of the creative process of the interaction between God and the world. And had creatures somewhere along the line responded differently to God, there might never have been the emergence of man. There might have been the emergence of some other form of intelligent life, perhaps from dolphins, but not from primates. Therefore, the character of God's address to the human situation is something contingent, not part of the eternal and necessary character of God. We have to wait on the situation itself to see how God is going to articulate his purpose precisely for man in his condition here and now. Therefore, what we should look for in the revelatory situation of Jesus as the Christ is God's creative word to the human situation.

God addresses each creature according to his kind. Hartshorne has said that philosophy considers what God is like for all beings, whereas theology addresses the question, what God is for us and means for us as human beings. The preaching of the kingdom of God is not merely a revelation of God's merciful nature. It is also an invitation for us to enter into a fellowship with God and Christ that can heal our brokenness and isolation. I see this fulfilled in the emergence of the body of Christ, for I understand the body of Christ itself to be a new product in the evolutionary development of the world which is also God's creative advance.

NOTES

1. *Adventures of Ideas* (New York: Macmillan, 1933), pp. 214f.

2. *Ibid.*, p. 216.

3. *Ibid.*, p. 216.

4. *Science and the Modern World* (New York: Macmillan, 1926), p. 275.

5. *A Process Christology* (Philadelphia: Westminster Press, 1973), p. 218.

SUGGESTED READINGS

Brown, Delwin, James, Ralph E., Jr., Reeves, Gene, editors. *Process Philosophy and Christian Thought*, Indianapolis and New York: Bobbs-Merrill Co., Inc., 1971.

Cobb, John B., Jr., *God and the World.* Philadelphia: Westminster, 1969.

Cousins, Ewert H., *Process Theology.* New York: Newman Press, 1971.

Hartshorne, Charles. *The Divine Relativity.* New Haven: Yale University Press, 1948.

Leclerc, Ivor. *Whitehead's Metaphysics: An Introductory Exposition.* New York: Macmillan, 1958. (Indiana Univ. Press, Midland Books, paperback, 1975.)

7 The Christological Symbol of God's Suffering

JOHN ROBERT BAKER

Professor Baker makes use of Charles Hartshorne's understanding of God as an insight into why the suffering of Jesus is a symbol (revelation) of God. If history really matters to God, then it must be the case that when things go badly God suffers over it. The suffering of Jesus is an important insight into God's intimate relationship with the history of man. Pastorally, this gives the interpreter of Christian life (teaching, preaching) a way of presenting the suffering of Jesus as essential to the economy of salvation. This approach is an alternative to the "atonement" interpretation that becomes more and more problematic in contemporary theology.

John Robert Baker is presently Assistant Professor of Philosophy at Louisiana State University in Baton Rouge. He received his theological training at Southwestern Baptist Seminary, Fort Worth, Texas. There he became interested in process theology as a means of reformulating traditional Christian belief. His Ph.D. dissertation was in process Christology. After several years in campus ministry he returned to school, completing a Ph.D. in philosophy at Vanderbilt University. His most recent work has been in logic. He has published in Process Studies, Southern Journal of Philosophy, *and has several articles forthcoming in* Notre Dame Journal of Formal Logic.

How can a modern man conceive of God? With the demise of traditional metaphors, what conceptuality is open to him? *Honest to God* surely

93

gave notice that the God "up there" or "out there" had lost its viability. And even the metaphors of depth and ground that arose out of Tillich's theology were reminiscent of earlier spatial conceptions and lacked wide appeal.

For a significant number of Christian theologians process philosophy provides a conceptuality that does justice both to one's experience as a modern and to one's religious sensibilities. Specifically, as D. D. Williams said, process philosophy "makes it possible for the Living God, the God who acts, the caring, saving God of the Bible to be made intelligible."[1] In this essay I want to sketch the conception of God that is presented in the philosophy of Charles Hartshorne, the foremost living exponent of process philosophy or "neo-classical philosophy," as he often calls it. Then I want to explore that aspect of the conceptuality wherein God is said to suffer. This exploration will be carried out in relation to a doctrine of Jesus Christ, particularly as that doctrine emerges from Hartshorne's philosophical work.

A complete statement of Hartshorne's doctrine of God would require a much larger space than is presently available. This study will have to be content with a brief introduction to his thought and an equally brief comparison of it with classical theism and classical pantheism. Hartshorne calls his doctrine of God "panentheism." Very simply stated, panentheism is the doctrine that God is "the cosmic or all-inclusive whole,"[2] "the all-inclusive reality."[3] Hartshorne sees the universe as one vast unified and eternal process with an increasing complexity. The life that permeates the organic process (or the social process) and creates its harmony is that of God.[4] By analogy, the universe may be construed as God's body, in that nothing exists outside of God; but God transcends his body in the sense that a man is more than his body.[5] If the universe, as Hartshorne conceives it, is a vast process producing novelty and change and if God somehow includes this process, what then of the notion of God's absoluteness?

This question leads directly to Hartshorne's concept of the divine dipolarity in contradistinction to traditional theism. In an early work Hartshorne characterized the God of classical theism as "a being in *all* respects absolutely perfect or unsurpassible, in no way and in no respect surpassible or perfectible."[6] Existing in the absolute bliss of eternity, this God needs nothing outside himself and can be affected by nothing outside himself. God is a self-sufficient, timeless Perfection, on the classical view. It is little wonder that the classical conception was severely strained when to it were added such Christian concepts as God's creating, knowing, and loving the world.

Taking as our two poles the ideas of absolute and relative, we readily see that classical theism is monopolar—only God's absoluteness is allowed. He is relative in no respect. For Hartshorne God is dipolar—both absolute and relative. God is absolute in that his existence is noncontingent; that is, God will exist regardless of what happens or does not happen in the world.[7] Thinking of the world at any given moment as a particular state in the ongoing life of God, Hartshorne claims that God is absolute in that his ethical character persists throughout his various states. "If, as religion says, God is perfect in goodness, wisdom, and power, then he is unchanging in these respects."[8] The *fact* of his character is absolute—present under any circumstance.

Yet God is relative. Whereas all other beings are but fragmentarily related or social, God is universally related and social. You and I know, are concerned for, and are influenced by a comparatively small number of beings (human and otherwise), whereas God is related to every element of the universe. Since God is eminently related to the world, and since the content of his experience and knowledge is dependent upon the world-process, it follows then that God's experience becomes richer and more complex, his knowledge fuller, and his love more content-filled in each continuing stage of the process. God possesses infinite potentiality for change and for incorporating the actual into his experience, yet he possesses as actual only that which has been actualized.[9] For instance, God remembers the past perfectly, knows the present (which we will designate T_1) in all its intricate detail; but since any future moment (T_2, say) is indeterminate, God at T_1 can know it only in broad outlines and as future. Yet at T_2 God knows the now-present world-process perfectly. Hence the content of God's knowledge at T_2 is greater than at T_1. God is the Self-Surpassing Surpasser, each state of the divine life surpassing every former state in knowledge. No other being rivals or surpasses God at T_1, except God at each future state.[10]

The question is often asked whether Hartshorne's panentheism is just classical pantheism in modern dress. For good reason

Hartshorne claims that it is not. Pantheism asserted the inclusiveness of deity yet balked at assigning contingency to this particular world. The present world had to be as it is, and with it the experiential content of the inclusive deity had to be as it is. The pole of absoluteness, as in classical theism, dominates. For Hartshorne there is radical freedom and creativity in all the beings of the universe, so that the present world could have been dramatically different contingent upon creaturely actions. Everything is contingent, in Hartshorne's view, except the character of God and the bare existence of God in some world or other. "God happens to include just this world; yet he did not have to in order to be himself, hence our acts are not required by the divine essence, and neither is the particular divine response to these acts."[11]

The dipolar conception of God offers a distinct and, I think, most interesting alternative to theism and pantheism. The christological doctrine that emerges from the dipolar conception is significant and is particularly useful here in directing our attention to an aspect of panentheism that has not been mentioned heretofore—the suffering of God.

Hartshorne states the matter concisely: "I have no Christology to offer, beyond the simple suggestion that Jesus appears to be the supreme symbol furnished to us by history of the notion of a God genuinely and literally 'sympathetic' (incomparably *more* literally than any man ever is), receiving into his own experience the sufferings as well as the joys of the world."[12] Elsewhere we find the more expansive statement:

> There is a way of interpreting Christianity . . . which would make Christianity truly a religion of tragic divinity. This is the view that Jesus as loving and altruistically suffering human being is, not indeed God, but yet a supreme symbol of deity. Jesus made no effort to immunize himself to suffering. He tried to alleviate the suffering of others. But he put himself at the center of human suffering, opened himself to it in more ways than other men. This suggests that God is the being with absolute *non*immunity or openness . . . to suffering. . . . Jesus is the man who deliberately and effectively embodies in his life the conviction that it is nobler and more God-like to share the sufferings of others (where these cannot be eliminated) than to escape into private joy. The Cross is thus the symbol of sympathetically suffering divinity, even though Jesus' sympathetic suffering is by no means the same as God's.[13]

Jesus is the concrete, historical symbol of God who suffers sympathetically with his creation. Jesus, as any creature, is not God, yet for the Christian Jesus is the most adequate means of symbolizing in human life the divine life. This then is how the decisiveness and uniqueness of Jesus are understood: The living God, though possessed of a character no man can possess, is imaged in Jesus with a clarity and definitiveness not to be found in other men.[14]

Jesus thus is the symbol *par excellence* of a God who loves and suffers with the world. How are we to understand the suffering of God? No simple Patripassianism is acceptable. Patripassian doctrine flourished in the early third century, and its exponents asserted that as Jesus God was born, suffered, and died on the cross.

Jesus died. God cannot; his existence is not contingent upon anything. Suffering always threatens our being; it cannot threaten the being of God. Without such a threat, can God *really* suffer? The traditional answer has been in the negative. For example, gods of the Homeric epics are spoken of as suffering, yet there is an unreality about it all because the gods are immortal. In the *Illiad* (Book V) Aphrodite is struck by a spear, and a messenger of the gods leads her away from the battle, "her lovely skin blood-darkened, wounded and suffering" (11. 353-354). Yet it is not blood that flows from the goddess' arm, but ichor, the fluid that runs in the veins of the gods. The gods "eat no food, nor do they drink of the shining wine, and therefore they have no blood and are called immortal" (V. 341-342). The pain of Aphrodite is short-lived and the arm is whole again, with the stroking away of the ichor. The suffering is transient and always reversible. Ultimate suffering and tragedy is only a human possibility. The Homeric gods are many things to the Greek audience, but never can they be tragic heroes like Achilles and Agamemnon.

Hartshorne answers the question in the affirmative, yet he urges that the remark, "God suffers," should be understood symbolically or analogically.[15] His implication is that the suffering of God, though real, is sufficiently different from that of men so as to preclude a literal construal of the remark. The suffering of God, as understood within Hartshorne's system, is bound up with the notion of God's omniscience.

Let's say that God knows Jones is suffering. This might

mean merely that God is cognizant of Jones's suffering. God, as the infallible spectator, is aware of the *fact* that Jones suffers. Hartshorne would reject this account of God's knowledge as inadequate. He believes that any intelligible doctrine of omniscience requires a complementary notion of divine participation—God experiences the experiences of creatures through "sheer, intuitive participation."[16] Concretely aware of another's suffering, God feels that feeling of the other. God feels the other's feelings, not as his own feelings, but as his creature's.[17] The suffering may be the result of insufficient information, as the mother who suffers because she has not heard recently from her son at war, but as a matter of fact the son is in perfect health and on his way home; nevertheless, God can sympathetically understand the mother's concern.

Surely any conception of God as loving requires his passivity, Hartshorne continues. To love is to be related to and influenced by the object of that love. Sympathy, participation, sorrowing with the sufferings of others and rejoicing with their joys, are not dispensable aspects of love; they are its essence. To be influenced by *all* creation is an unlimited positive power of God; the fragmentary, partial love of creatures pales beside the eminent Love.[18]

An objection sometimes made to the concept of divine participation in creaturely suffering is that one can help sufferers better if one does not feel their pangs. In considering this objection, one should first note that men have very limited passive powers. A man takes in strong feelings from another, and he is so incapacitated that he can take in very little else and has little energy left over to react creatively. This limitation as to the extent of passivity and as to the amount of energy is man's real weakness, and is not a limitation in the notion of passivity itself. "God, having unlimited scope of passive reception, can always assimilate *any* presented datum, including any strong emotion of another, and yet retain full freedom of attention for all other data and all relevant possibilities of creative reaction thereto."[19]

That God is sympathetically aware of the concreteness of creaturely suffering is one aspect of what Hartshorne calls "the tragedy in God."[20] There are other aspects that to me are more provocative. Given the idea of God's sympathetic awareness of the feelings of creatures, other feelings such as jealousy, envy, fear, and lust are likewise known by God. The feeling of suffering is but one among many such feelings, and thus far it has no particularly distinctive role in the concept of God.

Another aspect of God's suffering is inextricably related to the concept of divine governance of the world. In short, God's will for the world is frustrated and incompletely attained, with resultant loss both to the world and to God. Hartshorne speaks of God's power as "adequate"—adequate to set conditions that are maximally favorable to desirable decisions on the part of local agents (individual creatures).[21] This, of course, does not imply that the most desirable local decisions are inevitable, for decision is by its very nature partially free, not wholly inevitable. What then are maximally favorable conditions?

Hartshorne responds:

> An optimum setting of conditions for such freedom will mean neither a degree of safety, mitigation of risk, that would be too dearly paid for in depression of opportunity *nor* a degree of opportunity or promise that would be too dearly paid for in inflation of risk. A too tame and harmless order and too wild and dangerous . . . disorder—these are the evils to be maximally avoided in some golden mean.[22]

Note that the golden mean is not between amounts of evil balanced against amounts of good but between chance of evil and chance of good, between risk and opportunity. What actually happens is *not* some ideal mean determined by God; rather what happens is that the *conditions* under which creatures determine local happenings are optimized by deity. The resulting state is not ideal, for the local agents are neither optimally wise nor good. A certain degree of freedom makes both evil and good events possible, and the chance for these good things is divinely judged worth the risk of evil things.

The details of events, good and bad, are not determined nor divinely decreed. They just happen! What is divinely provided is that it shall be possible for them to happen, but also possible for other, and partly better or worse, things to happen. The reason their possibility is provided is that, in view of the state of things already determined by past decisions, divine and local, no other range of possibilities would involve a more favorable ratio of risk and opportunity. Therefore, "the chances of evil are subordinate to the chances of good, so that good is the primary overarching probability."[23]

How is the provision made for these optimal favorable conditions? Hartshorne seems to answer this in two ways. The first is a recourse to the divine decree of natural law that serves as a context for maintaining relative order and preventing sheer chaos.[24] Although the laws of nature are not eternal in that others could be decreed, thereby instituting a new cosmic epoch, they do not in themselves furnish the necessary flexibility and specificity of God's continuing provision of maximal conditions for the good.

Thus Hartshorne presents a second consideration, one couched in the context of God's control of creation by persuasion. God is uniquely influential because he is uniquely good, uniquely responsive. The power of God is the worship he inspires; his worshipfulness is his power. The world at every level has some primordial, unconscious awareness of God, as Whole and as Beauty. *All* of creation has this awareness of God, a fact that explains in part the universal influence of God in contrast to the fragmentary influence of local agents. It is in creation's response to God that God rules creation and provides optimal conditions for the possibility of the good.

God is presented anew to creation in every moment in that the content of his experience has been enriched by the just-past state of the world. Moreover, God is apprehended as presenting a range of possibilities, including the possibility preferred by God, for the particular local agent. This tends to narrow the limits of possibility as well as weighting the possibilities of response in the desired respect. The local agent's response to the range of possibilities is free. Even here response is not determined, though God's influence is uniquely (not totally) efficacious because of its eloquence and appeal.[25]

God prefers creaturely fulfillment over creaturely frustration, and it is such a possibility of fulfillment that God presents the local agent. When such a possibility is spurned, it is a misfortune both to the local agent and to God. Even if the individual never feels any sense of loss or frustration because of the choice, there is a resultant suffering and tragedy in the life of God. In this regard we have moved beyond the first aspect of divine suffering, that of sympathetic participation. God does not merely suffer *with* us but *for* us. By analogy, one suffers when he sees a friend miss some intellectual or social achievement because of alcoholism, even though the friend (for whatever reason) never experiences any sense of loss. In the case of God, moreover, he has an accurate, realistic view of the creature's possibilities, so God's awareness of the loss is even clearer and more poignant than any local agent's could be.

A further point needs to be made. The misfortune of the local agent occurs within the encompassing life of God; and since essentially it is creaturely fulfillment that enriches the divine life, creaturely frustrations are misfortunes for the very life of God.[26] God's own life is thereby limited. Of course, God makes the best use he can of such misfortunes. Hartshorne uses the following example to clarify this point:

> We ourselves derive optimal value from the health of our bodily cells, but we should do the best we can when they are unhealthy. They not only lose nothing by this, they gain something. If we do not make the best of their ills we add to them. So with God and his cosmic body.[27]

God decides what use to make in his own life of what happens through creaturely freedom; just how the course of cosmic history is to be evaluated and enjoyed in the divine perspective is free. *That* he will cherish creation is certain; *how* he will do so is his free decision.[28]

It should be clear now that the world poses risks even for God. Not in the sense that God's existence is threatened, but that the content of the divine experience and the extent of divine suffering are contingent upon the world-process. God cannot know how all the local agents will respond to the divine presentation of possibilities. Could there not be several alternatives for presentation, each of which promises optimal conditions for the possibility of good? Hence God must choose one alternative over the other, risking, not knowing the concrete response to any. What if the response of crucial local agents to that alternative is largely negative? Would God experience some form of self-reproach in that one of the other, perhaps more-productive alternatives should have been chosen? I do not see how such self-reproach is justifiable since God at the time of decision *could not* have known the local agents' responses. This focuses the elements of the freedom of creation and of the indeterminancy of the future. Nevertheless, there may be a speculative aspect to the divine life, a clear recognition without self-reproach of what-might-have-been. This focuses on the element of risk that is concomitant with God's suffering.

The aspect of risk involved in God's decisions raises a significant issue with respect to ethical valuations. Our valuation of a man's act on behalf of another, when that act involves risk to the agent, is largely dependent upon how we discern the extent to which the agent has transcended concern for his own future good. If the agent has not risked much, as in the instance of a man saving a drowning infant in a wading pool, we do not highly praise him. But if the agent risks much, as in swimming to the rescue of a drowning child in a shark-infested pool, our valuation of him is higher. Moreover, if the future good of the agent is intimately related to the welfare of the recipient of the act, then we tend to praise the agent less highly. Returning to the last example, if we were to discover the agent was the child's father, we would praise him less than some unrelated passer-by who performed the same act.

What does this have to do with the risks of God? Namely, this whole category of ethical valuation is transcended with respect to God's decisions. With God it makes no sense to speak of his acts being more or less intimately related to the welfare of the recipient. His life is completely related to every creature. Creaturely misfortune is his misfortune, and creaturely joy is his joy. Hartshorne concludes that

> omniscience and immortality make the whole issue irrelevant. God cannot benefit another without benefiting himself. In his case self-interest and altruism are indeed coincident, but not because he is clever enough to do us good so as to satisfy his own egoistic desires. He has no egoistic desires, if words are properly used. He wants only to enjoy creaturely good, seeking for the creatures the happiness they seek for themselves.[29]

Hence we can speak of Jesus as good, in his risk on behalf of the rejected and downtrodden. Such valuations tend to be misleading when applied to God.

Here again we see elements in the suffering of Jesus that defy application to God. But this is a limitation, not of Jesus specifically, but of any creaturely symbol to image literally the divine life. Nevertheless, the Church proclaims the cruciality in her life of the symbols connected with the Man of Nazareth. The symbols have served for nearly two millennia to inspire men to Christ-like and, by extension, God-like activity. The symbols of the first century could never be replaced in the Christian faith. However, there seems to be no theological (as opposed to practical) reason why these historic symbols should not be supplemented with more contemporary symbols that image afresh the divine life. The Christ symbol as understood within the tradition would serve as a theological yardstick for the selection of other symbols, and in this respect would always be definitive. Yet other symbols may well serve to enrich and inspire the Church. Thus Christology should be augmented by a hagiology. But God alone is "the unsurpassibly interacting, loving, presiding genius and companion of all existence."[30]

NOTES

1. Daniel Day Williams, *God's Grace and Man's Hope* (New York: Harper & Brothers, 1949), p. 42.

2. Charles Hartshorne, *A Natural Theology for Our Time* (LaSalle, Ill.: Open Court, 1967), p. 7.

3. Charles Hartshorne, "A Philosopher's Assessment of Christianity," in *Religion and Culture: Essays in Honor of Paul Tillich*, ed. by Walter Leibrecht (New York: Harper & Brothers, 1959), p. 167.

4. Charles Hartshorne, *Reality as Social Process: Studies in Metaphysics and Religion* (Glencoe, Ill.: Free Press, 1953), p. 135.

5. Charles Hartshorne, "God and the Social Structure of Reality," in *Theology in Crisis: A Colloquium on the Credibility of 'God'* (New Concord, Ohio: Muskingum College, 1967), pp. 20-21.

6. Charles Hartshorne, *Man's Vision of God and the Logic of Theism* (New York: Harper and Row, 1941), p. 11.

7. Charles Hartshorne, "God's Existence: A Conceptual Problem," in *Religious Experience and Truth*, ed. by Sidney Hook (New York: New York University Press, 1961), pp. 213, 217-18.

8. Hartshorne, *Reality as Social Process*, p. 160.

9. Hartshorne, *A Natural Theology for Our Time*, pp. 20-21.

10. Charles Hartshorne, *The Divine Relativity: A Social Conception of God* (New Haven: Yale University Press, 1948), p. 20.

11. Charles Hartshorne, "Interrogation of Charles Hartshorne," in *Philosophical Interrogations*, ed. by Sydney and Beatrice Rome (New York: Holt, Rinehart and Winston, 1964), p. 344.

12. Hartshorne, *Reality as Social Process*, p. 24.

13. Charles Hartshorne and William L. Reese, *Philosophers Speak of God* (Chicago: University of Chicago Press, 1953), pp. 162-163.

14. Cf. Eugene Peters, *The Creative Advance* (St. Louis: Bethany Press, 1966), pp. 116-17 and Norman Pittenger, *The Word Incarnate: A Study of the Doctrine of the Person of Christ* (New York: Harper & Brothers, 1959), pp. 236-44.

15. Charles Hartshorne, "The Idea of God—Literal or Analogical?" *The Christian Scholar*, XXXIX (June, 1956), 135; Charles Hartshorne, *Creative Synthesis and Philosophic Method* (LaSalle, Ill.: Open Court, 1970), pp. 155-56. See also Daniel Day Williams, *The Spirit and the Forms of Love* (New York: Harper & Row, 1968), p. 127.

16. Hartshorne, "A Philosopher's Assessment of Christianity," p. 175.

17. Hartshorne, *Creative Synthesis and Philosophic Method*, p. 241.

18. Hartshorne, *A Natural Theology for Our Time*, pp. 75-76.

19. Charles Hartshorne, "Whitehead and Berdyaev: Is There Tragedy in God?" *The Journal of Religion*, XXXVII (April, 1957), 83.

20. *Ibid.*, pp. 71-84; Hartshorne, "The Idea of God—Literal or Analogical?" p. 135.

21. Hartshorne and Reese, *Philosophers Speak of God*, p. 210.

22. Hartshorne, *The Divine Relativity*, p. 136.

23. Charles Hartshorne, "A New Look at the Problem of Evil," in *Current Philosophical Issues: Essays in Honor of Curt John Ducasse*, ed. by Frederick C. Dommeyer (Springfield, Ill.: Charles C. Thomas, 1966), p. 210.

24. *Ibid.*, pp. 208, 210-11.

25. Hartshorne, *The Divine Relativity*, p. 142.

26. Hartshorne, *Creative Synthesis and Philosophic Method*, p. 241.

27. *Ibid.*

28. Cf. Hartshorne, "A New Look at the Problem of Evil," p. 206.

29. Hartshorne, *Creative Synthesis and Philosophic Method*, pp. 309-10.

30. Hartshorne, *A Natural Theology for Our Time*, p. 137.

SUGGESTED READINGS

Ford, Lewis S. "Divine Persuasion and the Triumph of Good," *Process Philosophy and Christian Thought*. Edited by Delwin Brown, Ralph E. James, and Gene Reeves. Indianapolis: Bobbs-Merrill Company, Inc., 1971.

James, Ralph E. *The Concrete God: A New Beginning for Theology—Thought of Charles Hartshorne*. Indianapolis: Bobbs-Merrill Company, Inc., 1967. (Especially ch. 7 and 8)

Ogden, Schubert M. *The Reality of God and Other Essays*. New York: Harper & Row, 1966. (Especially ch. 1)

8 Holy Spirit: Compassion and Reverence for Being

DAVID GRIFFIN

Professor Griffin's reflections here respond to three important concerns in contemporary Christianity. The first is a very strong, renewed commitment to encounter with the Spirit. Theologically, at least, the Holy Spirit is probably the least elaborated "member" of the Trinity. Secondly, there is a new kind of openness within Christianity, both to variant traditions within Christian experience, and to learning also from other religious traditions. Thirdly, Christians (in consort with mankind, generally) are increasingly concerned with living in deep harmony with themselves and with their total environment. Out of concerns like this, and in a process perspective, Professor Griffin offers a "spirituality" of the Holy Spirit.

David Griffin received his theological training at Northwest Christian College (B.A.), the University of Oregon (M.A.) and the Claremont Graduate School (Ph.D.). He taught for five years at the University of Dayton, and is presently Associate Professor of Philosophy of Religion at the Claremont School of Theology. He is also Executive Director of the Center for Process Studies at Claremont. His publications include the book, A Process Christology *(Westminster, 1973), and numerous articles in journals such as* Theology Today, Journal of Religion, Process Studies, International Philosophical Quarterly, *etc.*

It is no secret that today many people in the West, especially among the young, seem to find more that is meaningful to them in religious traditions other

107

than the Judeo-Christian tradition that has been dominant in the West. I share the sense that there is much that is of value in other traditions that has not been present in the dominant forms of received Christian faith. On the other hand, thoughtful people realize that most of what is good in the West, and there is much, would not long survive apart from deep-seated convictions about life that have been instilled in us by this Judeo-Christian tradition. And the other religious traditions, which have particular attitudes and practices that we appreciate, do not have the overall vision of reality and of the meaning of human life within it that could undergird most of those aspects in our tradition that we, for all of our justifiable criticism of it, find of unquestionable value.

One of the reasons I have found process philosophy to be of great help to me in my attempt to be a Christian theologian is that it provides ways for Christian thought and sensibility to appropriate at least many of the elements that seem most attractive in other traditions. And, rather than this appropriation necessarily meaning a distortion of the basic Christian vision of reality, it can at least in some cases mean a deepening and fulfillment of it, in the sense of explicitly developing dimensions that have been implicit in it all along. In this essay, I will deal with three such elements: living by the Spirit, compassionate love, and reverence for all beings.

LIVING BY THE SPIRIT

In reaction against the rationalistic, calculating, dominating, even manipulating form of existence seen as required for success in our technological society, many find great appeal in ways of life advocated in the East, especially in the Taoism of the *Tao Te Ching*. The ideal of life is here seen as involving naturalness and spontaneity. Efforts designed to dominate other people and nature are seen as self-defeating. Above all there is conveyed the sense that there is a process behind, incorporating, and flowing through all beings, and that rewarding and truly successful living comes from being in harmony with this process. This process is called the Tao. It is said to be beyond conceptualization. It is known through experience, not through thought.

That Taoism is probably not by itself a satisfactory basis for life, at least in a community large enough to require much organization, is suggested by the fact that it has never been in China the basis for government rule (although, many scholars believe it was originally intended as such). But it has had a pervasive influence upon the Chinese spirit, and part of that which we find so attractive about the Chinese people is surely due to twenty-five centuries of Taoist influence. Also there is no reason that it need by itself provide a satisfactory basis for life in order for it to contribute an important element for good living. And most people who encounter Taoism find that it strikes a sympathetic chord in one part of their being. There is something appealing there that has been missing from the religious ideal of life as it has been conveyed to them.

But why has this element been missing from received Christianity? In the early Church there was much emphasis upon being led by the Spirit, whether this was called the Spirit of Christ or of God. The centrality of this element in early Christian existence is something that is both reflected by and advocated in the New Testament writings. For example, Paul says: "But you are not in the flesh, you are in the Spirit, if the Spirit of God really dwells in you. And one who does not have the Spirit of Christ does not belong to him" (Romans 8:9-9). And he continues: "For all who are led by the Spirit of God are sons of God" (Romans 8:14).

But it was not long before the experience of being guided by the Spirit waned. A Christian was increasingly defined in terms of certain doctrinal beliefs, and these were beliefs that did not concern the relation of God's Spirit to the actual experiences of daily life. Rather, they were beliefs about what God had done in the past, and what he would do in the future. The sense of a present experience of God that characterized Jesus and the early Church was largely gone. And, except for a few ecstatic movements, this situation has characterized the Church down to the present. However, in wide segments of the present-day Church most of the beliefs about the past have lost their hold. In this situation the absence of any distinctive experience is painfully noticeable, and membership in the Christian community becomes of doubtful value.

There are many reasons, of course, why the experience of being led by the Holy Spirit has not remained a central element in Christian life. But I believe one of the central factors is that Christian theology did not work out a genuinely Christian account of God's mode of acting upon the world in general, and human experience in particular. Alfred North Whitehead has said: "The essence of Christianity is the appeal to the life of Christ as a revelation of the nature of God and of his agency in the world."[1] But this represents what Whitehead thought Christianity ought to be, not what it has been. For whereas Christianity has to come extent said that Jesus, since he was the Christ, was thereby a revelation of "the nature of God," it has not drawn this conclusion in regard to "his agency in the world." That is, Christian thought, on the basis of Jesus, said that the nature of God is Love; but it did not, on this basis, work out a distinctively Christian understanding of how this loving God influences the world.

Reflection about God's agency on the world would have, of course, been carried out in the development of a doctrine of Holy Spirit. But this development was minimal. After the agreement at Nicea in 325 that the Son or Logos is *homoousion* with (of the same essence or substance as) the Father, it was added in Constantinople in 381, almost by way of a footnote, that the Holy Spirit was also *homoousion* with the Father. And, while the Son was said to be "begotten" by the Father, the Spirit was said to "proceed" from the Father. Further, there was disagreement between Eastern and Western Christianity when the latter added the word "*filioque*," which meant that the Spirit also proceeded from the Son.

The recognition of the deity of the Spirit implied that God, besides having been incarnate in Jesus, was incarnate or immanent in the world at large. And the "*filioque*" suggested that Jesus changed the way God's Spirit was available to the world. But beyond this there was little attempt to infer from the life of Jesus the manner in which God as Spirit is related to the world in general, and present and effective in human experience in particular. And what little attempt there was did not lead to a doctrine of the relation of God's agency that was either intelligible or distinctively Christian.

The dominant way of understanding the Incarnation of God in Jesus was such as to exclude the possibility of generalizing. Those theologians who won the title of "orthodox" rejected the idea that God's presence in Jesus was similar to the presence of the Holy Spirit in all persons. Rather, this incarnation was said to be unique, for several reasons. First, present in Jesus was not simply God's Spirit, but his "only begotten Son." Second, "God the

Son" was in many theological circles, and probably almost everywhere in the popular imagination, understood to be a being distinct from "God the Father," and not, for example, a set of attributes of God that were especially expressed in the life of Jesus. Third, in a wide portion of the theological community, and again probably almost everywhere among less sophisticated Christians, this second "person" of the Trinity was understood to be the person of Jesus of Nazareth; in other words, Jesus was God (the Son) walking on earth.

In the context of these beliefs the relation between God and Jesus was so different from the relation between God and ordinary human beings that the idea of generalizing from the former to understand the latter could scarcely occur. In fact, since the relation between God and Jesus was seen by most Christians as a mysterious kind of identity, the idea of generalizing this relation to themselves would have seemed blasphemous.

On the other hand, there is a sense in which orthodox theologians have generalized from God's agency in Jesus to his agency in the rest of the world, i.e., to his effective presence as Spirit. The Chalcedonian creed said that Jesus' actions were divine actions and yet fully human actions. Generalizing from this, God was said to determine all things in the world without in any way infringing upon human freedom and responsibility. In other words, events are caused *wholly* by God, and yet *wholly* by us.[2] It was admitted that how this was possible is beyond human comprehension. But the Christian is said to know that this type of "wholly-wholly" relationship is possible because he knows it was actual in Jesus Christ. Of course, the way Jesus could have been both wholly divine and wholly human is also admitted to be beyond comprehension. Hence, the way that God as Spirit is related to our experience was admittedly unintelligible. No images or even concepts of the relationship could be formed.

In this context, it is not surprising that the conscious experience of God waned, as there was no basis for Christian preaching, teaching, liturgy, stories, and proverbs to focus attention and expectation upon the working of God in human lives, to discern *Holy* Spirit from the other "spirits" or influences impinging upon present experience. People were taught: "Pray as if everything depended upon God, and act as if everything depended upon you." This separation of God from action is the precise opposite of the ideal of "being led by the Spirit." It means fully autonomous agency, based purely upon calculation; it excludes the idea of living in harmony with a Process greater than us, with a Wisdom surpassing ours.

Besides the fact that this "wholly-wholly" doctrine of divine and worldly agency was unintelligible, it was not distinctively Christian. Whereas Christian thought had allowed older doctrines of the *nature* of deity to be partly reformed under the impact of Jesus, so that the nature of God was said to be Love, there was not sufficient reflection upon the question of Love's *modus operandi*. Paul had said: "Love is patient and kind. . . . Love does not insist on its own way. . . . Love bears all things . . . endures all things" (I Corinthians 13:4-7). But the theologians implicitly said that this was not true of God's Love. For God insisted on his own way and got it, and immediately at that. Hence, he did not need to be patient, or to bear and endure anything (not to mention the fact that, in light of the tremendous evil in the world, it was difficult to understand how the being wholly controlling it was Loving Kindness). Hence a great hiatus existed between the nature of God and his *modus operandi*. His nature was said to be Love; but his mode of operating was the same old coercive power that characterized Middle-Eastern dieties in general. And I believe that this explains much of the violence perpetrated by Western man against both nature and his fellow-man, that has seemed such a paradox in a culture whose dominant religion has spoken of God as Love. It seems a paradox, since the basic religious drive of humanity is to be in harmony with that which is divine, in fact, to imitate God. Carl Becker says: "The desire to correspond with the general harmony springs perennial in the human breast."[3] Whitehead has expressed this desire by saying that, in a purified religion one studies the goodness of God in order to be like him.[4] The New Testament reflects this drive in the injunction: "Be ye perfect, as thy heavenly Father is perfect" (Matthew 5:48).

But if this desire is real and potent, one would have expected Western man to have been more gentle, more respectful of the integrity of others, less prone to resort to coercive tactics. However, I believe that the understanding of God's *modus operandi* as All-controlling Power has been greatly dominant over the understanding of God's nature as Love in determining the fundamental notion of what the word "God" means. The basic notion evoked by the word "God" both in orthodox theology and in the popular imagination has been that of the Power Controlling All Things. Only secondarily was it added that this God is Love. Accordingly, to be in harmony with the Ultimate Reality, to imitate God, has basically meant to exercise controlling power, to be in charge, to make things happen. (This theme comes through explicitly in the movie *Patton*.) Only secondarily at best has it been felt that admirable action must be for loving purposes. Effectiveness in controlling happenings has been the main criterion for "manliness." (I have been employing the masculine deliberately, since the dominant idea of God has been overwhelmingly masculine in the traditional sense that identifies masculinity with independent, controlling power.)

I have suggested that this aspect of Christendom is due in significant measure to the failure to think of God's incarnation in Jesus in intelligible and distinctively Christian terms. The traditional way of thinking of God's incarnation in Jesus was probably inevitable within the substantialist framework largely accepted for the discussion. In this framework, one individual cannot be present in another. Accordingly, if "God was in Christ," this had to mean that some element in Jesus was displaced by a divine substance. The early Church did, thankfully, resist all formulations that put it this way. But nevertheless, God's mode of operation in Jesus was, both in orthodox formulation and popular imagination, different in kind from his universal activity as Spirit.

However, in the way of thinking opened up by process philosophy, reality is made up not of independent substances, but of events, the very nature of which is to incorporate other events into themselves and then to become incorporated or "incarnated" into future events. Within this framework, it is possible to make intelligible the idea that God was incarnate in Jesus while seeing Jesus as fully human. And it is this combination of intelligibility and full humanity that is essential if God's efficacious presence in him is to provide a way for understanding God's relation to our own experience and agency.

Process thought suggests that each moment of our experience is called into being by an impulse from God. This impulse is called the initial or ideal aim. It provides us with a lure toward that possibility for the moment which would be most fulfilling in the present and would provide the basis for even greater fulfillment in the future. It is a lure to go beyond the achievements of the past into a greater future. Such an understanding of God's general *modus operandi* in the world is more in accord than are previous understandings with the notion suggested by the New Testament picture of Jesus. For Jesus is portrayed as a man who experienced a call from God to fulfill a task. He called others to share in this task. And the task was preaching, by deed as well as by word, the Kingdom of God, which symbolized the Greater Reality to which God was calling his people. And this Greater Reality was pictured as that which would bring fulfillment, as all obstacles to joy would be overcome. And this Kingdom was preached as both present and future, meaning that there can be partial fulfillment in the Now, but that this points to a More in the future.

According to this view, God's *modus operandi* is Persuasion. And this is much more appropriate to a God whose nature is Love than that of Coercion. Whitehead believed his doctrine of God's agency to be in harmony with "the Galilean origin of Christianity," which "dwells upon the tender elements in the world, which slowly and quietly operate by love."[5]

The obvious question at this point is whether the specialness of Jesus can be made sense of on the basis of process philosophy's idea of God's activity. I believe it can. I believe Jesus can be understood as special, or unique if you will, in terms of three factors: (1) the degree to which he responded to the divine aims for him; (2) the content of his initial aims, which were such that his actualization of them expressed God's nature and purpose, which can be considered the divine Logos; (3) and the fact that for Jesus these divine aims were not simply one factor among many, but became the center around which he organized his experience. It should be stressed that this third element does not, any more than the previous ones, nullify Jesus' full humanity, since this is a mode of human existence open in principle to anyone.

I have tried in some detail to show the intelligibility of these ideas elsewhere.[6] Obviously, I cannot do this here. I can only suggest that if such an idea of God's influence in Jesus is intelligible, it provides a basis for understanding and sometimes even consciously identifying God's presence in our own experience, and thereby of seeking to become more aware of this element in the future and of orienting our lives more fully in terms of it. In other words, we can seek to allow ourselves to be led ty the Spirit (while realizing that this very seeking is a response to the One who sought us first). And I suggest that if this understanding and practice came to the center of attention in our corporate and individual lives, we would find that a great void had been filled. Also, if the mode of life based thereon were to become sufficiently pervasive, we would find our present exploitative mode of being replaced by a gentler, less destructive stance. While giving thanks to other traditions for pointing out what we had lacked, we could recognize this new *modus operandi* as being in deeper accord than our previous one with the formal essence of Christianity as "the appeal to the life of Christ as a revelation of the nature of God and of his agency in the world."

COMPASSION

The other two themes will have to be treated very briefly. Compassion is primarily a Buddhist virtue. Compassion involves entering into the feelings of others, suffering with their sufferings, rejoicing with their joys.[7] It is distinguished from friendliness, which is wishing the other well. Compassion is passive, receptive, and internalizing, while friendliness is active, giving, and outgoing. Accordingly, friendliness corresponds more with Christian *agape*, at least the way it has come to be understood. For example, one oft-quoted definition of *agape* is "active good-will." And the most famous study of *agape* in modern theology portrays it as a completely downward or outward self-impartation that involves no sympathetic response to the value of the object loved but rather creates this value.[8] Further evidence of the almost entirely outgoing meaning of *agape* is provided by the connotations of the word "charity," which is the English translation of the Latin *caritas*, the medieval word for *agape*.

The negative reactions produced by the word "charity" suggest what has been wrong with Christian love. It has too often been an attempt to help that was not based upon an empathetic appreciation of the other's real situation. In fact, the word "empathy" has no doubt become so popular because this passive, receptive, appreciative attitude, which is necessary if genuine help is to be given, has not been connoted by the word "love." The words "welfare" and "do-gooder" also owe their negative connotations to the fact that programs and people thus characterized are notoriously devoid of any openness to the real situation of those they are seeking to aid. Like those who speak in tongues but have not love, those who have *agape* without compassion are like "a noisy gong or a clanging cymbal."

But why has the receptive element been so largely missing in Christian love? Surely, one can point out, *agape* as portrayed and preached in the New Testament was not devoid of what we now call empathy. Does not Jesus as portrayed in the Gospels manifest an uncanny understanding of the true situation of people, and a deep sympathy for them? Did not Paul say, in describing the Church as the body of Christ: "If one member suffers, all suffer together; if one member is honored, all rejoice together?" (I Corinthians 12:26).

I believe the explanation for the dropping out of this element in Christian existence is also significantly due to the doctrine of God that became dominant in Christendom. For if it is true that we form ourselves in large part on the basis of our understanding of deity, there was no basis in traditional theism for developing an empathetic love or compassion as one of the central virtues or "habits" of the Christian life. God was defined as being strictly "impassible" or unaffected in all respects. For example, Thomas Aquinas said that the creatures are related to God, but that God is not related to the creatures.[9] This meant that God affects the creatures, but that they in no way affect his experience.[10]

God knew what went on in the world, of course, but this knowledge involved no receptivity on his part. For there was said to be no distinction between his knowledge and his causation. Unlike ours, God's knowledge was said to be not receptive but creative.[11] This means that God's actions in the world are not based upon a prior, empathetic response to the previous state of the world, but are carried out independently of any such evaluation. But in what sense does God "love" the world if he is not sympathetic toward it? Thomas says that God loves his creatures in the sense that he gives them good things.[12] Is this not precisely the model of God as a cosmic do-gooder, a universal welfare agent? And of course, this doctrine was not unique to Thomas; it was shared by Augustine, Luther, Calvin, and Schleiermacher, to name only a few.

Again, I find that process thought provides the basis for overcoming the deficiency in traditional Christian thought about

God, and hence about the ideal human stance toward the world. God is not understood as a static substance, but as a process. The process understanding of God is sometimes called "di-polar theism." The dipolarity is formulated in differing ways. Whitehead distinguished between God's "primordial" nature, which is the source of the initial aims and hence represents the active pole of the divine love, and God's "consequent" nature. This latter term points to God's receptive dimension, to his experience that is "consequent" upon what happens in the world, and hence the passive or receptive side of the divine love. Charles Hartshorne distinguishes between God's abstract essence, and his concrete actuality. His way of making the distinction makes it clearer that God's activity, his provision of initial aims for worldly events, is based upon an empathetic evaluation of the previous state of his creatures. But in either case it is emphasized that God takes the world's experiences into his own experience, suffering with the sufferings and rejoicing with the joys. Whitehead referred to God as "the fellow-sufferer who understands."[13] This is the first major doctrine of God that has provided a basis for taking seriously Jesus' suggestion (e.g., in the parable of the Prodigal Son) that both compassion and rejoicing genuinely characterize God's experience. And, given the fact that our ideal of human being is based upon our ideas of divine being, this provides a basis for seeing the development of empathy as one of the most important things in human life. And Christian *agape* would become what I believe it was from the first meant to be.

REVERENCE FOR BEING

A third respect in which Christian thought, sensibility, and practice are widely seen as deficient by comparison with some other religious traditions, and rightly so I believe, involves the relation of humans to the rest of nature. Hinduism and Buddhism are especially noted as two post-primitive religions that inculcate reverence and ethical attitudes not only towards fellow human beings, but toward all sentient (experiencing) beings. Christianity, on the other hand. has seen ethics as relevant exclusively to the relations among human beings. The rest of the world entered into religious consideration exclusively as possessions. There was no thought about the intrinsic value, rights, and fulfillment of subhuman life in itself. Its only value lay in the instrumental value it had for human beings. It was there to be used. I have little doubt that this attitude has contributed both to the ecologic crisis, and to the feeling of estrangement from the world felt by so many modern humans.

On this issue the biblical tradition is somewhat ambivalent. On the one hand, God is certainly pictured as the creator of all beings, not simply human ones. And the basic dividing line is not between "persons" (divine and human) and "nature," but between creator and creation, and there is no doubt that humanity is part of creation. And there are suggestions that the entire creation will participate in the ultimate redemption. On the other hand, the divine-human drama is clearly the main act, and the nonhuman creation is regarded primarily as a backdrop. And man alone is said to be in the "image of God."

Traditional Christianity reflected about the same position on this issue as did the biblical tradition. But to whatever degree both the Bible and traditional Christianity were anthropocentric, they were mild in comparison with most modern philosophy and theology. Most modern thought has posited an absolute dualism between "man" and "nature." In its conservative forms this dualism gives intrinsic value to humans alone, and thereby by implication absolute value; nature has no value independently of its value to humanity. In its more radical forms, this dualism even empties nature of any reality independent of human experience.

There were many reasons for this development of modern thought, reasons based upon epistemology and ontology (as well as human pride). These cannot be discussed here. I can only mention that process philosophy provides a critique of the philosophical bases for anthropocentrism, and provides process theology with the basis for an alternative, nonanthropocentric view of the universe. In this view humanity is still seen as the apex of life on earth, but it is seen as differing only in degree from the rest of God's creatures. The processive view of actuality is applied consistently, so that no dualism is posited between beings with an internal process of actualization and those devoid of this. The other creatures are seen as beings with which we can feel a sense of kinship. And nature as a whole is seen as a vast process supporting a great variety of forms of life, forms which have their value in themselves and to God independently of their contribution to that form called humanity. In this view God is regarded not only as having created but also as loving all of the world. And we are called to treat all other beings with reverence, causing as little destruction as possible.

Because of the ambivalence in the biblical tradition, the appropriation of this third element is not as clearly a matter of being true to our own Christian roots as is the case with the first two points. However, it is certainly consistent with the idea that God created all things and that his nature is Love. And it can be regarded as one more step in the biblically rooted movement to overcome all forms of tribalistic ethics, as Schweitzer suggested.

CONCLUSION

The incorporation of these three sets of ideas, attitudes, and practices into Christianity would be a manifestation of its openness to learning from other religious traditions while at the same time representing a deepening and fulfillment of Christianity itself. There is an inner coherence among the three, so that each supports the others. The notion that the divine agency works on the basis of an appreciative evaluation of all beings will increase our own reverence toward all beings, and increase our feeling that it is right to let ourselves be guided by the divine Spirit. The attitude of openness to the divine influence will both support and be supported by an attitude of empathetic openness to the neighbor and even all beings. And the feeling of empathetic compassion and joy for others, including nonhuman others, will be increased by the awareness that the Holy Spirit is working in all of them, inspiring them toward the types of fulfillment possible to them.

The incorporation of these three changes that process theology suggests and makes possible would, I believe, bring about a considerable revolution in the nature of Christian existence. And it is a revolution, I am convinced, that would give Christians both the feeling and the reality of living more in harmony with themselves and their total environment. And it is therefore a revolution that would make Christian existence better, both intrinsically and instrumentally.

NOTES

1. Alfred North Whitehead, *Adventures of Ideas* (New York: Macmillan, 1933), p. 214.

2. Thomas Aquinas, *Summa Contra Gentiles* (henceforth SCG), III, 70, 8.

3. Carl Becker, *The Heavenly City of the Eighteenth-Century Philosophers* (New Haven: Yale University Press, 1932), p. 63.

4. Whitehead, *Religion in the Making* (New York: World Publishing Company, 1960), p. 40.

5. Whitehead, *Process and Reality* (New York: Macmillan, 1929), p. 520.

6. David R. Griffin, *A Process Christology* (Philadelphia: Westminster, 1973). The third of the three factors has been especially worked out by John B. Cobb, Jr.; cf. "A Whiteheadian Christology," D. Brown, R.E. James, Jr., and G. Reeves (eds.), *Process Philosophy and Christian Thought* (Indianapolis: Bobbs-Merrill, 1971), pp. 382-398.

7. Actually Buddhist thought distinguishes between "compassion," which involves suffering with the sufferings of others, and "sympathetic joy." I have combined these two passive or responsive dimensions for the sake of simplicity. I have compared Buddhist and Whiteheadian thought on this subject in "Buddhist Thought and Whitehead's Philosophy," *International Philosophical Quarterly* (September, 1974).

8. Anders Nygren, *Agape and Eros*, trans. by Philip S. Watson (Philadelphia: Westminster, 1953), pp. 75-78, 95, 151f., 733-737, and *passim*.

9. Thomas Aquinas, *Summa Theologica* (henceforth ST), I, q. 13 art. 7.

10. SCG I, 16, 6.

11. ST I, q. 14, art. 8; SCG I, 65, 7.

12. ST I, q. 20, arts. 2-4; SCG I, 91, 2 and 12.

13. *Process and Reality*, p. 532.

SUGGESTED READINGS

Griffin, David. *A Process Christology*. Philadelphia: Westminster, 1973.

————— "A New Vision of Nature," *Encounter* 35, 2 (Spring, 1974).

————— "Buddhist Thought and Whitehead's Philosophy," *International Philosophical Quarterly*, XIV, 3 (September 1974).

9 The Holy Ghost Is Dead—The Holy Spirit Lives

G. PALMER PARDINGTON III

It is one of the convictions of process theology that God's way of moving history and transforming it is through reality's insides. Interpreting the Spirit as "creative-transforming Love," Dr. Pardington develops the role of the Spirit in the world's self-transcendence from within structures, and not as some alien force invoked from outside them. The element of "divine discontent" that moves communal structures in the direction of greater humanity for its members is a work of the Spirit. The Spirit finds expression not only in human history, but in the evolutionary development of the universe itself. In relating the Spirit to both the historical and the cosmic orders, Pardington's theology of the Spirit leads man to apprehend, to respect, and to foster his organic roots in the natural order.

G. Palmer Pardington III received his training at Washington and Lee University (B.A.), General Theological Seminary in New York (M.Div.), and Graduate Theological Union, Berkeley (Ph.D.). He is ordained in the Episcopal ministry and has served in parish work and college chaplaincy. Following his work at Graduate Theological Union, he served a year as teacher and chaplain at Chatham Hall, Virginia. At present he is Vicar of Christ Church in Danville, Virginia, and assistant at the Church of the Epiphany; he also teaches part-time at Central Virginia Community College.

The implications of process thought for our thinking about the Holy Spirit are vast and far-reaching. Therefore this essay can suggest only a few areas in which process philosophy can make an important contribution to the doctrine of the Spirit, and thereby also contribute to the renewal of Christian life and spirituality.

The title of this essay suggests that the most basic implication of process thought is that we need no longer describe the Holy Spirit in terms of a pale and bloodless phantom, but rather in terms of life and creativity and transformation. In fact, it is my position that the Holy Spirit can be most accurately described from the process standpoint as "creative-transforming Love."[1] The contemporary sense of the *un*reality of both human spirit and Holy Spirit is rooted in metaphysical presuppositions about the nature of reality that belong to earlier ages of thought. The arrival of process philosophy has now made it possible to reconsider the nature of God and his Spirit in relation to the world so that the Holy Spirit need no longer be regarded as a "ghostly" or "other-worldly" reality.

Three interrelated considerations arising out of the process perspective on reality make this dynamic and full-bodied view of the Holy Spirit possible. The first is the vision of the social interrelatedness of reality, the second is the denial of the traditional classical dualism of body and mind, and the third is a redefinition of the natural in such a way as to include the action of God.

The social character of reality in the Whiteheadian schema is provided not only by the prehensive unification of each event, but also by the fact that all actual entities are found in the context of societies of entities, and it is these societies, which become more and more complex as they approach the human level, that form the everyday entities which we perceive and use. Some of these societies are "democratic," as is the case with most plants and inorganic entities, and others are "monarchical," with a dominant, controlling member, as in the higher animals and man. "Democratic societies," as applied to the inorganic world, and to most plants, are so called because the entities making up the society are relatively independent of each other, with no one actual entity dominating the rest. A rock would be a "democratic" society, because no one part of the rock dominates, or controls, the rest of the rock. Likewise, a tree would be "democratic" because, although some parts of the tree, such as the tap root, are relatively more important than others, there is no dominant controlling entity in the tree. The tree cannot act or react as a unified whole to outside stimulation. It has nothing corresponding to the brain in animals. A "monarchical society," on the other hand, can act or react as a unified whole owing to its control of the brain and nervous system. Any stimulus felt by a constituent part of a monarchical society is also felt by the controlling part of that society and the entire organism can react accordingly. A tree does not recoil or struggle when a branch is removed from it, whereas one could expect a severe reaction on the part of an animal if one were to try to remove one of its arms or legs. God in his concrete or world-inclusive aspect can then be considered the supreme "monarchical" Organism or Society that provides the context for all less inclusive societies.

Charles Hartshorne, in his book *Reality as Social Process*, points out that this vision of the universe means that deity is the supreme sharer of all experiences of the creatures. This conception is of God as "a social being, dominant or ruling over the world society, yet not merely from outside, in a tyrannical or nonsocial way, but rather as that member of the society which exerts the supreme conserving and coordinating influence."[2] This view implies that God has social relations with man, receiving as well as giving, and thus implies a departure from that view of God which conceives him in nonsocial terms, as absolutely perfect independently of man.

How then does this view of reality as social relatedness form the context for the Holy Spirit as creative-transforming Love? It would seem that the Holy Spirit as creative Love operates continually to produce the sort of community or communal relatedness with an atmosphere in which the creativity of each member is elicited, both for his own sake, and for the enrichment of the whole. Also, under the stimulus of the Holy Spirit as creative-transforming Love, each person finds the resources for his own creativity within the surrounding cultural matrix, which is a communal creation. Similarly, out of the encouragement and stimulus of interpersonal relationships pervaded by the Spirit's impetus of loving concern, each man draws resources that stimulate his own sense of identity and self-transcendence. He also finds his existence enriched simply by the encounter with the other in friendship, love, and mutual support. The element of transformation through the Spirit comes by the Spirit's providing a "divine discontent," a force that moves toward the reshaping of communal structures in the direction of greater opportunity, justice, wholeness, and humanity for each of its members. The Holy Spirit as creative-transforming Love works to challenge structures of repression and injustice, and the weight of dead habit and tradition. Because it is embodied within these structures, however, the Holy Spirit creates and transforms from *within* the structures, and not as some alien force invoked from outside them.

With regard to the second consideration, the process denial of the dualism of mind and body, we need to recall first that process metaphysics defines itself over against what may be described as a "Renaissance-Newtonian" cosmological paradigm, which prevailed from about 1450 to the beginning of the twentieth century and even later.[3] The Renaissance-Newtonian paradigm made a radical distinction between the realms of mind or spirit and the realm of lifeless matter. It was the latter that became predominant in the Newtonian scheme because it could be described and measured in precise quantitative terms. The Newtonian view of the universe as a giant machine, completely mechanical, and completely determined, seemed to leave no room for purpose, mind, value, or spirit within nature. These elements had to find their home in the basically subjective realm of mind. The nonquantitative, nonmeasurable aspects of reality having to do with the intangible features of human consciousness and experience seemed by comparison to have less importance or reality. Man's rational faculty did continue to be highly valued, but the religious aspect of the human consciousness came under much suspicion and skepticism on the part of many scientists. After Kant, many scientists and philosophers tried to reduce religion to morality or to a noumenal realm completely apart from the phenomenal realm that was the province of science. Process philosophy challenges this dualism of mind and matter, and in so doing, makes it difficult for us to talk about the Spirit as operating only upon the mental or spiritual part of man. Rather, the Holy Spirit, in the processive viewpoint, performs its creative and transforming work through man as a concrete experiential unity, a unity that transcends any dualism of body-mind, or of subject and object.

There are two main ways in which process philosophy overcomes the dualism of the mental and the physical. One is the way followed by Whitehead and Hartshorne, that of unifying mental and physical factors within an all-embracing metaphysical structure. The other is the method found in the work of such figures as Conwy Lloyd-Morgan and Teilhard de Chardin: that of describing the psychical factors as they emerge from the more strictly physical level in the course of evolution. We will look briefly at one example of each approach.

The thought of Whitehead on the relation of mind and body can be at least partially summed up in his dictum that "process is the becoming of experience."[4] In Whitehead's view, concrete units of experience are the most basic elements or entities in the universe, and "body" and "mind" are no more than factors abstracted from the concreteness of experience. Whitehead calls this the "reformed subjectivist principle." This principle, "that the whole universe consists of elements disclosed in the analysis of experiences of subjects,"[5] he takes to be a central tenet of most modern philosophy since Descartes. Whitehead's view is a "reformed" subjectivist principle because it rejects the substance-quality, subject-predicate categories that led much modern philosophy into solipsism and skepticism about the existence of the external world.

In place of "mental substances," which somehow have to be brought into relationship with "physical substances," Whitehead suggests that each event or "actual entity" is the product of the combination of physical feelings, or "prehensions," and conceptual feelings, or "prehensions." If it might be objected that this is simply the old dualism with a different set of labels, it should be pointed out that Whitehead has met this possible criticism by suggesting that there is a special complex kind of physical feeling, one that "feels" the object in both its physical and conceptual aspects. As he puts it, "the disastrous separation of body and mind, characteristic of philosophical systems which are in important respect derived from Cartesianism, is avoided in the philosophy of organism by the doctrines of hybrid physical feelings and of the transmuted feelings. In these ways, conceptual feelings pass into the category of physical feelings. Also conversely, physical feelings give rise to conceptual feelings. . ."[6] It should be noted that Whitehead places our apprehension of God in this special category of complex, or "hybrid," physical feelings, so that "the objectification of God in a temporal subject is affected by the hybrid feelings with God's conceptual feelings as data."[7] Thus it would seem that we could say that man's experience of

God's Holy Spirit could be described in Whiteheadian terms as a "hybrid," or complex physical feeling of God. That which is divine is neither simply "spiritual" nor simply "material," but a complex unification of both.

Teilhard de Chardin, who takes the evolutionary approach to the mind-body problem, sees psychic elements at every level of reality, even the most apparently insentient matter. He expresses this insight by postulating a "within" to all things. Physicists generally confine themselves to the "without" of matter, that quantitative aspect of it which can be weighed and measured. Whatever "within" there is to the matter of the physicist can be safely ignored, for the most part. However, the case is different when we come to the levels of plant and animal life, and finally to that of man. At these levels, the "within" of things must be taken into consideration. Teilhard postulates that, since there is a "within" to some levels of being, there must be a "within" at all levels, no matter how attenuated. Teilhard sees the overall evolutionary movement as one of progressive "complexification" of the primordial matter, with the different phenomena of life, mind, and spirit emerging as the process of increasing complexity reaches certain critical transition points. Lower levels of complexity have relatively low levels of psychic development, while at higher levels of complexity, there are also higher levels of mentality.

One of the latest developments in the process of complexification is the envelopment of the earth with a layer of mentality which Teilhard has labeled the "noosphere." It is this noosphere that will form the matrix for a new global consciousness marked by what Teilhard calls the "spirit of the earth." The distant goal of an increasingly interdependent noosphere will be the convergence of all separate consciousnesses upon one suprapersonal center called the Omega Point. In order to insure that the converging forces of the world will not end in a nightmarish totalitarian state, Teilhard feels that it is important that Christians emphasize the Personal nature of the convergent goal and affirm that it is the Spirit of Love which is moving man toward that goal. Most important for our understanding of the incarnate nature of the Holy Spirit, however, is Teilhard's affirmation that the Omega-culmination of the evolutionary process will be the fulfillment and completion of the physical and social world, and not the sudden and arbitrary incursion or intrusion of a supernatural order at the end of time.

The Holy Spirit as creative-transforming Love, then, works in this fully embodied context that we have just set forth. The Holy Spirit finds expression not only in the totality of man conceived as psychophysical unity, but in the very evolutionary development of the universe itself. Considered as a concrete experiential unity, as in Whitehead, man is at one with the entire universe understood as a system of societies of concrescent events. Man differs from the other societies of events only in that in him the Spirit as creative-transforming Love finds self-conscious expression and response. Considered from the point of view of his evolutionary roots, as in Teilhard de Chardin, man as self-transcending spirit, and therefore as a vehicle of the Divine Spirit, is the highest product that we know to have been created by a process of increasing complexity and differentiation of primordial matter. These convergent perspectives on man and God as embodied or incarnate thus remove effectively any basis for seeing the Holy Spirit as a disembodied, ghostly substance inhabiting a body that is nothing but a collection of chemical interactions. Rather, the Holy Spirit continually re-creates and re-constitutes man in his total personhood. The Holy Spirit so conceived also leads man to apprehend, to respect, and to foster his organic roots in the natural order.

A third main consideration arising out of the process perspective that has a direct bearing upon our thinking about the Holy Spirit has to do with a redefinition of nature and the supernatural. The elements of mind, purpose, beauty, value, and so forth that had been excluded from nature in the Newtonian cosmological paradigm are not restored to the concept of nature in the process paradigm. Whitehead, in his well-known *Science and the Modern World*, has given a thorough analysis and criticism of the Newtonian cosmology. One of his principal objections to that cosmology is that the Newtonian scientists committed the "fallacy of misplaced concreteness," by mistaking abstract aspects of nature for the concrete. He also objected to their exclusion of the so-called "secondary," or nonquantifiable, qualities from nature.

Along with the redefinition and enrichment of the concept of the natural, process thought has also raised questions about whether it is any longer desirable or even possible to conceive of God as a supernatural being. Any implications for a doctrine of the Holy Spirit must be drawn out indirectly, but it seems apparent that if we cannot speak of *God* in supernatural terms, we can use supernatural language even less justifiably with reference to the Holy Spirit.

The grounds for rejecting the idea of the supernatural in process thought are to be found basically within the panentheistic model of God as set forth in the writings of Whitehead and Hartshorne. That model of God basically rejects any picture of God as a completely self-contained being existing outside and apart from the natural order. God does surpass or transcend the world in a certain sense in the panentheistic view, but only as the supremely inclusive organism of the world, as surrelative and ever-growing Perfection, and not as already-completed perfection. He also transcends the world by his primordial nature, but this is only one aspect of the divine. Hartshorne terms his view of God's transcendence of the world that of "dual transcendence."[8]

This notion implies that God is transcendent, not only negatively, as the supremely *un*conditioned, but also transcendent positively, as the supremely conditioned. God would therefore be not only supreme cause of the world process, but also its supreme *effect*. This is possible because God's perfection need not be conceived as a static, unchanging affair, but can be seen as a self-surpassing perfection. Traditionally, the notion of transcendence could be reached only by denying any form of limitation or dependence to the transcendent. However, Hartshorne thinks that God's transcendence must be so understood that God not only influences the world, but is subject to its influence. God receives as well as gives to the world. Man's responsibility is heightened because the transcendent is described in such a way that man can make a definite contribution toward it. God is also conceived in such a way that there is no need for the postulation of a completely self-contained supernatural order over against the natural.

In commenting on this panentheistic view of God, Schubert Ogden notes that it provides a necessary ground for man's confidence in his ultimate value and significance. The Panentheistic God is able to do this because he is a "reality which is genuinely related to our life in the world, and to which, therefore, both we ourselves and our various actions all make a difference as to its actual being."[9] This God who is supremely related to us must himself be related to nothing outside of him, however, and here Ogden is pointing to the absolute aspect of God's being, based on

Hartshorne's distinction between the noncontingent "that" of God's existence and the contingent "what."

Let us now look at some of the more specific implications of a nonsupernatural concept of God for the doctrine of the Holy Spirit. In speaking of the Holy Spirit in terms of creative transformation, we can contrast it with the notion of the Holy Spirit as supernatural assistance. Bernard Meland, in his book *The Realities of Faith*, has described how it is possible to experience grace through the natural social structures of our existence. His discussion provides a good illustration of what it might mean to speak of God's grace or of the grace of the Holy Spirit in the context of a view of the world in which the supernatural as a separate realm is meaningless. His remarks also further illustrate our earlier point about social relatedness as a context for the Holy Spirit. Meland suggests that we encounter the Holy Spirit intermittently in those social situations in which we become aware of an extra margin of sensitivity and love. As we come more and more to transcend our self-assertive "first level of freedom," we come more and more to experience a "second level of freedom," in which we find ourselves responding and being transformed rather than asserting ourselves. This charismatic power to live on the second level of freedom has the primary characteristic of undeserved gift. "The flowering of spirit in the human personality in the saint, as in more common instances of grace in the human structure, is not a charismatic power or capacity which the individual himself possesses or controls. It is, I am persuaded, a consummation of what occurs or can occur when, out of this margin of sensitivity that is our freedom to respond to the spontaneity of the spirit, the gift of God's grace actually reaches the human structure to transform or heighten its every power and response. The realm of spirit, then, is no mere figure of speech or symbolic doctrine; nor is it a remote or esoteric sphere that a few rare souls encounter. It is a reality of grace that presses upon our common experience, a depth of sensitivity and power awaiting our response and our participation . . . The gentle might that occurs in acts of love, in forgiveness, in the exploration of one another's good, in the care of one human being for another, in the negotiable life among sensitive human beings, is not just one man or woman dealing with another, not just a variation of moral or ethical good. It is the wonder of the realm of spirit made manifest again and again in human relations, in human history. It is the mystery of the Kingdom made luminous in common events."[10]

In another place, Meland notes that the new view of nature fostered by process thought recognizes its depth and plural dimensions. There is more room for "grace" within the horizons of an expanded "nature." He points to the relational ground of man's individuated existence as presenting him with a level of freedom that goes beyond what he could achieve for himself. The resources of goodness and judgment not one's own that are to be found in these structures offer "a surplusage of meaning and opportunity beyond the calculations and effortful designs of one's own inherent nature."[11] Grace is found in the "depth of innovation and spontaneity attending the whole of created realities."[12] Grace is "moments of heightening, moments of release, moments of freedom and joy."[13]

The question may be raised as to how we can be sure that, in these "extra margins of sensitivity," or in these moments of heightening and release, we experience the Holy Spirit rather than simply human spirit. This question is related to the broader question of the shift in apprehensions of reality and of the Spirit brought about by process modes of thought. We experience the Holy Spirit in these "extra margins" and in these "moments" because, in terms of the process outlook, this is where we *expect* to find the grace of the Holy Spirit operating. If the Holy Spirit is creative and transforming Love, we would expect to find the Spirit in situations where we find ourselves recreated and transformed by love. A certain amount of ambiguity and uncertainty remains, of course, and the Holy Spirit may not always be present when we think it is present. However, the same point could be made about some of the more traditional mediators of grace and the Holy Spirit: prayer, the sacraments, and the reading of the Word. In none of these traditional ways of access to the Holy Spirit can we be sure that the human element may not obscure or take the place of the Divine.

We have now looked at three ways in which the process paradigm of reality can have an important influence upon our thinking about the Holy Spirit. The Spirit as creative-transforming Love operates in the context of social relatedness, and we saw how process thought describes reality as social process. In that social context, the Holy Spirit produces a certain quality of community that elicits the creativity and fulfillment of each of its members in an atmosphere of reciprocal and loving concern. As transforming Love, the Spirit works to transform social structures in the direction of greater wholeness, justice, humanity, and sensitivity.

Creative-transforming Love also works in the context of reality conceived as a complex network of concrete psychophysical experiences. Since he works in terms of that nondualistic framework, the Holy Spirit can no longer be considered a disembodied ghost. The Spirit finds expression in the total bodily and living experience of man, and not in some "spiritual experience." He transforms and re-creates man in his total personhood.

Finally, the Holy Spirit as creative-transforming Love depends upon the natural structures of the world and of man's existence for his expressive embodiment, with the result that grace is not a supernatural substance that simply operates *through* natural structures. We saw how the panentheistic concept of God makes this approach possible by removing the basis for the postulation of a realm of supernature over against the realm of nature. In process thought, nature is reconceived so that it has room for the elements of value, purpose, and transcendence that are aspects of man's experience; and, likewise, God is reconceived so that he includes nature as part of his consequent and surrelative perfection. Man is given the sense that he can make a significant and permanent contribution to the world process. In the process view, since God is no longer conceived apart from the world in a supernatural realm, but is rather understood as embodied in the world, there is no natural structure that cannot be the expression of God's creative and transforming Love.

NOTES

1. See the writer's unpublished Ph.D. dissertation: *Spirit Incarnate: The Doctrine of the Holy Spirit in Relation to Process Philosophy.* Berkeley: The Graduate Theological Union, 1972.

2. Charles Hartshorne, *Reality as Social Process* (Glencoe, Illinois: Free Press, 1953).

3. For a discussion of paradigms in the history of science, see Thomas

Kuhn, *The Structure of Scientific Revolutions* (Chicago: University of Chicago Press, 1962).

4. Alfred North Whitehead, *Process and Reality* (New York: Harper and Row, 1960), p. 252.

5. *Ibid.*

6. *Ibid.*, p. 376.

7. *Ibid.*, p. 377.

8. The following assertions are based on Hartshorne's discussion of this issue in his recent work *Creative Synthesis and Philosophic Method* (London: SCM Press, 1970).

9. Schubert M. Ogden, *The Reality of God* (New York: Harper and Row, 1963), p. 47.

10. Bernard Meland, *The Realities of Faith* (New York: Oxford University Press, 1962), p. 241.

11. Bernard Meland, "New Perspectives on Nature and Grace," *The Scope of Grace*, ed. Philip E. Herner (Philadelphia: Fortress Press, 1964), p. 156.

12. *Ibid.*, p. 160.

13. *Ibid.*

SUGGESTED READINGS

Hartshorne, Charles. *Reality as Social Process.* Glencoe: The Free Press, 1953.

Meland, Bernard. *The Realities of Faith.* New York: Oxford University Press, 1962.

Ogden, Schubert M. *The Reality of God and Other Essays.* New York: Harper and Row, 1966.

Teilhard de Chardin, Pierre. *The Phenomenon of Man.* New York: Harper Torchbooks, 1961.

Williams, Daniel Day. *The Spirit and the Forms of Love.* New York: Harper and Row, 1968.

PART THREE

CHRISTIAN CONCERNS

The Church
Hope
Grace
Faith and Belief
Revelation and Ecumenism
Eucharist
Ethics and Human Experience
Spirituality
Commitment
Death and Dying
Prayer

THE CHURCH

Joseph M. Hallman
J. Gerald Janzen

10 Toward a Process Theology of the Church

JOSEPH M. HALLMAN

Professor Hallman is offering here some propositions about the Church that stress its dynamic
character—the tradition has perhaps overstressed its
stable character. His focus is upon reunderstandings
that must be forged out in Catholic thought in a
post-conciliar Church, so that "the aim of authority
and the aim of the Church is the construction of significant or important Christian experience." For example, the prophetic function is essential to lively
growth through self-criticism, but the priestly function has gotten so much more attention than the prophetic function that we have had to pay the price of
triviality of experience. While the focus is often upon
Catholic experience, there are clear messages for
anyone who wishes to keep Christianity lively. One
remembers Whitehead's reflection that the death of
religion comes with the repression of the high hope
of adventure.

*Joseph M. Hallman received his theological training
at Marquette University (M.A.) and Fordham Uni-
versity (Ph.D.). He taught for several years at Web-
ster College in St. Louis. Presently he is Chairman of
Religious Studies at Wheeling College, Wheeling,
West Virginia, where he is Assistant Professor of
Religious Studies. He is active in the American
Academy of Religion, and he has also published in
Process Studies.*

U ntil quite recently, it was common for
American Catholics to relate to the
Church in terms of its authority. The Catholic Church was con-

ceived as a benevolent mother who made the rules within which one worked out his individual salvation, and all questions that an individual had regarding faith and morality were referred to her ordained representatives for decision. The *ordinandi* were responsible for relating the general salvific rules to the particular individual, whether young, middle aged, or old, married, single, or celibate.

During the Second Vatican Council, this understanding of the Church was replaced by one that is more biblical. Faith is understood in a more personal way as fulfilling the deep aspirations of the heart, and the responsibility for religious and moral decisions has now shifted from priests and bishops to the individual Catholic. It has shifted quickly and at the expense of some very powerful beliefs.

The "new" understanding of the Church within Catholicism does not have the same power to involve Catholics emotionally that the old understanding had. Perhaps it never will. American culture and many of the ideas contained in the documents of Vatican II depend greatly upon the secular understanding of the world —an outlook that is deeply committed to individualism, democracy, and empiricism. It is opposed in principle to strong emotional attachment to authority. Some writers have mourned the growth of this new outlook, and others have celebrated it. Ecclesiology must separate itself, however, from both mourners and celebrants, and gain evaluative distance.

One method for attaining this distance is the adoption of an empirical point of view regarding the Church. I here suggest that the Church be analyzed by using the categories of an empirical philosophic system. One advantage that this point of departure has is that it avoids the idea that any theological doctrine, whether old or new, is normative and must therefore be justified by contemporary theology. It rules out our uncritical adoption, for instance, of the biblical ecclesiology found in *Lumen Gentium* since it mostly tells us about what the Church thought of itself in the distant past. It is also opposed to the subordination of ecclesiology to eschatology.

The renewal of eschatology in Catholic theology has produced a one-sided understanding of the Church, and a promotion of futurism at the expense of realistic ecclesiological appraisal. The normative future is no more attractive theologically than the normative past. According to A.N. Whitehead, whose philosophic system will be utilized here, the aim of life is richness of experience in the present moment, and I will argue that the aim of the Church ought to be the promotion of important experience in a Christian style.

In the arguments which follow, I suggest that Whitehead's theory of causality can be applied to the Church as a social institution. Once applied it affirms the importance of the ongoing Christian tradition without taking as normative any particular past forms. It also affirms the importance of novelty and creative self-expression.

Secondly, Whitehead's notion of divine authority is utilized to interpret the Christian ideal of kingship as a leadership of service. Thirdly, Whitehead's analysis of important human experience and how it is constructed is applied to the Church. Here I explicate prophecy and priestliness in Whiteheadian fashion.

THE CAUSAL PAST AND THE LIVING PRESENT

Whitehead's analysis of the causal role of the past as material for present experience implies the importance of the existence of the Church as historical society that is rightfully concerned about its traditions. There is social order, according to Whitehead, where "there is a common element of form illustrated in the definiteness" of each individual.[1] The common element is experienced by individuals as shared with one another, and the experience of this identity (the definiteness) by the individuals is positive and affirmative. When they are together, they feel that they "belong" together.

The nature of the form indicated by a term such as "Christianity" or "Catholicism" is complex. This means that it contains an indefinite number of related forms (subforms) which can be experienced by the various members of a society with varied intensity. Some would define patriotism in America, for example, as necessarily including an intense adherence to capitalism. Others think that it includes the universal applicability of the Bill of Rights. Still others harbor the belief that an American is patriotic if he fences his property and learns how to operate a rifle. The history of Christianity also contains many varieties of definitions about what it means to be a Christian.

Some of the various forms included in a society's definition must be felt positively and affirmed by each individual relative to the importance to him of other related forms. Since societies are continually in process, the individuals will experience and evaluate the various related forms differently (grade them in terms of their importance) while maintaining membership in a given society. For Whitehead, pluralism and tolerance of diversity are not only modern social attitudes; they are at the heart of reality at its deepest levels. The manner in which Americans are patriotic varies. The Berrigan brothers thought of themselves as patriotic and so did Richard Nixon. And what is more interesting for our purposes is that all three consider themselves to be Christians.

Present experience is to a great extent determined by its past. The past in Whitehead's view does not refer only to those moments of experience that are chronologically distant. The relevant past is the concrete material that is close at hand and giving itself in terms of causal influence for present experience. This means that some fairly recent events can exert as much influence on the present as certain chronologically past events can, while the reverse is also true.

To put it bluntly by way of example, the Second Vatican Council, although recent and influential, is a far less important event, for some Catholics at least, than the death and resurrection of Jesus. On the other hand, what happened to me yesterday (e.g., a death in the family) might be more influential today than Jesus or the Second Vatican Council.

Whitehead's use of the term "past" refers to all of the important influences (chronologically near or distant) that press upon the present moment of experience.[2] For purposes of clarity, I will call this the near-past, although Whitehead does not use the term. Near-past, then, is the relevant concrete material out of which present experience is constructed.[3]

Much of the material of the Church originates in the more distant past. This includes the books and letters of the New Testament, early creeds, rituals, laws, doctrines, etc. Some of this early material has taken on a normative character. And some of it, normative or otherwise, has had new forms throughout the centuries of Christianity that are the outgrowth of the manner in which the old forms were experienced. The "new" forms create the possibility of having "new" experiences of the old material. The many forms are all indicated by the term "Christianity" when used empirically. Christianity is the total content of the actual past lived religious moments of Christians, all of whom have had some positive experiences of the common complex form, and have felt the various subforms with varying intensity.

Christians have continually attempted to determine the true and proper common forms to preserve, and to exclude the false doctrines as heresies. Yet not all of the materials of the Christian past have been consciously evaluated with as much care as others. Certain materials of the past are accidently forgotten, such as various liturgical practices, theological arguments, etc. This is an inevitable and necessary result of the process of tradition. Some doctrines, creeds, laws, and practices simply lose their past power to inspire new and relevant experience. A current example of this is the doctrine of the Assumption of Mary into heaven. American Catholics do not usually deny the truth of the doctrine. And yet, it scarcely ever comes up in conversation. The Church forgets by accident as well as by design.

Is there an absolute or impulsive power that determines the direction of these changes? One theological reply states that the divine Spirit is present in the Church and that ultimately this is the *élan vital* for Christian change. Whitehead's nontheological answer differs but does not necessarily contradict this doctrine. For him, the fundamental purpose of existence is the creation of as significant a form of present experience as possible.

When this idea is applied to the Church, it means that the materials of the near-past ought to be so constructed as to be the best possible environment for significant Christian experience to occur. If the construction of this environment fails, the institution declines, and if it succeeds, there is progress. The question before the Church is this: given all the materials of the Christian near-past that are open to analysis, how should they be constructed so that significant Christian experience can occur? Which of the particular available forms ought to be promoted as most nearly able to effect intense Christian religious experience, which is the aim of the Church?

It is necessary for the Church to make judgments about the relevance or irrelevance of Christian forms. It is also necessary to analyze other aspects of the near-past that have to do with man's immersion in the wider societies of which he is a member. The Church is inextricably bound up with culture and with nature.

Each environment of faith lives within a particular historical-natural context, and must perceive and evaluate the influences that it feels.

Let us imagine the near-past of any Christian community as a bundle of many multicolored threads variously tangled, reaching backward to the disciples of Jesus and continually extending themselves forward into the present. Let this represent the totality of human culture since the beginning of Christianity, including the Church and the wider societies (cultural and natural). For the sake of clarity, we will bracket those threads that belong to the history of the nonhuman world.

Each Christian community experiences a limited number of historical threads and their relationships. Those that are consciously perceived can be evaluated. They will be affirmed or rejected and possible rearrangements can be considered. Yet because the bundle is never totally open to analysis, and since individual perceptions differ, mistakes and conflicts will always occur. There are obvious differences between prominent Christians such as the Berrigans and the former President. Exactly how the "threads" that they represent are relatable is very difficult to understand. Or one can consider two Baptist Christians arguing about the superiority of the white race on the basis of scriptural interpretation. The Church as a whole ought to be able to decide something about the Christianity of the Berrigans and the former President, and something about the two Baptists. It must exclude things that obstruct Christian religious experience at any given time, and include those that promote it. The questions to be raised here are the same for all societies: how much difference is tolerable before survival is threatened? How much sameness can we have before boredom sets in? How are the final decisions to be made? This leads us to the question of authority in the Church.

AUTHORITY

According to Whitehead, divine agency in the world is persuasive.[4] God persuades by offering an ideal aim for every moment of experience that creates the urge for a new experience—an aim that brings together as much of the near-past as possible into some intense and significant unity. Although the divine ideals are never fully attained, the role of God is to urge the best possible experience for every creature at every moment. God persuades creatures to create themselves by giving them their aim; the aim is directed to the highest experience of which creatures are capable.

The traditional Christian ideal of kingship can be explicated in this manner. Those within the Church who have a high degree of Christian religious experience and have the ability to lure others toward the creation of these experiences ought to have authority. Those who are most akin to the divine ought to function as persuasive agents for the religious self-realization of believers. This agency involves an ability to analyze and evaluate the near-past. It also involves a personal holiness that is open and generous. This concept of authority can be useful even if one continues to think of Church government in hierarchic fashion. The credentials for authority that it promotes are based solidly upon the Christian ideal that demands true holiness of those who lead, as well as a commitment to service to the Church. It demands skill in the noncoercive exercise of authority that allows freedom.

CHRISTIAN EXPERIENCE

The aim of authority and the aim of the Church is the construction of significant or important Christian experience. The essential condition for important experience is that it have contrast or discord as well as harmony.[5] I apply this ecclesiologically to the functions of prophecy and priestliness.

If human experience has too many of the same elements from moment to moment, it becomes repetitive and trivial. No experience can be endlessly repeated, no matter how high a degree of intensity was attained. Each moment of life must be seen as a challenge to unify one's past and present experience at as high a level as possible. This, according to Whitehead, is life's adventure.

Ecclesiologically speaking, the function of unification of Christian religious experience is the function of priestliness. Here one must think of priestliness as an adventure in the unification of Christian experience—an adventure that is the responsibility of all believers.

Whitehead also believed that important experience must have contrast or discord. Thus all believers are challenged to be prophetic—to destroy and criticize, to pull things apart. Richness of Christian experience depends upon a dual ability to unify and to separate, or better, to experience unity amidst the separate. Catholics tend to believe too much in the priestly and not enough in the prophetic, and hence pay the price of triviality of experience.

If one has faith in the Church, one ought to believe that the relevant discordant elements can be included in Christian religious experience, and that the cost of repressing them is triviality of experience accompanied by the lack of zest. Persuasive credible leadership must demonstrate its recognition of the prophetic as well as the priestly elements of experience. One must love and hate the world; one must also love and hate the Church. One must be for the destruction and the creation of both, as the Bible is. And whoever does not appreciate this seeming paradox ought not to lead in the Church.

With the threefold exercise of ecclesiological function we have persuasive credible leadership, diversity of values and harmony of final result. Without contrast we have harmony that is religiously trivial, and this contributes directly to decline. Without harmony, we have contrast and intensity that becomes undirected enthusiasm. This also leads to decline. And if we lack persuasion to create significant and important Christian experience as well, we reduce ourselves to the fundamental question that faces Western Christianity as it faced Ezekiel: can these bones live again?

THE FUTURE

A future ecclesiological effort might analyze the various relationships between Christians and the world of nature. A better understanding of these relationships could contribute to Christian ecological thinking as well as to the growing dialogue between Christianity and other religions, especially those of nature. Future ecclesiological reflection in this style must show how Whitehead's concept of God is related to the Church, and evaluate the Christian notions of grace and sacraments, as well as redemption, eschatology, and Christology. A new ecclesiology may provide direction for a religion that is sadly in need of theological repair and renewed orientation. Process theology has many of the resources necessary for this reconstruction.

NOTES

1. *Process and Reality*, p. 50-51. See also and especially *Science and the Modern World*, ch. X.

2. See. *Process and Reality*, pt. III for Whitehead's most analytic treatment of causality.

3. This material is much more than its merely formal content. Hence the term "concrete" designates the totality of experience, while the "forms" are only its intelligible or recognizable content.

4. Lewis S. Ford, "Divine Persuasion and the Triumph of Good" in *Process Philosophy and Christian Thought*, ed. by Brown, James, and Reeves, p. 287-304. Also John B. Cobb Jr., *God and the World* (Philadelphia: Westminster, 1969).

5. See especially Whitehead's *Adventures of Ideas*, ch. 17.

SUGGESTED READINGS

Lee, Bernard. *The Becoming of the Church: A Process Theology of The Structures of Christian Experience*. New York: Paulist Press, 1974.

Pittenger, Norman. *The Christian Church as Social Process*. Philadelphia: Westminster, 1971.

11 Modes of Presence and the Communion of Saints

J. GERALD JANZEN

Church exists wherever the Jesus-event has a hold on human lives in individual and socially cohesive ways. Sometimes the Jesus-event gets at us out of its long-ago past, sometimes it touches us through its pervasive spread in the present of our world, and sometimes it moves in on us from the future. In this chapter, Professor Janzen is dialoguing with Bernard Lee's presentation of the Church in *The Becoming of the Church*. He wants to make sure that the Spirit gets full credit for a continual role in the Church's becoming. And he elaborates a very important sense of "communion" that we do not miss the full, active sweep of the Communion of Saints. These developments, he feels, are necessary for understanding the creative presence of the future (a work of the Spirit) and the creative presence of the present (the Communion of Saints).

J. Gerald Janzen is a Canadian by birth and by part of his training: the University of Saskatchewan (B.A.), and Emmanuel College (L.Th.). He received his Ph.D. from Harvard University. He is Professor of Old Testament at Christian Theological Seminary, and a priest of the Anglican Church of Canada, with regular liturgical duties in an Indianapolis Episcopal Diocese. He is the author of Studies in the Text of Jeremiah *(Harvard University Press, 1973). He has published articles on hermeneutics and biblical theology in* Interpretation, Encounter, *etc.*

Whitehead was fond of describing his philosophy as "the philosophy of organism." By this phrase, he expressed his understanding of the living interconnectedness of all things, from God on the one hand to the merest microcosmic puff of existence on the other. While he fully recognized and even urged the importance of individual existence for its own sake, his philosophy provides a healthy corrective to those philosophies that so isolate individual things as to leave them, in the case of human beings at least, with only a "terrible loneliness in which one shivering consciousness looks over the rim of the world into the cold unfathomable lifeless abyss."[1] For a world whose critical problems include the challenge to achieve community both within and among nations, and to recover a viable relationship with the nonhuman environment, his philosophy offers ontological foundations for solutions. But a corollary—and a component—of these problems for the Christian is the need to rediscover the nature of the Church in its internal relations. In terms of an old phrase, what should we understand by "The Communion of Saints"? Whitehead's philosophical metaphor of "organism" converges with the biblical metaphor of the Church as "the Body of Christ" so as to suggest the promise of a fruitful reinterpretation of the Church—the Communion of Saints —with the help of his categories.

In his book *The Becoming of the Church*, Bernard Lee has offered one such reinterpretation. Taking as fundamental Whitehead's notion of causal efficacy, Lee expounds the nature of the Church in terms of the mutual organic indwelling of its members, inclusive of God and of Jesus as Head of the Body. His emphasis on causal efficacy (the capacity of a past occasion to affect the becoming of a present occasion by being *present* in it) is such that he characterizes it as the ultimate, the deepest and essential, the most real, and indeed the only mode of presence.[2] On the basis of this emphasis, Lee develops a persuasive and existentially clarifying understanding of the Church as the Body of Christ, and of the sacraments as symbolic means to the realization of the Church. Indeed, so effectively does he exemplify his own thesis, in heightening our own awareness of this mutual indwelling and this organic interdependence, that the image of the Body, for all its metaphorical character, seems to be the only adequate way to convey a proper sense of what is literally the case.

However, Lee's exposition must be taken as only a partial exposition of a full reinterpretation of the Church in Whiteheadian terms. In my view, what he has done achieves a solid beginning. But except for two brief and partly implicit references,[3] he deals with only one aspect of Whitehead's view of the relations enjoyed by an occasion of experience; and therefore he ends up with only one dimension of the experience of the Communion of Saints. (If I may anticipate one aspect of the following discussion: He provides a rationale for the Church as the *Body* of Christ, but omits to account for the importance of the *Spirit* for the Church. Indeed, for all its historical connection—through Pentecost—with the origins of the Church, and for all its close credal connection with the Church's self-understanding, the Spirit is not once mentioned in Lee's chapter on "Church.") This essay will attempt to sketch the outlines of a fuller view. While I will deal with some of the emphases that Lee has made, I intend my argument to complement his by concentrating on what he has left unsaid. If my paper therefore seems to be one-sided, it should be balanced by his discussion, which I accept in substance. In the following section I will review and build upon some of Whitehead's relevant notions. Then from this standpoint, in the last two sections I will explore the nature of the Communion of Saints.

II

Whitehead's understanding of the organic character of reality arises out of his understanding of the dynamic history of the basic entities that go to make up reality. These basic entities he variously calls actual entities, actual occasions, and occasions of experience. In one of his accounts, he says of such an occasion that it arises as

> a certain immediate individuality, which is a complex process of appropriating into a unity of existence the many data presented as relevant by the physical processes of nature. Life implies the absolute, individual self-enjoyment arising out of this process of appropriation.

He goes on to say,

> The data appropriated are provided by the antecedent functioning of the universe. Thus the occasion of experience is absolute in respect to its immediate self-enjoyment. How it deals with its data is to be understood without reference to any other concurrent occasions. . . . In fact this mutual in-

dependence in the internal process of self-adjustment is the definition of contemporaneousness.

And later in the same chapter he concludes,

Life is the enjoyment of emotion, derived from the past and aimed at the future. . . . The emotion transcends the present in two ways. It issues from, and it issues towards. It is received, it is enjoyed, and it is passed along, from moment to moment. Each occasion is an activity of concern, in the Quaker sense of that term. . . . The occasion is concerned, in the way of feeling and aim, with things that in their own essence lie beyond it. . . . Thus each occasion, although engaged in its own immediate self-realization, is concerned with the universe.[4]

For the purposes of this essay, we may note the following points. First, the "togetherness" or organic connectedness of the universe may be said to be experienced primarily in respect to the *temporal* aspect of reality. An occasion is "concerned with the universe" in a twofold way: through its causal relations with its past and its causal relations with its future. In the first place, the occasion arises as an appropriation, a taking into itself and making its own, of other occasions as they enter into it from the past. These past occasions influence it in the literal sense that they flow into it so as to contribute, by their *presence* in it, to its peculiar emergent character. Each occasion of experience is thus bonded organically to all other past occasions by the way in which they enter into it.

In the second place, the occasion of experience, once complete, becomes a datum for subsequent occasions of experience. Thereby it becomes bonded to them by their appropriations of it. But this bond with future occasions is augmented by another factor. Insofar as an occasion can, in principle, envisage types of subsequent occasions, and in some way "aim" itself at them or dispose itself toward them, a present occasion can be said to be related to the future in the more tenuous but nevertheless real mode of types or forms of anticipation. This relation enters into the self-determination of the prior occasion, insofar as its anticipations help to shape its self-determination. In the sense, then, that the future as anticipated shapes present self-determination, the future may be said to enter into, and thus to be present in, the present.[5]

If we wish, now, to speak of this twofold organic togetherness of the universe in terms of *presence* (as Lee does), we may say that the universe is present *in* an occasion of experience in two ways: The *past* is present in the occasion as an actual, completely determined ingredient in that occasion. The *future* is present in the occasion as a limited, but within these limits indeterminate, set of possibilities, experienced in the form of certain aims or hopes or anticipations that the present occasion entertains both for itself and for other future occasions which it will influence.

What has been outlined to this point I take to be in accord with Lee's argument. But, as Lee several times points out, Whitehead does not write only of the organic togetherness, the community, of the universe. He places equal weight upon unity and plurality, upon togetherness and separation. In the strongest terms he asserts the individuality—and the uniqueness of the individuality—of each actual occasion. This individuality and separateness may be said to be experienced primarily in respect to the *spatial* aspect of reality. An occasion of experience achieves its individuality in its independence of, and its absolute freedom from, any causal relations with *contemporary* occasions. In fact, he writes,

> The vast causal independence of contemporary occasions is the preservative of the elbow-room within the Universe. . . . Our claim for freedom is rooted in our relationship to our contemporary environment. . . . The causal independence of contemporary occasions is the ground for the freedom within the Universe.[6]

This independence accounts for the irreducible solitariness which is one aspect of experience, and is the metaphysical basis for the great importance Whitehead places upon solitariness as a mark of higher religious experience.[7]

Now, is it possible to speak of the relations between contemporary occasions in terms of *presence*? At first glance it would seem not. Indeed, in one place Lee asserts flatly that "there is no other mode of presence than that of causal efficacy."[8] Yet Whitehead clearly thinks otherwise. According to him, there are at least two senses in which we can speak of the relations between contemporaries in terms of presence. First, affirming that

> [contemporary] occasions originate from a *common past* and their objective immortality operates within a *common future*.

he goes on to say,

> thus indirectly, via the immanence of the past and the immanence of the future, the occasions are connected.

And he concludes,

> there is thus a certain *indirect immanence* of contemporary occasions in each other.[9]

He explains this indirect presence by reference to his earlier account of the presence of the future in a present occasion. Given two contemporary occasions B and C, each was once in principle present in A, in the form of the anticipation with which A aimed at its future. Now, however, A as a completed datum is actually present in B and C. But A's presence in B includes the presence of C in A, and therefore, through its presence in A, C is also indirectly present in B. In the same manner, B is indirectly present in C. In this sense, though they do not directly influence one another, but rather are absolutely free in relation to each other, they may be said in a special sense to be present in one another. Now, this argument of Whitehead's may seem more cute than cogent, or at best, of speculative rather than practical or existential interest. But it ought not to be neglected in the attempt to formulate a Whiteheadian understanding of indwelling spirit.

Meanwhile there is a second, and I think more important, sense in which we may describe the relations between contemporaries in terms of presence. This becomes clear from a brief consideration of Whitehead's technical description of the modes of perception. According to him, we perceive in two modes, to which he gives the descriptive labels *causal efficacy* and *presentational immediacy*.[10] The first indicates the process already discussed, by which we appropriate past occasions into ourselves where they contribute efficaciously to our becoming. The second mode refers to the fact that we are aware not only of our past as past, but also of a contemporary world made up of those items, objects, persons, that we perceive as being out-there-*now*. The question is, how can we perceive them, since they cannot influence us? Whitehead argues that we extrapolate from their past which has just flowed into us, and we project what we have just received (that is, perceived) upon that spatial region where we suppose them now to be. (It is to be noted that perception in the mode of presentational immediacy cannot arise by itself, but arises out of perception in the mode of causal efficacy. This will be important for my argument concerning the inherent relationship between the two modes of presence, and between the Church as the Body of Christ and the Church as the Fellowship of the Spirit.) This extrapolation is usually practiced unreflectively, for example when we hear the sound of a jet plane and know where to look for it in the sky. Though, for one who grew up learning to spot infrequent propellor-driven"bush" planes by the sound of their droning motors, there had to be a quite conscious period of relearning to extrapolate for jets, because at first one was always looking at where the jet plane had just been. Another example: A pitched baseball that passes from sunlight across a sharp line into deep afternoon shadow, sometimes seems almost to retain its sunlit whiteness for just a split second after it has already entered the shadows. In such instances, we project the last causally efficacious perception of the bright ball onto that space where, from our estimate of the trajectory and velocity of the ball, we expect it to be—and that next space, in this instance, is just inside the shadowed part of the infield.

In general, then, though other occasions do not influence us as contemporaries, yet we "see" them as "there-*now*." And to be sure, they *are* "there-now," in their own right, in their own "absoluteness of self-enjoyment." In themselves they will be somewhat different from what we see them to be, or even pronouncedly different. This is a function of the solitariness of contemporaries. Yet our perceptive experience includes an impression of their *presence*. And that presence has an *immediacy* which, for all the absoluteness of the spatial chasm between us and them, is generally move vivid, and more intensely conscious, than is the case with past occasions perceived in the mode of causal efficacy. It is not insignificant, then, that when Whitehead wishes to describe our perceptual relations with contemporaries, he carefully chooses the two terms that give him the phrase *presentational immediacy*.

According to my argument, then, the relations between *all* occasions—whether in the past, the present, or the future—can be spoken of in terms of presence. But it is necessary to distinguish two modes of presence. One mode may be indicated by the phrase *presence in*. It is the mode by which the past and the future are present *in* the occasion of experience. This comes about as the occasion feels what is *there-then* (in the past or the future) and transforms it into what is *here-now*.[11] Only indirectly can contemporaries be said to be present *in* one another.

The other mode may be indicated by the phrase *presence to*. It is the mode by which contemporary occasions are present, immediately, *to* the occasion of experience. This comes about as the experiencing occasion extrapolates from what is perceived as *there-then*, to envision what it believes to be *there-now*. The details of this belief may be well founded (as when a batter connects with what he took to be a sinking curve ball, or when we guess what someone is thinking); or it may be mistaken (as when the batter strikes out, or when we miscalculate someone else's mood and commit a social blunder). As will be appreciated, the component of belief perforce enters—sometimes prominently and fatefully—into this second mode of presence. Truly, "seeing is believing"!

Within the frame of reference of the above understanding of modes of presence, I wish now to explore the modal character of the Communion of Saints.

III

Let me introduce this section by recurring briefly to some aspects of Lee's discussion of the Church. As I have pointed out, he speaks of the Church only as the Body of Christ, and omits to deal with the Church's connection with the Spirit. In a brief modish cartoon, he seems not even to allow for the existence, or for the Church's experience, of the Spirit. For in this cartoon, there are only the Beckoner (God) and the Fellow (Jesus). Of the Beckoner he writes

I know from the other times he whistled that when I get to

his "corner" he'll be whistling a couple of blocks further on, and that it'll be my corner now.[12]

Here Lee catches perfectly the implications of relations in the mode of causal efficacy. They have the character of memory and of anticipation, but never of contemporaneity. What we possess is what the Other *was*, and is no longer, since He is already Other than He was. The incompleteness, and indeed the unsatisfactoriness, of this mode of communion taken merely by itself, is tacitly acknowledged a few pages farther on:

> [to follow our Fellow] makes us feel actually a little more personal about the Beckoner, for we never did run fast enough to catch him at the next corner.[13]

Here Lee almost discovers the dimension that would complete his picture of the Church. He implies that to feel a little more personal about the Beckoner, we have to overcome the limitations of relations purely in the mode of causal efficacy. But, I suggest, he aborts this lead by identifying the agency of this more personal feeling as the *Fellow*. For it is unclear to me how the Fellow solves the problem of the time-lag, since we are not running *beside* the Fellow, but following *behind* him—indeed, by now some nineteen hundred and fifty years behind him. As my own argument will imply, the term "fellow" is in fact a good term for the One who "makes us feel actually a little more personal"; but as such it ought to refer, as the New Testament has it refer, to the Spirit (II Corinthians 13:13). If I may put my critique in one comprehensive statement, I suspect that Lee's failure to speak of the Spirit, and his assertion that God never stands "on any corner long enough to be caught up with"[14] can be accounted for—at least on the level of philosophical rationale—by his failure to discuss the Church in terms of relations between contemporaries, that is, in the mode of presentational immediacy. As a result, the preliminary modish cartoon accurately conveys the suggestiveness, and the limitations, in his subsequent more extended and elaborated discussion. Let me indicate one rather practical limitation. Lee makes much of Whitehead's emphasis on individuality, and applies it to the notion of diversity and plurality as marks of the Church. And he embraces and sensitively exegetes Whitehead's valuation of solitariness as the mark of high religious experience. But failing to note that individuality and solitariness are grounded in the nature of contemporary relations, he can give no rationale for them, nor interpret them meaningfully as modes of God's self-giving to us and of our self-giving to one another. In the absence of such a rationale, one wonders how his admirable vision of the Church as the Mystical Body can be saved for long from regression to an indiscriminate herd.[15] In what follows, now, I will attempt to indicate such a rationale, and to suggest some of the characteristics of a Communion understood in its terms.

The foundations of interpersonal communion are laid by relations in the mode of causal efficacy. The necessary condition for any communion is the interchange of embodied existences, in the form of acts of concrete reciprocity, especially but not exclusively expressed in material modes. As Lee points out, we should understand "Body" in a sense wide enough to embrace all relations that are causally efficacious. Drawing upon some notions of Teilhard, he suggests that

> Body is . . . the totality of the world that has become partially mine. It is what has become mine because I have made it part of my own becoming—I have allowed it a participation in my self-hood.[16]

This has reference to the bodily relations that an occasion has with its past. A similar character may be given to the bodily relations which that occasion will eventually have with its future. Lee quotes Whitehead as saying

> the Human Body is that region of the world which is the primary field of human expression.[17]

By expression, Whitehead means the self-offering of the completed occasion for experience by its successors. From his statement, one may say that whatever form this expression takes, whether physical, or political, or linguistic, it establishes bodily relations between an occasion and its successors.

In general, then, one may say that communion germinates in the body. Perhaps the archetypal, as well as the temporally primary, instance is the relation between mother and child. The prenatal interchange, by which the fetus grows into human shape, and by which the mother redefines not only her physical profile and hormonal functions, but also her self-understanding, is pronouncedly biological. And if, after birth, the embodied relationship becomes much more diversified to include such rarified forms of bodily relation as speech and memory, yet the bodily basis for whatever else may spring up is essential. Similarly, *all* human relationships begin in palpable interchanges. And some of these interchanges are marked by such positive emotional intensity that the deepening, widening, and prolongation of them becomes one of the highest values. Parties to such relationships often are loath to admit any limits to the "togetherness" that they may yet mutually achieve.

But communion that strives to progress only in this mode is immature, and if confined to this mode may run into grave problems. What began as a coming together of separate individuals may become a desire for such a fusion as will blur the necessary boundaries between the parties. Where the willingness for such absorption is mutual, it may provide a certain sort of continuing satisfaction. But it will be of a relatively arrested and low grade. On a wider social level, it produces conformist communities marked by a mass or herd mentality. On a more local level, it produces small groups or couples whose relationship may have an "old slippers, and tea every day at five" comfortableness that will strike outsiders as dull and lacking in intensity or freshness or discrimination. Where the desire for such absorption is one-sided, the positive tone of mutual regard becomes marred by negative feelings. On one side there are feelings of encroachment and suffocation, of being invaded and deprived of "elbow room." On the other side arise feelings of both starvation (because one "cannot get enough of the other"), and naked loneliness (because one cannot get sufficiently close inside the other's warmth). And on both sides resentment or one of its emotional cousins is bound to ensue.

For the achievement of higher—one wants to say qualitatively distinctive—forms of communion, it is necessary to recognize that, as important as embodied communion is, communion is completed and crowned in the spirit.

In Whitehead's terms, communion is not perfectible without a recognition and acceptance, and indeed a positive affirmation and celebration, of the "absolute, individual self-enjoyment," which is to say the irreducible solitariness, that is at the heart of every creature. This involves the affirmation that, apart from my relations with others, I have intrinsic worth; and that I, and I alone, will ever have access to my own subjectivity. And also this involves the affirmation that all others have like intrinsic worth; and that they rightly enjoy a solitary subjectivity to which I will never gain access.

Now, this recognition may at first seem to place an unsurpassable limit or restriction upon the possibilities for communion —as though the fact of our solitariness said to each of us, "thus far, and no farther." But oddly enough, this need not be the case. Rather, I suggest, it is this very fact of our solitariness that provides the condition for an unlimited opportunity and a widest possible horizon for a more intimate mode of communion. As I understand and partly experience it, this arises out of the nature of the two modes of presence.

Let me restate some things that I have already argued. Bodily relations arise whenever we mutually indwell one another. This means that a new bond of such communion arises every time I receive the other into myself to become part of my own becoming— whenever I feel the other person as *there-then* and receive that person into myself *here-now*, to become present *in* me. Such bonds are palpable, and become incrementally rich as they are multiplied. But then the desire to intensify them may become limitless, and with it the attempt to draw the other into a relation of complete immediacy. What is the result? Though I seek to draw the other into my immediate here-*now* experience, what I receive is the warm *after*glow of what the other was in himself or herself, there-*then*. It is not only Bernard Lee's Beckoner, but every other creature, that "we never [do] run fast enough to catch . . . at the next corner," if we pursue only along the one-way streets of causal efficacy. For the past is the past. It cannot be relived as present, only enjoyed as the presence of the past. This means that, however much I may enjoy what the other *was*—sometimes was just a tantalizing moment ago—I cannot, in this mode of communion, enjoy the other as my *contemporary*. That is, I cannot enjoy the desired immediacy of communion. And time, which is the bridge enabling mutual indwelling, becomes the uncrossable chasm and the unyielding limit to my desire for immediacy. If this were the only mode of presence, we would all be doomed to a communion marked by just-missed train schedules. And at the same time, it would be a communion marked also by congested train terminals. For, though we would never be able to get close enough to the just-departed afterglow of one another's interior selfhood, yet we would in another sense be altogether too close for comfort, because of our frantic attempts to close the gaps in our *time*tables, and we would all suffocate from the loss of the fresh air of our individual freedom.

What we need to learn, at such junctures, is implied in some of the last thoughts of the priest, just before his execution, in Graham Greene's *The Power and the Glory*:

> It seemed to him, at that moment, that it would have been quite easy to have been a saint. It would only have needed a little self-restraint and a little courage. He felt like someone who has missed happiness by seconds at an appointed place.

But of course, the priest did not miss it. In the end, and unrecognized by himself, he found the self-restraint and the courage, little as it was, to accept his own solitariness before man and God. It is this acceptance, and with it the self-restraint of the insatiable desire to eliminate the chasm between one self and another, that begins to discover in the independence of contemporary presence a higher mode of communion.

For once one's own solitude and the other's own solitude are accepted, suddenly the other as fully existing, not in the past, but in the living present, becomes a contemporary—and the other becomes present *to* one, there-*now*! What arises to intensely vivid consciousness is the fact of the other, not as one's benefactor, nor as one's beneficiary (as important as these efficacious aspects undoubtedly are), but as a person charged with intrinsic worth in the absoluteness of that person's own self-enjoyment, actually present-to-himself-there-now. It is the recognition of the other as a "Thou." In the nature of this mode of experience, it perhaps can be better illustrated than explained. Let me offer some actual experiences, and then some testimony of two modern poets.

Two colleagues became closely attached during the years of their work together. There is something about the senior colleague, a personal restraint—the sort of restraint that puts an almost intolerable edge of beauty on his performances of baroque music—which does not detract from the mutual indwelling, but contributes to it an indefinable tone, as of a clean resonant freshness and an uncloying sweetness. Then the senior colleague retires. Both in anticipation and in retrospect the younger colleague is desolate. At night he lies in a twilight zone between sleep and wakefulness, and time flows through his body—his arms and legs and chest—and it flows unresisted, like wind through a screen door, and the flow is time and transiency and mortality. Then, sometime later, he makes a discovery. He realizes that not only is the historical, past colleague present *in* him, in the mode of memory, and sweet influence for good English and good music and clarity of tone in all things; but that the contemporary person is present *to* him! Where? *There-now!* At any given moment, somewhere unknown and beyond ready bodily contact, Carley is present to himself, having his own experiences, interacting with his own specific situation, with his own appropriate and unique self-awareness. But this awareness makes Carley also, in some strange way, present also to the younger colleague, with an interior immediacy. The historical presence dwells within, efficacious, gladdening, strengthening; and the contemporaneous presence dwells alongside, in a freedom and a communion of solitudes that provides its own, at times intolerably taut, beauty and strength. But this second mode does not take its beginning just at the point of bodily separation. In retrospect it is realized that the stage for it was set already by the restraint which was not an aloofness, nor a drawing back from friendship, but rather a clear-eyed recognition of the essential selfhood out of which all friendships arise. This earlier experience, in fact, was already an unrecognized form of the experience of Carley there-now. The more recent radical separation by a wide space now only throws into sharp relief what was already coming into being along with the more palpable bodily fellowship. Conversely, the earlier stage of the communion of solitudes makes possible the recognition of the true nature of the present more radical solitude.

A second example: A young couple, who trained for ministry together, are now to be ordained together at a home church in the Rocky Mountain foothills. Some friends come from the Midwest for the service; but most who would come cannot. During the service there arises a strong sense of the palpable bonds of community among those who are there. Then, unexpectedly, the thought of those who could not come becomes, not a sense of regret and limitation, but a sense of the *width* of the present occasion. For one discovers that those others, present to themselves *there-now*, become also present *to the ordination here-now*. And the ordination, while it is bodily centered in the church, suddenly takes on as many centers in the spirit as there are "con-celebrating" persons whose distribution across the continent marks the width of the occasion. In this there is no sense of deprivation or of naked aloneness, but of fullness and of being surrounded by a whole cloud of witnesses, *now*.

Robert Frost returned again and again to the theme of the need for boundaries as a condition for good relationships. Only because the poem is so often misquoted is it necessary to remind ourselves that the point of "Mending Wall" comes, not in the opening line, but in the last, with its reiterated "good fences make good neighbours." In this poem the tone and treatment are pleasantly pastoral, with no particular emphasis upon how the fences perform their function. The pastoral setting becomes the means for a more intense statement, in "The Tuft of Flowers." In this poem, a farm hand goes out to turn the mown grass

> after one
> Who mowed it in the dew before the sun.

He looks about for his early co-worker in vain, then concludes that he must be, as the other had been, alone,

> "As all must be," I said within my heart,
> "Whether they work together or apart."

Yet by the end of the morning the farm hand has come to think quite otherwise. Something has happened that makes him

> feel a spirit kindred to my own,
> So that henceforth I worked no more alone.

For the rest of the day, the hand works "as with his aid," and at the noon break in an interior immediacy rests with him and talks with him as

> one whose thought I had not hoped to reach.

"Men work together," I told him from the heart,
"Whether they work together or apart."

What has brought about the change? A tall tuft of flowers left standing by the mower's scythe. And what invests those flowers with the power to evoke such a sense of communion? A desire on the part of the mower to enrich the experience of some subsequent flower fancier? Or to break his early-morning loneliness by a message to some later field worker, and thereby to console himself in the anticipation of being thought of after the fact? Not for the farm hand. To his eye,

The mower in the dew had loved them thus,
By leaving them to flourish, not for us,

Nor yet to draw one thought of ours to him,
But from sheer morning gladness at the brim.

What this tuft of flowers does, is to bring vividly to the farm hand's consciousness the solitary presence of the mower, in the latter's own freedom and self-enjoyment. And this vivid presence issues in a transforming sense of communion in the spirit. What is further noteworthy in this poem is its exemplification of the way in which communion with "a spirit kindred" does not emerge ethereally out of nowhere, but is necessarily connected with a factor of bodily communion, in the form of the tuft of flowers. In this instance, the material object acts not only as conveying its own efficacious beauty, but as signifying, sacramentally, another kind of reality. It becomes, as all bodily expression can become, an outward and visible sign of the inward and spiritual grace of one who, in my second mode, is "really present." Finally, though there is no space to discuss it here at any length, there is the sonnet "The Master Speed," composed for the marriage of one of Frost's daughters. The sonnet celebrates the inseparability of the young couple, so long as they know how to live as contemporaries, "Together wing to wing and oar to oar."[18]

The treatment of the tuft of flowers in passing indicates a dimension of communion that, although I cannot develop it here, deserves at least to be recognized. That is the sense of communion with nature, as an integral part of the communion among all of God's creatures. From Psalm 148, through St. Francis of Assisi's Canticle to Brother Sun, down to Wordsworth's celebration of "the haunting presence of nature,"[19] to name only a few noteworthy examples, this dimension of communion has always existed. In what does it consist? Let me suggest that it consists in an appreciation of the creatures of nature, not merely as benefactors of man—not merely as put here to serve and supply us—nor as beneficiaries of our too often fumbling attempts to "improve" our environment, but as creatures in their own right, enjoying a certain absoluteness and intrinsic worth. What led the mower to spare the tuft of flowers but a solitary gladness that recognized in the flowers an intrinsic worth which answered to his own? Is it not on this basis that we may recover the ability to say "Thou," with St. Francis, to the creatures who are our fellows? And does this not also mean that, as vehicles of sacramental presences, they not only serve as vehicles, but also participate in their own right in the communion of solitudes?

Let me call in one more poet in testimony, this time not through his poetry, but through his letters. Though Rainer Maria Rilke can write of mutual influence, and often does, he writes most powerfully when he stresses the mutual solitude that marks all deep relationships. Such relationships, in his view, arise when

one is willing to stand guard over the solitude of a person and . . . is inclined to set this same person at the gate of one's solitude, of which he learns only through that which steps, festively clothed, out of the great darkness.

Again, he writes,

I hold this to be the highest task of a bond between two people; that each should stand guard over the solitude of the other . . . Out of this . . . alone will joys come to it by which it will live *without starving*.[20]

These personal experiences and literary evidences I have come to understand more definitively in terms of the existential symbolism of the old Israelite sanctuary. The presupposition here (which it would not be difficult to argue) is that religious sanctuaries are architectural metaphors for the persons of the parties to religious communion. Now, the Israelite sanctuary was characterized by a forecourt where the people could congregate. Beyond this was a Holy Place where only the priesthood officiated. Finally there was the Holy of Holies that contained the invisible presence of Yahweh, whose solitariness there was qualified only under the rarest and most special conditions. True enough, God and Israel engaged in what we might call embodied relations. For God provided Israel with "the corn and the wine and the oil," and with Torah to live by. And in return, Israel offered herself to God through the ethical shape of her national life, and symbolized this bodily self-offering in the metaphor of animal sacrifices. But this bodily relation was complemented by the mutual recognition of the privacy of the other. On the one side, the Decalogue, as the epitome of the Torah in negative terms, set the limits or conditions of viable community existence, within which Israel enjoyed the freedom, the "elbow room," to define her life as she saw fit. (And the rise of legalism was the transformation of law as the shaped offer of freedom into law as the specific determiner of actions.) On the other side, the service of Yahweh in the sanctuary was carried out, not *within* the presence of Yahweh, but *before* his presence, on the outer side of the intervening veil. In Rilke's words, this was Israel's highest task: to stand guard over the solitude of Yahweh, making no idols of him, but allowing him to be "there-now" as he who he should there choose to be. The sanctuary architecture thus symbolized the supreme *mysterium*, which existentially would mean, in New Testament words, to "sanctify the Lord . . . in your hearts" (1 Peter 3:15). That is, the solitariness of the other over which one stands guard exists not only in the other, but somehow is to exist also within one's own solitude. But this line of thought leads into the final section of this paper, in which I will explore the possibility that communion in the mode of mutual solitude is communion in the spirit.

As I have indicated above, Bernard Lee argues that we should understand causally efficacious relations as giving rise to embodied community. What I wish to argue is that the Communion of Saints in the Spirit arises out of embodied relations, in a specific way; but that while it displays one feature of bodily relations (mutual indwelling), this feature is yet in some respect different in its "effects"; and that this indwelling of the spirit gives rise to yet another mode of relations in which spirit is experienced as contemporary. Let me trace this rise and development by considering, once more, the dynamic history of personal relations.

To begin with, I arise out of my immediate past. More specifically, my body arises in part out of the data presented by past occasions. These data themselves have arisen from the past decisions of others, and the past decisions of myself. That is, I inherit bodily from my own embodied past and the embodied past of others. But my body does not come to me completely ready-made. My body is an emergent, arising out of my capacity in the present for making decisions for myself now, and as contributing to what I and others will become in the future. So my own embodied self is a result of the determinate influence of others and of my own past self upon me, and a result of my self-determining activity in the present. This capacity for making decisions, this freedom for self-determination, is a mystery, even to myself who display this capacity. It is my own inner solitude of which I myself learn, in Rilke's words, "only through that which steps, festively clothed, out of the great darkness." This inner capacity, I suggest, is what we mean by spirit. As St. Paul says, "what person knows a man's thoughts except the spirit of the man which is in him?" (I Corinthians 2:11). In his only two references to spirit in his discussion of the Church, Bernard Lee calls this inner capacity "the interior spirit of the individual." Of this spirit, he writes, "it is . . . in the interior assent of the individual that society itself is created. That is equally true of the Church."[21]

Where does this capacity, this interior freedom, come from? I suggest that, in part, it arises out of certain specific past conditions, in some respects similar to, and in other respects crucially different from, the way in which my body arises out of certain specific past conditions. My past self, and past others, contribute to my *bodily* existence, my determinate existence, by making determinate decisions to which my own existence must conform. But they *may* also contribute to my *spiritual* existence, by making a type of decision that does not exact my conformity, but which, within limits, sets me free from the necessity for conformity—sets me free to determine myself. What sort of decision would this be? Let us suppose that these others, in my past, are aware that their actions and decisions will affect me, or at any rate persons in general, in their future. Let us imagine them undertaking to stand guard over my own potential solitude, and in this way to "sanctify" me, to recognize my irreducible worth as a person and freedom as an individual, in their hearts. What does this mean? It means that, not only in their actions toward or in behalf of me, but also in their own secret thoughts about me, they will leave an area of indeterminateness within which they will allow me to be who I shall choose to be. But this area of indeterminateness is not "out there" in their future. In the manner in which Whitehead speaks of the immanence of the future in the present, they will allow this indeterminate me to "indwell" them by anticipation. They will make no idol of me even in their imaginations, but will allow me to "be there," in them, as he who I shall there choose to be. Now, when subsequently I experience them in the mode of causal efficacy, I will receive from them not only the embodiment of their specifically shaping influences upon me, but also this strange noninfluence, arising out of their self-restraint—for it will come to me embedded in the bodily influences like air bubbles in whipped cream or microscopic granules of fat in a cut of choice steak.

Now, the Bible speaks of God as giving us the spirit of life (e.g., Genesis 2:7). Analogously, Whitehead speaks of an initial endowment from God—an initial aim—that becomes a kind of nucleus around which the emerging occasion builds itself. In my terms, this would mean that the eminent gift of solitude arises out of the eminent instance of standing guard over the dignity and worth of my solitude, that is, from God. My present freedom, then, my present spirit, arises as a gift from God, from my fellow creatures, and from my past self who may have had the courage not to determine the future finally but to honor its indeterminateness. This last endowment is usually very frail, very tentative. We would rather conform to the momentum of our achieved selves, and deal with the future on the basis of knowledge and certainty. And often our frail self-endowment is in danger of being overrun by our own past momentum. But when we experience others as reinforcing this self-endowment by their guard over it, and when we experience God as also standing guard over it (how often, in the Bible, God confronts man, not with directives, but with an open future calling for man's own decision!), the chances are increased that we will act "in the spirit" and not merely obey the "dictates of the flesh."

In these last remarks, I have attempted to talk about indwelling spirit in terms both similar to and yet unlike the experience of bodily indwelling. In this way, I hope to have suggested that communion in the spirit does not arise purely on an ethereal plane, but out of—and only out of—communion in the body. Let me further indicate the indivisibility of these two modes of relation.[22] As psychosomatic unities, we do not live just to produce spiritual communion out of the compost heap of the body. For the realization of communion in the spirit has its final result in enhancing the intensity and quality of communion in the body. That is, at one time I enjoyed communion in the body, as a communion of what was there-*then* with what is here-*now* in me. But my enjoyment was limited by the discovery that the vividness of my own immediate enjoyment was not matched by an equally vivid sense of the other "at the other end," for the other was no longer, in Lee's figure, at that street corner. Then I discover the reality of the other's selfhood there-*now*, and in that solitary reality I discover a presence whose vividness matches my own. This is communion in the spirit. And the final discovery is that, in the intensity of my realization of the other, I now receive the other's bodily indwelling itself with the intensity of a spiritual presence. But, after all, this is not the final discovery. For the heightened sense of bodily communion itself leads, by extrapolation, to a renewed sense of the mystery of the other's contemporaneous solitude—and the interaction between body and spirit is reciprocal in a fashion that would make any eschatology other than bodily resurrection something of a letdown.

The reference in the last sentence to extrapolation leads however to another important aspect of communion in the spirit, beyond that of indwelling spirit, though perhaps arising out of it. For if spirit is to be defined in terms of freedom, we should not expect relations in the spirit to have primarily a historical, but rather a contemporaneous character. For as Whitehead's statements quoted earlier indicate, it is the causal independence of *contemporary* occasions that is the ground for the freedom of the universe. But how may contemporaries be experiences with feelings of *positive* spiritual communion, and not just in terms of strangeness and unreachableness? By analogy with the experience of indwelling spirit. The more basic experience of bodily communion may already contain within it the seeds of spiritual communion, in the form of the self-restraint with which one occasion stands guard over the solitude of its successors, and which the successors then receive and experience as the gift of freedom.

Since this gift is experienced along with bodily communion, this form of solitude already has the character of a *communion* of solitudes stamped upon it. When, now, one realizes the absolute independence of one's contemporaries, one is led to extrapolate from the experience of spirit as indwelling to an experience of spirit as contemporaneous. It is in this mode, in which we experience one another as present *to* one another, that the Fellowship of the Spirit reaches its apex. So that a full analysis of the Communion of the Saints in the mode of the Spirit will be given in terms of both presence *in* and presence *to*. This would seem to correspond to the implications of John 14:17, where although the tenses of the verbs are textually uncertain, the connotations of the prepositions are not. For the presence of the Paraclete is referred to by the phrases *en humin*, "in you," and *par' humin*, "with you." (The basic meaning of the latter preposition, significantly enough, is "nearness in space.") This last reference leads to a few words about the relation of Jesus to his Church.

Jesus indwells his Church both bodily and by the indwelling of his Spirit. His bodily indwelling may be understood in terms of the actual historical concatenations of causal efficacy of which we are beneficiaries. Here we may speak of the visible Church, in its concrete institutional and generally structured forms, material, doctrinal, and so on. His spiritual indwelling may be understood in terms of what St. Paul calls the freedom for which Christ has set us free (Galatians 5:1, and the whole context with its emphasis on freedom and Spirit). Jesus envisages us, his followers, so intensely in terms of our own potential intrinsic worth and absolute selfhood, that when this gift of freedom is mediated through his Body the Church, it may be experienced as having the capacity to set us free from the coercive and overwhelming momentum of our own past and of the world as settled. We are set free to become children of God, free to inherit the selfhood that God himself endows by his own envisagement of us as in his own image. In this way of understanding it, the Church *does* in fact act as the mediator of the Spirit of Christ.

Yet, though the Spirit is thus related to the Church, the Spirit is not imprisoned in the Church. This arises out of the fact that Jesus is not just our historical Pioneer. He is our contemporary. This, surely, is the testimony of the Book of Acts and of the early Church—that the Jesus whom they serve, and indeed worship, is *"there-now!"* And this is no idolatrous worship, because as there-now he transcends settled forms of the past. It is the cry "Jesus there-now!" that gives eminent expression to the *esprit de corps* which animates the Church at work and at worship. And where the Church as Body quenches the indwelling Spirit, and thus inhibits the endowment by which the members of the Body might be liberated, there is this other mode of communion that remains unquenchable, between individuals in their solitude and the risen Lord there-now in his. It is this mode that ultimately saves the Church from regression to mass or herd mentality; for by it come those movements of critique by which the Church is renewed in the Spirit. (On the function of the Spirit as critic of the Church, compare Revelation 2:7, 11, etc.) But this last motif, of the contemporaneousness of the risen Lord, with the "Church Triumphant," brings us to the brink of the final scope of the Communion of Saints.

That brink is the brink of death. It is one thing to discover a new mode of presence and communion, in the ability to say freely of an absent friend "Carley there-now." In this case, such an act of communion is a self-transcending celebration of the other's existence. But is such a communion discoverable with the dead? What if the other is in fact no longer there? If death finally cancels out the other's thereness, do not our attempts at such communion become a self-serving device for avoiding our own sense of loss and loneliness? Does not death open up a "cold unfathomable lifeless abyss" lying just over the rim of the world—a space that sets the final limits to communion even in the second mode?

We should not easily deny this possibility. For in this instance the sort of extrapolation required in all perception in the mode of presentational immediacy, comes to its most tenuous venture of belief—or of unbelief. (Is it superfluous to point out that neither is less tenuous than the other?) At this point in this essay I will not debate the issue, but simply suggest a way of practicing such a belief within the perspective of this paper. As I "see" it, death does not so much break off our communion as to throw it decisively, for the time being, into the mode of the Spirit. But this in no way should encourage an esoteric trafficking with spirits. Quite the opposite. For our relationship with the dead will be one in which we stand guard over their solitude, leaving them to be whatever and however and wherever in God's providence it is appropriate for them to be. And yet, since to stand guard over their solitude means to "sanctify" it, within our own hearts, this involves accepting their death, their silence, into ourselves. Accepted as the solitude of those who are *there-now*,

> all the silence is like space between us, but not like time: it does not separate us, it only determines the extent of what we have in common and makes it very wide.[23]

NOTES

1. *The Autobiography of Bertrand Russell*, Vol. I, 1872-1914 (New York: Bantam Books, 1969), p. 3.

2. Bernard Lee, S.M., *The Becoming of the Church* (New York: Paulist Press, 1974), pp. 183, 211, 218, 227.

3. *The Becoming of the Church*, pp. 80, 276.

4. Alfred North Whitehead, *Modes of Thought* (New York: Free Press, 1968), pp. 150, 151, 167.

5. Some of Whitehead's comments may further safeguard this notion from misunderstanding: "The future is to the present as an object for a subject. It has an objective existence in the present. But the objective existence of the future in the present differs from the objective existence of the past in the present. . . . There are no actual occasions in the future to exercise efficient causation in the present. What is objective in the present is the necessity of a future of actual occasions, and the necessity that these future occasions conform to the conditions inherent in the essence of the present occasion." *Adventures of Ideas* (New York: Free Press, 1967), pp. 194-195.

6. *Adventures of Ideas*, pp. 195, 198.

7. Alfred North Whitehead, *Religion in the Making* (New York: World Publishing Company, 1969), pp. 16-19, 86, 132.

8. *The Becoming of the Church*, p. 227. On page 276, there is a reference to "surrendering one mode of presence for another." The reference is to "time given to pulling away for reflection." My general thesis would appear to fit exactly into the implication of this latter discussion.

9. *Adventures of Ideas*, pp. 195-96. The italics in quotations one and three have been added.

10. It is in respect to these two modes that Lee deals with only part of Whitehead's view of the relations enjoyed by an occasion of experience. Now, for Whitehead, what we customarily have is perception in the mixed mode of what he calls *symbolic reference*. As his monograph on *Symbolism* demonstrates, a Whiteheadian discussion of sacramental symbolism should properly employ the categories of both pure modes of perception. As should become clear below, a discussion of the Eucharist only in terms of causal efficacy leaves the liturgical action of the *epiclesis* in the prayer of consecration unexplained. On the other hand, if my thesis has any merit, it will suggest the integral place of the *epiclesis* at that point in the Eucharist.

11. One may well question whether this sentence properly describes the nature of our relation to the future, since the future is not really "there" yet. After rethinking the sentence, I believe it is not an incorrect statement, provided we understand it carefully. For one thing, I believe it is correct and necessary to say that the present occasion does *feel* the future as an *object*. To be sure, "the objective existence of the future in the present differs from the objective existence of the past in the present," as Whitehead says (*Adventures of Ideas*, p. 194). But it is alike in being *felt*, with feelings of anticipation, more narrowly specifiable as feelings of types of possibility clothed in emotions of joy, dread, bewilderment, curiosity, and so on. And these feelings are experienced as indicating a referent beyond the subject, i.e., the future, which is thus experienced as a *there-then*. Granted, the future does not yet exist. Yet, as Whitehead points out, what does exist is the necessity of a future, and a further necessity that the future will have a shape that conforms to conditions "inherent in the essence of the present occasion" (*ibid.*, p. 195). And a felt awareness, both of the necessity and of the dim character of the possibilities for the future, takes the form of specific emotions. These emotions can be pushed away (as when one refuses to face the future) or accepted into oneself. In this sense I think that my sentence is metaphysically correct and phenomenologically faithful. For a remarkable description of this kind of awareness and its "uses," see the Eighth Letter in Rainer Maria Rilke, *Letters to a Young Poet*, revised edition, translated by M. D. Herter Norton (New York: W. W. Norton, 1954). This letter reveals the immense existential import of what Whitehead discusses metaphysically.

12. *The Becoming of the Church*, p. 155.

13. *Ibid.*, p. 158.

14. *Ibid.*, p. 158.

15. Compare Alfred North Whitehead, *Religion in the Making*, p. 28 and context generally.

16. *The Becoming of the Church*, p. 178.

17. *Ibid.*, p. 178. The quotation is from *Modes of Thought*, p. 22.

18. "Mending Wall," pp. 47-48; "The Tuft of Flowers," pp. 31-32; "The Master Speed," p. 392; all in *Complete Poems of Robert Frost* (New York: Holt, Rinehart and Winston, 1964).

19. The phrase is Whitehead's, in *Science and the Modern World* (New York: Free Press, 1967). p. 83.

20. *Letters of Rainer Maria Rilke, 1892-1910,* translated by Jane Bannard Greene and M. D. Herder Norton (New York: W. W. Norton, 1969), pp. 58, 65-66.

21. *The Becoming of the Church,* pp. 168-69.

22. It may be of interest to relate this general perspective to the two classical ways of describing our knowledge of God, the *via positiva* and the *via negativa* (in the Eastern Church, the *kataphatic* and the *apophatic*). In the first way, God is spoken of in terms of human attributes and of the world generally. In the second way, God as he is in himself is said to be unknowable, at least intellectually, and therefore to be beyond description in terms drawn from the world. My argument in this paper may be taken to suggest how these two ways are related. The first way may be said to arise out of our relation to God in the body, and the second way out of our relation to God in the spirit. The two ways, then, are complementary. While the second arises out of the first, it in turn intensifies the first with heightened significance and preserves it from the idolatry of literalness. The first, thus heightened and chastened, would again in turn save the second way from either an esoteric agnosticism or an incommunicable gnosticism. These two ways of describing our knowledge of God are exemplified in St. John of the Cross, who balances his famous "nothing, nothing, nothing" with his vividly anthropomorphic Stanzas of the Soul whose exegesis forms the content of his *Dark Night of the Soul.* Similarly, the central thesis of *The Cloud of Unknowing* would have to do with the sense of God as present within and to the contemplative in the solitary otherness of His contemporaneity. This is implicit in the words with which the Fifth Chapter closes: "Although it be good to think upon the kindness of God, and to love him and praise him for it (i.e., to relate to God efficaciously): yet it is far better to think upon the naked being of him, and to love him and praise him for himself."

23. *Letters of Rainer Maria Rilke,* 1892-1910, p. 196.

SUGGESTED READINGS

Buber, Martin. *I and Thou,* 2nd edition. Translated by Ronald Gregor Smith, New York: Chas. Scribner's Sons, 1958. (In retrospect, I would suggest that Whitehead, at least as I interpret him in the above article, provides a rather exact metaphysical basis for Buber's two "modes of relation," I-It and I-Thou.)

HOPE

William A. Beardslee
Schubert M. Ogden

12 Sex: Biological Bases of Hope

WILLIAM A. BEARDSLEE

We spend energy, if we take Christianity seriously, probing human experience for what it has to teach us about God. That being true, it is somewhat amazing how little we have probed human sexuality as a resource for Christian spirituality. (How often have you heard the word "eros" get a good press in a sermon?) Professor Beardslee explores growth and reproduction as a basis for understanding hope and God. He deals also with Whitehead's philosophy as a framework for his interpretation.

William A. Beardslee is Professor of Religion at Emory University. His theological training was at Harvard (B.D.), New Brunswick Theological Seminary, Columbia University, Union Theological (M.A.), and the University of Chicago (Ph.D.). He is an ordained minister in the Reformed Church in America. Under a Fulbright Senior Research Fellowship, he did post-doctoral work at the University of Bonn in 1961-62. He has published widely in the areas of the New Testament and process theology. His book A House for Hope *is published by Westminster.*

Awoman living in an urban ghetto is asked by a reporter what hope she has, living as she must. She points to her children: "They are my hope," she says. This simple episode shows how profoundly mysterious hope is, how it is often present in the most discouraging of circumstances, though it often evaporates when times are easier. The episode also shows how deeply rooted hope is in the biology of reproduction. The child is the fundamental focus of hope and, more broadly, the paradigm of hope. This point is important to make, since at first sight, hope may seem to be more dimly related to our biological nature than almost any other mental-emotional response. The style of interpretation that emphasizes man's closeness to his biological roots usually downplays hope. In the theological sphere this latter stance is impressively and consistently developed by Richard L. Rubenstein, who combines a sensitive Freudianism with a deep appreciation for the archaic or pagan elements in Judaism, and who explicitly holds that the directional, hope-oriented aspect of Judaism and Christianity is without basis.

"'Eschatology is a sickness.' . . . It was our Jewish sickness originally. We gave it to you [Christians]. You took us seriously. Would that you hadn't! . . . If you are a Christian, you cannot avoid it. If you become post-Christian, choose pagan hopelessness rather than the false illusion of apocalyptic hope."[1]

In the face of the widespread mood of rejecting hope and of establishing a more "realistic" and less idealistic view of man by rediscovering his body, it is important to see that hope does have inescapable biological roots. These will not prove that hope has an inevitable or rightful place in human existence. But to see them clearly and to clarify the physical rootage of hope will not only balance a prevalent one-sided interpretation of man's bodily nature, but will help us to see the depth in which the self-transcendence of hope is based.

The biological basis of hope can be taken to be the directionality of biological growth or the directionality of sexual reproduction. There is much to be said for taking the former alternative, growth, as the biological perspective from which to understand hope. Then growth can be understood as an "open" side of self-preservation; starting this way, hope is openly and unashamedly hope for oneself. Such an approach helps us to understand how hope is a characteristically youthful property—the potential of growth is associated with the young self's reaching forward to the future in hope. This way of approaching hope would not only illuminate some of the connections between hope and creativity, but would tie in with the easily observed fact that hope is most obviously a property of children. The children of the American urban ghetto or of an Asian metropolis show the unfolding of hope as readily as do the children of the economically privileged, as anyone knows who has been among them. As the inexorable closing-off of opportunities takes place, as growth reaches its term, hope contracts. The horizon of hope closes with the passage of time, and the hopelessness of age replaces the hopefulness of youth.

Such a perspective has the merit of making contact with psychological studies that indicate the healthfulness or wholeness of the self which is open to growth; at least under certain circumstances the hopefulness of youth does not have to be abandoned in maturity. Hope may still be meaningful in terms of realistic growth and openness to new possibilities. Important work by psychologists shows the fruitfulness of this approach.[2] Furthermore, hope as an expression of the self's readiness to respond openly to the next moment can be related to a basic religious insight that the utter core of faith is the stance of receiving the next moment as a gift. An interpretation of hope connecting man's basic biological tendency to preserve himself, his openness to biological and cultural growth, and his religious stance of receptivity to the gift of the next moment of existence can create an avenue to an impressive recovery of hope.

THE CHILD AS THE FOCUS OF HOPE

Nevertheless, we propose a different biological function as a paradigm to clarify the nature of hope. It can be simply put:

To have a child is to hope,
And to hope is to have a child.

The most illuminating biological basis for hope is sex. The peculiar drive and texture of human hope arise in part, it is true, from the tendency for self-preservation modified toward the growth of a new self. But sex as the process by which the line of life is projected forward through time is the best key to hope. Hope for the child is the most persistent form of hope, and in fact the only concrete form of hope available to the greater part of humanity under the terrible economic pressures that have been the lot of most men, as is dramatically shown by such a book as that by James Agee and Walker Evans, *Let Us Now Praise Famous Men*.[3] So far as we can penetrate animal existence, the nearest analogue to human hope that we see there is the care of animals for their young. In that phase of animal existence in many forms of life, there is an intense channeling of energy into the protection and nurture of the young life—anthropomorphically speaking, a self-denial for the sake of the coming reality—that is well known to all who have observed the life, for instance, of mammals or birds. The willingness to forgo immediate satisfaction for the sake of a coming reality is a basic mark of all hope, and this aspect of hope is most decisively expressed on the biological level in the parent-child relationship, which in so many of the more complex forms of life functions unconsciously in this very pattern of deferring immediate satisfaction for the sake of the child.

THE GAP BETWEEN THE TWO PHASES OF SEX

Thus we come to a striking feature of sex—one highlighted by the way in which it functions in our culture—namely, the separation between its immediate phase of sexual union and its long-term consequence of offspring. Animals, and it is said certain archaic tribes, have no consciousness of the connection between the two phases. These two phases, inexorably built together by biological fact but separable in experience, have to be welded together by some cultural structure. The family, varied as its forms are in different cultures, functions in all of them to hold together the two phases of sex, so that the care of children is the consequence of sexual union. In our own culture, probably partly as a reaction against a period of strong emphasis on a close connection between the two phases, sexual union and the care and hope for children are now tending to fall apart. This trend hardly needs to be documented, and it is interestingly shown in the use of language: having children is hardly a sexual act, as we use the term "sex."

Our culture means by sex the first phase of biological sex, sexual union. The celebrations of sex in the American arts from advertising to writing, the film, and the theater have almost entirely to do with this phase of sex. The separation of the immediately erotic from the rigidities of the traditional family structure has been widely hailed as liberating and hopeful. This trend is understandable as a reaction against the cultural suppression of much of the freedom, beauty, and excitement of the erotic. No doubt it has been immensely aided by the technological developments summarized under the term "the pill," though it should not be forgotten that techniques of contraception and abortion have been known and practiced for centuries. It seems that this trend toward separating sex and children has been even more basically furthered by the general affluence of so much of the area of the world dominated by Western culture. An offhand first response to those who see the separation of the two phases of sex as hopeful would therefore be to see how sex and affluence have worked together in other cultures. A reading of the Roman satirists and historians should be a sobering experience in this connection.

That is only a first response to a very complex change. It is not intended as a polemic against the recognition of ourselves as deeply constituted by our bodily sexuality, nor as a denial of the profound insights of Freud into the immense influence of the unconscious on our behavior and into the large sexual component of the unconscious. In point of fact, the very Puritan heritage that is so widely blamed for its repressiveness of sex was one of the channels through which an appreciation of sex, and even of its playful aspect, was brought to expression in our culture. The Puritan rejected the ascetic ideal of celibacy and emphasized the healthfulness of the sexual side of marriage. The modern sex manual has its literary ancestor in the frank Puritan marriage sermon.[4] But more than this: sexual union affords a direct if often mute avenue toward awareness of the sacred. A remark attributed to a modern theologian is puzzling: He who longs for the infinite while in his beloved's arms is guilty of bad taste. One would think it more natural to ask, What else would he be longing for at such a time? Instead of opposing the association of sex and the sacred, I would affirm sexual union as a fundamental access to the mystery of existence.[5]

The current emphasis on the immediacy, the freedom, and the longing for totality that sex as union symbolizes is highlighted by the particular cultural situation in which we find ourselves, a situation in which freedom is emotionally associated with aversion from long-term goals. But the direction of this symbolization is built into the delight and intensity of the sexual encounter itself. It is of the moment, not of the future. The liberation of sexuality in our culture is profoundly connected with a rejection of long-term satisfactions. But the second pole of sex—the birth of children—is just as profoundly connected with a long-term process moving into the future. Love as erotic union expresses a longing for totality which becomes a longing for death. The affiliation between erotic love as a longing for totality and the desire for death as also a longing for totality is made clearer when erotic sex is detached from the life and future-oriented consequence of children. Thus the medieval courtly lover, whose love was in principle outside the family, had the connection between love and death explicitly drawn out for him in the poetry of courtly love.[6] Until not long ago the modern imagination, by drawing erotic love back into marriage and thus bringing to expression its movement beyond the moment into the future, has concealed the affinity between erotic love and death. But in still more recent times the connection between love and death has again become evident, and with a force and violence that the medieval mythical structure was able to channel and control. Many of the perplexities of our time with sex can be illuminated from this point of view: the rigidities of marriage were rejected as not life-giving either. Erotic love is biologically life-giving only in terms of the next generation, and if this connection is canceled out, the intensity of love, its thirst for totality, soon discloses its affinity with the longing for the totality of death.

It is true that the affinity between total intensity and death does not come out so clearly when biological growth is taken as the basic biological model. Then the tensions between the intensity of immediate satisfaction and the achievement of long-term goals can be seen as manageable, and the moments of intensity, including sexual intensity, can be seen as finding their place within a life of growth which accepts the fact that death is the terminus of growth. Such a pattern lies behind some of the most penetrating psychological interpretations of the structure of existence. But it is noteworthy that such interpretations usually do not make much either of the procreative function of sex or of hope as a fundamental human stance. Thus Abraham Maslow's important book *Toward a Psychology of Being*,[7] sets up a model of cognition that contrasts "deficiency-cognition" with "being-cognition." In this model, deficiency-cognition is oriented toward the future as the focus of active striving, or of self-projection, but being-cognition is disoriented to time, and is a perception of a pure present. Maslow's study of "self-actualizing" individuals and of "peak experiences" is extremely fruitful in dispelling the notion that the overcoming of deficiency is the fundamental energy of the self. His emphases on growth through delight and on the future as dynamically active in the present are important for an understanding of hope. Further, he has shown that peak experiences are not simply momentary but have profound aftereffects. But his strong emphasis on the way in which peak experiences are sufficient unto themselves leads us to inquire whether Maslow has overlooked other, more future-oriented experiences, which disclose linkage toward the future.

Maslow does not find empirical data which would lead him to modify his model to include a forward-looking hope that is transformed into something more than self-actualization, and it may be that he has not found these data because hope for the future is eroded in our culture. But more important is the fact that hope does not readily express itself in a moment of detachment, illumination, and totality such as that expressed in ecstasy including the ecstasy of erotic sex. Maslow's data, like the important work of Marghanita Laski on ecstasy,[8] are gathered from reports of moments of psychic intensity, and both Maslow's and Laski's materials emphasize the aspects of disorientation, timelessness, and detachment of the peak experience or ecstasy. Such cherished moments are obviously of immense human significance. The preoccupation with sex in our culture and the pursuit of ecstasy through the deserts of desacralized sexual experience testify to a longing for this moment of totality even when it cannot be found. But this line of investigation will remain opaque to the search for the phenomenon of hope, since hope and disorientation to time do not belong together. Ernst Bloch has pointed to a different type of psychological experience as the field in which to explore hope—the daydream, in which the ego (with its orientation to time) remains dominant in the imagination, even though "reality" is transformed into the dreamed-of world.[9]

We shall have to return to these two styles of pointing toward "perfection," the style of loss of self in totality, and the style of projection of self forward into an open future. For the moment, however, we return to the biological level, to point out (what is obvious) that biologically the whole point of the moment of erotic intensity is that something comes out of it; through it the energies of life are projected into the future. The second phase of sex, biologically just as "sexual" as the first—the coming of the child—orients the parents toward the future rather than toward the moment. In this phase the relationship of caring for the other cannot remain the closed totality that it proclaims itself to be in the moments of making love. From the biological point of view, this second phase is what sex is there for. In a sense, therefore, our culture's use of sex is a Promethean effort to liberate one phase of sex from its total biological meaning.

From this point of view, the reactionary pronouncements of the papacy about birth control gain a different perspective from that in which the thoughtful modern viewer usually first sees them. The traditional Roman Catholic view has the wisdom of the continuing effort of culture not to put asunder what biology has joined together. The family is the traditional means of effecting the union of erotic concern for the moment and child-oriented concern for the future. But the particular way in which the two phases of sex are held together in the papal position will not find wide support. Social and technological changes have made the traditional Roman Catholic opposition to birth control no longer tenable—as indeed is widely recognized by urbanized Catholics. However, it is important to note that while one thrust of criticism of this traditional position faults it for its downgrading of what we have called the first phase of sex, the clinching pragmatic argument against it comes from its failure to do justice to the real requirements of the second phase. For the papal position completely fails to come to grips with the conflict between the "natural" consequence of the production of children and the social consequence of the population explosion. That is, the traditional view has to be rejected primarily because it obstructs care for the child.

But all this should not lead one to overlook one of the basic intentions behind this rigid and unacceptable position. The claim of the future, the child, is fundamentally more important in sex than the claim of the longing for total presence, for ecstasy in the moment. The trouble with the papal position is not that it affirms this, but that it affirms it unintelligently and in a way that chokes off the fundamental meaning of hope that is expressed in the relationship to the child. It is true, however, that the task of finding an adequate way, functional in terms of our present knowledge, by which the fundamental biological connection between the present and future in sex and the family can be expressed is enormously difficult. Despite all the freedoms that modern knowledge gives men, there is little reason to think that we are at the point of being liberated from the basic structure of concern for the future that the traditional view expresses. The view of our biological nature that we find so widely expressed today is a singularly one-sided one. Biological sex taken as a whole expresses openness to the future in its total rhythm, and not just in the intensity of the moment—an openness to the future of which the child is the biological symbol and the biological reality.

For our purposes, it is not important to settle the question how far we can liberate human life from its original biological patterns, or to decide what the consequences of such liberation will be. On the one hand, social changes in the role of women will mean that the child will be (and indeed has already been) increasingly recognized as the concern of both parents. On the other hand, the threats to ecological balance may bring about a strongly conservative attitude toward biological and technological innovation. But in spite of this possible and well-grounded reaction, the discoveries which are now being made will bring us into a period of hitherto unsuspected "biological freedom," freedom to reshape the mechanisms of heredity and reproduction as well as many other biological processes, to an extent that would have seemed fantastic only a few years ago. For better or worse, we shall enter this realm of experimentation. Technical considerations—what can actually be done—will determine many of the results. But fundamentally the results will be shaped by our aims, by what we intend. We will be changed in unexpected ways by biological technology, but we need not be its slaves, even though many of the changes will be irreversible. If our aims are to be wise, they must take account of the whole meaning of the processes upon which we exercise our freedom.

The manipulative freedom of modern science and technology has tended to reinforce the focus of consciousness on sexual union as the meaning of sex, while those who have had a grasp of the need for some social cement to hold the two phases together have often appeared to be repressive reactionaries with no grasp of biological reality. We are not appealing here for a traditional solution to any of the problems raised by biological experimentation, but are pointing to the necessity of keeping the functional meaning of both phases of sex in view as we grapple with the new issues. The biological root of hope in sex as procreation, the transcendence of the moment which comes as one is taken beyond himself into the next generation—this is the basis of hope's persistence in the face of hopeless situations as well as the root of hope's willingness to defer immediate satisfaction. That the specific forms which express this biological hope vary from society to society must not obscure the fact that this claim of the future is as "bodily" and as deeply rooted in our nature as is the more immediate satisfaction of sexual union.

THE PROBLEM OF WASTE

At the same time, the connection between biological processes and human hope is a painful one, most evidently because the biology of reproduction involves a fantastic amount of "waste." The animal may devote an immense portion of its energy to taking care of its young, but most of the young cannot survive for long. If young birds are taken from the nest by a cat or a snake, the parents return to the nest for a day or so, but very soon the biological signal that directs them to do this is turned off; if it is early enough in the season, another signal soon directs them to mate and raise another brood. So short is human memory that it will be hard for many of the readers of this book to realize that the conditions of human family life, for most of the world's population, function in a pattern very similar to this, or did so until a generation or two ago. Through the years it has been the way things work that a large family was born, of whom in most cases few survived. But this "waste," this harsh pattern, did not close off hope. Indeed, it is of the essence of hope that it does not always have to be satisfied. The basic biological-social unit of the family is so illuminating as a model for hope not only because it juxtaposes hope, precariousness, and waste, but because it brings to light more decisively than the alternate biological model of growth can do the element of self-denial for the sake of the future which is in a strange way also a projection of one's self.

HOPE AND THE CONFLICT BETWEEN PARENT AND CHILD

There will be those who will object that our model for hope is based on an unreasonably simple or even sentimental view of the relationship between parent and child. The child is also a symbol of death to the parent, and the parent is a symbol of death to the child. We know this all too well today, and we are indebted to

Freud for bringing into the open aspects of the meaning of the child which we do not readily recognize. Freud's view that religion originated in the murder of the father by the "primal horde" in order that they might get possession of the father's females is not taken seriously by historians of religion as a description of how religion actually arose. But that does not lessen the significance of this vision of conflict at the core of the relation between father and son.[10] The relevance of this Freudian insight for the question of hope is that it points to the problematic of hope, that hope is dependent upon a future beyond ourselves, and in some sense implies an effort to control the future. But the future may resist control, may take the power and direction of life into its own hands. The most hopeful parent may be the most tyrannical, and may from the child's point of view be thrusting him toward death and not life, whereas the vitality of the younger generation appears as a death-dealing threat to their elders, as we can so plainly see from the headlines we read in the last third of this century.

The mutual desire for the other's death is real enough in the relation between parent and child, and the fact that this competitive desire has been so largely papered over by social control, repressed, and then discovered in the unconscious has given many interpreters of modern life the feeling that by getting at this aspect of the relationship, they were getting at the "real" relationship, whereas the older sustaining and transmissive model was a social fiction. But a balanced view will see it the other way around. The child is a threat because he is an object of hope: the child as hope is primary, and without that meaning, the whole structure of conflict which Freud analyzed would be without profound significance.

Further, the turmoil in the relation between the generations so evident in our culture does not undermine the fundamental structure of hope that moves from generation to generation. The conflict between the young and the old is a sign of readjustment in their relationship, and it is the fruit above all of the extended period of preadult existence which a complex technological society has forced upon young people. The older generation has extended the notion of the child beyond the age in which it is appropriate, and the younger generation is rejecting the style of adult life prepared for it by its elders, but these facts do not destroy the meaning of the new generation as the focus of hope. The point is that hope, with its pattern of anticipation, movement toward and waiting for a goal, and deferment of immediate satisfaction in favor of a creativity that will be operative in the future, is as deeply rooted in our biological nature as is the more accentuated stance of intensity or ecstasy, in which the present moment is "all." This is a simple enough point, but it is worth stressing, since it is so often said that the second stance, the stance of immediacy, is more "natural," and the stance of hope, waiting, and intentionality is imposed on human nature by culture. Human biological nature does not provide an organized specific relationship between the two stances, as animal life does, but nonetheless no distinction between the one stance as natural and the other as imposed can be made. Both stances have deep physical roots; each finds its most powerful biological expression in one of the two phases of sex—and both are shaped by culture, for human nature apart from culture is an abstraction. That the two elements are often in tension with each other has nothing to do with the supposed secondary or imposed nature of restraints on immediacy and intensity of experience.

On the contrary, as far as a purely biological view of man's nature is concerned, one would have to say that deferment and hope express a more fundamental biological reality than immediate intensity does, for the child is the fundamental and functional reason for the intensity of sexual encounter. It is not my purpose to suggest that people enjoy sex because they expect to have children! The point is that the retrospective view, which can be aware of and appreciate both phases of sex, and can therefore be future-oriented, is more revealing than the awareness of the moment. It is one of the oddities of our supposedly knowledgeable age that we restrict the word "sex" to only one part, and in the long run the less central part, of its meaning. This narrowness of vision expresses a longing for a single moment which totally unifies experience, for sexual ecstasy promises such a unitary moment. But as we shall see in our study of the cultural forms of hope, the linear vision reaching into the future is as unifying as is the total moment, though in a different way. This linear vision, springing from the biology of sex and yet reaching beyond it, is the one that needs to be clarified and emphasized today.

A FRAMEWORK FOR INTERPRETATION:
WHITEHEAD'S PHILOSOPHY

Before we turn to the cultural dimension of hope, it is important to explore the setting of the biological thrust into the future by sexual reproduction in a wider understanding of the physical world. This is a most complex question, to which our answers must often be tentative. At the same time, the question is a real one that we must try to face.

The problem of the relation of such a human stance as hope to the workings of the physical world is almost impossible of solution if we are bound to the presuppositions of most modern science and theology. For both of these disciplines have for the most part accepted a total separation between the subjective and objective worlds, so that a "subjective" reality such as purpose or hope could have nothing to do with what can be observed objectively. Both the immense success of the scientific method in explaining, without recourse to subjectivity or purpose, and the desire to free theology from conflict with the details of scientific findings have pressed these two disciplines so far apart that they have almost no ground for common dialogue. The reasons for this split lie in the history of philosophy, above all in the critical work of Hume and Kant, who proved how different the objective and subjective sides of reality are. Furthermore, Darwin's work and its further developments have shown that a detailed purposeful design determined in advance is not a meaningful way of interpreting the evolution of life.

In spite of all this history, the divorce between objectivity and subjectivity is an impasse, for our commonsense perception of the world shows us that subjectivity and objectivity interact— our intentions result in action. And the pressing practical problems of our, or any, time cannot be met without bringing the two together, even if only pragmatically. Hope and purpose must have something to do with an objective, external world, if they are to be trusted.

It is possible to confront this impasse, and the most constructive approach is along the lines worked out by Alfred North Whitehead.[11] Whitehead was able to accept the sharp distinction, which Kant had stressed, between subjectivity and objectivity without letting them fall apart. His central insight was that neither subjectivity nor objectivity are enduring realities, but that they alternate as aspects of the concrete occasions which are real. Reality is not smoothly continuous in a preformed time and space, as it had been supposed to be in the Newtonian model. Rather, it consists of an infinitely complex sequence of successive actual occasions. Each actual occasion is both subjective and objective. Each occasion, whether an occasion at the very simplest subatomic level or an occasion in my conscious experience, has subjectivity in its unique moment of concrescence or coming-to-be (though in the simpler grades of occasions, of course, the subjective elements of freedom and purpose are trivial). Each occasion derives its data from the now objectively real (because completed) preceding occasions and in its turn becomes objectively real as a datum for later occasions. Although there are immense differences in the complexity of actual occasions, in principle subjectivity and objectivity thus are aspects of all reality. Purpose, associated with subjectivity, is directly known to us only in our own experience, but it is seen to be a characteristic, in varying degrees, of the subjectivity of all occasions. The efficient causality of previous occasions which shapes the feeling or "prehension" of new occasions, is likewise a characteristic of all reality. Freedom and purpose always operate within the limitations set for a given occasion by its data.

Such a perspective is congenial for exploring the problem we have set. Since it does not recognize a sharp line of distinction between living and nonliving or between human and nonhuman reality, at least the question whether a human reality such as hope can be related to the physical universe is a meaningful question in this perspective.

For the question of hope, it is important to see that Whitehead worked out his vision of reality as process not only to bring subjectivity and objectivity into some intelligible relationship, but also to take account of the forward movement of things in time. Mathematics and physics rather than biology were the scientific disciplines that brought his grasp of the problems into focus, but Whitehead was also deeply struck by the biological and evolutionary processes which have brought into being increasingly complex forms of existence with increasing amounts of freedom. The emergence of novelty was one of his central concerns, and he did not think that novelty could be accounted for apart from the aims of actual occasions at intensity of experience both in their own coming to be and in their relevant future, that is, their fore-seeable possible impact on later occasions. Thus the aim of the present toward the future is a central feature of his vision, a feature that quite notably sets it apart from the many systems which have essentially static views of reality. But the aim at the future is, so to speak, decentralized and localized in the actual occasions themselves. There is no one fixed aim in detail for the whole of things, but there are specific aims of specific occasions. While these are taken up in turn (felt or "prehended") by succeeding occasions, each occasion has its own privacy and freedom, and does, within limits, set its own aim.

But the coherence and order that we experience are not adequately understood merely in terms of localized and decentralized seeking of aims by actual occasions, even if these do have to express some continuity because of the influence of past occasions on them. When novelty emerges it is related in an orderly way to previously existing order. Whitehead saw that this interrelationship between order and novelty required that there be an actual entity which offers to each occasion its initial aim, and which sets the initial aim in terms of the maximum intensity of contrasting unity which is possible for that occasion in that situation. The actual entity which does this, of course, is God. God's further function, to be discussed later, is to preserve the achievements of all actual occasions.

We shall examine the meaning of Whitehead's view of God for an understanding of hope in later chapters. Here we note only one point: God is the source of the aim toward the future, but Whitehead is resolutely pluralistic in his view of reality; each actual occasion has freedom, within limits, to set its own subjective aim, by modifying the initial aim given it by God. God does not determine the outcome; his power is the power of persuasion. How extensive and effective the power of divine persuasion can be is one of the central questions for a process theology of hope, and a question to which we must return.

For the moment another consequence of the process perspective must be emphasized: both God and the actual occasions are involved in process. This means that whereas our unreflective experience of subjectivity is of *continuing* subjectivity, in reality the continuing identity of a subject in time is a derivative rather than an ultimate reality. Just as experience comes in "droplets" or "buds," in discrete bits, the real subject (or self) is the subject of each bit of experience. The ultimately real subject is the concrescing occasion. Continuing identity in time is to be understood as a "personal order" of actual occasions, in which each successive occasion inherits from its predecessor. It is clear that this system could allow for greater or less importance for personal continuity in time, and that a use of Whitehead's thought to explore the meaning of Christian existence will find this question of continuing personal identity a central one.[12] But it is important as well to note that the paradigm of hope which we have used (the child) affirms that hope is not merely based on the continuation of personal identity. If one can look for some equivalent to the "child," then the death of one personally ordered sequence of occasions is not in itself a reason for abandoning hope.

Whitehead's vision affirms as fundamentally real some things that run counter to widespread scientific presuppositions; his work was a resolute effort to alter the scientific perspective. Basic to his view is the conviction that there is a tendency in things toward complexity and intensity, which runs counter to the tendency in measurable concentrations of energy to dissipate or "run down." The second law of thermodynamics (entropy tends toward a maximum) suggests that the physical universe is headed toward an eventual increase of disorder or randomness to the point where significant concentrations of energy will finally no longer exist. Life is an important instance of a tendency in the other direction—toward the intensification of energy. Instead of seeing life as an accident or aberration, Whitehead saw it as a striking instance of a creativity that is everywhere at work. He speaks of a "three-fold urge: (i) to live, (ii) to live well, (iii) to live better. In fact the art of life is *first* to be alive, *secondly* to be alive in a satisfactory way, and *thirdly* to acquire an increase in satisfaction."[13] Final causation, or purpose—the central way in which we men experience what life is—is not to be understood either as an illusion (as in a mechanistic interpretation) or as a uniquely human property. Our experiences of purposeful action, on the contrary, supply us with the clue to an aspect of all actual occasions. Furthermore, "purpose" is not adequately conceived as the limited response of seeking a definite goal (purposing to cook a meal or do a day's work). Such a view of purpose is too static. Purpose tends beyond the known model that it is striving to achieve. The tendency of purposive action continually to reach beyond its original models or goals is the great evidence of human creativity, and Whitehead took it as an instance of a far more widespread creativity.

The evolution of life is one of the most striking instances of a pattern of continually reaching beyond an existing and functioning model, and experimenting with new forms. A central question of biology has been whether this evolutionary questing can be understood in terms of purpose. Since sexual reproduction is a central feature of the process of most evolutionary development, the tantalizing question is raised whether there is any connection between the phenomenon of hope in concern for the child and the evolutionary questing for a "better" form of life.

Most of the current interpretation of evolution would reject such questions out of hand. The attempt to view evolution in terms of an élan vital has not stood up. Most students of evolution see no need to bring in any element of purpose. Natural selection working on chance variation within the gene pool of a population seems a sober and adequate approach to most. The brilliant research on the structure and function of the DNA molecule has not been carried out with models that include any element of purpose. Furthermore, more generally it can be said that many activities of living organisms which seem purposive to us are better explained simply as repetitions of successful innovations. In spite of the fact that purpose or final causation is uncongenial to most current interpretation of evolution, however, from the point of view of the perspective we have outlined it can be seen to play a real and central role, along with chance and efficient causation.[14]

"Life is a passage from physical order to pure mental originality, and from pure mental originality to canalized mental originality. It must also be noted that the pure mental originality works by the canalization of relevance from the primordial nature of God. Thus an originality in the temporal world is conditioned, though not determined, by an initial subjective aim supplied by the ground of all order and of all originality."[15] The technical Whiteheadian vocabulary is making the point that an element of purpose ("pure mental originality") is involved in the emergence of novelty, and that if it is to persist, the novelty must be stabilized ("canalized"); if this occurs, it may become the basis for further originality. The foci of living energy at various levels of complexity have an aim at intensity; their departures from established patterns are not *merely* random but involve *also* the intention of increasing the kind of satisfaction that is appropriate for them.[16] This does not mean that the various constituent parts intend the development of the emerging creature, but that in the complex processes of development which result in a variety of living creatures, the tendency toward intensity of experience is at work, and specifically at work in the actual foci of experience at various levels in each organism. "Viewed this way, evolution appears as *a general movement toward societies of organisms with more complex mentality*, even though the movement has been sporadic and never has had any one type of organism as its goal."[17] In this general sense there is a connection between the thrust toward the future which we see in the child and which becomes conscious in human culture on the one hand, and the process of biological evolution on the other.

It is important not to try to make this argument prove too much. Since this concept of purpose is coherent with the freedom of the actual occasions, no one outcome (e.g., man) could have been the predefined purpose of the whole process—though once man has come to be the particular form of life peculiarly susceptible to intensity of experience, to freedom, and to the reach toward the future, it is not unreasonable to see him as of special meaning because of his potentialities. Beyond this, there is no reason to suppose that any one form or order will last perpetually; the question remains to be discussed whether and in what ways the forms that pass away can be understood as still contributing to the future. We have already noted, in considering the symbol "child," the immense amount of "waste" in the process of life, and this same impression is left by a survey of the evolutionary process. The individual is not important from the point of view of the developing species; many lines of evolutionary development "fail," and most seem to show a tendency to become static after a time of development. Thus any attempt to correlate man's drive toward the future with that which is discernible in the development of life must deal seriously with waste and loss.

Once this sober fact is accepted, however, it does seem reasonable to affirm that the alternation between intensity of the moment and concern for the future, so characteristic of human experience, is also characteristic of a much wider sphere. We see this alternation most clearly, beyond ourselves, in other living things. But we shall be on soundest ground if we follow Whitehead, and interpret also the inorganic realm as dimly characterized by subjectivity as well. The alternation between two phases of experience is basic; both are essential. But what appears from this survey of the physical rootage of our nature is that while the thirst for totality, for the infinite, is a basic and wonderful part of our makeup, it tends to claim more for itself than it really can achieve. Total unity is of the moment, and the other element of longing, the longing for the "more" of the future, is if anything more essential.

NOTES

1. Richard L. Rubenstein, "Thomas Altizer's Apocalypse," in John B. Cobb, Jr. (ed.), *The Theology of Altizer: Critique and Response* (The Westminster Press, 1970), p. 133.

2. For instance, Erik H. Erickson, *Childhood and Society* (W. W. Norton & Company, Inc., 1950).

3. James Agee and Walker Evans, *Let Us Now Praise Famous Men* (Houghton Mifflin Company, 1941).

4. See Roland M. Frye, "The Teachings of Classical Puritanism on Conjugal Love," *Studies in the Renaissance*, Vol. II (1955), pp. 148-159.

5. As by Abraham H. Maslow, *Religions, Values, and Peak Experiences* (Ohio State University Press, 1964).

6. Denis de Rougemont, *Passion and Society*, tr. by Montgomery Belgion (London: Faber & Faber, Ltd., 1940).

7. Abraham H. Maslow, *Toward a Psychology of Being* (D. Van Nostrand Company, Inc., 1962).

8. Marghanita Laski, *Ecstasy: A Study of Some Secular and Religious Experiences* (Indiana University Press, 1961).

9. Ernst Bloch, *Das Prinzip Hoffnung*, 3 vols. (Frankfurt: Suhrkamp, 1959), Vol. I, Ch. I.

10. Sigmund Freud, *Totem and Taboo* (New Republic, Inc., 1931).

11. The fundamental work is Alfred North Whitehead, *Process and Reality: An Essay in Cosmology* The Macmillan Company, 1929). Also basic for Whitehead's thought are *Science and the Modern World* (The Macmillan Company, 1926); *Religion in the Making* (The Macmillan Company, 1926); *Adventures of Ideas* (The Macmillan Company, 1933).

12. Thus, Hans Jonas, *The Phenomenon of Life: Toward a Philosophical Biology* (Harper & Row, Publishers, Inc., 1966), p. 96, holds that Whitehead's emphasis on the actual occasion as the unit of reality, by breaking life up into a series of moments, makes it impossible to deal seriously with the continuity of a living being's life and with death as the final term of its existence. As will appear, we recognize that Whitehead's system can be seen in this way, but it does not require this interpretation.

13. Alfred North Whitehead, *The Function of Reason* (Princeton University Press, 1929), p. 8.

14. The discussion here on evolution is indebted to Richard H. Overman, *Evolution and the Christian Doctrine of Creation: A Whiteheadian Interpretation* (The Westminster Press, 1967).

15. Whitehead, *Process and Reality*, p. 164.

16. Overman, *Evolution*, p. 210.

17. *Ibid.*, p. 211.

SUGGESTED READINGS

Beardslee, William A. *Literary Criticism of the New Testament*. Philadelphia: Fortress Press, 1970.

—— (with Jack Boozer) *Faith to Act*. Nashville: Cokesbury Press, 1967.

—— "Openness to the New in Apocalyptic and in Process Theology," *Process Studies*, III (1973), pp. 169-178.

13 *The Meaning of Christian Hope*

SCHUBERT M. OGDEN

Hope is the criterion for judging the mythological symbols of hope, and not the other way around. And Professor Ogden thus proceeds to assess the hope symbols of "resurrection of the body" (a horizontal symbol) and "immortality of the soul" (a vertical symbol). Apart from whether or not there is such a thing as continuation of personality beyond physical death, Professor Ogden argues that personal immortality is not an essential element to Christian hope. Hope has to do with the ultimate significance of the world and of man, because of God's love. God's love is his boundless acceptance of the entire world in such a way that ultimately there is neither loss nor destruction, despite the world's own transience and death. Professor Ogden feels that the noninclusion of personal immortality in the essence of hope protects us from the Garden of Eden temptation to be like God—rather, in his understanding, God alone is the ultimate significance of your life; you shall make nothing else besides him (i.e., your personal immortality) essential to its significance.

Schubert M. Ogden is Professor of Theology at Perkins School of Theology, and Director of the Graduate Program in Religion at Southern Methodist University in Dallas. He received his education at Ohio Wesleyan University, the Johns Hopkins University, the University of Chicago, and Philipps-Universität in Marburg, Germany. *From 1969-72 he was Professor of Theology at the University of Chicago. He is an ordained elder in the United Methodist Church. He is best known for his books:* Christ without Myth, A Study of the Theology of Rudolf Bultmann, *and* The Reality of God and other Essays.

195

Essential to Christian faith, as I understand it, is belief in the reality of God as distinct from and more than the reality of the world, taken either in its individual parts or as the collection thereof. God in the Christian sense is neither a mere part of the world nor all of its parts together, but is a distinct center of activity and reactivity, and so a genuine individual in his own right. At the same time, Christian faith involves the belief that God is the beginning and the end, the ground and the consequent, of every other individual whatever, so that he himself is not merely an individual, but is *the* individual, the one whose own reality coincides with reality itself or as such. Whatever is, or is so much as even possible, has its beginning and end in God's love for it and, but for the reality of his love, would have neither being nor value in any public or objective sense. Thus while God as individually distinct from the world is believed to transcend it, he is also believed to be immanent in the world as its primal ground, even as it is immanent in him as its ultimate end.

But now, how is this essential Christian belief to be effectively elaborated and expressed? My suggestion is that the truth of Christian theism may be stated most appropriately and understandably in our situation today by developing the analogy based on the relation of the human self to its own body. Given the contemporary understanding of the body as an incredibly complex microcosmos of molecular and cellular activities, the self must be conceived in relation to the body not as "the ghost in the machine," but as something like a little indwelling god. This is so, at any rate, unless one is prepared to deny that the human person as a whole is not simply many things but one thing, an individual center of activity and experience as well as the complex of activities and reactivities comprising its bodily life. But if the self in this sense may be said to be the god of the body, the God affirmed by Christian faith may be said to be in an analogous sense the self of the world. For of all the analogies available to us for understanding God's relation to the world, none so well clarifies the peculiar unity of difference and identity, of transcendence and immanence, that is of the essence of Christian faith in God.

My purpose here, however, is not to argue any further for the appropriateness of this analogy. I ask, rather, that my readers simply assume its appropriateness and consider with me, briefly, the belief-system that results when it is more fully elaborated.

The first point to notice is that the human self is incarnate in its body, and thus in the wider world beyond, only in what is, after all, a radically limited manner. Although the interaction between self and body at its height is as intimate as any known to us, the fact is that the self directly interacts only with its own brain cells or, at most, with the cells of its central nervous system. What goes on in its body as a whole, not to mention the wider environment, is largely a mystery to it, and it in turn can effect changes in the remote bodily regions or in the world beyond it only through the mediation of its brain and spinal cord. All of which is to say that the human self as we experience it is but a fragmentary or localized self, encompassed round about by an external environment with which it interacts only indirectly. And this explains why the self's relation to its body is, after all, only an analogy for our understanding of God. For in the case of God's relation to the world, any such limitation is removed. The field of God's interaction with others is nothing less than the world as such, or the entire universe, with every individual of which his relations are unsurpassably direct. Because his love for others is literally boundless, what goes on in the world is completely open to him, and his power over every region of the world is correspondingly direct and immediate. In a word, God is the one integral or strictly universal self, whose only environment is wholly internal to his all-encompassing love. The only thing excluded from his love is the future as such or as not yet actual, and even that in its way belongs to him (in the only way it could belong to anyone) as his own possibilities for further actualization in and through his creation of others and thereby also of himself.

The second point to be made about the human self is that it is also fragmentary or localized with respect to time. The whole venture of human selfhood in which each of us is involved is always bounded by the two limits of our birth and our death. Although what we think of as our self is the principle of identity through the entire sequence of changes that is our human career, it itself at some point comes to be and at yet another point passes away. Thus the sequence of bodily worlds of which each of us is, as it were, the god or the unifying center is neither unbegun nor unending, and so is temporal rather than eternal. Hence, once again, we are forced to recognize that the self-body relation is at most an analogy of God's relation to the world. For the difference between God and all other individuals is that he alone neither begins nor ends but simply is, as the strictly eternal principle of identity of the infinite sequence of worlds that is his own career as divine.

> Evermore
> From his store
> New-born worlds rise and adore.

Throughout all the becoming whereby, without beginning or end, new worlds come to be and pass away, God is the one individual who himself neither becomes nor perishes. Although through his limitless love for the world he does indeed share in its becoming, and in *that* sense becomes himself, his love as such has never begun nor can it ever end. Rather, he always has been and always will be the boundless acceptance of others, ever creating himself in and through his creation of them and their own attempts to create themselves and one another. Furthermore, God's radical difference from the human self implies that he is free from yet another of its limitations with respect to time. Since this point is important for the argument I shall presently be developing, we must make a special effort to understand it.

On any profound understanding of the matter, the death that is one of the limits of human selfhood cannot be restricted simply to that final termination of our subjective experience of which I have previously spoken and which we ordinarily mean by the word "death." Viewed in its actual context, such termination of our experience is but the last and most radical instance of a process that constantly occurs throughout our life—namely, the loss of any vivid awareness either of ourselves or of others or of the whole of life in which we share. The fragment of our experience that we are able to retain in memory is never more than infinitesimal in comparison with all that is continually swept away into the vast oblivion of our forgetfulness. And this is as true of the collective memory of mankind as of the individual memory of each of us. The trials and triumphs of the fathers are so poorly appreciated by their sons that it is almost as though they had never lived. Thus, from time immemorial, no theme has more preoccupied sensitive minds than the essential transience of life—the fact that each moment is, as it were, a little dying, a prefiguring already in the present of the final loss of experience as such.

But if God is the self of the world in an analogical sense only, or in other words, is the one truly perfect self, it belongs to his perfection that he should be free of death also in this extended sense of the word. Radically unlike ours, his memory is infallible, and so for him the transience of life is overcome or, rather, simply does not exist. Because his love of others is literally boundless, whatever comes to be is fully embraced by his love, where it is retained forever without any loss of vividness of intensity. Such value as it has, whether positive or negative, becomes an integral part of his own divine life, and thus is in the strict sense immortal or of everlasting significance. Because this is so, we must always speak with caution of the perishing of things or of their passing away. Although everything other than God does indeed perish or pass away, in the sense that it sooner or later reaches its term, it is only for such narrow sympathies as our own that anything ever ceases fully to count or to make a difference. For God, by contrast, everything always counts for exactly what it is and never ceases to make just its own unique difference.

This, then, very generally, is how I should try to express at the more fully reflective level of theological understanding the essential structure of theistic belief that is implied in Christian faith. But the question, obviously, is whether the essence of Christianity can really be expressed in some such terms. Granted that such a system does indeed express faith in God as the self of the world, as the encompassing love of others whereby all things are bound together into one integral whole of life, is this by itself sufficient to constitute a *Christian* theism?

In order to speak to this question, I now wish to show how this belief-system also provides for a theological understanding of Christian hope. I shall argue that the essential meaning of Christian hope can be appropriately expressed in these terms and, further, that by so expressing it, we are able to meet a fundamental criticism of Christianity that is often made by its secular critics. In so arguing, however, I shall be forced to make a claim that I suspect many of my readers will not be at all inclined to accept—namely, that the meaning of Christian hope may and must be so redefined that the hope for our own subjective immortality can no longer be held to be essential to it. Because I am well aware that this is an unusual claim for a theologian to make, I must not only ask my readers to withhold judgment until I have presented my case, but also state at the outset that I have no intention whatever of questioning that immortality is in a profound sense essential to the Christian hope. Although I frankly prefer to speak with the Apostles' Creed rather of "the resurrection of the body" than of "the immortality of the soul," I nevertheless firmly believe that it is of the essence of Christian hope to hold that the limit of our death is finally overcome—that the end of our life, just like its beginning, is nothing less than the everlasting life of God himself. But exactly how this does and does not imply that we ourselves are immortal seems to me the very thing to be considered, and it is to such consideration that my argument shall be directed.

II

I begin by recalling briefly the characteristic features of Christian hope as it is classically attested by Scripture and tradition. If we ask of the New Testament what it is that Christians hope for, the answer at first glance seems clear enough. Christians hope for "the day of the Lord Jesus Christ," that is, for the "coming" or the "appearance" of Christ, whereupon the final judgment and salvation of God will at last take place. Thus Paul writes, "the Lord himself will descend from heaven with a cry of command, with the archangel's call, and with the sound of the trumpet of God. And the dead in Christ will rise first; then we who are alive, who are left, shall be caught up together with them in the clouds to meet the Lord in the air; and so we shall always be with the Lord" (I Thessalonians 4:16 f.). Implied by this hope is not only that, with the resurrection of the dead in Christ, the whole world will be judged and all mankind consigned to its final destiny, but also that all this is going to happen at any moment. But this is to say, in effect, that the hope attested by Paul, along with most of the other New Testament witnesses, is really only the Christianization of the characteristic hope of late Jewish apocalypticism. The sole important difference is that, whereas Jewish hope looks forward to "the day of God" and to God's coming, Christian hope replaces this with the imminent coming of the Lord Jesus Christ as God's Messiah.

In a few places in the New Testament, however, we encounter a quite different way of interpreting Christian hope. In part, certainly, because the original expectation of a near end of the world proved illusory, but also because as Christians more and more found themselves in a non-Jewish cultural environment, the apocalyptic hope tended to recede in favor of a typically Hellenistic interpretation of man's destiny. According to this interpretation, which was popularly represented by the important religious movement of Gnosticism, the decisive happening is not the resurrection of the dead and the judgment of the entire world, but the death of each individual person, when, provided he is properly instructed, he ascends at once to the heavenly world of light whence he originally fell. In other words, while the apocalyptic hope is projected along the horizontal line of historical development and anticipates the resurrection of the body, the Gnostic hope is really a vertical projection, which envisages solely the immortality of the human soul. The chief witness to such a hope in the New Testament is the author of the Fourth Gospel, for whom the earlier apocalyptic hope expressed by Paul has completely lost its power. Although John, as we call him, fully retains the traditional Jewish belief in God's creation of the world, and thus rejects Gnostic dualism, including its doctrine of the self's preexistence, the forms of his understanding of hope are taken straight out of Gnosticism. This is especially evident from the well-known words in the fourteenth chapter of his Gospel, which reflect the Gnostic picture of the soul's ascent upon death to reunite with its heavenly Redeemer: "In my Father's house are many dwelling places; if it were not so, would I have told you that I go to prepare a place for you? And when I go and prepare a place for you, I will come again and will take you to myself, that where I am you may be also" (vss. 2f.).

But now the striking thing about the subsequent development of the theological tradition is that this Gnostic interpretation of hope did not generally displace Christian apocalypticism, as it clearly had in John's Gospel, but was rather superimposed upon apocalypticism to express the hope of Christian orthodoxy. As is indicated by the way it figures in the major Christian creeds, the apocalyptic hope for the resurrection of the dead more and more receded into the background of orthodox eschatology. The foreground was held by the Gnostic hope for immortality, which was believed to be fulfilled immediately upon the death of each individual. Provided he had received the sacraments of the Church and thus died in a state of grace, the individual could expect that his soul would survive the death of his body and be united at once with God in heaven. And yet, because the original apocalyptic picture of hope was never completely abandoned by the Church, it continued to provide the larger setting of traditional Christian doctrine. Even though the resurrection of the dead and the final judgment were now envisaged as events of the remote, rather than, as in most of the New Testament, the imminent future, the claim of the tradition was and is that their occurrence alone will constitute the fulfillment of the whole of Christian hope.

Now, without supposing that this is more than the briefest summary of the traditional hope of Christianity, I would make two observations about it.

First of all, given contemporary standards of meaning and truth, there can be no question that these terms in which Christian hope is classically attested are through and through mythological and must be interpreted accordingly. I do not mean by this, of course, that traditional Christian eschatology is simply false. The popular assumption that what is mythological in its form of expression cannot be true only evidences the extent to which all of us today are under the spell of secularism. The ground of this assumption is the secularistic denial that there is any truth other than the truth of empirical science, from which it follows that, since mythology clearly cannot be taken as science, one can only assume it is false. Yet, even if one rejects this denial and the assumption that follows from it, the fact remains that mythology cannot be construed as science, even though it is the mark of mythological terms to invite such misconstruction. Thus, in speaking as it does of the resurrection of the dead and of the last judgment, the myth of apocalypticism appears to refer to cosmic events of the near or distant future in something like the way in which scientific language might refer to them. On closer examination, however, it becomes evident that the use to which mythological terms are actually put is quite different from the use of language—even of the same language—in science. The real intention of myth, and in this lies its distinctive kind of meaning and truth, is not to speak of the various details of reality in the manner of science, but to express our own most basic understanding of ourselves in relation to reality as such. Whereas science by its very nature is concerned with the parts of reality or with everything taken distributively, myth as the language of faith or religion is concerned with everything taken collectively, or with reality as a whole. Because this is so, however, all mythology, and therefore the traditional language of Christian hope as well, has to be interpreted so that its real meaning and truth. so far as it has any truth, can be understood. In a word, the language of hope must be demythologized. It must be interpreted in terms of its own real intention to disclose the truth of our own existence in relation to reality as a whole.

And this leads to my second observation. The traditional mythology of Christian hope is, in fact, an amalgam of Jewish apocalypticism and Gnosticism, and therefore as such nothing specifically Christian. Neither the collective hope for the final fulfillment of all creation nor the individual hope for the soul's ascent to heaven immediately after death is original with Christianity, although both hopes were adopted by it and eventually worked together into its traditional teaching. This is not to say, naturally, that there could not have been specifically Christian reasons why these pictures of hope were adopted and retained throughout the Church's history. On the contrary, the Christian community almost certainly came to express its hope in these terms because, in addition to their being terms in which men once naturally thought and spoke, they were recognized as being somehow appropriate to Christian hope itself. The point, however, is that this hope is the criterion for judging the mythology—not the other way around. Even if we can understand the meaning of hope only by critically interpreting its mythological forms of expression, it is nevertheless a *critical* interpretation that is called for if we are not simply to mistake Christian hope for something else. Recalling, then, my first observation that the language of hope, being mythological, has to be demythologized, or interpreted in terms of its understanding of existence in relation to reality as a whole, we may now add that the criterion of our interpretation can only be the specifically Christian understanding of man's relation to God.

If this is our theological task, however, I hold that it cannot be especially difficult to accomplish. I do not mean, of course, that the essence of Christian hope is so obvious and simple that something less than a complete eschatology would be sufficient to interpret it. My contention is simply that there can be no doubt as to the Christian understanding of man's relation to God and therefore as to the criterion of interpretation of Christian hope as well. So far as Christianity is concerned, the ground object of man's hope, even as of his faith and love, are precisely and only God as decisively re-presented in Jesus Christ. This is to say that, for the Christian understanding of existence, the ultimate whole of reality to which man is related is understood to be the boundless love whereby all lives are knit together into one integral and everlasting life. Even as this love is at once the ground and object of man's faith, of his trusting consent to reality as such, so it is also the ground of his own capacity to love and the one inclusive object toward which all his love is directed. Being freed to love by God's limitless love for him and for the whole creation, he loves both himself and all others in his returning love for God. But, in the same way, the love of God is also the ground and object of Christian hope. Because what is ultimately real is not merely the world but God's all-inclusive love of the world, there is a ground for hope beyond the limits of the world with its death and transience. Although it is the destiny of the world and of everything in it that it should come to be and pass away, the world is nevertheless the good creation of God and the object of his everlasting love. Thus whatever is created is also redeemed, in the sense that it is fully embraced by God's love and there cherished forever for exactly what it is. But this means that the love of God is itself the object of Christian hope as well as its ground. For while this hope is indeed the hope for a significance of the world beyond the limits of its own transience and death, God's love alone is sufficient to constitute such significance and therefore is itself not only, if I may say so, the *why* of Christian hope but also its *for what*.

In general, then, it is clear how an adequate interpretation of traditional Christian mythology ought to proceed. Such mythology should be interpreted simply as the symbolic expression of Christian hope, of hope that is grounded in the love of God decisively re-presented in Jesus Christ and which is directly to that self-same love as its only proper object. Without going into the details of such interpretation, I would now like to make two further points concerning it.

The first is that an interpretation of this kind would have no trouble at all agreeing that there are in fact specifically Christian reasons for the Church's traditional way of expressing its hope. Indeed, such interpretation could readily explain why the pictures of hope of both Jewish apocalypticism and Gnosticism could have been adopted and retained by Christianity. The virtue of apocalypticism, with its horizontal projection of hope and its central symbol of the resurrection of the body, is that it brings to expression the truly cosmic dimensions of Christian hope, which sees in the reality of God's love the promise of fulfillment not only for the individual person and the whole of mankind, but for every created thing. Even as the symbol of creation expresses that whatever is has its primal ground solely in the divine love, so the symbol of resurrection affirms that it is in this same divine love that all things also have their only ultimate end. Thus, even though the terms of apocalypticism are mythological, they may still be taken to affirm that the whole of history, including the larger history of nature, is ultimately significant, and thus serve as symbols of Christianity's truly collective hope. On the other hand, the merit of the Gnostic picture is to symbolize the meaning of hope for each individual person. As surely as man belongs to nature and is continuous with it, he is also distinguished within nature as the one point where, so far as we know, nature can become fully conscious of itself and of its ultimate ground and end. In fact, it is this very capacity to be fully conscious of himself, and thus, in a way, of reality as such, that explains why man is said to be created in God's own image, and therefore to be uniquely the creature of hope, even as he is also the creature who uniquely believes and loves. Because of its projection of hope along the vertical and its central symbol of the immortality of the soul, Gnosticism in its way expresses this distinctiveness of man from the rest of nature. Therefore, as mythological as it certainly is, the Gnostic picture can still be taken as a symbol of the uniquely human relation to God, and thus of the meaning of Christian hope for man.

The second point I wish to make, however, is that neither the apocalyptic hope for resurrection nor the Gnostic hope for immortality can be taken as anything other than a symbol of specifically Christian hope—by which I mean, of course, hope in God's love as itself the ultimate significance both of the world and of man. Whether Christian hope is expressed in terms of the horizontal projection of apocalypticism, or expressed, rather, through the vertical projection of Gnosticism, it is in either case expressed in symbols that point beyond themselves. Since the reality of God's love, and hence the ultimate significance of our life, is neither one more event in the future ahead of us nor real only in some heavenly realm above us, both projections are inadequate to the real meaning of Christian hope. At best they but provide pointers to its essential truth—to the truth, namely, that in spite of the death and transience of all things, their final destiny is to be embraced everlastingly by God's love for them and that man, at least, through faith and love in the present, can already share in this his eternal life in God. In other words, the symbols of resurrection and immortality must be taken as pointing not to some other life beyond this life but to the abiding significance in God of this life itself. Which is to say that the only immortality or resurrection that is essential to Christian hope is not our own subjective survival of death, but our objective immortality or resurrection in God, our being finally accepted and judged by his love, and thus imperishably united with all creation into his own unending life.

III

But now it is this claim that, as I admitted earlier, many of my readers are likely to find unacceptable. So deeply rooted is the assumption that Christian hope includes our subjective immortality, or even essentially consists in it, that any statement to the contrary is certain to meet with considerable resistance. As a matter of fact, I have the impression that there are many in the Church for whom none of its traditional certainties is as important as the certainty that they themselves will somehow continue as subjects beyond the limit of death. Even so, I trust it will be granted that any hope for subjective immortality is itself extremely problematic and is, if anything, still more so in a secular age such as our own. Involved in the secular affirmation of the reality and significance of our life in this world are the most serious reservations about any hope that, like the conventional hope for immortality, appears to compromise it. Whatever one's own personal beliefs, then, he is hardly equal to the present theological task unless he is willing to ask as honestly as he can whether any such hope is, in fact, included in the essence of Christianity. If my own answer to this question is negative, this is not because I have simply accepted the reservations of secularity and then so redefined Christian hope as to conform it to them. Rather, as the preceding discussion should have made clear, I have looked first to the New Testament itself and tried to determine the only proper object of Christian hope, and then, finding this to be nothing other than God's boundless love for us, I have inferred that our own subjective immortality is not to be counted as belonging essentially to it. But since the precisely contrary inference is so often drawn, I owe my readers still more in the way of an argument for my counterposition. And so I turn, briefly, to what I see to be serious objections to the usual view that God's immortal love for us implies that we ourselves are subjectively immortal.

It will be observed that the objections I shall offer are strictly theological, and thus prescind from other more broadly philosophical objections that might also be made—such as, for example, that subjective immortality is no solution whatever to the really fundamental problem of life's transience, of which death, as we usually think of it, is merely the most extreme instance. I should also explain that the only thing I am objecting to is the notion of our subjective immortality in the strict sense of the words. Whether or not we somehow manage to survive death for a longer or shorter period of time I regard as a question of no particular theological interest. So far as theology is concerned, the only interesting question is whether we are in at least one respect like God himself in continuing to exist as subjects for the strictly infinite future. And to the affirmative answer to this question I see two basic objections.

The first is that this answer obscures the witness of Christian faith to the essential difference between God and man, the Creator and the creature, the Redeemer and the redeemed. According to the Genesis account of the fall, man's primal sin is precisely his desire to be like God, his refusal of the fact of his creaturehood and his attempt to live by and for himself, rather than under the gift and demand of God's love. Instead of acknowledging that we are dependent on God absolutely, that we live at all only from him and for him, we all try in various ways to become independent and to have life in ourselves. Small wonder, then, that the different pictures in which we as a race have expressed our ultimate hope also give expression to our sinful self-assertion. This is particularly evident from our usual doctrines of the immortality of the soul, according to which the human self is in principle immortal, being a very spark of divinity itself. Significantly, the Church has been sharply critical of such doctrines at the point of their correlative affirmation of the self's eternal *pre*existence. This affirmation has generally been held—and I believe rightly held—to be incompatible with essential Christian faith in the creation, which affirms that everything other than God himself, not excluding the human person, is God's creature, and therefore is in no sense eternal. It belongs to every creature, as essentially different from the Creator, that there once was when it was not, and in this sense it is said to be created out of nothing by God (*ex nihilo a deo*). But my question is whether the Church has not failed to follow out the logic of its own witness by not recognizing that a precisely parallel criticism must be made of the affirmation of the self's eternal *post*existence or, in other words, of our usual doctrines of subjective immortality. Does it not also belong to the redeemed, as radically different from their Redeemer, that there shall be when they shall be no more, save in that their lives are everlastingly loved by God, who, in the words of Scripture, "alone has immortality and dwells in unapproachable light, whom no man has ever seen or can see" (I Timothy 6:16)?

The usual reply to this question is that, if God really loves man, is his Redeemer as well as his Creator, he cannot permit the object of his love ever to be lost or destroyed. But aside from the fact that this reply betrays a narrow concern for man to the exclusion of the rest of creation, it misses the point of the question. As we saw earlier, the reality of God's love as his boundless acceptance of the entire world means that ultimately there is neither loss nor destruction, despite the world's own transcience and death. Even if all creatures eventually perish or pass away, in that they reach the term of their own subjective participation in life, their lives nevertheless are objectively immortal through God's loving participation in them, and thus are in no sense lost or destroyed. All that they are and ever have been, for good or for evil, is raised beyond their own death and transience into the eternal life of God himself, where it abides forever as imperishably significant. This being so, I find as little reason in God's love that man should postexist eternally as that he should preexist eternally; and I see in the one notion as surely as in the other something that, in obscuring the essential difference between God and man, is doubtfully consistent with the essence of Christianity.

Related closely to this first objection is another equally basic. If man's primal sin is his desire to be like God, the fact remains that all his attempts to fulfill this desire are doomed to failure, since, whether he acknowledges it or not, he is and remains God's creature, absolutely dependent on the divine love for the ultimate significance of his life. Even so, because man's sin is precisely his refusal to acknowledge his dependence on God, his faith takes the inauthentic form that Scripture speaks of as idolatry—that is, the setting up of something alongside of God's love as alone justifying his life by finally making it worth living. "I am the Lord thy God; thou shalt have no other gods besides me"— which is to say, "God alone is the ultimate significance of your life; you shall make nothing else besides him essential to its significance." But even as authentic faith in God is the fulfillment of this commandment, so the inauthentic faith of sin is its transgression. It is the refusal to let God really be God by acknowledging his love *alone* as the ultimate end of one's life.

Now, maybe I am mistaken, but it is this very refusal to live, finally, solely from God's love for us that I find involved in the setting up of our own subjective immortality alongside of our objective immortality in God. This seems clear to me simply from the structure of the argument whereby theologians commonly try to infer that we ourselves are immortal subjects. I refer to the argument already considered, to the effect that, if God really loves us, he will somehow see to it that our existence as subjects is not terminated by death but continues forever. Whatever the force of this argument, and I have already explained why it does not seem to me to have much force, I find it structurally identical with rationalizations that could be offered for any idolatry, even the crudest imaginable. I fail to see, in other words, how it differs logically from arguments which would hold that, if God really loves us, he will not permit our nation to suffer reversal or defeat, will see to it that our children grow up just as we wish them to, will guarantee our success in business, or will make certain that we are always prosperous and sleep on full stomachs. Furthermore, the way theologians usually develop this argument for subjective immortality makes clear that it, too, can be reversed, permitting identically the same inference, namely, that if God would *not* see to it that we continue as subjects, then he would *not* really love us—just as some infer from national defeat or their own personal failures that God has abandoned them and that their lives are no longer worth living.

But what does this show if not that the inference of subjective immortality from the reality of God's love involves the same refusal to live solely from that love itself which is the very essence of man's sin and idolatry? Perhaps there is some way of making this inference that avoids so profound a distortion of essential Christian faith and hope. But, so far as I know, such a way has not yet been found; and the usual arguments for subjective immortality appear, however unintentionally, to be witnesses more to man's persisting sin than to God's abiding love—the love that is the only object of Christian hope just because it is by it alone that our sin as well as our death is finally overcome.

These, then, are my objections to the view that our own subjective immortality is essential to Christian hope. If they are as sound as I think them to be, the understanding of hope for which I have argued is not merely theologically acceptable but is far more appropriate to the essence of Christianity than more conventional interpretations.

Furthermore, and this seems to me quite as important, such an understanding clearly meets a fundamental criticism of Christian hope that is commonly made by secular men. The most serious secular reservations about the Church's hope are not due to its being held to be, at best, extremely problematic on strictly theoretical grounds, but to its alleged diversion of man's concern and responsibility away from his present life here and now to some other life beyond. By focusing our ultimate hope on our subjective existence beyond death, Christianity appears to many of our contemporaries to belittle the urgent problems of a humanity struggling for greater justice and enlightenment and to provide at least a negative sanction for the social and political status quo. And this appears all the more certain to them because, with its virtual abandonment of apocalypticism as expressing a truly collective hope, much of modern Christianity has, in fact, focused man's ultimate expectations on the existence beyond death of individual persons. Thus it has been widely taught in modern Churches that all that finally counts is the other-worldly salvation of individuals, with the result that efforts for the fulfillment and humanization of this world have been deprived of any ultimate significance. But aside from the fact that any such teaching seriously neglects important elements in traditional Christian mythology, it is obvious that it has been radically called into question by the interpretation of this mythology offered here. On this interpretation, such mythology in no way expresses hope in some other life beyond this life but, precisely as symbolic of Christian hope in God's love, expresses hope in the ultimate significance of this life itself. Therefore, so far from compromising our concern with this world and our responsibility for humanizing it, Christian hope is disclosed to be the best of reasons for having such concern and responsibility. Just because it is hope in God's love, it is also hope in the world's significance, and this means that it is the kind of hope that issues in concerned and responsible action for the world's fulfillment.

Yet, if Christian hope as interpreted here is in this respect accessible to a genuinely secular outlook, there is another respect in which it has been understood to involve infinitely more than any merely secular hope for the future. And this, too, has an importance that ought not to be overlooked. Given its dominant interests and direction, the most serious danger confronting contemporary theology is hardly that it will succumb to a false otherworldliness which obscures the truth that Christian hope has to do with this world's ultimate significance and fulfillment. The greater danger, rather, is that in its concern with developing such things as political theologies and theologies of hope and liberation, theology today will repeat the mistake of the social gospel and reduce Christian hope in God's love to little more than a secular hope for man's this-worldly fulfillment. Theology seems apt to forget, in other words, that although Christian hope does indeed have to do with this world, and thus is open to all that secularity itself can hope for, it nevertheless is not in this world but in the boundless love embracing it that such hope has its sole ultimate ground and object. To the extent of this danger, therefore, the interpretation of hope offered here has its contribution to make to theology's encounter with the secular world. For while fully affirming man's secular hope, it does not make this its only or even its primary affirmation. Its first witness, rather, is to the ultimate reality of God's love, which alone embraces not only our future in this world but also our transience, our death, and our sin, and thus creates that "hope against hope" by which, as we may believe, all men are finally sustained.

SUGGESTED READINGS

Bultmann, Rudolf. "The Christian Hope and the Problem of Demythologizing," *The Expository Times*, LXV (1954), pp. 228-230, 276-278.

Hartshorne, Charles. *The Logic of Perfection and Other Essays in Neoclassical Metaphysics*. La Salle: Open Court, 1962, pp. 234-262.

Ogden, Schubert M. *The Reality of God and Other Essays*. New York: Harper and Row, 1966, pp. 206-230.

GRACE

David A. Fleming

14 God's Gift and Man's Response: Toward a Whiteheadian Perspective

DAVID A. FLEMING

One characteristic of man today is that he wants to get his worlds together, not to have a natural world and a supernatural world each with its own metaphysical rubrics. That "one world" understanding is precious to Whitehead. But that makes it necessary to raise again the question of grace. Process theology espouses "one world," yet needs to account for the abiding religious instinct that God enters history in ways that are pure gift. Professor Fleming addresses himself to that question.

David A. Fleming, a Marianist priest, is Chairman of the Graduate School of Theology at St. Mary's University. He has a Ph.D. in literature from the University of Chicago, and an S.T.L. from the University of Fribourg. He has also done theological study at Münster and Nijmegen. He is the editor and translator of several French and Latin works. His publications have appeared in such journals as Southern Humanities Review, Humanistica Lovaniensia, The American Ecclesiastical Review, *and* Review for Religious.

A t the heart of man's religious experience lies the conviction that God touches man and gives rise to a relationship. "Religion" may even be defined, I believe, as "having a sense of the giftedness of life," recognizing the gratuity of our experience, realizing that this life is not something we have to earn or deserve, but rather something which is given to us. The religious man experiences his life as something coming to him from without or beyond, as something that he did

215

not initiate and originate and that he surely did not need to deserve. Both the *tremendum* and the *fascinosum* Rudolf Otto saw as the components of religious experience come together in this religious sense of the giftedness of life.

To say that life is a gift is not to say that it is mainly heteronomous. One may respond to gifts in the most diverse ways. To be religious, to recognize gratuity, is not necessarily to be passive, but rather to recognize an influence from without that touches and in some sense has a shaping role in my life.

The question of "God's gift and man's response" is one of central importance for the Christian life. Without a clear theology on the matter, man's recognition of such personally central religious issues as grace, vocation, doing the will of God, prayer, and providence is lost in confusion or in wordless fideism. If any place for a genuine Christian theology is to be found in philosophical categories, these categories must be capable of dealing with these issues. If one is a traditional religious person, and even more so if one is a Christian, the viewpoint possible on the question of gratuity and on the synergism of God and man in human acts takes on a crucial importance in authenticating any philosophy as a framework of thought.

The aim of this essay is to make a beginning attempt to express the religious sense of gratuity with the help of the philosophical viewpoints of Alfred North Whitehead. The essay is subtitled "Toward a Whiteheadian Perspective," because it wishes simply to be an "essay," in the sense of Montaigne, a probe toward a conceptuality, not an attempt to exhaust the subject. The essay presents only one Whiteheadian perspective, surely not the only view on the matter that is possible for a follower of Whitehead. Whitehead, like Aristotle, has followers who are deeply religious and other followers who are atheists. The attempt here is to show how the issue of gratuity, judged important out of a religious framework, can find a nesting-place within the compelling world view of Whitehead. The essay is quite frankly an exercise in "faith seeking understanding."

II

In the history of the Church, the question of God's action in man's life has been a central and recurring theological problem. It surfaced as the central issue in two key theological debates:

that concerning Pelagianism in the fifth and sixth centuries, and that concerning justification in the sixteenth century.

Pelagius himself has surely been much maligned by history, outargued as he was by the much superior intellect of Augustine. It may be that in attacking him Augustine was in fact attacking a straw man. But in any case the Church's intuition that emerged from the debate was central: any theology which suggests that man can earn his own salvation by his unaided merits is one that fails to recognize the central role played by God, and particularly by God in Christ, in each man's personal salvation history. Man is not able to save himself and the need for a redeemer is absolute in the present order of history.

Luther's sixteenth-century reassertion of the belief that man can be saved by grace alone, and by faith (as he understood the term) alone, was reaction against what the Reformer rightly judged to be the latent Pelagianism of much late-medieval piety. His challenge brought about a new stress on gratuity in Catholic circles as well as in the Reformed Churches. There emerged on all sides a stress on the gratuity of God's gift and the utter lack of proportion between this gift and man's merit, condemning once and for all any attempts at self-justification on the part of man. In reacting against such attempts, sixteenth-century theologians were surely reacting against a tendency that is all too prevalent in any Church in any time, for we are all implicitly Pelagians in the sense that in any Church in any time we all implicitly fall into the habit of thinking that somehow we are capable of justifying ourselves and saving ourselves from our own sin.

This traditional doctrine of God's graciousness and the gratuity of his dealings with man is at least as much a problem in the twentieth century as it was in the fifth or the sixteenth. Our modern problems seem to me to arise from at least four factors:

1. Modern man, at least as he is perceived by the existentialists, is very convinced of his autonomy, his radical freedom, and his personal responsibility for his own life. If the doctrine of grace, i.e., of God's gratuity, means that man is merely passive, an instrument picked up and justified by God, like Bernini's swooning St. Teresa, waiting limply to be enlivened by the arrow of God, then this doctrine goes against the most powerful views of man elaborated in the twentieth century. A purely extrinsic justification, a sort of legal fiction in which man is thought of in a

new way by God, somewhat as a child might be indulgently forgiven by a father who is resigned to infantile weakness, cannot give the basis for a radically free and responsible life. Any view that stresses a blind and unthinking obedience to absurd commands supposedly emanating from the Creator is rightly regarded by modern man as an affront to his own power, freedom, and responsibility.

2. Modern man is more aware than ever before of the subconscious and unconscious, psychic and sociocultural factors that influence his behavior. Indeed these factors are perceived as setting limits, more or less severe, to the autonomy that we have just considered. This awareness of the unconscious and the socially structured nonreflective aspects of man's life leads man in our time to be quite suspicious of any doctrine that calls him to yield to an external power and transcend himself. "Submission to the Spirit" may sometimes be a delusion cloaking and justifying the dynamics of unconscious desire. Our own desires and eager drives may well trick us, in the name of following the impulse of grace, into doing precisely what we secretly long to do, even into finding a masochistic pleasure in self-chastisement. Thus the "will of God" may become a pseudoreligious projection of our own secret desires. Hence a life lived out of a conscious effort to follow the promptings of that will is suspect to some thinkers.

3. The awareness of evil on a massive scale makes modern man sceptical of any doctrine of the ultimate graciousness of life. If our world is truly a world of providence, one which is subject to the loving power of God, then how can we explain the holocaust of six million Jews in the Nazi era—to take only the most striking of the massive evils we have witnessed in the twentieth century? Since the doctrine of graciousness implies a sense of God's loving, gracious care for all man, it seems suspect indeed.

4. Finally, the twentieth century seems to have brought with it, at least in its second half, a heightened desire for justice. In religious terms, this desire leads to universalism. We want a God who is fair, who treats all with equal concern, not a capricious and intolerant deity who predestines some but not others, gives special graces to some but denies them to others. Insofar as the traditional doctrine of God's graciousness seemed to imply a particular providence for each individual, a special grace or set of graces reserved for him, it is difficult for many to accept that doctrine.

The hope that the Whiteheadian conceptuality may allow us to express a doctrine of gratuity that avoids or answers the four objections is based partly on the realization that Whiteheadian thought includes a sensitivity to this modern problematic. Like most other twentieth-century thinkers, Whitehead stressed man's freedom and autonomy in a radical way, with emphasis on his creativity and his capacity for introducing novelty into the world. At the same time, through his doctrine of "prehension," Whitehead left room for a full awareness of the limitations on our freedom and the powerful conditioning of our behavior and even of our conscious motivations by psychological and sociocultural factors. And in his own doctrine of God, Whitehead manages to deal in a compelling way with the problem of evil.

Yet precisely because of the radical stress on human autonomy and creativity—a stress characteristic of process thought —some process thinkers and even some interpreters of Whitehead have tended to deny the personal giftedness of our religious experience, or at least to lessen it greatly. Theologians within other philosophical traditions have often criticized "process theology" as "Pelagian." In fact, certain interpreters of Whitehead tend to make God seem a rather passive being, one who is surely able to be influenced by man but one who hardly seems able to take an initiative in influencing man. This view comes from what seems to me an inadequate understanding of Whitehead's description of the "primordial nature of God" and God's "subjective aim for every actual occasion." And even if most process thinkers have not entered into this precise discussion, the tenor of some of their statements and the "pathos" of their systems seem to leave little room for a God who "intervenes" in a decisive way in history. In this regard, of course, process thinkers are hardly different from some of the existentialists.

I believe, however, that a perspective which takes full account of the religious and mystic tradition of Christianity, with its emphasis on the gratuity and initiative of God's action on man, is available to us in the conceptuality provided by Whitehead's work. In what follows I would like to sketch an outline for such a theology of gratuity in a Whiteheadian framework, and then make a few applications to various areas of Christian life, specifically what has traditionally been called "petitionary prayer," "vocation," "the will of God" and "particular providence."

In order to understand Whitehead's contribution to the understanding of these problems, it will be necessary to start with a brief sketch of some of the basic assumptions of Whiteheadian "process philosophy." Taking a cue from modern science, process thinkers regard the ultimate constituents of reality as "energy-events" rather than static substances. Each of these energy-events is best understood as the focus of a dynamic field of relationships rather than as a strictly bounded and self-sufficient entity. Every actuality exists in constant movement and change; being and identity are explained in terms of becoming and process rather than vice versa. Creativity is the supreme category necessary for the understanding of reality, for to be actual means to be creative, to become constantly more in oneself and in relationship to the rest of the universe. The Whiteheadian world view may thus be termed a "processive-relational" one.

In accord with this basic world view, Whitehead sees God not as a changeless being, unaffected by creaturely actions and reactions, not as an exception to all metaphysical principles, but rather as their "chief exemplification."[1] (In this basic methodological principle, Whitehead is at one with Aquinas.) Consequently, Whitehead has developed a view of God that Charles Hartshorne (a great follower of Whitehead and an important American philosopher in his own right) has termed a "dipolar conception."[2] God is seen, according to this line of thought, to enter into real, not merely "logical" relations with creatures. Thus man can affect and change the actuality of God himself, in a real and not merely metaphorical way. God is supremely powerful and supremely knowing, but his omnipotence and omniscience do not destroy the real knowledge and real autonomous creativity of free creatures. God is the supreme type of social relationships. (Thus a new meaning is given to the Johannine definition: God is Love.) His supremacy is manifested especially in the fullness of his relatedness with all. He surpasses all others precisely by being fully and positively related to all others. Yet he is always able to surpass himself, for each moment of creation presents God with new actualities for his relating.

The "dipolarity" of God is the conception used to clarify his supreme yet multirelational quality. On the one hand, God is seen to have a "primordial nature" (or in the terminology suggested by Hartshorne, an "abstract aspect") in which all the possible forms of definiteness for the cosmos are conceptually present. This aspect of God is unchanging, since the forms of definiteness, ordered in "graded relevance" to one another, are eternally available for acts of creativity. The "primordial nature" expresses this eternal, "changeless" face of God, by which he is the eternal ground of possibility for the world. The changing, relational, social aspect of God is called his "consequent nature" (or, in Harthshorne's terminology, his "concrete aspect"). This is the aspect of God by which he constantly receives and harmonizes all energy-events in the cosmos and thus becomes the supremely processive, supremely relational being, the "great companion" and "the fellow sufferer who understands," in Whitehead's words. He accepts the consequences of all actions of creativity in the universe and "saves" them (again a term employed by Whitehead), finding and creating harmony and beauty in every way he can. Thus the consequent nature is the supremely changing, and ultimately the supremely loving, face of God.

This very summary statement of Whitehead's view of God and the world, fragmentary as it is, already provides us with keys to dealing with the question of gratuity.

The first Whiteheadian insight that seems helpful is his concept of the "primordial nature" (or aspect) of God as the ground of possibility for all possible human actions. In itself, the images of God as a "ground of possibility" seems at least as rich for the Christian imagination as Tillich's comparable image of God as the "Ground of Being." It is a beautiful, even (as is often the case with Whitehead's natural theology) poetic insight, allowing us to see God as the source of all the possibilities that stand before us in life. My actions, decisions, choices are fully my own, the work of my own creative energy, yet they are possible to me because of their existence, precisely as possibilities, in God. Thus God is the source of my every action, even though I freely choose which of the many possibilities open to me I wish to actualize. In faith I can see this God as loving, one who offers to me the springs of life and the forms of definiteness for all my own creativity. Moreover in this primordial nature of God, all these possibilities are available to me in an order, in a "graded relevance." Some are more immediate to me than others; some exercise, through God's gentle, persuasive, but never coercise "lure," a greater attractiveness than others. And yet it always remains my prerogative to choose. I am free at each moment of choice to decide, out of a multitude of possibilities, those which I will actualize. I can truly build my own world, and yet the possibilities that lie before me are in fact ordered in importance and immediacy, and thus some have greater potential than others for creating that beauty which Whitehead sees as the end of the creative process. God offers to man all the possibilities there are, and man chooses and freely creates out of these possibilities, thus structuring his own reality.

Already it should be clear that the "lure" of which Whitehead speaks is very similar to the "grace" of traditional Christian theology, provided we understand by "grace" something that is available (in different degrees perhaps, but still truly available) to all men and in every one of their actions, and provided we are willing to admit that grace works only persuasively, never coercively, that man is radically free to ignore this "lure" of God at any moment. (The Jansenist notion of "irresistible grace," condemned by the Roman authorities in the seventeenth century,[3] is clearly excluded by this view.) Thus we have sketched, in the considerations flowing from Whitehead's doctrine of the primordial nature of God, a theology that gives ground for no overly supernaturalistic action of God, totally out of the realm of nature, but rather for a kind of synergism in which both God and man find a place of creativity in every human act. Gratuity is possible without destroying autonomy or insisting on a deterministic kind of predestination.

Further light is offered by Whitehead's view of the "consequent nature of God." Once man has made his creative choices, good or bad, accepting the seemingly ideal aim of God or not, these choices are taken lovingly into God. Our choices affect him and he works with them, in order to "save" them, to bring good even from evil, and to preserve all the beauty and all the richness of any choice. Whitehead tells us: "The image—and it is but an image—the image under which this operative growth of God's nature is best conceived, is that of a tender care that nothing be lost. The consequent nature of God is his judgment on the world. He saves the world as it passes into the immediacy of his own life. It is the judgment of a tenderness which loses nothing that can be saved. It is also the judgment of a wisdom which uses what in the temporal world is mere wreckage."[4] Our actions affect God very concretely, and he aims to save them so that our choices, no matter how faulty, can be integrated into his lure for the greatest beauty of the moment in each human occasion.

Through this saving action the good harmonized by God once again becomes a source of new possibilities that he offers for man's choice—each human choice determines in some degree the range of possibilities available at the next moment. Man has through his own creative action opened up these new possibilities, and these new possibilities are once again ordered for man and informed with new "lures," new ideal aims and loving invitations of God. Thus at each moment man can (metaphorically) modify the call of God in accord with the new realities alive in the world, and at each moment God adapts himself in a new, saving, and loving way to man's situation. What we have done causes God to present to us a new aim and a new personalized order of graded relevance among the inexhaustible possibilities for choice presented to us.

In order to understand this action a bit better, Thomas Stokes has suggested that we might think of it as that of a friend upon a friend. The love between friends is "a dynamic relation whereby the lover places himself in the state of a gift, and this relation finds full maturity in the free responses of the one loved."[5] When we love another person, we offer him the free gift of our concern. We invite him to act, we have our own persuasive, "luring" action toward what we think are the best aims of his action—we are not indifferent to his choices—but at the same time we are never coercive; and when our friend chooses in ways we think second-best, we adapt to his choices and attempt anew to bring the best out of the situation. We are not uninterested, but ideally we leave our friend free. Stokes applies this analogy to God as follows: "God wills to be a lover waiting upon man's free return of love. God wills to be what He is eternally in part by reason of man's free response to His call to place himself in a state of gift. The paradox is that the autonomy of man's free response is nothing but God's gift of self to man."[6] This analogy shows clearly how the good we do in every action is fully received from possibilities in God and accords with his subjective aim for the good (thus it is gratuitous), while at the same time our good actions are fully our own (autonomous). The giftedness of life and man's free creativity are fully affirmed, without one overshadowing the other.

If we pass on to sketch some possible applications of this interpretation of grace and gratuity, I believe that we will discover the congruence of the Whiteheadian perspective with much that is traditional in Christian discipleship.

One of the problems in modern Christian thought and life has been in the area of petitionary prayer. Even in the traditional view, petitionary prayer presented a problem because it was hard to see what our prayer could do to change an all-knowing, all-foreseeing and omnipotent God to whom the total course of history was already fully present in every way. At best, petitionary prayer seemed to be a kind of exercise in dependence before the Almighty. Its justification has sometimes seemed to rise or fall with a world view that sees man as a humble and rather helpless petitioner before an Oriental potentate, fully aware of his own indignity and his total dependence. Moreover, petitionary prayer has often been associated with an excessively supernaturalistic view of God's action in the world: we seemed to be begging an omnipotent God to "intervene" in a totally abnormal way in history and change the arrangement of the cosmos or the direction of human intentionality to suit our convenience.

Yet in the Whiteheadian view there is a definite place for a kind of prayer that might be seen as the "sharing of our concerns" in collaboration with the creative work of God in the universe. In this view we can prevail upon God to "change" in a dynamic and creative sense: we freely contribute to the building of the universe by our acts, and God's concrete manner of caring for the universe will be influenced by our creative choices. The prayerful sharing of concerns in this view is surely not a way of asking the Omnipotent to come down and supernaturally transform reality in accord with our wishes; rather it is a presentation of concerns regarding our own creative involvements, so that this concern may enter through God's consequent nature into the constant reshaping of the initial aim and the order of relevance he provides to the universe in response to the free and creative actions of creatures. In this sense we can truly bring about a change in God's purposes for the universe, and petitionary prayer is a valid effort to bring this collaboration with God in creation more fully to our own consciousness and even into the responsive reality of his life.

Another key question about Christian discipleship today concerns the traditional complex of doctrines concerning the "will of

God" for individuals, the "calls" we receive from God, and the sense of "vocation" in life. To many moderns these doctrines seem to represent a mythological pattern of thought, and to have the unfortunate result of making man fearful to exercise his autonomy, too ready to respond passively to what is naively thought to be the will of God but what is in fact merely a bowing to heteronomy. Moreover, these doctrines sometimes seem to foster scrupulosity, to force man into an anxious and generally futile search for what is absolutely the best in each action, thus hemming him in with inhibitions and impeding his creative freedom in the building of the universe.

I believe that Whiteheadian thought, as sketched above, allows us to speak of God's "call," his "will," and our "vocations" in life, but helps us to understand these realities of discipleship in ways that do not detract from, but rather enhance and fully valorize our human and autonomous creativity. The "will of God" and the "calls" he makes upon us may be understood as that which in the immediate context of each actual human occasion is most relevant in the order of possibilities presented to us in the primordial nature of God, as that which most accords with the subjective aim of God for our human actions. God is the ground of possibilities, presenting all of them to us in order and luring us toward those which he wills for the fullest beauty and harmony of the cosmos; this lure, based on his "aim" for each actual occasion, is Whitehead's way of speaking of the fact that God is not indifferent to our choices: he calls us to create with him all the goodness and beauty possible in every decision. Yet he never coerces, but works only by persuasion. We have our own autonomous creativity, our own causality, our freedom in responding to the gift that is given and the gratuity of possibilities presented to us.

Even when we make choices outside the subjective aim of God, even when we ignore or mistake his "lures," God still saves our creative choices, bringing the good out of the less than good, and presenting still new proximate possibilities for good even on the basis of the imperfect choices we have made. We need not, in fact, think of God as having a single, fully determined subjective aim for each human actual occasion. Yet there are always some possibilities preferable to others, and we cooperate with God in creative activity by choosing the precise ones we wish to actualize.

Thus we can have a sense of the "will of God" and of real "calls" and "vocations" in our lives, while at the same time maintaining our own autonomy. We need not become overly anguished about each choice, realizing the broad range of possibly valid choices and the constant saving action of God to bring out the best of each actual occasion, no matter how imperfect it may be. Our choices are important, but God will always labor to bring out the best from them, no matter how imperfect they may be.

The question of God's particular providence for creation is resolved by the Whiteheadian framework in basically the same way. "Particular providence," for Whitehead, consists in the aims that God presents for our choice at any given instance and which grades the relevance of possibilities for our action. Evil in the world is the result of choices made at variance with the aims of God. It is not his responsibility, except insofar as he has established the order of the cosmos with freely creative agents—and since, in the Whiteheadian understanding, to be actual means to be creative, we cannot clearly envision a deterministic universe in which actual occasions were not free and creative. Such great evils as the holocaust of the Jews at the hands of the Nazis need not be blamed on God, and yet we need not deny his particular providence. Evil is the result of man's refusal to cooperate with God's subjective aim in the work of creation. Particular providence is the work of God's saving power, seeking to salvage the good from the most evil and to present new possibilities, inevitably conditioned by man's previous free choices, for the creation of beauty even in the midst of evil. Particular providence is God's adaptation to man's choices, and his consequent attempt to bring the best out of them in each case. It is based on the interaction of the consequent nature of God (in which he is truly a "fellow sufferer"[7]) and the subjective aims with which he cocreatively constitutes each actual occasion.

The entire interaction of God in man's life is summed up in a beautiful passage on the last page of *Process and Reality*. Whitehead sees this action taking place in four steps:

There are thus four creative phases in which the universe accomplishes its actuality. There is first the phase of conceptual origination, deficient in actuality, but infinite in its adjustment of valuation. Secondly, there is the temporal phase of physical origination, with its multiplicity of actualities. In this phase full actuality is attained; but there is deficiency in the solidarity of individuals with each other. This phase derives its determinate conditions from the first phase. Thirdly, there is the phase of perfected actuality, in which the many are one everlastingly, without the qualification of any loss either of individual identity or of completeness of unity. In everlastingness, immediacy is reconciled with objective immortality. This phase derives the conditions of its being from the two antecedent phases. In the fourth phase, the creative action completes itself. For the perfected actuality passes back into the temporal world, and qualifies this world so that each temporal actuality includes it as an immediate fact of relevant experience. For the kingdom of heaven is with us today. The action of the fourth phase is the love of God for the world. It is the particular providence for particular occasions. What is done in the world is transformed into a reality in heaven, and the reality in heaven passes back into the world. By reason of this reciprocal relation, the love in the world passes into the love in heaven, and floods back again into the world. In this sense, God is the great companion—the fellow-sufferer who understands.[8]

Despite the technical Whiteheadian language, the thrust of the description of divine-human synergism is evident: God offers possibilities, man actualizes them, and the realities thus created are accepted and given permanent significance in the "consequent nature of God," thus becoming available for all future creative events. Man's action enters into God and qualifies the action of God for all future moments. God is thus, in Bernard Lee's suggestive image, the Beckoner who calls us ahead into new experience —a new experience in which we are always free to do what we want, to accept or reject. This Beckoner stays ahead of us, but not too far, so that he can always respond and even readjust to the decisions we have freely made. He draws us on, and his gratuity never deserts us; yet with him it is we who freely fashion our own history.

NOTES

1. Alfred North Whitehead, *Process and Reality* (New York: Macmillan, 1929), p. 521. All references to *Process and Reality* are made to this edition.

2. See, for example, Hartshorne's essay "Whitehead's Idea of God," first

published in 1941 and now reprinted in Hartshorne's collected essays, *Whitehead's Philosophy* (Lincoln: University of Nebraska, 1972), pp. 63-97.

3. The condemnation was included among errors of Cornelis Jansen noted in the bull of Innocent X *"Cum Occasione"* (May 31, 1653). See Denzinger-Schonmetzer, 32nd edition, no. 2002.

4. *Process and Reality*, p. 525.

5. Walter E. Stokes, "A Whiteheadian Reflection on God's Relation to the World," in *Process Theology: Basic Writings*, ed. Ewert H. Cousins (New York: Newman, 1971), p. 138.

6. Stokes, p. 149.

7. *Process and Reality*, p. 532.

8. *Process and Reality*, p. 532.

SUGGESTED READINGS

Hartshorne, Charles. "Whitehead's Idea of God," *Whitehead's Philosophy*. Lincoln: University of Nebraska, 1972, pp. 63-97.

Stokes, Walter E., "A Whiteheadian Reflection on God's Relation to the World," *Process Theology*. Edited by Ewert Cousins. New York: Newman, 1971, pp. 138-50.

Whitehead, Alfred North. *Process and Reality*. New York: Macmillan, 1929.

FAITH
AND BELIEF

Eugene Fontinell

15 Religious Truth: A Pragmatic Reconstruction

EUGENE FONTINELL

In an earlier chapter in this book, Professor Fontinell laid out, in a general way, the characteristics of an understanding of religion that was rooted in a pragmatic-process framework (especially in the thought of William James and John Dewey). Here he deals specifically with understandings of truth, faith, and belief. There has been a strong tendency in Western Christianity, and particularly in Roman Catholicism, to intellectualize the notion of faith and to absolutize verbalizations of intellectual understanding. Fontinell deals with "belief" as "any affair of leading, as a pointing ahead," and faith as "a belief or a set of beliefs which bear upon human life in its comprehensive effort."

My task in this chapter is most properly described as the initiation of a *probe* in the direction of a radical reconstruction of religious truth, morality, God and religion. I am concerned simply to delineate the conditions for a viable theory, or, to use a less ambitious term, a viable *approach* to these realities, given a thoroughly processive view of man and reality. In each of these areas, there are classical controversies and highly technical questions which must be bracketed or merely referred to in passing. I will not presume to resolve, for example, the classical conflicts surrounding the "proofs" for the existence of God or the reality of moral "absolutes." Though I make no pretense of solving these problems I will in each instance take a position and give some indication as to why I think such a position is justified, or, as a minimum, what are some of

231

the positive possibilities to which such a position gives rise. The justification for this non-polemical approach is that reflective men must continue to think and act in spite of the absence of definitive resolutions to many profoundly complex problems. There is no avoiding taking sides on these great issues but this does not mean that there is no merit in the position which one rejects. A pragmatic attitude of openness, as I will stress below, allows us to make a commitment, whether intellectual, moral or religious, without closing us off from insights achieved by others who operate from different and even opposed commitments and perspectives.[1]

I express my belief that the human situation has a richness which cannot be exhaustively grasped or expressed by one metaphysics. Hence, while the fundamental framework throughout this essay will be supplied by a processive-relational metaphysics, there will be no hesitation in drawing upon insights developed in other traditions whenever it is judged that they further the question under consideration. If the result is an uneasy amalgam of pragmatism, existentialism and phenomenology, this is not necessarily an eclectic disaster. The primary obligation of any philosophical endeavor is to better a problematic situation, not to maintain some kind of ideological purity or abstract intellectual consistency. Why, then, have I described in such detail a particular metaphysics? Three reasons seem pertinent: first, because particular problems are most fruitfully handled within a relatively integral and consistent metaphysics; secondly, while all philosophical approaches are to some extent eclectic, they also involve a controlling set of principles and a dominant angle of vision; finally, because the metaphysics opted for is congenial to whatever has been assimilated from other traditions.

FAITH NOT A MODE OF KNOWLEDGE

Given a processive-relational world, let me try now, most tentatively and hypothetically, to draw out the implications for religious truth. The first condition for a pragmatic reconstruction of religious truth is a willingness to surrender the "knowledge" bias which has for a variety of reasons, many of them quite good ones, dominated Western culture and the Christian religion from the time of the Greeks. To state my position in its sharpest and starkest form, let me say that religious truth is characterized by faith and faith is *not* knowledge, whether about God or man or the world. Now, such an assertion is for many people, specifically those within the Roman Catholic tradition, quite disconcerting. It immediately conjures up such specters as voluntarism, emotivism and subjectivism. To say that faith is not knowledge would seem at best unnecessarily confusing and misleading and hence there is a great temptation to substitute for it a position which would affirm a variety of modes of knowledge, among which we would have one called "faith." I readily concede that there are a number of impressive efforts to account for much of the data with which I am concerned and to do so without denying that faith is knowledge in some sense.[2] Nevertheless, I feel that the formulation "Faith is not knowledge" should be retained for at least two reasons. First, and perhaps less important, knowledge, like science, has come, in Western civilization, to have an increasingly precise and restricted meaning. It seems fruitless to insist on using knowledge (or science) to cover a variety of admittedly different experiences simply because classical philosophy used the term first, in a broader but less precise sense.

The second and more important reason is that to make faith a mode of knowledge is like making love and art modes of knowledge; in doing so we risk losing the truly distinctive quality of all these experiences. In the final analysis such an approach betrays as its hidden assumption the belief that only knowledge is of value. The classic example of such an attitude is to insist that sex is a form of knowledge principally on the basis of the Hebrew use of the term "know."

Instead of *knowledge*, I will employ the term *experience* as my primary category or metaphor. I will affirm a variety of modes of experience without ranking them hierarchically.[3] This is not to imply that all experiences are of equal value. The worth of an experience or of a type of experience will be assigned on the basis of its contribution to the development of man. One immediate advantage of such an approach is that it removes any artificial competition among our experiences. A variety of experiences has a claim upon us simply because no one kind of experience suffices for the continuing realization of man.

The contention that faith is essentially noncognitive is so central to my position and gives rise to such controversy that, before proceeding further, I think it would be helpful if I spelled out a bit more fully something of what a doctrine of faith as noncognitive implies. First, it should be noted that in any dispute concerning the relation of faith to knowledge no one seriously asserts their identity and no one seriously asserts their radical separation. In evaluating the competing explanations, therefore, every effort should be made to avoid caricature. Though this essay attempts an explanation of faith which denies that it is essentially cognitive, there is no implied claim that every explanation of faith as cognitive is crudely rationalistic and abstractionist. On the other hand, I do not accept a characterization of the position here offered as fideistic, emotivist or anti-intellectual. In the long run the crucial question is: Which better accounts for that which must be accounted for—an explanation in terms of a variety of knowings or one in terms of a variety of experiences?[4]

Recall the key principle asserted by Dewey to the effect that experience is wider than and inclusive of knowledge. Knowledge is but one among the variety of experiences that may be had by the human person. I contend that faith is also a mode of experience distinct but not separable from knowledge. It is important to stress that I am presupposing a living person as a concrete relational unity. Traditionally all worthwhile theories of man have to a greater or lesser degree admitted the ultimate mystery of personal unity while attempting to account for personal complexity in terms of principles or faculties or functions. While there are strengths and weaknesses accompanying all approaches, I think, following James and Dewey, that some form of functionalism has the most possibilities for handling the issues involved. On such a view man can be described in the concrete as a believing-knowing-loving-feeling being. Since the distinctions are made in terms of functions, one keeps to a minimum the risk of fragmenting the person. The need to make the distinctions and the distinctions themselves must be justified pragmatically, that is, in terms of their contribution to the development of man. This procedure, of course, is but a specification of the controlling pragmatic principle (some would say assumption) that everything, including knowledge and metaphysics, must be evaluated on the basis of its service to human life rather than in terms of correspondence or coherence (internal conceptual consistency). Such an approach does not rule out, as I shall later indicate, the presence of some kind of correspondence and coherence, but these are not the ultimate determinants of the worth of a theory. Such features are not sought for their own sake but only because cumulative human experience has shown that without some degree of correspondence and coherence a theory or a metaphysics will not be serviceable.

In like fashion, faith and knowledge are not ends in themselves, sought for their own sakes, but ultimately they take their value from the enrichment of human life which they provide. They are functionally different modes of experience, both indispensable and not reducible one to the other. This does not mean, however, that they can ever be totally separated. They play different but not isolated roles, therefore, in the development of human life. Recognition of both their distinct functions and their intimate relation will make it possible to utilize them to the greatest possible extent.

RELATION BETWEEN FAITH AND KNOWLEDGE

Up to this point the terms belief and faith have been used interchangeably, but it might be helpful if they were now distinguished. Henceforth belief will be understood as any affair of leading, as a pointing ahead—a going out beyond that for which there is evidence, or at least for which evidence is not present or consciously attended to. Every moment of our lives, from that of everyday routine to the most sophisticated scientific endeavor, is permeated by beliefs so understood. Faith as the term will now be employed will refer to a belief or a set of beliefs which bear upon human life in its comprehensive effort. Faith plays the role of holding together or attempting to hold together the diverse aspects or modes of human life or experience. It might be described as an integrating experience whereby knowing-experience, affective-experience, aesthetic-experience—in short, all forms of experience—are brought into a relatively cohesive whole which is expressed in the life of the person. Faith thereby serves to order, direct, illuminate and render meaningful human life. If the objection is made that this assertion surreptitiously transforms faith into knowledge, the reply would be that this follows only on the prior assumption that the *sole* way in which life is ordered, directed, illuminated and rendered meaningful is through some form of knowledge. I would insist that there are a variety of experiences, functionally and qualitatively different from knowledge, such as faith, love and art, which supply order, direction, illumination and meaning to the human condition.

Now beliefs, as the term is used here, are capable of verification upon which they become knowledge, or better, knowing-experiences. Faith, however, is such that only a lifetime of commitment and lived affirmation is adequate witness to its authenticity. I do not deny that there may be, and even to some extent must be, evidences of authenticity such as a degree of personal fulfillment or a more humane community which flows from faith. These, however, can never be definitively compelling; they can never have the kind of verification which characterizes knowledge.[5] (It should be mentioned that this holds as much for the faith of a non-theist as for that of a theist.)

In making such a sharp distinction between faith and knowledge, there is no intention of advocating a sentimental fideism or a naive anti-intellectualism. Actually, the position being proposed recognizes a much greater influence of knowledge and science upon faith than does the traditional viewpoint. I would insist that faith inevitably *involves* knowledge and, further, that a reflective faith ought to embody the very best knowledge of the culture at every moment of the culture's history. This hypothesis excludes, however, any identification of faith with a culturally and historically determined mode of knowledge.

It is the inevitable involvement of knowledge in any faith, particularly a reflective faith, which gives support to the view that faith is in some sense cognitive. It is at this point that the contention that faith is noncognitive experience appears most suspect. Nevertheless, I still insist on the difference between faith which involves or employs knowledge and faith which is knowledge— however that knowledge might be designated or qualified. No one today would deny that the history of the Christian faith manifests numerous knowledge-claims which have been subsequently judged erroneous. The dominant response to this on the part of Christian thinkers is to admit that these claims were excessive and that faith has often strayed into territory in which it did not belong. On this view, the task of the Christian thinker, specifically as Christian, is to discover that knowledge which belongs to the Christian faith in distinction from that achieved in other ways. On this basis, most Christian religions have long since surrendered their knowledge-claims in the realm of the so-called natural sciences, but the situation is quite different in metaphysics and moral philosophy. Without pretending to handle the enormous difficulties involved in this question, I would simply state that, on my hypothesis, no religion, including Christianity, has any more competence in the realms of metaphysics and moral philosophy than it does in the realm of the natural sciences. Whatever knowledge is accessible in these spheres must be so to all men and not only to the initiates of a particular religion. Christian philosophers must be accorded the same autonomy that has only recently been granted to Christians who are scientists.

This hypothesis, however, should not be understood as calling for an isolation of faith or religion from whatever knowledge man has achieved. On the contrary, religion should be influenced by, and also influence, the knowledge of a culture. In my opinion, however, it cannot properly achieve these ends by placing itself in competition with the various sciences and philosophies.[6] Faith or religion can make its contribution best when its adherents recognize that it has a different but no less important function than knowledge.

Rather than isolate or separate faith and knowledge, then, my intention is to render the relation between them more intimate and dynamic. My contention is that to characterize faith as knowledge leads to an isolation of faith inasmuch as it then must remain untouched by the ever-changing knowledge which characterizes man's intellectual endeavors. Hence, the alleged knowledge which results from faith has to be assigned to a distinct realm of being which is basically, if not totally, irrelevant to knowledge in other realms. Thus knowledge-claims for faith emerge which, in order to avoid such destructive conflicts with science and philosophy as have taken place in the past, form a protective isolationism whereby more and more our "faith-knowledge" is emptied of experiential content and relevance. In this way, regardless of what new facts or theories emerge in science, religious faith is safe, since it supposedly is concerned with a methodology and a sphere of reality which is only peripherally related to that with which science is concerned.

The relation here suggested between faith and knowledge distinguishes them but neither assigns them to separate realms of reality nor puts them in competition with each other. Any living and reflective faith will inevitably attempt to express itself in concepts, metaphors and symbols and in doing so it will be obliged to utilize the concepts, metaphors and symbols which the culture makes available to it. I believe that this has always been the situation but now we are conscious of it. Today no one can doubt some influence of the historical and cultural context upon one's faith, but the dominant Roman Catholic tradition has been to insist that its beliefs, at least in their fundamental or essential dimensions, are independent of historical and cultural conditions and hence can be continually affirmed without need for or the possibility of any fundamental and radical change. In my opinion, this is equivalent to an absolutizing of historical and cultural forms, and results in a freezing of the faith into relatively static doctrines. Paradoxically, perhaps, by admitting the necessary and ever-present historical and cultural features of the faith expression of any moment, we are able to liberate the faith from any reduction to or identification with any particular historical and cultural forms. Such an attitude should maximize the possibilities for creative and imaginative reflection upon the faith-mystery. At the same time, it must continually maintain dynamic and relatively coherent and consistent relations both with its earlier expressions and the best knowledge and experience of its time. This, of course, is a very big order and I am not suggesting that in asserting it as a goal I have proved that it can be accomplished, much less that I have accomplished it. The aim here is much more modest—it is merely an attempt to indicate that the insistence on the uniqueness of faith and its noncognitive function and quality is not a call for some kind of anti-intellectualism or pseudomystical kind of faith. As will be stated again and again, what is being asked for and suggested is the possibility of a new approach which will avoid both the rationalism of a religious objectivism and emotionalism of a religious subjectivism.

Actually such a position as I am arguing for would seem to be to the advantage of both knowledge and faith. As far as knowledge is concerned, it will not be asked to serve an apologetic role which distorts its characteristic function and historically has too often been an obstacle to its free development. Faith, meanwhile, would cease to rest on the shaky and ever-changing foundation of what happens to be the dominant science of the age. It too, given my viewpoint, is able to serve better as a liberating force in the human situation by expanding man's vision beyond his knowledge and constantly energizing him and spurring him on to greater realization. Faith can successfully perform such functions, however, only if it does not try to transform itself into a knowledge which supplies man with absolute certainty concerning the so-called important questions of life. The claim that we have knowledge supplied by religion inevitably diminishes the importance of knowledge achieved in other ways; this may take place subtly and indirectly, but the history of religion (Eastern perhaps even more so than Western) provides ample evidence of the harm that results from the various religions asserting that they possess some privileged knowledge. On the other hand, such "knowledge" and the faith involved are continually in jeopardy from new discoveries in the various spheres of man's intellectual life. Thus we have witnessed an increasing diminution of the knowledge supposedly "revealed" or given by faith.[7] It is not so much that religion is fighting a losing battle in its knowledge assertions as that it is fighting the wrong battle. Religion is, or should be, oriented toward the continued expansion of human life and it should be a continuing challenge, sometimes directly but most often indirectly, to philosophy, science, art, literature and the like, to make their distinctive contributions to this end.

As I am describing it, faith would in a very real sense be serving knowledge, and we can also see how knowledge would serve faith. Knowledge would serve faith positively by continually supplying it with new and possibly more adequate concepts and symbols by which faith could develop and deepen. Negatively, knowledge would serve faith by criticizing the expressions of faith; it would thereby continually oblige the believer to be wary of his symbols and to avoid transforming them into idols.

In making this proposal, there is no intention of either resolving or bypassing the traditional tension between faith and reason. The hope is, rather, that the approach here suggested would lead this relation to a new depth and richness. In the final analysis, of course, this is an existential relation which is always inadequately described when presented abstractly. Reflection upon the relationship can be helpful only if it eventually results in a deepening of the living experience of the person and community as a whole. At best we can have but a continuing dialectic between distinct aspects of human experience in which both faith and reason are enriched. It is most important to underscore, however, the unacceptability of any dualism whereby, in Dewey's terms, we partition the territory, assigning one kind of reality to faith and another to reason. The relationship between the two is best expressed in terms of the processive-field metaphor which I have employed repeatedly. The relation is an "all at once, through and through," in which the aspects of faith and reason are interdependent, each suffusing the other. Faith and reason are thereby able to be differentiated interiorly—or to say the same thing, distinguished within the concrete field—but they are not able to be divided either horizontally or hierarchically.

TRUTH IN GENERAL

I have been discussing at some length faith and knowledge but so far very little has been said directly about "religious truth" which supposedly is in the process of being reconstructed. The simplest thing I could do, consistent with the viewpoint thus far advanced, would be to say that there is no religious truth any more than there is religious knowledge. Most of the arguments against asserting that faith gives a kind of knowledge, namely, religious knowledge, could be used with great force against a view that faith gives a kind of truth, namely religious truth. If truth is understood in dominantly and exclusively intellectualistic categories as a correspondence of the mind to reality or as a kind of rational coherence so that what results is a knowledge *about* reality, then, of course, I would deny that there is any religious truth. But the term truth has always had a richer and more varied connotation than knowledge. There is a long tradition of truth as a mode of life, as existential and personal.[8] I would like, therefore, in briefest outline, to suggest an approach to religious truth which would be personalistic, processive and pragmatic. I am not presuming to prove anything but merely to indicate a possible direction which would be consonant both with the processive and relational world already portrayed and also with a religion such as Christianity.

Recall that the world to which I have been referring is made up of "fields" rather than substantial things, and that while each field has an identifying focus and an irreducible quality, these are interdependent and interpenetrating. A person in these terms is not a substantial entity capable of entering into relations but is rather a being who is constituted by his relations—physical, cultural, familial and the like. "My central point is that the human person does not exist as an isolated atom but is actually *constituted* by his relationships—to the world, to his family, to his fellowmen, to the Church and to God. It is important to stress that these relationships are not extrinsic or spatial but intrinsic; they belong to the very fabric of the person's being. Further, these relationships are not given once and for all. They change in small matters—a new job—and in great—joining the Church. By these changes a man modifies his person."[9]

Bearing these points in mind, allow me to propose the following working description of truth: truth in the primary though not exclusive sense of the term, refers to personal experience insofar as the relations constituting this experience are *satisfactory*. "Satisfactory relations" are to be understood here as those conducive to the developing life of the person.[10] Thus truth is existential and participational rather than abstract and representative. Such a view does not deny the legitimacy of some form of abstract and representative truth but the ultimate justification for even this truth would be its relation to the life of man. For example, scientific propositions might be said to be true insofar as they represent certain relatively constant relations which, for the purposes of science, are considered in abstraction from the concrete existential situation in which they operate. Ultimately, however, science is true not because it represents or corresponds to a reality existing independently of man, but because it enables man to participate more fully in the ongoing processive reality with which he is continuous.[11]

Given this pragmatic meaning of truth, knowledge can be designated true insofar as it establishes or enables man to establish satisfactory relations within the relational-continuum of reality. Consider a simple example. A people live along a river and are dependent upon it for their sustenance. For most of the year their situation ("field" or relational-complex) is relatively satisfactory. One month during the year the river floods and this renders their situation unsatisfactory inasmuch as their houses are destroyed. They eventually learn, however, that by raising their houses on poles, they can avoid the annual disaster. This knowledge results in more satisfactory relations, in a better situation, and hence can be called true.

I admit that the example chosen clearly supports the pragmatic theory of truth and that the life connections are not so easily demonstrated when we are dealing with higher mathematics or theoretical physics or formal logic. The controversy surrounding this question is of long standing and I shall not presume to resolve it in a few words. In defense of pragmatism, however, I would simply say that none of its major proponents has ever denied the value and necessity of so-called theoretical knowledge—knowledge whose implications for life were not immediately evident. There is a *sense* in which knowledge is sought "for its own sake," but this refers to the immediate end and not to the ultimate purpose of knowledge. Actually, the justification for temporarily prescinding from the so-called practical application of knowledge is that such an approach ultimately proves more *fruitful* in the over-all human endeavor.[12]

All of this adds up to the conclusion that man the knower is a participant in the development of reality and not merely a mirror or spectator of reality. But knowing is but one of a variety of ways by which man contributes to the development of reality, and hence truth, as I am describing it, is a more extensive category than knowledge. Following Dewey, I would assert that knowledge renders the human situation more satisfactory by resolving problematic situations. But all human experience is not restricted to responding to problems. Human development is achieved not only by overcoming difficulties and problems but also by adding to or enriching the human situation through creative activities. Thus painting, music, poetry, architecture and the like add a richness and dimension to reality whereby it can be designated "more satisfactory." It is an analogous contribution, in my opinion, which is made by religion. Hence the denial that religion gives knowledge does not lessen its importance. Rather, it is an effort to spur religion to make its own distinctive and irreplaceable contribution. Given this view of different roles for different kinds of experience, it is then possible to assert that art, literature, crafts, religion—in short, any experience—can be called true to the extent to which it renders the human situation relatively satisfactory.

In defining satisfactory as conducive to the life and development of the person, I must underscore again the point that the person is not an isolated entity and hence there is no question here of advocating a destructive individualism. When the person is viewed as essentially communal and the community as essentially personal, as they must be in the relational world here proposed, many artificial aspects of the tension between person and community are removed. Further, much of the fruitless debate centering around truth as subjective or objective can be avoided because it is possible to account for the respective values of subjectivity and objectivity by differentiating them functionally rather than ontologically.[13]

Since our world is not only rational but also processive, no set of relations can ever be more than relatively satisfactory. It is true that certain relations, those we call physical,[14] are changing at such a slow pace that for most practical purposes we can treat them as regular or constant. In an organism as complex as the human person, however, in which the constituting relations are so numerous, the change is more evident and rapid. Any pattern of immutable truth can only be an abstraction from the concrete flow which characterizes all reality in general and human reality in particular. If truth is understood as a mode of life, this lack of immutability is to be rejoiced in rather than lamented.[15] Truth, on these terms, therefore, is essentially and necessarily developmental because the life or living relations which it signifies is such.

TRUTH AS CREATED AND DISCOVERED

The assertion that "truth is developmental" has become a commonplace even within the Roman Catholic community, which has been traditionally identified with the position that truth, especially religious truth, is immutable. The radical and disturbing implications of changing or developmental truth are, however, for the most part avoided or glossed over. Upon closer analysis most theories of the development of truth, particularly those concerned with religious truths, are merely asserting that man's grasp of these truths is never exhaustive. Hence, his understanding of them can develop indefinitely. Thus we can discover more truths than we now possess and we can discover more about those truths already in our possession. The pragmatic claim, however, to the effect that man actually *creates* or *makes* truth remains for most people an absurd and repugnant doctrine. Such a radical developmental view of truth must appear absurd as long as one retains a view of reality as permanently structured independent of human activity. Within such a framework man's task as far as truth is concerned can only be to discover those ideas or judgments which represent or correspond to the essential structure of reality. If, however, we posit a radically processive world such as was earlier described—a world or reality which was becoming, changing, developing in every dimension of its being, then a "truth" which becomes or is made appears less absurd. The very process whereby man "makes" reality "more satisfactory" involves a truth dimension.

Again, I must stress that I am not so presumptuous as to imagine that such an assertion refutes the many objections which have been and are still raised against pragmatism. James's contention that it means exactly the same thing to say that an idea " 'is useful because it is true' or 'it is true because it is useful' "[16] remains a scandal to many reflective men. I fully realize that the serious implications of the classical objections against a pragmatic theory of truth have not been overcome merely by describing truth in terms of "satisfactory relations." The critic can still ask, "Is idea or judgment 'A' true because it issues in more satisfactory relations or does it issue in more satisfactory relations because it is true?" I do not believe that pragmatism can give a satisfactory answer to such a question—at least none which would satisfy one for whom this is a vital question. The best that can be done is to suggest that from a pragmatic perspective such questions are not really significant.

If the emphasis in the pursuit of truth is placed, as it is in pragmatism, on rendering more satisfactory the human situation in general and specific situations in particular, the question of "truth in itself" becomes irrelevant at worst and uninteresting at best. The energy and efforts of man from this perspective are best directed toward changing the present world—making it truer. That is why the method or process of verification is so central to any pragmatic concern for truth. Indeed those critics are not completely wrong when they say that pragmatism gives us a method of verification rather than a theory of truth. This critique loses most of its force, however, when we recall the radically processive world posited by pragmatism. In such a world, verifying becomes, in part at least, a process of creating. Further, creating and discovering are not antithetical or mutually exclusive. This follows since only by creating various concepts, ideals and patterns of life can we discover those which further the development of man and the world and those which impede or retard it.

I cannot emphasize too strongly that throughout this consideration of truth I am attempting to describe an approach to what has been called "lived truth" rather than simply "propositional truth." As has already been indicated, the primary and ultimate ground of truth is the human person viewed as essentially relational and processive. I must stress that this does not mean that the human person is the primary or ultimate ground, absolutely speaking. Even, however, if one *believes* that the human person is related to and developing with an *Other* who is not confined by the limits of humanity, the only truth which man can possess, be, discover or create is that which has its locus within the human reality. In other terms, God can be true for man or be man's truth only to the degree to which man, individually and collectively, is involved in an existential, living relationship with him. Hence, to approach truth or God by way of the concrete human person is in no way to subordinate God to man. Rather it is to recognize that whether we speak of man building himself into nature, reality or God, there is no possibility of bypassing the human situation—no possibility of judging the success of his efforts with reference to any reality, norm or standard "outside" man himself. It is in this sense, then, that all truth must be relative—relative to the human self understood as at once individual and communal.

The classical dangers of relativism such as whimsical individualism or crass subjectivism can be avoided by a pragmatic approach to truth inasmuch as it does not admit the human subject as an atomistic individual. There can be no true fulfillment or satisfactory experience for the person in isolation from the various relations whereby he is constituted.

The approach to truth as primarily a mode of life rather than a characteristic of propositions follows from pragmatism being a life-oriented rather than knowledge-oriented philosophy. In so describing the orientation of pragmatism, I must again deny that there is implied here a lack of respect for and appreciation of the importance of knowledge. As was pointed out in the preceding chapter, however, it does explicitly deny that knowledge is the sole means by which man gains a hold on reality. Knowledge, as we have seen, is but one of a variety of experiences by which man participates in the process of reality. Knowledge, then, is a function in the service of human life, and its worth, justification and truth is *ultimately* justified in terms of the contribution which it makes to this life. Such a viewpoint does not exclude or diminish the importance of activities such as abstracting, theorizing and speculating, but it does insist that such efforts cannot be evaluated definitively in isolation from the long-range influence they have upon the developing human community. Hence, pragmatism will always insist that the "nature" of truth is intimately bound up with the criterion of truth.

PRAGMATIC CRITERION OF TRUTH

In the history of philosophy there have emerged, with numerous variations, three fundamental theories of truth—the correspondence theory, the coherence theory and the pragmatic theory. The correspondence theory, which is the oldest and most enduring, affirms the correspondence of the mind with reality as the basic criterion of truth. The various coherence theories maintain that the only reliable criterion of truth is the internal consistency of a set of ideas. Pragmatism, in its many forms, insists that the fundamental criterion of truth lies in the fruitful consequences which follow from an idea or judgment. To some extent, I believe that in any significant theory of truth there is an attempt to involve or take account of each of these criteria. Eventually there will emerge some genius who will give us a new synthesis whereby we can move beyond the classical conflicts that still surround these three theories. At this moment, however, it would seem that reflective men must select one of these approaches as more fundamental and proceed to develop a theory of truth accordingly. As I have already indicated, I make no pretense to be developing anything which would merit being called a "theory" of truth. I am, however, suggesting an approach to truth which I believe has the most possibility for further development. Allow me, therefore, to indicate briefly something of what such an approach would involve.

The primary criterion of truth presupposed by the pragmatic approach here being suggested is quite simply—too simply perhaps—the life of the community. Does a particular idea, theory, doctrine, poem, painting, building, practice and the like contribute to the enrichment, illumination, development—in short, to the quality of life of the community? If it does, then it can claim some measure of truth. I am well aware of the fact that such a succinct description of the pragmatic criterion of truth will raise more questions than it answers. What, for example, does one mean by "quality of life"? Which community is to be the determining one in any evaluation of an idea, belief or action? How is one to determine whether or not something really does contribute to the quality of life of a community? These and many other objections inevitably and properly have been and will be raised against any pragmatic approach to truth.

Without presuming to handle all the levels and implications of the classical objections against pragmatism, allow me to give at least a preliminary response—positive, not polemical—to these questions. It should be acknowledged at the outset that to make the life of the community the central and ultimately decisive criterion in evaluating the truth or worth of any idea, belief or action is itself an option or act of faith which is irreducible and unprovable. I am not concerned to argue here whether this is the best criterion available to man—though I obviously *believe* that it is. The point made earlier concerning the faith dimension at the base of any metaphysics, however, should be kept in mind.

Granted that the life of the community is to be our ultimate determinate for thought and action, how are we to understand the phrase "quality of life"? Negatively, it does not refer to any external or transcendent norm according to which particular ideas and actions are judged. Every life, individual and collective, is permeated by a pervasive quality which is directly experienced. The judgment that the quality of life of a person or community is better or truer or higher is always a comparative judgment. Just as it is possible to judge the quality of one painting as better than another although there does not exist some absolute quality against which both are judged, so it is possible to judge the quality of life of one community as better than that of another though there exists no absolutely perfect community.

Because it is also possible and indeed necessary to project an ideal in terms of which actual communities are to be formed and developed, there has been the tendency since the time of Plato to conclude that we can judge one reality better than another only if we have some absolute norm as the ultimate basis for our judgment. Pragmatism, however, is able to assign a role to ideals which avoids either positing them as absolute antecedently existing entities or reducing them to useless subjectivistic fictions. "Ideals," James asserted, "ought to aim at the *transformation of reality*—no less."[17] Dewey links ideals to possibilities, novelties and creative imagination. In contrast to the classical meaning, Dewey contends that in modern life "potentiality" means "the possibility of novelty, of invention, of radical deviation."[18] In another place, he insists that "all possibilities, as possibilities, are ideal in character," but, he goes on to say, "the reality of ideal ends as ideals is vouched for by their undeniable power of action. An ideal is not an illusion because imagination is the organ through which it is apprehended. For *all* possibilities reach us through the imagination."[19] Here again is an instance of a running theme of this essay, namely that pragmatism offers us a third alternative beyond both subjectivism and objectivism.

Up to this point I have been using the term "community" without further specification. One of the problems to be confronted by the approach which I am taking is that there are many communities: how are we to decide which is to be the criterion for judgment? It might appear that this question can be answered easily by simply stating that the human community is to be our touchstone. Now, there is a sense in which I believe this to be true, but a few qualifications are in order. To begin with, as of this moment of history, there are really many human communities. *The* human community is still in a very real sense an ideal, a project, a task—it is what we believe should be created and that which, hopefully, we are creating. True, we have at this juncture of man's development a few clues as to what will further this development and what will obstruct or retard it. Most important, perhaps, is the awareness that in the life of communities as in that of persons, whatever cuts them off from others, whatever isolates them or turns them toward themselves, tends to impede their growth and leads to such destructive forms as egoism, racism and religious and political nationalisms. Hence, any community, religious or other, must continually reflect upon its beliefs, doctrines and actions in order to determine whether they are contributing to or obstructing the movement toward the realization of the human community.

There remains the all-important question of just *how* we determine whether our beliefs, ideas or actions do further the well-being of the human community. As is well known, the pragmatic response is at once deceptively simple and highly controversial—only by observing the consequences which follow from an idea or an action, according to pragmatism can we discover those which are worthwhile—those which are "true." Numerous objections immediately spring to mind—among them: which consequences? Actually any idea or action might and does give rise to numerous consequences, sometimes conflicting ones. For example, a consequence may be, or at least appear to be, good for an individual person but bad for the community. Or, an early consequence might appear good and later issue in consequences which are bad. There is no necessity to multiply these objections, since they are familiar to most, nor will I claim to be able to refute them. Actually I do not believe they can be refuted, simply because I think they are describing the complexity of the human condition rather than presenting difficulties peculiar to a theory called "pragmatism." Again, of course, one of my crucial assumptions is showing. I am assuming that there are no absolute or definitive resolutions to significant human problems—further, that while we do advance in many different ways, each advance gives rise to new problems or difficulties. If one objects that pragmatism is deficient because it cannot give, a priori, absolute once-and-for-all resolutions to human problems, pragmatism can only reply that it cannot give such resolutions because it does not believe that the human situation allows them. At the same time, pragmatism refuses to accept, as an alternative to absolutism, a destructive individualism, subjectivism or nihilism. Whatever shortcomings or difficulties are to be found in such thinkers as Peirce, James and Dewey, it is simply a failure to read them on any but the most superficial level which would interpret them as saying that "anything goes" or that every individual can make up whatever values or truths he *feels* like. No, each of these men in his own way believed and endeavored to show that men can live and live more fully without the aid of absolutes and in the absence of absolute certainty even on those matters which bear most deeply and intimately upon human life.

What is often overlooked in criticizing pragmatism is that there is no pretense on the part of the pragmatist of starting from scratch or thinking or acting as if man had no past. "We can be aware of consequences," Dewey tells us, "only because of previous experiences."[20] Experience cumulates and it is this cumulative experience, funded with intelligence, which is the basis for projecting beyond the present. Ideas, beliefs, ideals are all in a sense hypotheses—they are guides to further thought and action, but the only way we have of winnowing out and developing those which are of worth or are true is by continually attending to the consequences which ensue—or by observing the quality of life to which they give rise. Hence, the human community is, in the broad sense, experimental and self-correcting; while it does achieve consummatory moments, these are never absolute or final but simultaneously serve as instruments for further development.

If these are the general conditions for all beliefs and actions, then the belief in God and other religious activities are not exempt from them. I am, of course, rejecting any claim to a privileged source of knowledge or experience which enables a religion or its beliefs or doctrines to escape the demanding test of service to the human community as the measure of its truth.

RELIGIOUS TRUTH

Within this pragmatic framework how are we to understand religious truth? Religious truth will differ from other truth only in its comprehensiveness and not because it pertains to a different kind of reality. Now, the comprehensiveness referred to is not a kind of knowledge but the comprehensiveness of faith as earlier described. Religious truth primarily refers to personal life (which, remember, is essentially communal) considered in its fundamental integrating, ordering, directing and meaning-giving activities. The person performing such activities may *believe* that they are performed in the presence of and on the basis of a continuing encounter with an *Other*; in such instances the religious truth may be called theistic. Again, since religious truth is here described in life categories, it is evident that immutability is ruled out, but this does not mean that there is no continuity or cumulative community experience which quite possibly expresses an irreversible direction. Hence, an eschatological religious vision such as the one embodied in Christianity should, in this respect at least, find the pragmatic view of religious truth most congenial.

Given such a view of religious truth, what, if any, role can be assigned to creeds, or dogmas or sacred writings? To begin with it is evident that from such a perspective they cannot supply us with information or knowledge about God. Further, any God which might be affirmed in this religious truth could never be an object of knowledge. Here again I can only allude to one of the great philosophical questions. I can only state that the approach which I am making does not exclude the possibility of faith in God or even experience *of* or *with* God, but it does rule out any knowledge, however minimal, *about* God. If one insists that the only worthwhile function of creeds, dogmas and sacred Scripture is to give knowledge, then I think that the game is finished and we are forced from the evidence supplied by historical experience to conclude that they are worthless. But, in my opinion, this is not their function. Rather, they must be seen as efforts of the community to articulate its continuing "encounter" with the "nameless one." These articulations are always necessary for the deepening and development of the life of faith. They serve as religious energizers insofar as they intensify and expand the life of the person and the community. They do this by continually enlarging man's vision, by stimulating him to better modes of action, by spurring him to move beyond the relatively inadequate situation in which he finds himself and by adding to human life a quality and dimension which can be achieved in no other way.

It is permissible, in accordance with the viewpoint here proposed, to believe that these community expressions are formed in response to a divine "call"[21] but it is not permissible to overlook the fact that the response is always given in human terms which are essentially cultural and historical. This does not rule out the possibility that some of these articulations have a unique and indispensable role in the continuing life of the community. In the case of Christianity, this would most assuredly hold for Sacred Scripture. Even, here, however, I would insist that the Bible is the work of the human community though I *believe* that it proceeds from a community experience with that *Other* who is not reducible to the human community.

I do not wish to minimize the radical nature and serious implications of the change which I am suggesting in the Christian understanding of and relationship to the Scriptures. Nor do I imagine that any hypothesis that I advance does not demand extensive development and refinement. From a crude pragmatic standpoint, however, it would be well for the Church not to rule out all explanations of the role of Scripture except those which made knowledge-claims for the *Word* of God. As one bit of knowledge after another must be surrendered in view of new experience and insights, the "Scripture gives knowledge" advocate retreats to a gradually diminishing base of knowledge. Consequently, it becomes more and more difficult to maintain any kind of "revelation as knowledge" interpretation of the sacred writings. It is rather ironic that Roman Catholics should feel particularly defensive concerning the knowledge dimension of the Scriptures since they have traditionally avoided placing all their theological eggs in the scriptural basket. The Catholic emphasis upon the primacy of the community and upon its historicity lends itself to the kind of interpretation I am suggesting.

The great fear of those who hold out for some knowledge content in the Scripture is that the *only* alternative is to see the Scriptures as a collection of subjectivistic myths resulting from the psychological projection of man's desires. I would argue that we are not confronted with the alternatives of either a hard core of knowledge, essentially untouched by psychological, historical and cultural factors, or a radical subjectivism, historicism and cultural relativism. Let me try to sketch briefly a mode of scriptural interpretation which frees it from any particular knowledge content and at the same time keeps the Scriptures from being reduced to a subjectivistic production of man. To begin with, we must surrender the notion of a self-contained text embodying its meaning independently of man. As a working hypothesis I would suggest viewing the Scriptures as a unique and continuing locus of the divine-human encounter. On this hypothesis both man and the sacred text are living and thus developing. The Scriptures serve as the focus and "meeting place" of the continuing and ever-new dialogue between man and God. The marvel and the mystery is that though originally expressed in the language and thought patterns of a particular culture and moment in history, the Word can be received by all men according to their development—cultural and historical, as well as personal. This means that while there is continuity there is not identity of meaning, understanding or truth. What is ruled out here is any notion of a static meaning or static truth combined with a dynamic understanding. Instead, what is being affirmed is a developing man and community of which the Scriptures are also an organic and developing factor. On this hypothesis the Scriptures would not be viewed as *merely* subjectivistic projections of man. On the other hand, they would not be books that embody meaning apart from their relation to man; they would not, in consequence, be outside the cultural, historical and sociological realities which enter into the continuing formation of man.

Now, as anyone knows who has even a superficial awareness of what has been happening within biblical theology in recent years, much of what I am suggesting has already been recognized and to some extent accepted within the Church. In general, however, there is still a conviction that a core of knowledge about man and God, if not the world, escapes the conditions of history and culture. This leads to a certain irony, for many who would readily concede that the Church has been misled by too great a dependence on Aristotelian metaphysics feel that the way out is to return to the Scriptures where "Christian knowledge" is to be found in its pristine form. The way back draws upon the tools of cultural and historical criticism, but the assumption is that what results is the discovery of a transcendent eternal verity rather than the experience of a particular "encounter" in history between God and man. It further assumes that we then possess that knowledge, however minimal, that God wants us to have. This is another manifestation of an unhealthy dualism, since it tends to make all other knowledge relatively superfluous. The faith-knowledge distinction here suggested avoids such a dualism since it refers to two necessary and indispensable modes of human experience both of which are oriented to the one world and one God.

What all of this reduces to is a denial of the claim that God has sent us a message in the form of the Scriptures. Surely, if God were a message sender, he would do a better job—his message would not be expressed in such a way that those who claim to be following it would end up hating and killing each other. Whatever difficulties attach to my approach, and they are legion, at least I think it avoids picturing God as an incompetent wireless operator.[22]

RELIGIOUS SYMBOLS

In any developed reconstruction of religious truth, it will be necessary to present a doctrine of religious language in general and the role of religious symbols in particular. This, needless to say, is a formidable task particularly within the framework of a pragmatism which cannot settle for any restricted linguistic analysis but must draw upon the data and insights produced in anthropology, psychology, sociology and art. For my purposes, it will suffice to indicate what I believe to be a few of the basic features of any philosophy of religious language which would be consistent with the pragmatic world view advanced earlier.

In the first place all religious language and indeed all religious rites, practices and institutions must be regarded as in some way symbolic. Without necessarily accepting every aspect of Paul Tillich's famous theory of religious symbols, I would, nevertheless, insist upon the following text as a minimal and controlling axiom for any adequate theory of religious symbols:

> Whatever we say about that which concerns us ultimately, whether or not we call it God, has a symbolic meaning. *It points beyond itself while participating in that to which it points*. In no other way can faith express itself adequately. The language of faith is the language of symbols.[23]

A corollary of the axiom that whatever we say about God is said symbolically[24] is the assertion that religious symbols are not representative but functional and participational. John Herman Randall gives just such an interpretation:

> A symbol is in no sense representative: it does not stand for or take the place of anything other than itself. Rather, it *does* something in its own right: it provokes a characteristic response in men. . . . What is important to recognize is that religious symbols belong with social and artistic symbols, in the group of symbols that are both *nonrepresentative* and *noncognitive*. Such noncognitive symbols can be said to symbolize not some external thing that can be indicated apart from their operation, but rather what they themselves *do*, their peculiar functions.[25]

What, then, are the "peculiar functions" of religious symbols? I would suggest that they serve to order, direct, integrate and intensify the developing life of the community and those persons who are expressions of the community.

In addition to the functional and participational dimensions of religious symbols, pragmatism must also insist that they are in some way—whether individually or collectively or both, consciously or unconsciously or both—creations or constructions of the human community.[26] Now, nothing is more upsetting to most Christians than the suggestion that the symbols, rites and practices by which they order their lives are products of the human community. Yet it would seem that the Christian as much if not more than any other believer would insist upon the constructed and tentative aspects of those concepts, symbols or institutions concerning that inexpressible mystery whom we have termed "God." Such an attitude is a protection against that temptation designated "idolatry," which attributes human expressions to God, thereby avoiding our responsibility for them. Further, the recognition that our concepts and symbols concerning God are products of our own making enables us to avoid that fanaticism and intolerance which follows from believing that we are the chosen defenders of God's attributes. In my opinion, only a faith which allows—indeed which demands—continual reconstruction of its conceptual, symbolic and institutional expressions can enable man to avoid worshiping his own handiwork. It is this very awareness that the symbols which we employ and by which we live are *our* creations that continually protects the "moreness" of the mystery which Christian faith affirms. Nor does the "construct" aspect of our concepts or symbols render them subjectivistic or unreal. Since symbolization and conceptualization are means by which man participates in and contributes to the development of reality, the worth and truth of such symbols and concepts depends upon their serving this function.

The objection might be raised that while religious symbols can be shown to have served an illuminating and energizing function in the past, they were able to do this because they were not consciously recognized as symbols. The contention here is that the pragmatic efficacy of these symbols was due to the belief that they were "given" by God or some power beyond man. Hence, the question which now must be confronted is whether we can be conscious that we are the authors of our symbols and still have them serve the function which they have served in the past. Of course, the only convincing evidence that they can so function depends upon the life of the community which employs symbols with this awareness. The best that a speculative effort such as this can do is to suggest what the positive fruits of a particular symbol might be. It is also possible, however, to call attention to the fact that works of art and literature play similar and analogous roles to that suggested for religious symbols and no one seems compelled to deny that they are human constructs or creations. "Art," Dewey contends, "has been the means of keeping alive the sense of purposes that outrun evidence and of meaning that transcend indurated habit."[27] I believe that the function which Dewey here assigns to art is pre-eminently the function of religion in general and religious symbols in particular.

Religious symbols, then, are always constructions of some human community and must continually be evaluated in terms of their service to the ongoing life of that community. While they are constructions of the community, however, it is not legitimate to rule out, a priori, the possibility that the constructing is done in the *presence* of or in an experience with this *Other* whom we traditionally call God.

NOTES

1. Cf. Morris R. Cohen's introduction to Charles S. Peirce, *Chance, Love, and Logic* (New York: George Braziller, Inc., 1956), p. xxv. "Man is bound to speculate about the universe beyond the range of his knowledge, but he is not bound to indulge the vanity of setting up such speculations as absolutely certain dogmas."

2. Three such efforts are: Michael Polanyi, *Personal Knowledge* (Chicago: University of Chicago Press, 1958); Michael Novak, *Belief and Unbelief* (New York: The Macmillan Co., 1965); and Richard C. Hinners, *Ideology and Analysis* (New York: Desclée De Brouwer, 1966).

3. I do not rule out the possibility of a relative ranking or hierarchy. For example, it is permissible to rank one food better than another food, one poem better than another poem and one religion better than another religion. I am calling into question, however, the advisability of attempting to establish an over-all hierarchy in which religion would be ranked higher than science or art, or the other way around.

4. Cf. Gabriel Moran, "The God of Revelation," *Commonweal* (February 10, 1967), p. 502: "If the word 'knowledge' connotes the gathering in of objective data and the quantitative increase of facts about the world, then God's revelation cannot be identified with knowledge. God does not compete with finite objects for man's attention; he does not fit into our schema of known things. On the other hand, if 'knowing' can designate man's primordial receptiveness to being and man's thrust forward to the fullness of life, then the Christian would claim that he knows and is known by God."

Moran is describing two distinct kinds of human "transactions" which characterize reality. In my terminology they are two kinds of "experience" rather than two kinds of "knowledge." More important than the language employed, however, is the recognition of the distinction of activities. That I do not consider the "language employed" unimportant is evident from my attempt to change this language.

5. I am not restricting "verification" to a specific form but I am presupposing, as I have already indicated, that any verification designated *cognitive* will differ in kind from "verification" through faith, love, art and the like. Cognitive verification admits of a precision and control which is neither possible nor proper in other experiences. This is in no way a defect in these other experiences but simply indicates a difference in them. My position allows for a variety of modes of verification, one of which can be designated *cognitive*.

6. This, of course, is the central point of Dewey's critique of religion. Cf., for example, *The Quest for Certainty*, pp. 303 ff.

7. John Herman Randall, Jr., *The Role of Knowledge in Western Religion* (Boston: Starr King Press, 1958), p. 11. "Each new attempt to set up an assailable preserve for religious truth has had to surrĕnder more territory than its predecessor."

8. I concede that to a great extent the same can be said of knowledge. Still, it can be argued that the term "truth," because it lacks the relatively precise meaning which knowledge has increasingly received, can be employed in reference to religion without the distortions that accompany a similar use of the term "knowledge."

9. Eugene Fontinell, "Contraception and the Ethics of Relationships," *What Modern Catholics Think About Birth Control*, William Birmingham, ed. (New York: New American Library, 1964), p. 246.

10. For a fuller development of the category of "satisfactory," see below, pp. 139 in my book, *Towards a Reconstruction of Religion—A Philosophical Probe* (New York: Doubleday, 1970).

11. Although Leslie Dewart presents a developmental theory of truth which differs in many respects from the approach I am making, there is complete agreement on the following: "Although truth is not the adequation of the *intellect to being* (insofar as understanding consists in the assimilation of being by the formal mediation of concepts), truth might nevertheless be called an adequation of *man to reality*, in the sense that it is *man's self-achievement* within the requirements of *a given situation*. . . . In this context *adequation* would not connote *conformity, correspondence, likeness* or *similarity*. It would connote *adjustment, usefulness, expediency, proficiency, sufficiency* and *adaptation*." *The Future of Belief* (New York: Herder and Herder, 1966), p. 110. For a fuller treatment of Dewart's theory of truth, see his, *The Foundations of Belief* (New York: Herder and Herder, 1969).

12. Josiah Royce noted the twofold aspect of "disinterestedness" and "prac-

ticality" which characterizes science. Cf. *The Spirit of Modern Philosophy* (Boston: Houghton Mifflin Co., 1892). "The value of higher insight is seldom immediate. Science has an aspect of noble play about it. It is not the activity, it is the often remote outcome of science, that is of practical service" (p. 7). "Even the hardest and least popular reflective researches are to be justified, in the long run, by their bearings upon life" (p. 24).

13. See above, pp. 61; also below, pp. 140 ff.

14. By which I mean both the relatively constant relations grasped by "common sense" and those described in the physical sciences.

15. It is significant that what we ordinarily call the lower forms of existence come closest to immutability in the monotonous repetition of their actions.

16. James, *Writings*, p. 431.

17. James, *The Letters of William James*, Vol. I, p. 270.

18. John Dewey, *Reconstruction in Philosophy* (Boston: Beacon Press, 1957), p. 58.

19. Dewey, *A Common Faith*, pp. 23, 43.

20. Dewey, *Experience and Education*, p. 79.

21. The terms "encounter" and "call" are placed within quotes to indicate that they are to be understood symbolically rather than literally.

22. Cf. Dewart, *The Future of Belief*, p. 8. "Christianity has a *mission*, not a *message*." Also Gabriel Moran, "The God of Revelation," p. 503. "The last glimmering hopes of man for sacred messages and divine institutions were extinguished with Christ. What had been implicit has now become an unavoidable fact, namely, that man is the high point of creation and that there are no messages or truths above him. If God is to be sought, it can only be in human life. God can be for man only as man takes up his own responsibility and frees himself from every form of slavery."

23. Paul Tillich, *The Dynamics of Faith* (New York: Harper & Brothers, Torchbook Edition, 1958), p. 45 (italics added).

24. At the risk of scandalizing most of my coreligionists for whom symbol always means "mere symbol," I must insist that trinity, incarnation, resurrection, eucharist and the like are symbols. This view does not exclude the possibility of some "historical" dimension to such symbols. Without presuming to resolve the enormously subtle and complex questions which such a view raises, I would simply suggest that reflection upon these beliefs within the metaphysical framework already proposed may enable us to avoid both a literalistic objectivism which places these "events" in the same order as Caesar's crossing the Rubicon, and a superficial subjectivism which reduces these "symbols" to *mere* psychological projections.

25. Randall, *The Role of Knowledge in Western Religion*, pp. 113-114. Randall has noted the similarity of his position on symbols to that of Paul Tillich. Cf. *The Journal of Philosophy*, Vol. LI, No. 5 (March 4, 1954), p. 159.

26. For an acknowledgment of the "constructive" and the "functional" aspects of symbols by a sociolgist, cf. Hugh Dalziel Duncan, *Symbols in Society* (New York: Oxford University Press, 1968), pp. 46-47. "Machines signal through built-in message tracks, animals communicate through gesture and sound, but man, and man alone, *creates* the symbols he uses in communication. He is able not only to communicate, but to communicate about communication. No matter how 'fixed' a meaning may be in ritual, magic, or tradition, it must always pass the test of relevance; that is, it must help men to deal with problems which arise as men act together."

27. Dewey, *Art as Experience*, p. 348.

SUGGESTED READINGS

James, William. *Essays in Pragmatism*. Edited by Alburey Castell. New York: Hafner Publishing Co., 1948.

McDermott, John J., editor. *The Philosophy of John Dewey* (2 vols). New York: Capricorn Books, G.P. Putnam's Sons, 1973.

Randall, John Herman, Jr. *The Role of Knowledge in Western Religion*. Boston: Starr King Press, 1958.

REVELATION
AND
ECUMENISM

Jan Van der Veken

16 Can the True God Be the God of One Book?

JAN VAN DER VEKEN

For a long while there was a kind of a popular version of ecumenical unity that hinted at a single super-church as the achievement of Christian unity. Today, Professor Van der Veken points out, we have learned to live with many particular instances of Christianity dialoguing with one another without having to melt into that single super-church. He is concerned to take the discussion still further in order to provide a theoretical basis for the task of the future, which is a dialogue between religions. This chapter is highly recommended for anyone engaged in inter-Christian or interreligious discussion—or for that matter, for anyone with religious interest in the brotherhood of man. It is Professor Van der Veken's conviction that God could not be the God of a single book, be it the Upanishads, the Koran, or the Bible. But with that said, he sets himself to discussing how Christians might make valid claims to a uniqueness and finality for the Jesus-event. The discussion makes large use of Whitehead's philosophy of religion.

Jan Van der Veken is a Professor of Philosophy at the University of Louvain in Belgium. He received his Ph.D. from Louvain with a thesis on Maurice Merleau-Ponty and the Problem of the Absolute. *His special interests are in natural theology and in the relationship of Christianity to modern thought. He has been a guest lecturer at the University of San Francisco and at the Claremont Graduate School. He has published on the problem of God in contemporary thought in Dutch, French, and German.*

"**I** distrust the reader of one book." We are all familiar with the saying and with that distrust. Some may find, I am afraid, the question "can the true

263

God be the God of one book?" a bit arrogant. "Of course," they reply, "the God of the Bible is the true God, the only true God there is." Then it is obvious that the "book" in question is the Bible. This indeed seems to be the heart of the biblical doctrine of God: He, the God of Israel, is really and truly God; he is the God of heaven and earth.

Others may object that the Bible is not just one book. To be sure, the Bible is closer to a library than to a book. The Bible is the expression of a whole cultural tradition, and yet is God's Word to his people. My question can then be rephrased as follows: can the true God be the God of one cultural tradition? Is not there at least a tension between being the God of one people —the God of the Covenant—and the fact that he is also the true God, and in this sense the God of all men and the God of the universe?

I think there really is a tension here. In a way, the tension is present in the Bible itself: the mighty God of Israel is indeed confessed as the God of the nations.

In this paper I want to shed some light upon the tension between the particularity of the religious language of Israel and the God who revealed himself to that people, and the obvious fact that if the expression "true God" is to have any meaning at all, it points to the fact that the true God is necessarily the God of all men, the only true God there is. There can be many gods, but there can only be one God. After all, the problem of the relation between the God of the Bible and the God of the nations, or more generally, the problem of the relationship between the particularity of religious experience and the universality of reason, thought and mankind, is but a new instance of the old problem of faith and reason, of revelation and thought, of theology and philosophy. It is my contention that the philosophy inspired by Alfred North Whitehead and Charles Hartshorne has developed conceptual tools that are subtle enough to illuminate in a new way the old problem of the relationship between the God of religion and the God of philosophy.

Biblical scholars are at home in the particularity of the scriptural text: texts are always particular. There is no such thing as a Universal Book of Mankind. Theology, on the other hand, adds precision to man's experience of God, expressed in the Bible, through the application of a coherent and adequate scheme of interrelated notions. The theologian speaks the language of reason, but "the perspective by which it is governed is received from a community of faith."[1] He is basically a member of the community of believers. Speaking the language of reason, he is a little bit suspect to the "readers of one book" (even if that book is the biblical library), but he is still accepted as "one of the club."

The philosopher urges to greater generality what both the members of a community of believers and their theologians are saying. He is a "minister of mankind," not of any particular religious community. He is therefore a minister of restlessness (*un ministre d'inquiétude*): he is a real threat for all particular religions, or more correctly for the particularity of religion. Nevertheless, a particular religion needs his light, for a religion that gives up saying something ultimate about human existence and about "how all things hold together" reduces itself to a mere subjectivistic way of looking at man and his destiny in an unfathomable universe.

Let me now come to the specific thesis of my presentation: First, we should refrain from speaking of God in general. There is no God-in-general (no more than man-in-general). The only God there is, is the God that religions worship. Worship, not understanding, is the basic religious category. Philosophy has to take that into account. The *real* God, the God who is worshiped, is always the God of a particular religious tradition, and therefore in most cases the God of a Holy Book. It is quite obvious that God's Word in the Bible is really incarnate: it has all the features of the particular literature of a gifted but not too important people of the Near East. We can trace the lines of development of the belief in the true God of Israel. It is striking how the growth of the belief in the true God of Israel accompanies the awareness of his uniqueness *and* universality. The gods of the neighbors were in the early stages of the Bible still very powerful, but no longer had a dominion over Yahweh's chosen people. Then we see how more and more the gods of the heathens are reduced to powerlessness (but still existing?) and ultimately to sheer nonexistence. The logic of this evolution is that the God of Israel cannot be the true God if there are others besides Him. We share the logic of that claim; we hardly can share the way in which it sometimes was practiced.

Further (and this is my second point), if a dialogue with other religions is to remain open, we have to see how the claim of uniqueness does not destroy the possibility of generality. There must be a sense in which the unique God of Israel is "worshiped" in all religions (at least in the higher types of monotheistic religion). Therefore, we have to think of the relation between the particularity and the universality of reason in a new way, without resolving the problem by the disappearance of one of the poles of the tension. The human mind has often been tempted to resolve paradoxes in that way: if one pole is reduced to insignificance, the problem is "solved," in the literal sense, as a lump of sugar is dissolved in a glass of water.

In the concluding part of the article we will have to face the theological claim of the finality of Christ, and how it relates to both particularity and generality. It will be important not to overlook the quite different "logic" of each of the three parts of this essay: the distinction between abstract generality and concrete particularity is a philosophical issue. The question of the uniqueness of Christianity as a historical religion is to be studied in comparative religion, although it has obvious theological implications. The claim of finality and decisiveness of God's revelation in Christ is a typical instance of self-involving (D. Evans[2]) or convictional (W. Zuurdeeg[3]) language.

I

The particularity of revelation has always been a crucial difficulty for rational believers, and surely so for philosophers. John Locke still tried to prove the "reasonableness of Christianity," but after him the philosophers of the Enlightment concluded that it was more reasonable to trust reason alone, even in religious matters. The result was deism. God, grasped by reason alone, conceived as a supreme being, orderer of the world, which could be discovered by all men who were able to see that there can be no clockwork without a clockmaker. The particularity of Christian faith is reduced to a contingent expression of a more general, common belief in "God." For M. Tindal, Christianity was as old as creation. The Gospel is a reedition of the religion of nature. No religious experience can reveal the true God; that would be the God of desire. The true God, the totally Other, reveals himself in the Word. This Word comes to us "from above." Revelation "posits," or accounts for, the whole content of Christianity. There is no such thing as universal religion. This theory can be called revelational positivism (*offenbahrungspositivismus*).

It is very tempting, of course, to preserve the originality of Christianity in that way. The originality is surely saved, but the price is too high: for the word of God has to be accepted by a human mind and to be conserved in a human heart. Hermeneutics and linguistic analysis are the stumbling blocks for such an approach. The message has to be understood, and the language of the Scripture appears to be human language. My honest fear is that a Barthian condemnation of natural theology leads sooner or later to atheism. This may be a startling insight. Yet there comes a moment when a reasonable mind no longer "buys" revelational positivism. "Hear and accept the word or perish" would be a non-poetic translation of Bonhoeffer's rendering of the same idea: "Eat, bird, or die" (*"Frisch, vogel, oder stirb"*). If the only alternative is to die, faith will die. It seems likely to me that the survival of faith in the twenty-first century will have something to do with our ability to conceive of both the particularity of religion and its generality. I sincerely hope that the ecumenical problem in the traditional sense will be solved at that moment: that we will have learned to live with many particular instances of Christianity, dialoging with one another without having to melt into one super-church. When Christians will love and respect one another more fully—and the theoretical basis for such an attitude is already there—then they will be better equipped for the great task of the future: the dialogue between religions. My single confidence is that Whitehead's insight into the relationship between particularity and generality of religion can provide a better conceptual framework upon which to base such a dialogue than conceptions on the Continent. Lessing, the philosopher of the Enlightment *par excellence*, was impressed by what he called "the terrible gap" between the rational and the historical, the necessary and the concrete, the universal and the contingent.

In his own way Hegel broke the fascination of the Enlightment by broadening the concept of reason. Merleau-Ponty said that Hegel had been at the roots of all important contributions to philosophy during the last century and a half, by broadening the concept of reason (*"une raison élargie"*). In his rational system Hegel saved some place for the contingent and the historical. He showed how the rational (the Spirit) has to incarnate itself in a concrete history. Hegel reconciled to such a degree the rational and the historical, that he claimed that historic Christianity, when understood, is rational religion, in fact *the* rational religion. Hegel's approach in its recent interpretations (I mention only the names of A. Chapelle, C. Bruaire, G. Van Riet, André Léonard) has proved to be most fruitful in the philosophy of religion. He speculatively reconciled the God of reason and the God of historical faith. But something was lost. From the theological point of view, there is no room in Hegel's system for the gratuity of God's saving love. From the point of view of world religions, a dialogue with Hegel's understanding of Christianity is hardly possible. He reduced all religions to a dim preparation, an early and even necessary step toward their fulfillment in Christianity.

The reaction against Hegel has been equally forceful. The basic and true insight that the only God worthy of faith is the concrete, living God has often led to the other way of solving the problem of faith and reason, namely, fideism—which is in fact reversed deism. Luther came close to this; Kierkegaard is its chief exemplification, and the less subtle categories of deism or fideism (which are just labels for the attempts to solve the problem of faith and reason by destroying one of its poles). Whitehead's approach seems even more promising than Hegel's, as far as the possibility of dialogue is concerned. For, after all, Hegel reduced the significance of non-Christian religions to being a preparation or step toward their fulfillment in Christianity. For Hegel, Christianity, fully understood, is Hegelianism. Whitehead accounts for both particularity and high generality, but within the same cultural sphere. He writes: "Two levels of ideas are required for successful civilization, namely, particularized ideas of low generality, and philosophic ideas of high generality."[4]

For Whitehead the necessity of generality arises within the realm of particularity, as a universalizing force, pervading more and more the whole life of that community, but respecting its own cultural idiosyncracies. In Hegel's system particularity disappears once the Spirit has entered his homeland, the reign of truth.

Let us now come to a more precise elaboration of this viewpoint. Whitehead discovers two stages in the rhythmic growth in man's experience and knowledge of God.

The first stage is the dimension of "romance": experience is really open to novelty; there are seers and prophets. Holy books are written. (I cannot develop here how such a view need not imply that religion is a merely subjective creation. On the contrary, I am quite convinced that the seer and the prophet are really "see-ing" and not inventing something; that something has been "disclosed" to them. Ian T. Ramsey's categories can be most helpful in this context.) The second stage is the stage of precision, which adds to man's experience the coherence and adequacy of a scheme of interrelated notions. Those notions depend as far as their content is concerned on the previous stage of romance. What could be the meaning of the God of the covenant if God had not shown his power and his concern in leading his people out of Egypt? And yet, the mighty deeds of God are more than just past history: they receive an illuminating (elucidatory) power for all occasions of experience. At this stage "religion claims that its concepts, though derived primarily from special experiences, are yet of universal validity, to be applied by faith to the ordering of all experience."[5]

Religion has surely been for Israel "the central element in a coherent ordering of life."[6] In this sense Whitehead can call it "rational religion." "The Bible is by far the most complete account of the coming of rationalism into religion, based on the earliest documents available."[7] God has not saved just one generation (our fathers), but he is also *our* saving God. In the end, he will show his power to all nations: then he is truly God. Only as the result of a long struggle toward a greater universality can we too be "the heirs of the religious movements depicted in that collection of books." Thus, according to Whitehead, "the peculiar position of religion is that it stands between abstract metaphysics and the particular principles applying to only some among the experiences of life."[8] I would add, applying to the experiences of life of only some people. What Whitehead called "rational religion" is far away from deism, which is in fact the creation of a new religion, the religion of Reason.

Rational religions—the main exemplifications being the Eastern Asiatic religions and the religions resulting from the Judeo-Christian Bible—are really historical religions: "Buddhism and Christianity find their origins respectively in two inspired moments of history: the life of the Buddha, and the life of Christ. The Buddha gave his doctrine to enlighten the world; Christ gave his life."[9] Whitehead never suggested replacing the historical forms of religious belief by one super-religion, or the God of faith by the God of reason. Yet, he was quite convinced that "Religion requires a metaphysical backing. Thus dispassionate criticism of religious belief is beyond all things necessary."[10]

How can we account for the difference in principle between the God of faith and the metaphysical concept of God? My answer is as radical as that the God of metaphysics is abstract, not actual. It has been said many times that God is not an object of thought, but a subject of encounter. I agree fully with this saying, if correctly understood. This insight should not imply that rational talk about God is impossible or that rational talk is not "about God" (as G. Marcel puts it); on the contrary, we should think about all reality as rationally as possible. Religion that refuses to think is not human and very soon is less than human.

It can be argued, of course, that God is more than rational, the Supreme Thou. I am not denying that. On the contrary, my thesis can be stated as follows: God is both the object of rational metaphysical reflection and the Supreme Thou, but not under the same aspect. The God of metaphysics is abstract, devoid of actuality, and in this sense not the "real" God. The God of faith is concrete and eminently real. The God of metaphysics is by necessity abstract: which is a key insight. Abstraction is the price for generalization. I apply here in a new way Charles Hartshorne's basic distinction between the abstract and the concrete. It seems to me that this distinction is not only fruitful when applied to God-language, but that it is also very illuminating when we talk about man and his culture.

Let us first try to explain how abstract, objective, rational talk about a person, a subject, is possible.[11] A good attempt is to be found in Heidegger's existential analysis. Although man is always a subject and never an object, the basic structures of his existence can be analyzed. Man is "in-the'world" ("*in-der-Welt-sein*"), his existence is qualified by "thrownness" ("*Geworfenheit*"), he is directed with others toward the world ("*Mit-Dasein*"). The essential structures of his existence can be the object of a phenomenological analysis. Heidegger would not admit that such talk about man reduces him to an object. It is not even talk "in the third person," as Merleau-Ponty would put it. On the contrary, the existential analysis really concerns *me*, as a subject. I am the one who has to be-together-with-others-toward-the-world. These essential structures of my existence can be the object of philosophical analysis, without reducing me to an object. It remains true, however, that existential analysis can never reach the concreteness of *my* existence. We can put it in this way: existential analysis speaks objectively about the abstract features of my existence as a person in the world. Only the concrete I is the real one; in a very true sense it can be argued that the abstract subject of existential analysis *does not exist*. It is only real when actualized or concretised in a real human person.

Another comparison may be helpful. When a psychologist speaks about the human person, about love between man and woman, about friendship, joy, and sorrow, it can be argued that the man and woman of a psychologist's treatise, just as the parents and the children of a book on education, do not exist; nevertheless they are real in an abstract sense, and talk about this abstract feature of human existence makes a lot of sense, although lacking concreteness and "life."

Why could not the same be said about God-talk? In one sense objective talk about God is possible: it is the endeavor of all metaphysics to say something which is applicable to reality as a whole. Metaphysical categories are by necessity applicable to God (univocally or analogously, it remains to be seen), if it is the task of metaphysics to provide a set of coherent, intelligible, and relevant categories to talk consistently about all-inclusive reality. To say the contrary is either to deny the reality of God or the fundamental rationality of religion's basic concept. With metaphysics rational reflection about God is at home.[12] Of course, if some would argue that metaphysics as such is impossible, they are making another point. That problem would have to be answered in another way, with other conceptual tools. But let us admit for the sake of argument that if some talk about reality as a whole is possible, although abstract, then we should be able to talk objectively, though in an abstract way, about God without reducing him to a thing or to an object of thought. I have no difficulty in allowing for the fact that the God of philosophy is not the real God of personal encounter. But it is not a different God either. It is the same God in his abstract features. For Hartshorne God can be an object of philosophical thought without in any way being reduced to a worldly being. Philosophy does not seek to explain the God of personal encounter, God as concretely actual. In one sense God may be the object of philosophical analysis, in another sense solely the subject of personal encounter (or the God of history). Only the God of personal encounter is concrete and real. It makes a lot of sense to me to interpret Pascal's saying in that way. The God of the philosophers is *not another* God than the God of Abraham, Isaac, and Jacob, and of Jesus Christ; he is not the real God either, called to replace the God of faith for those who do no longer believe in myths but have the true gnosis. The God of philosophy is the same God as the God of Abraham, Isaac, and Jacob but from an abstract point of view. The abstract is not real in the full sense of the word. For that reason it can be said that the only true God there is, is the God who reveals himself in personal encounter, in history. How God reveals himself is not rationally deducible. There is no such thing as general revelation: revelation and encounter are always particular, and for that reason historical events.

I think this is a significant point, as far as the topic of this paper is concerned: namely, that only the real and true God is God communicating himself in history. It will never be possible to argue that the God of faith, the God of personal encounter, has to be replaced by the God of Reason. Philosophy should not replace religion. God as fully actual, as fully personal and self-related to me, can be known by faith alone. Faith is directed to God as concretely actual. The true and real God is the God of Abraham, Isaac, and Jacob, the God of Jesus Christ and *my* God. It has often been said that one cannot relate in prayer to "the ground of our being" or to "the Absolute." That seems very true to me. One can relate in prayer only to the concrete, living God, who made himself available in history. Nevertheless, the fact that one can relate in prayer only to the God of faith need not imply that God is not the ground of our being, or the absolute, or all-inclusive reality, or Eminent Becoming (depending upon the philosophical conceptuality one adopts to speak about the abstract features of God).

More is true about God than what can correctly be said about God in philosophical theology, not less.

II

When this point has been made, the question of the uniqueness of historical religion such as the Judeo-Christian can be asked in a more correct way. Although a Christian recognizes that "in the past God spoke to our ancestors many times and in many ways" (Hebrews 1:1), the revelation of God in Christ is unique and decisive. I think that the conceptuality developed in this presentation allows for the uniqueness of the revelation of God in Christ, precisely because I accept that the only real revelation of God is historical and concrete. Of course, I cannot prove that the revelation of God in Christ is unique in the sense of being the only true one there is. The claim of uniqueness should not be confused with the semantically related claim of "onlyness." Both have often been confused. A considerable degree of work is involved in analyzing the "logic of uniqueness." Here I can only give some hints.

1. Uniqueness centers in particularity. You can say, when you are really impressed by a piece of art, "This painting is unique." What do you mean? Surely you mean that it is a true, real piece of art (there is no such thing as real art-in-general, no more than real abstract religion). A real piece of art is always concrete. Do you mean that you have seen all the art there is in the world, and that after careful examination you came to the conclusion that this is really a unique piece of art, because it is comparable to nothing else in the world? Surely not. No piece of art could be called unique during our lifetime. What then do you mean? I think one could say this painting *in its particularity* has disclosed to you, in a brilliant moment of esthetic experience, what art is all about. It seems odd in this context to stress the difference between the claim of uniqueness and the claim of "onlyness." No one would want to say that this painting is the only one there is. Even if he says, to make his point, "That's what I call real painting," everyone will understand.

2. Would it seem too far-fetched to say that esthetics is talking about art and even about beauty in its generality and that the object of esthetics as such does not exist? Nevertheless, esthetics may well be about the abstract features of art and beauty in the universe. An abstract analysis of the general features of art is not excluded but rather implied by the assertion of the fact that real beauty is unique.

3. The claim of uniqueness does not exclude but rather implies generality; "onlyness" excludes other particularity. Let us take the same example: someone who is struck by the uniqueness of a work of art "sees" that this definite work of art, in its utmost

concreteness, mediates that which art is all about. The claim of uniqueness does not exclude but rather reveals that something universal is present here and now. To confess Jesus as Lord does not exclude that an analysis of the abstract features of the higher world religions, where somehow God's presence is experienced, is possible and highly desirable, once the stage of early Christian romance has born its fruits. A structural analysis of the most general features of theistic world views would be most illuminating. The study of the different religions in their particularity—in their distinctiveness and similarity—is the task of comparative religion. The claim of distinctiveness is a historical claim. The claim of finality, as we will see, has another logic and seems to me to be a theological claim, although it can and must be historically under-girded.[13] There is no point in saying that all religions are particular and unique because they are culturally situated; there is no point either in accepting that all religions are saying basically the same thing. But it can be exciting to try to figure out how and why they can be compared with one another, although they are particular, and to see how they differ, although the great types of religion of mankind can be called rational religion. Some good examples of comparative religion are available, avoiding both the pitfalls of syncretism and exclusivism. Syncretism would make all religions equivalent and reducible to some vague "superreligious" synthesis of human fashioning. Exclusivism would say that only *my* religion is valid.[14]

Comparative study of religions has to focus on content, and for that reason has to take the differences between the various particular religions into account. A structural analysis of rational religions and world views would be a most illuminating supplement to comparative religion because it would focus less on the particularity than on the abstract features of all world views, much in the same sense as a structural analysis of texts in the manner of V. Propp and Claude Lévi-Strauss who have found similarity of pattern in very different myths and folktales. Claude Lévi-Strauss's approach has been inspired by Vladimir Propp's study of Russian folktales. Propp has found a clue to classify over 600 folktales, all very different and particular, by focusing attention exclusively upon the formal structure of the narratives. Personages are considered not in their individuality, but as "actants": the protagonist, the opponent, the adjuvants. The action narrated in the tale is not considered in its specificity, e.g., a prince ultimately liberating his beloved, or a warrior-king winning a battle; but in its generality, viz., accomplishment of a difficult task, overcoming of a major threat, etc. Louis Marin has applied these hermeneutic devices to Gospel texts and has offered a structural analysis of the passion and resurrection narratives. It is amazing to see how the differences between the four Gospel accounts tend to disappear. Structural analysis has introduced a new type of rationality in areas where until recently only the content was taken into account (such as linguistics, psychology, ethnology, sociology). The defendants of structuralism even claim that only in this way can the so-called human sciences attain scientific status.

One of the drawbacks of this almost exclusive stress on scientific method is that a merely structuralistic approach may lead to a new and strange kind of relativism. There is, they say, no such thing as absolute truth, revealing to us how things are in themselves. The only thing there is, is a "text," an interrelated set of symbols, concepts, words, narrative schemes, combined in ways that can be described and even computerized. There is no way to jump out of the system. The only universality is a set of universal structures, wherein nothing really happens. Mikel Dufrenne has called structuralism a new form of eletism (like Parmenides' or Zeno's).

My contention is that structuralism can be a most helpful tool, but philosophical conclusions about the very nature of rationality should be avoided. A structural analysis is necessarily abstract. It cannot and should not replace living faith. For that reason I am completely opposed to the reduction of living religion to its residue in history or to an abstract philosophical outline. Religion will not gain universality by denying its particularity.

III

This leads us to a last point, where the *theological* claim of the finality of Christ enters into the picture. The question that is now to be asked and which has a quite different logic—in fact "the logic of faith"—is how a historical and in this sense particular revelation can claim to be a decisive revelation of the true God. The confession that Jesus is the revelation of the true God, the only God there is, makes Jesus for those who believe the touchstone of all divine revelation in the past and the future. To say this is the idiosyncracy of Christian faith: only a Christian will say that. It is a matter of faith and cannot be proven. The claim of finality is the claim of a believer, of someone who accepts Jesus as *the* way, as the Lord of his life. The language of faith is highly self-involving language. It is the language of someone who has experienced God's saving presence in Jesus as the Christ. That God is decisively present in Jesus means for me that God's presence in Jesus has not only established Jesus as the Lord, but has also qualified God. For all ages to come God has compromised himself with that man. Dying on the cross, he truly is the Son of God. God is truly the father of that man. In other words: the particularity of Jesus dying on the cross and rising from the dead has to be incorporated by all future ages in all God-talk which is to be acceptable for Christians. There is for Christians no God-without-Christ. It does not follow, however, that for Christians the true God cannot be accessible in other religions. On the contrary, by believing more fully that God is really present and decisively acting in the Jesus-event we will grasp something of God's universal saving power.[15] That the true God has revealed himself in a particular history need not imply that this particular revelation of God is the only revelation of the true God there is. Rather it implies that this particular revelation of God in Jesus is true revelation of the only God there is. This seems to me implied by the confession of Jesus' Lordship: Jesus, being the true revelation of God, must be the Lord of all nations. He cannot be claimed to be the true revelation of God, without sharing somehow in God's prerogatives. It is exactly that which has been affirmed by Christian faith. The particular revelation of God in Jesus has to be related, therefore, to the whole creation. Jesus is confessed as the Lord of the universe, as the cosmic Christ. The implication is that a Christian, when dialoguing with other religions, will have to *recognize* the presence of God as revealed in Christ, even if Christ is not confessed in any explicit way. I am not very much at ease with Rahner's notion of "anonymous Christians," although what he is trying to say is acceptable to me. We should not be amazed when we recognize the Lord of History and of the Universe at work everywhere. The expression "anonymous Christians" seems to be ambiguous. We should not impose our frame of reference upon the confessions of others. We should be willing to confess that God's love encompasses all mankind; that Jesus has revealed to us the love of God, for which there are no boundaries of race, social status, and should we add "religious confession"? It is ultimately a matter of faith to recognize the same spirit at work everywhere there is true religion. This is certainly not a purely descriptive statement, but an expression of Christian hope, which opens new ways for understanding.

Let me conclude by juxtaposing three different attitudes of religious men, Christians in fact, confronted with the problem of the plurality of religions, and their belief in the true God of Jesus Christ.

The first, a faculty member of the School of Theology at Brussels, tells of a personal experience in India. "I saw all these religious people praying, offering, reading their sutra's, and I thought what they are doing is just the same as what we are doing in our churches. But then I rejected that idea, and I said No, No, there is only one name in which we can be saved, and that is the name of Jesus." I would call this minister a representative of revelational positivism. Another traveler to India related in a beautiful article in *Concilium*, a year or so ago, that he attended a "Krishna play," and how it dawned upon him that the glory of Christ was shining from the faces of these young children, acting in the play. He humbly confessed that he was quite sure about his experience, but that he hardly could give a theological rationale for it. I think I share somehow that experience but I would like to be more theologically demanding. A third approach, with which I identify more fully, has been brought to my attention by Albert Nambiaparambil, secretary of the Commission on Dialogue of the Catholic bishops' conference of India. In January 1974 the Conference stated that "Inter-religious dialogue is the response of Christian faith to God's saving presence in the religious traditions of mankind and the expression of the hope of the fulfillment of all things in Christ."[16]

Let us share that faith and that hope.

NOTES

1. John B. Cobb, Jr., *A Christian Natural Theology: Based on the Thought of Alfred North Whitehead* (Philadelphia: Westminster, 1965), p. 252.

2. Donald D. Evans, *The Logic of Self-involvement: A Philosophical Study of Everyday Language with Special Reference to the Christian Use of Language about God as Creator* (London: SCM Press, 1963).

3. Wilhem F. Zuurdeeg, *An Analytical Philosophy of Religion* (New York: Abingdon, 1958).

4. Alfred North Whitehead, *Adventures of Ideas* (New York: Free Press, 1967), p. vii.

5. Alfred North Whitehead, *Religion in the Making* (New York: World Publishing Company, 1960), p. 31.

6. *Ibid.*, p. 30.

7. *Ibid.*, p. 29.

8. *Ibid.*, p. 31.

9. *Ibid.*, p. 55.

10. *Ibid.*, p. 81.

11. I owe this comparison to Schubert M. Ogden, "Bultmann's Demythologizing and Hartshorne's Dipolar Theism" in *Process and Divinity*, The Hartshorne *Festschrift* (Lasalle, Ill.: Open Court, 1964), p. 500.

12. Alfred North Whitehead, *Religion in the Making*, p. 41. "Rational religion is the wider conscious reaction of men to the universe in which they find themselves."

13. See John B. Cobb, Jr., *The Structure of Christian Existence* (Philadelphia: Westminster, 1967). For Cobb "the finality of Jesus Christ is *first* [my italics] a historical question." "The Finality of Christ in a Whiteheadian Perspective," in Dow Kirkpatrick, ed., *The Finality of Christ* (Abingdon, 1966). As a historical question I would rather use the word uniqueness. Cobb will also allow "a second dimension to the claim of the finality of Jesus. From the very beginning Christians have affirmed that God was present to and in Jesus in a precise way" (*Ibid.*, p. 138). Here he clearly comes to the theological problem. It seems to me that the conceptuality he adopts (God providing Jesus with a unique subjective aim) allows more for the uniqueness of Jesus than for his universal importance. I thank Professor Cobb for indicating, in a Claremont conversation, that he will give more stress in his forthcoming Christology to the cosmic dimension of Christ than in the quoted article.

14. Jacques-Albert Cuttat, "Christian Experience and Oriental Spirituality," in *Concilium*, Vol. 49, *Secularization and Spirituality*, 1969, p. 132.

15. In *Christ Without Myth* (New York: Harper and Row, 1961), Schubert M. Ogden relates the decisiveness of Jesus to God's universal love.

16. Consolidated report of the Workshop of the Bishops of India (Jan. 6-14 session, 1974).

SUGGESTED READINGS

Cobb, John B., Jr. *The Structure of Christian Existence*. Philadelphia: Westminster, 1972.

Kirkpatrick, Dow, editor. *The Finality of Christ*. Nashville: Abingdon, 1966.

Whitehead, Alfred North. *Religion in the Making*. New York: World Publishing Company, 1960.

EUCHARIST

Bernard Lee

17 The Lord's Supper

BERNARD LEE

The last twenty years have seen a lot of theological reinterpretation of the Eucharist. Professor Lee explores the possibilities of a process interpretation. The deepest meaning of "presence" is not the nearness and hereness of "substance," but it corresponds rather to what shapes or creates one's reality. What is present is what participates in the real constitution of one's identity. That highly relational notion of presence is brought to bear upon the eucharistic notion of "real presence." Further, Professor Lee feels that recent New Testament scholarship on the institution texts suggests that "events" rather than "stuff" (physical bread and wine) are the symbols of which the sacrament is created—the essential "matter" is inclusive of, though larger than, bread and wine.

Bernard Lee, a Marianist priest, received his training at St. Mary's University (B.A.), Catholic University (M.A.), the University of Fribourg (S.T.B. and Ph.L.), and the Graduate Theological Union (Th.D.). He is Associate Professor of Philosophy and Religious Studies at Maryville College, and Chairman of the Department of Religious Studies. He also taught at St. Mary's University, St. Louis University (Divinity School), and was visiting Professor at the University of San Francisco. In 1973 he directed the Process Theology Institute in St. Louis. He is author of The Becoming of the Church: A Process Theology of the Structures of Christian Experience *(Paulist, 1974). His writings have also appeared in such organs as* Worship, Review for Religious, National Catholic Reporter, *etc.*

The eucharistic celebration has been a central event of Christian life since the beginning of Christian community. It has been a constant in the faith of that community that the risen Lord is present in the eucharist. The eucharist is the central dynamic in re-creating the church over and over again. All theologies of the eucharist have in common that they try to provide rational, conceptual understandings of the church-creating presence of Jesus in the eucharist. No system of rational elaboration intends to prove the presence—presence is rather the "given" in experience to which theology wishes to add the support of understanding.

There are two good reasons for theologizing anew on the real presence of Jesus in the eucharist. The first is that the world view in which most of the previous elaborations were worked out is not the world view today. Nor is our world view today simply different. We are confident that in human experience we accumulate insights. We change world views only when patchwork on the old fabric cannot handle the accumulation of new intuitions, not only because these are so numerous but because they are of such marked difference. That seems to be the case with today's accumulated insights and the Greek world view which so long supplied the conceptualizations with which we elaborated our faith experience. The notions of substance and accidents reflected and respected the state of physics (i.e., the best understandings of nature) in the world of Aristotle. That was still largely true for the world of Saint Thomas. Those notions are not supportable today.[1] I wish to suggest process modes of thought as a contemporary world view which has a rich contribution to make to elaborations of the real presence in the eucharist.

A second and equally cogent reason for undertaking a theological reexamination of the eucharist is recent New Testament studies on the accounts of its institution. In every sacrament the sacramental symbols[2] mediate and particularize the presence of the Lord. What recent exegesis suggests is the need for an enlarged understanding of what is present and an enlarged understanding of the symbols through which that presence "becomes." Not just Jesus, but the Jesus event is made present. Not just bread and wine (though they are essential), but the larger events (in which the bread and wine are central) mediate the presence of the Jesus event. What is made present is an event. And the sacramental symbols are likewise events.

In this article I want to examine the possibilities of elaborating anew our experience of the eucharist.

Process Modes of Thought

Alfred North Whitehead is neither the first nor the last to devote his philosophical synthesis to the experience of becoming. But at this juncture his work is without doubt the most systematic and in its reaches the most thoroughgoing. It would be too simple to say that he took up the Heraclitian option,[2]* although that is certainly true. But if he moved in that direction, it was in response to what he surely considered the coercion of contemporary science, and the intuitions that have emerged from science to become increasingly normative in the contemporary mind. Foremost among these is the conviction that becoming and reality are coterminous. Our scientific intuitions enable us to know what eludes our unsophisticated, unaided perception: that trees and tables are not the solid things they appear to be but that they are made of molecules, which are made of atoms, which are made of electrons, which, to the best of our knowledge, are not bits of matter but expressions of energy characterized by prodigious activity. Hamlet has finally got his wish: the too, too solid flesh *has* melted.

Any philosopher who gets a hearing today has to account for two primary experiences, that of identity or sameness and that of becoming or change. Greek thought tended to make identity or sameness primordial, and change was a function of substance; thus the eucharist had to be worked out in terms of substance. In process thought, becoming is primordial. The event is the tiniest building block of reality. And the experience of identity is expressed as function and character of event. In this setting I wish to examine the process understandings of presence and symbol for their relevance to sacramental theology. And though this analysis relates to each of the sacraments, I prefer to deal with the eucharist as a way of exemplifying and exploring the implications of a process sacramentology.

Presence

The largest process understanding of presence situates itself in the presupposition that the entire universe is an organic community of interlocked events. The interrelation of all that is real is without exception. In that sense, the entire universe is mutually present to itself. This mode of universal presence has two aspects, one spatial and one temporal. The law of universal gravitation exemplifies in some degree the spatial aspect. There is a formula which expresses the force of gravitational attraction between any "bits of matter," regardless of size and distance. The attraction may be negligible because of its minuteness and because of the multitude of intervening forces. But it is there nonetheless. The negligibility of the force merely points to the imperceptibility of effects.

The temporal dimension of the world's mutual presence to itself points to our conviction that at any given moment we stand on the shoulders of *all* past history. Some events may be so remote that we do not know what their shoulders feel like. They may be negligible in their impact on us, but the historical facticity of any event that ever occurred is irradicable. It's always there.

Whitehead makes an important practical distinction between the whole world and the "actual world." The latter expression indicates what there is in the whole world that contributes to something's real internal constitution. Let us use Whitehead's name for the basic realities: actual entities or actual occasions. (The two are apparently not completely interchangeable—but the small distinction is not important here; and sometimes Whitehead seems to equate them.) The actual world is that part of the whole world which contributes to the configuration of an actual occasion. Presence, therefore, has a more limited meaning in reference to an actual entity's actual world. Whatever shapes or creates me in any way is present to and in me. Presence refers to whatever has a hold on my becoming. This is a slight paraphrase of Gabriel Marcel's description of presence as what has a hold on my being. The deepest meaning of presence is causal efficacy, and the most poignant experience of it comes with the addition of conscious awareness.

It is often the case that temporal and spatial proximity accompany the experience of presence. I easily notice what is close in time and space. But if I want to make an accounting of my reality, I will often have to say that some event much more distant temporally than a phone call this morning contributes far more to my configuration than the phone call. And I might have to say that there are people miles away who have a greater influence on the shape of my life than those in the same room with me now. Those who largely create me are more present to me than those who create me but a little.

Once we begin with a world view that understands the whole world to be mutually present to itself (and contemporary experience and intuition seem to support that), we no longer think precisely in terms of "present" or "not present"; we presume presence and ask about its size. We distinguish between the general presence of a whole world, and the more specific presence of one's actual world—i.e., of those factors which contribute to the real, internal constitution of an actual entity. We hold that while it often happens that what is "here" or "very near" is more likely to be experienced as present, the deepest meaning of presence is causal efficacy—what has a creative, formative hold on an actual entity's becoming. Whatever in the world nourishes my becoming is what is present to me. And I in turn am present wherever my influence is felt. That is the deepest meaning of presence; and when speaking of the real presence of Jesus in the eucharist, I must also heed that presence in terms of what focuses most clearly upon its deepest meaning.

SYMBOL

One of the significant features in the process understanding of symbol is that it has its basis in metaphysics. Given the longstanding penchant of Catholic theology for a metaphysics, there is an impressive congeniality between process thought and traditional theological instincts. Most of our recent eucharistic theologies have tended to draw their sense of symbol from phenomenology and anthropology. I think that in the long run Whitehead's approach to symbol can also sustain these other insights while retaining its own metaphysical underpinnings.

Whitehead says in *Process and Reality* that the whole of that work could be understood as an attempt to elaborate how one actual entity is present in another.[3] And it is out of a close analysis of presence-making dynamics that an understanding of symbol emerges.

Even the simplest of entities which we experience is so incredibly multifaceted that no relationship could embrace it in all its aspects. Every entity is experienced through some of its aspects. To a certain extent every object we experience must be simplified. An object of experience is commended to our attention through one or more of its aspects in order to become a manageable item of data.

We get to know someone only when we get "handles" on our experience of him. What there is about a person that reveals him to me can be quite different from those aspects that someone else fixes upon in coming to know the same person. But whatever aspects are singled out, it is the very condition of an experience that *some* aspects give me a hold on what I experience, and those aspects in their turn mediate and particularize the kind of presence that someone has in my becoming. Until such handles are found, someone can be "there" in time and space but not part of my actual world and not, therefore, shaping my reality. What is "there" breaks out of its neutrality when its general presence in my whole world becomes a particular presence in my actual world, that is, when something about it commends it to my attention. That commendation is always particularized through those aspects which invite and excite my attention. Of course my own subjectivity has much to do with what I attend to and with what there is about a thing that makes me attend—but this is only to say that in every experience something is contributed by the subject and something by the object.

Such simplification of data, which is a necessary operation in every relational act, Whitehead calls "transmutation." It is not a human phenomenon alone—it is metaphysical in import, in that transmutation facilitates and mediates each transaction whereby anything's real, internal constitution is affected by other actual entities. For example, no two plants experience the soil in the same way. Each does it in terms of what it needs and what is there.

Symbolic activity is a highly complex expression of transmutation. The basis upon which "something about" an actual entity is able to stand for that entity, is that the "something about" really participates in the reality into which I am led; or, I might also say, it participates in the reality which it leads into me. The important implication is this: *every human experience of presence is mediated through symbol.* The tendency to distinguish between mediated presence and unmediated presence is misplaced. Symbol is what makes anything stand up and stand out so that it is inserted into my experience and becomes present.

Symbol not only mediates presence but particularizes it. The impact that someone or something has on my becoming is conditioned by the symbol which mediates its presence. Jesus as the primordial sacrament of God (in Schillebeeckx's fine phrase) is nonetheless a particular symbol of God. The reality of God cannot be exhaustively presented in human history—history is not a large enough medium for the immensity of God. The transmutation of God's reality in the Jesus event is a particular way in which God stands up and stands out to call for the attention of humankind.

The life of the church in its turn is symbol—shares in the reality—of the Jesus event. Each sacrament is an ecclesial way of taking hold of critically important aspects of the Jesus event and offering them to human life to be part of life's becoming. Presence is intrinsically dialogic: it occurs when what is offered there has effects here.

I want to recapitulate briefly before looking at the New Testament accounts of the institution of the eucharist. The deepest meaning of presence is "what has a hold on my becoming." Presence is defined and measured by causal efficacy. The size of presence is the breadth and depth of its reaching into my becoming. Secondly, transmutation is a factor at work throughout reality whenever something is present to and in something else; symbolism is a particular expression of transmutation in conscious human experience of presence. *Every* presence is mediated for us through symbolic activity. Every presence is shaped and particularized by the symbols that mediate it. The effects which constitute presence depend on the shape of the mediating symbol.

It becomes increasingly important to turn attention again to the eucharist because recent scholarship suggests that we have very likely trimmed our understanding of the symbols of the eucharist to too small a size. If the symbols are larger than we thought, there may be more in store for us than we thought too.

THE INSTITUTION ACCOUNTS

Cultural symbols demand a certain immediacy of comprehension for their effectiveness. Symbols always require some act of interpretation so that they can give their yield; but belabored acts of interpretation weaken symbols. I mention this because the eucharistic symbols are deeply rooted in Hebrew culture, especially in the covenant. If Jesus used those symbols to point to a new covenant, it would seem reasonable that their old covenant character would count for much among the "whats" of the new covenant which the eucharist singles out and presents.

The Exodus is the controlling metaphor of the Old Testament experience of God. The Exodus was and is an event which then and now constitutes the identity of that people who let their becoming be shaped largely by that historical *event*. While it is true, of course, that the presence of Jesus as Lord creates Christian community, we seem more faithful to those symbols which Jesus chose when we say that the church is created by the ongoing appropriation of the Jesus *event*: his life, his death and resurrection, his teaching, his caring, his anger at repression, his joy in encounters with faith, all his saving acts. Jesus is in all of them with huge presence. We want to say that the presence-making symbols of the eucharist direct themselves, and attention, to the Jesus event. This seems to be supported by New Testament studies.

I can do little more than point to some conclusions from work done on the institution accounts of Matthew, Mark, Luke and Paul. There are readily available resources.[4] There is far from universal agreement, even in recent studies; but there is much common ground. Considerable study is still needed on this New Testament topic. Process theology is relatively new, and much work lies ahead here too—on the relation of the process philosophical method to theological method, on the process presuppositions and other such topics. I mention this to indicate the tentativeness of probing into a process theology of the eucharist. But it seems to me that there is sufficient material to justify the undertaking.

All the institution accounts are somewhat conditioned by the fact that they form part of cultic, or liturgical, formulas. Of the four accounts, Paul's in I Corinthians is the oldest written record; it also seems to represent the oldest tradition. In the Pauline account, which is reflected in Luke, the blessing, breaking and sharing of the bread are separated in time from the cup of the covenant in Jesus' blood which is shared *after the meal*. These are two individual actions. In the setting of the paschal meal each is a symbol, in a related but different sense, of the Exodus event. The symbolism of each action mediates and particularizes the eucharistic presence.

Very early in Christian community the eucharist was removed from its setting within an actual meal—which the eucharist still seems to have had when Paul's account of the institution was written. As soon as this change occurred, the eucharistic actions centering on the bread and the cup of wine stood side by side, facilitating the movement from bread and wine to the strict parallel with body and blood. Further, under the influence of Greek thought, attention was easily fixed on the substances of bread and wine in far more restricted fashion than was likely in the original context.

The words of institution in Paul are not the same as those given in Matthew and Mark concerning the cup of wine. In Paul (and Luke) Jesus says, "This *cup* is the new covenant in my blood. . . ." In the other accounts Jesus says, "This is my blood, the blood of the covenant. . . ." For at least three reasons the Pauline account, which presents "cup" more prominently than "blood," would seem closer to what Jesus actually said.

First, there is the fact that Paul's account is older and earlier. In Paul's account the eucharist is still set within the context of a meal, as was the eucharist celebrated by Jesus with his followers.

Secondly, and I think more decisively, the many Hebrew injunctions concerning blood would make it unlikely that Jesus could say to the Hebrews with him at table, "This is my blood . . . drink it." That would be unthinkable. But blood as a symbol of covenant is familiar. And sharing a cup as a symbol of covenant has a wide cultural base even outside Hebrew history.

Thirdly, in Pauline theology the eucharist symbols are more than bread and wine. He speaks of eating the bread or, more largely, of sharing the "table of the Lord" in parallel with drinking the cup of the Lord. Paul's body-of-Christ theology would surely suggest that when he does speak of the body of the Lord, even in the eucharistic context, he does not have in mind the physical substance of Jesus.

The one symbol, it seems to me, is larger than bread. It at least includes the action of breaking the bread and sharing it; it may refer to the entire meal experience. In Acts, when Luke speaks of the early Christians as praying in the temple each day and returning home to break bread together, it is unclear whether that reference is specifically to a eucharistic celebration or not. But what is clear is that the breaking of the bread refers to the whole action, whether meal or eucharist, much as breakfast refers not just to the first morsel that breaks the night's fast, but to the meal. And the second symbol also seems quite clearly to be more than wine. The cup [of wine—but cup is indicated and not wine] is the cup of a new covenant in the blood of Jesus—and the cup of the Lord is shared, covenanting those who share it in Jesus' blood.

The Johannine discourse at the Last Supper provides an adequate hermeneutic for the shared table or shared bread, however we take it. One of the reasons why the eucharist has been and is the primordial sacramental experience is that it transmutes the Jesus event in symbols that point to the heart of its meaning. The eucharistic symbols have a hold on the larger, overall configuration of the Jesus event. Saint Thomas intimates this conviction in holding that all the other sacraments point to the eucharist. The symbol of Jesus' relation to God is that of Son to Father. And the intimacy of that union is the symbol of the union that should mark the relation of brother and sister Christians with each other and with God: "That they may be one as we are one. . . ." Sharing the Lord's table is a symbol of that unity. All those Hebrews and only those Hebrews who were already one people in virtue of entering into covenant with God, had the right to sit together at the Passover table (Ex 12). In the action of sharing a table according to the Passover ritual, they reconstituted themselves as God's people. The Exodus event is continued in its presence because it has new effects.

The New Testament meal shares deeply in the basic symbolism of the Old Testament meal. To come to the Lord's table is to be one who has already said Yes and wishes to say Yes again. It is to know that saying Yes to God through the event of his Son and saying Yes to fellow Christians are not two actions but one. Sharing the bread elicits that Yes. The Yes is the effect. In the Yes the Jesus event (whose Yes to me preceded my own) enters into my becoming. But because presence is dialogic, my Yes is as necessary as the Yes of the Jesus event, though the latter Yes far outsizes my Yes in its importance for the dialogic encounter.

Because my Yes is expressed existentially through historical appropriations of the Jesus event, I must say Yes to my Lord in the same Yes I say to my brothers and sisters. If I have been saying No to them, I must first go and say Yes to them and then return to the table. I have no right there otherwise. The Yes that makes the union that brings us to the table is part of the eucharistic symbol through which the Jesus event becomes present. I must make bread and bring that; but I must also pledge Yes and bring that.

I am not suggesting that this kind of assent is a spiritual concomitant of the eucharist. What I am suggesting is precisely that the full sacramental symbol includes what makes it possible, and gives the right for us to break bread. It has long been the position that the faith of those experiencing a sacrament is requisite to the effectiveness of the sacrament. I am proposing a still more intimate relation: that in the eucharist the unity which has already been carved out by faith is a necessary part of the essential sacramental symbol. It is that "already union" which provides the interpretative context which *makes* the breaking of the bread the symbol that it is. And this is another way of insisting that the real presence of the Jesus event whose hold on human existence is already becoming the church in reality.

The cup of the covenant carries a multiple symbolism (such as its relation to blood offering), all of which participates in the transmutation (in Whitehead's sense) of the Jesus event. I will call attention only to some of the aspects of covenant which mediate and particularize the eucharistic presence. In earlier Hebrew history there is a very strong consciousness that God relates to Hebrews primarily as a people. The individual is taken up into God's love when he is a member of a faithful people that is taken up into God's love. One does not make it alone. The tendrils of the covenant between God and his people are as immediately horizontal as they are vertical. This orientation weakens in later history as personal ethical consciousness develops; but it is never lost. The effects of covenant are responsibility to God as well as to and for our brothers and sisters: faithful caring. The Second Vatican Council's Pastoral Constitution *Gaudium et spes* speaks of the emergence of a new humanism in which man is *defined* by his responsibility to history and to his brothers.

It goes to the heart of the Jesus event to understand it as covenant. That, in fact, is its most common name: New Testament. The Jesus event is present when and to the extent that covenanting is its effect. It is really present when covenant seriously shapes my becoming and our becoming. What the cup of the Lord demands of us in response to what it offers is the assumption of active responsibility to, for and in Christian community, alone and together before God in Jesus' name. That is how the cup of the covenant in the blood of Jesus mediates the real presence of the Jesus event and particularizes the effect which is necessary if one is even to speak of real presence.

One of the liturgical implications of this process formulation is that communion under both species should not be the exception but the rule. Pastorally the poignancy of the experience of the eucharist will of necessity be enhanced by clear attention to the particularity of the real presence as shaped by each of the eucharistic symbols. Because of both the scope and the intent of this article, I have dwelt upon the particularity of the two symbolic actions of the eucharist. It is of equal importance to understand the complementariness and interaction of these symbols in the unity of what is *one* sacramental experience.

I have tried to indicate, first of all, that the most real meaning of presence is that of causal efficacy: what is present is what has a hold on my becoming. The substance/accident paradigm must be surrendered in deference to the current state of human knowledge. But even beyond that, the nearness and hereness of a substance would not get at the heart of what it means to be really present. Secondly, I have pointed out that *every* human experience of presence is mediated and particularized through symbolic activity.

Each of the sacraments is a particular way in which the Jesus event is transmuted and proffered. Something about the Jesus event is embraced by each sacramental symbol and offers presence. The symbol is a dimension of event, of Jesus event. We are asked to let the "something about the Jesus event" which the symbol catches be also "something about us." As a celebrating community we are asked to let a particular something about the Jesus event become a particular something about our shared life. In this we know presence.

The eucharist catches hold of the Jesus event in bolder strokes than the other sacraments, and this is why they are in a real sense directed to the eucharist. More than any other sacrament, the eucharist is at the heart of the life of the church. The "something about" the Jesus event that is offered in the eucharist is mediated and particularized not merely through bread and wine as things—but these and more: bread that is blessed, broken and shared by a people who are and who become the people of God by becoming the body of Jesus, the primordial symbol of God. The sacramental symbol is a realizing symbol. The cup of wine which is the cup of the covenant in the blood of Jesus is blessed and shared by a people already responsible to and for each other before God and in Jesus, but now assimilating that covenant anew into the pattern of life which constitutes the becoming, and therefore the reality, of Christians.

For many reasons it is a fearful task to undertake a reexpression of the eucharist, though easier now than before. Fresh enough is memory of the painful reactions when "transignification" and "transfinalization" were proposed as alternatives to "transubstantial" understandings of the real presence. Our instincts about the centrality of the eucharist to our life are so keen that we are uncomfortable with any tampering. Process theology, like any theology, is an effort to elaborate faith experience, and no theology can do that exhaustively or definitively. In this process-foray into eucharistic teaching, no claim is made to offer a thorough accounting for faith experience of the real presence. Ours is rather a quest for reasonable adequacy. In exploring anything more that needs to be accounted for, it must be remembered that the presuppositions of process thought differ in some basic ways from the presuppositions of most of our accumulated theology. Whatever more needs to be accounted for should reflect our experience and not conclusions from another world view: what is there in our faith that still yearns for more understanding?—*fides quaerens intellectum*. Not, what is there in an alternative system of formulations that I do not find in this system.

I would like to conclude with the closing sentences of Whitehead's *Symbolism*: "It is the first step in sociological wisdom, to recognize that the major advances in civilization are processes which all but wreck the societies in which they occur:—like unto an arrow in the hand of a child. The art of free society consists first in the maintenance of the symbolic code; and secondly in fearlessness of revision, to secure that the code serves those purposes which satisfy an enlightened reason. Those societies which cannot combine reverence to their symbols with freedom of revision, must ultimately decay either from anarchy, or from the slow atrophy of a life stifled by useless shadows."[5] It is not at all far afield to consider the sacramental system as the mainstay of the symbolic code of that society which is the church, and theology as the historically conditioned symbolic code which ongoingly explores and develops, keeps alive and immediate the sacramental appropriation of the Jesus event. In other words, theology wants to help keep real presence unstifled by useless shadows.

NOTES

1. There is ample discussion of this elsewhere: for example, Eugene Peters, *The Creative Advance* (Saint Louis: Bethany Press 1966), esp. chs. 2, 3 and 4; Edward Schillebeeckx, *The Eucharist* (New York: Sheed & Ward 1968), esp. the early sections of part 2.

2. In deference of modern usage I use symbol rather than sign, but in the sense in which traditional usage spoke of the sacramental sign.

2*. Of the Greek philosopher Heraclitus (died c.470 B.C.), to whom was ascribed the saying: "Everything is in a state of flux."—Editor.

3. Alfred North Whitehead, *Process and Reality* (New York: Harper 1960), 79-80.

4. For example: Willi Marxen, *The Beginnings of Christology* (Philadelphia: Fortress Press 1969), esp. ch. 4, and *The Lord's Supper as a Christological Problem* (Philadelphia: Fortress Press 1970); Eduard Schweizer, *The Lord's Supper According to the New Testament* (Philadelphia: Fortress Press 1967). I do not agree with all of the conclusions, but I cite these books as good summaries of much of the recent work in this area.

5. *Symbolism* (New York: Capricorn 1959), 88.

SUGGESTED READINGS

Guzie, Tad W. *Jesus and the Eucharist.* New York: Paulist Press, 1974.

Marxsen, Willi. *The Beginnings of Christology.* Philadelphia: Fortress Press, 1969. (Especially ch. 4, "Jesus and the Lord's Supper.")

—— *The Lord's Supper as a Christological Problem*. Philadelphia: Fortress Press, 1970.

Pittinger, Norman. *God in Process*. London: SCM Press, 1967. (Especially ch. 5, "The Christian Fellowship and the Sacramental Action of the Church.")

Schillebeeckx, E. *The Eucharist*. New York: Sheed and Ward, 1968.

ETHICS AND HUMAN EXPERIENCE

Charles Hartshorne
Bernard M. Loomer

18 *Beyond Enlightened Self-Interest*

CHARLES HARTSHORNE

Charles Hartshorne did not write this chapter as a "homily" to the American Experience—his reflections are, indeed, upon universal human experience. But given religious and philosophical persuasions about the brotherhood of man, it becomes increasingly difficult to make sense out of "free enterprise" that is not conducted in a manner that is beyond enlightened self-interest. To care for others beyond enlightened self-interest, Professor Hartshorne insists, is not just a requirement of the gift of grace—it is a command of reason. That is a basic intuition shared by both Christian and Buddhist traditions. But we have had to wait a long time in the West for philosophical understandings that might adequately sustain those religious intuitions.

Charles Hartshorne is one of the seminal figures in whom process theology is rooted. Even a list of his published writings goes on for pages and pages. His impact on the movement grows. His early training was at Haverford College. This was followed by two years in the U.S. Army Medical Corps in the First World War. He received his Ph.D. from Harvard in 1923, and then studied abroad for two years. He was Instructor-Professor at the University of Chicago 1928-55, and Professor at Emory University 1955-62. Presently he is Ashbel Smith Professor of Philosophy at the University of Texas where he has been since 1962. Among his books are: The Philosophy and Psychology of Sensation *(University of Chicago Press, 1934),* The Divine Relativity: A Social Conception of God *(Yale University Press, 1948),* Philosophers Speak of God, *with William L. Reese (University of Chicago Press, 1953).*

The world, according to common sense, consists of a great many individual things and persons, each individual remaining identical through change but losing some qualities from time to time and acquiring others. This view has obvious truth, but it easily misleads in serious ways.

I. THE ILLUSIONS OF EGOISM

Consider the human species. At a given time it consists of a number of persons, each the same person from birth to death. At every moment I am Charles Hartshorne, and John Smith is John Smith. Never have I been anyone other than Charles Hartshorne, and never has John Smith been anyone other than John Smith. That each of us is always the same human individual is true; but that each of us is always simply the same thing, the same reality, is false. We are identical through life as human individuals, but we are not identical as concrete actualities. The identity is abstract, the nonidentity is concrete. Without this distinction the language of self-identity is a conceptual trap. Into this trap have fallen most philosophers. Of all the great traditions, only Buddhism has entirely escaped the error. However, Buddhists have tended to be intuitionistic or anti-intellectual and so have failed to develop conceptual devices altogether adequate to their insight.

Personal identity is a partial, not complete identity; it is an abstract aspect of life, not life in its concreteness. Concretely each of us is a numerically new reality every fraction of a second. Think of the difference between a newborn infant and an adult person; also, of that between an adult and a senile octogenarian. These differences are not slight. The infant is only potentially a "rational animal"; actually it has no rational thoughts. A senile person may also scarcely have any.

Another difference is that between a person in dreamless sleep and the person dreaming; also between the dreamer and the person awake. In addition there may be aphasia, loss of any clear sense of one's past history, delirium, insanity, intoxication, weird drugged states, multiple personality. Personal "identity" must span all these differences. We say that at some moments a person is "not himself." The New Testament speaks of being "born anew." Personal identity as many philosophers construe it leaves out all that these expressions report. To abstract from such vast contrasts and say that from birth to death the person is one and the same entity is to emphasize the abstract or the potential at the expense of the concreteness or actuality of life. This one-sided emphasis has momentous consequences.

Let us be clear on one point. I am not disputing that there is a definite sense in which each human individual is distinguishable from any other. A person's bodily career is continuous in space-time. People could have been observing me from birth on and would have seen no gap in my physical development and persistence from infant to adult, from middle age to elderliness. Also there have been scarcely any abrupt changes in my habits, my personal style. But this physical continuity is an extremely abstract feature of one's existence. It allows very radical changes in quality from a nearly mindless infant with incomplete brain cells to full maturity, from dreamless and apparently mindless sleep to being wide awake, from irritated or furiously angry states to happy or benevolent ones, and so on.

Consider, too, that many minute portions of one's body were once parts of the environment, and vice versa. So far as these portions are concerned, spatiotemporal continuity connects one not with oneself in the past or future so much as with the environment, that is, other individual beings, in the past or future.

Forget about the bodily continuity, and think instead about the mental one. Of my thoughts or bits of knowledge, many go back to thought or knowledge not my own, and some will in the future become part of the thought or knowledge of others. If I am influenced now by what I have been in the past, I am as genuinely influenced by what others have been in the past. If I can plan now to bring about results in my future bodily and spiritual career, so can I plan to bring them about in the future bodily and spiritual careers of others. Where, in all this, is there any absolute distinction between relation to self through time and relation to others—apart from the abstract physical distinction already granted?

If we forget how relative, partial, or abstract, as well as primarily bodily, personal identity is, we pay serious penalties in our interpretation of fundamental issues. For instance, it then seems natural to adopt a self-interest theory of motivation. I am I, you are you, neither of us is the other. If I care about my future, it is because it is mine; so runs the thought: but if I care about your future this must be because that future, or what I do for it, will benefit my own. My future advantage is then the end, while contributing to your advantage is but a means. For over fifty years I have rejected this view, and my original reasons still seem valid, though they have become enlarged and fortified. I think the view is bad psychology, even bad biology, and bad ethics and metaphysics. It also contradicts the imperative of all the higher religions that one should love the other *as oneself.* If loving the self is a sheer identity relation and loving the other a sheer nonidentity relation, then one can never do anything like loving the other "as oneself"; for on the hypothesis this is a metaphysical or logical impossibility.

My position, since 1918, but rendered much clearer by exposure, first to Hume, James, Peirce, and Whitehead, and then to the Buddhists, has been that self-love and love of others are alike, both being relations of partial, not complete, identity or nonidentity. This view is to some extent recognized in common speech but usually denied in philosophical and theological doctrines in the West, with of course some notable exceptions. The exceptions include post-Kantian idealism, Marxism, and the doctrine of Saint Paul in his saying, "We are members one of another"—an epigram closer to the truth of this matter, in my opinion, than anything to be found in Aquinas or Kant, not to speak of Hobbes or Bishop Paley. But none of the writers mentioned does full justice to the degree of nonidentity abstracted from by the common-sense notion of the "same" individual. Only in Whitehead (most nearly anticipated by Peirce) does the West, after more than two millennia, come to meet the Buddhists on the question of selfhood and motivation.[1]

In common speech occur such remarks as that we "identify ourselves with" a friend, or with offspring or fellow advocates of a common cause. We have the expression "alter ego" for such cases, or "better half" for a spouse. But where are the absolute limits of these qualifications of self-interest? I take the qualifications to show that the really basic principle of motivation is not regard for the future of one's own bodily and mental career. This regard is merely a principal derivative of the truly basic principle, of which regard for the future of other organisms or careers is another derivative.

The basic principle is the appeal of life for life, of feeling for feeling, experience for experience, consciousness for consciousness

—and potential enjoyment for actual enjoyment. One's own future is interesting, appealing, motivating. Why? Because it is the future of a sentient and conscious career—and present experience more or less vividly and sympathetically anticipates this future. If we find means to be as aware of the prospects of others as of our own, then we may take a similar interest in their prospects. The interest may or may not be very sympathetic, it may even be more or less sadistic. But this is because of some lack of harmony between the career of the other, as we envisage it, and our own present currents of thought or feeling. It is not because the abstract thread of individual identity leads only to one's own past or future rather than to the others' past or future. The grounds of antipathy, as of sympathy, are much more concrete. And parallel to sadism is masochism. The difference is relative.

1. The first illusion of egoism, then, is the notion that motivation depends basically upon the mere spatiotemporal continuity of organic careers. True enough, it is normally the case that we are more vividly and steadily aware of and sympathetic to our own future prospects than to those of others. But this difference of degree provides no reason to make an absolute of self-interest as compared with interest in others.

To value oneself *rationally* is to value oneself for the same reasons, and by the same criteria, as are used in valuing others. In short, "love others as oneself" is a command of reason, not just a requirement or gift of grace. We should not give the prestige of reason to the fact that every animal tends to feel its own weal and woe more vividly and steadily than the weal or woe of any other animal. To use reason (and it requires reason) to extend self-interest to include one's own entire future, but not to use it to extend interest in others so as to include in principle their entire futures, seems misuse of the power to generalize, to seek truth and value wherever they may be and as being "there" for any impartial spectator. Reason should universalize our ends as well as our means.

The value of one's own life is more in one's power than is that of other lives; one can understand it more easily, and so it is one's greatest single responsibility. But there are times, as when one is close to death, when one may be able to do much more for another than for oneself.

Mortimer Adler eloquently urges that we should have as our

concern the goodness of our own lives as entire careers and, only as derivative from this concern, care about the future of others. But why should I now care infinitely for my life or career as a whole? Adler admits that this whole will never be experienced, possessed, or enjoyed by me. I have glimpses of it, and so do my acquaintances. But none of us will ever really possess it.[2] Why then is it so important? I agree that it is important, but for the same reason that makes anyone else's life important, not just to him but to any rational spectator. It is not my entire life's goodness that I have to have right now, but only the satisfaction of having a rational aim right now. The reward of virtue, which, as Spinoza said, is in virtuous action itself, is not the whole of happiness, but it is the only reward that one needs to take as absolutely essential. For a rational being it is the pearl of great price. The rest is additional good fortune to be utilized by practical wisdom.

Like Adler, though in an interestingly different way, Michael Scriven derives the motive for good conduct from rational concern for one's own career. Both writers show some realization of the limitations of the project, but neither seems to see clearly that ethics has a deeper and more rational ground elsewhere.[3]

There is of course partial agreement between the aim at future well-being for oneself and the aim at the good of others. But the value of knowing this is to weaken the force of man's natural though relative self-centeredness, not to enthrone this animal limitation as the voice of reason. A great deal of self-interested action is self-defeating, and there are often great rewards for bringing genuine good to others. I do not envy anyone the benefits he gets from selfishness. On the other hand, I cannot see any need to make the future rewards to self for now acting upon a rational aim *the* reason for having this aim or acting upon it. Nor can I see that giving self-interest an absolute priority is in any good sense rational.

The lower animals, which I have been studying most of my life in one way or another, are not merely selfish, but selfish and altruistic, both of course in the same largely instinctive or genetically determined fashion. (What they cannot do is to generalize either self-interest or altruism; for they cannot symbolize abstract ideas, they cannot deal with the absent or potential as definitely as with the given situation.) The basic instincts are to keep the species going; the individual's preservation is subordinate. A male spider may risk his life in courting the female, but in running this risk he serves the species.

2. The primary egoistic illusion about motivation tends to associate itself with another. This illusion is the unexpressed but felt anticipation of living virtually forever. That one is mortal is known, but not genuinely realized and acted upon. What matters is thought to be one's own future. But which future? One's life prior to death? Or one's future altogether? Our ultimate destiny, so far as we know it, is to be heaps of dust. What then will it matter to us that we have, perhaps, been happy—or unhappy? For us there will then be no such truth. But we put this out of our minds almost completely, and face things as though we would always be there to reap any harvest we may sow. This, I hold, is an illusion, and one of the commonest. St. Exupéry wrote that, of the many persons he had seen facing their own imminent death, not one thought primarily of himself. If we lived in the full light of the truth, this would be our attitude all along.

The future that matters is not our own future as such, but rather any future we can influence, sympathize with, and in some degree understand as good or bad *for someone.* To serve this future can be our present aim, whether or not the good we do to the other will also be our own future good. It is our good, right now, to promote what we care about for the future, whether it be a child's welfare, even a pet animal's, or our country's, or mankind's —and one could go further still. Other things being equal, one prefers that persons, even animals, should be happy, not only while one can share in their happiness but afterward as well. Anyone of whom this is not true is insofar a subnormal or irrational human being, and may be a sick one as well.

So, far from our valuing others only for their usefulness to ourselves it is in no small part for our usefulness to others that we value ourselves. Convince yourself that you are no good to anyone, and how much will you love, rather than hate and despise, yourself?

There is a great Buddhist passage that goes something like this. "You say, 'He injured me, he insulted me, how terrible!' " "But," the writer goes on, "this is writhing in delusion." Why so? It is writhing because it is unhappy. It is delusion, first, because the self that insulted you has been partly superseded by a new concrete actuality, the other person now, which may be indefinitely different from the insulting self. It is delusion, second, because the insulted self has also been superseded. There is incomplete identity on both sides. But third, there is only incomplete nonidentity between the two persons. The other's past has entered into your present being, your past into his, and both share a partly overlapping causal future. Each helps to create a new self in the other and will influence some of the same future selves. Finally, fourth, both you and the other, as individual animals, are passing phenomena, whose careers may cease at any time.

The angry man is reacting like an injured animal, using his reason only to articulate the animal's lack of perspective rather than to overcome it. This is a misuse of reason. The human power of abstraction and generalization is ill-employed if it merely generalizes the means and leaves the end the same, or if it merely generalizes the self-protective aspect of instinct and not the species-serving aspect. The rational aim is the future good that we can help to bring about and take an interest in now, whether or not it will do us good in the future and whether or not we shall be there to share in the good. We share in it now, and that is all that present motivation requires. It is a luxury, not a necessity, if we can hope to have a future share in the good we make possible for others. Moses did not need to enter into the promised land.

3. A third illusion generated by overemphasis upon self-identity is the misconceptiion of the meaning of death and the real problem of immortality. Thinking in terms of self-identity we seem to face the stark alternative; eventually "I" become nothing at all, or—what seems virtually the same in value terms—a heap of dust, or I survive death in some heaven or hell, or in some new animal body in which I have further experiences of a scarcely imaginable kind and for even the bare possibility of which I have no clear understanding or evidence. Thinking in terms of concrete momentary states of experience, the alternative is quite different. Concretely I am not a mere self, the same through change, but a "society" or sequence of experiences, each inheriting its predecessors, so far as memory obtains. But our human memory is very selective and for the most part highly indistinct or faint. Thus, shortly before death, even though we are fully conscious, the wealth of experiences we have already enjoyed is almost entirely

lost to us. Death is merely the definitive form of a lack of permanence which pervades our entire lives.

The basic question of "transience," as Whitehead profoundly and perspicaciously insists, is not what happens to our identity at death but what happens at every moment to what we were the previous moment. As Santayana put it, every moment "celebrates the obsequies of its predecessors." Santayana saw also, though not so clearly as the Buddhists or Whitehead, that the concept of substance, at least in the form of individual identity, is not the illuminating one at this point.[4] The concrete permanence, if there be one, must be something very different from self-identity as we human beings have it. For that is, at best, an extremely partial preservation of the actual quality of life.

If death means that the careers we have had become nothing, or a heap of dust, what is history about, or biography? And what is autobiography, if the past experiences and actions are now reduced to mere faint and partial recollections and a few records, photographs, and the like? On this hypothesis, the very idea of truth grows problematic. Truth about the past, it seems, must be one thing, and truth about nothing, or about humanly accessible traces of the past, quite another. Thus the great doctrine of the "immortality of the past," found in Bergson, Peirce, Montague, Whitehead, and some others, is an answer not simply to the frustration we tend to feel in thinking about death and the mutability of all individuals, but to the puzzle of historical truth, the most concrete and inclusive form of truth.

My personal view is that the complete rational aim is the service of God, whose future alone is endless and who alone fully appropriates and adequately appreciates our ephemeral good. What some term "social immortality" is literal immortality only so far as God is the social being who is neighbor to us all. For he alone is exempt from death and able to love all equally adequately. He is the definitive "posterity."

The egoist, I have been arguing, subordinates the concrete to the abstract, the whole to the part, the really inclusive future to a limited stretch of the future, and is in a poor position to see the meaning of life and death. This meaning is that the passing moment is, first, self-enjoyed, valuable in itself, and beyond that, so far as it is rational, an intended contribution to the future of sentient life, or whatever part of that life it can best hope to enrich with itself or its consequences. The future career of the same individual is normally a prominent part of future life as proximate receptacle for the present contribution. But the ultimate receptacle of values must lie beyond any one human career, and even, I hold, beyond human life as such. Of course the self, and its future, is interesting. But how much else is interesting?

Long ago I made my decision: No one will ever compel me to shut myself up in a prison of self-interest; compel me to admit that others are for me mere means and myself the final and absolute end. In that case how ghastly an affair my death should appear! And how seriously I should have to take every misfortune to myself, and unseriously every misfortune to others. "Writhing in delusion"—what else is it? But many a philosopher and many a theologian, tragic though this be, has in effect told us that such is the rational way. How grateful we may be to the Buddhists, and to Whitehead, and to the Judeo-Christian insight (indeed the insight of every great religion), when taken at its best and not explained away, for showing us another possibility!

True enough, saying that one rejects the primacy of self-interest does not prove that one is living unselfishly. But it might help at least a little to strengthen our generosity, and weaken our self-serving, self-pitying tendencies, if we gave up the theoretical adherence to self which disfigures so much of our philosophical tradition and opened our minds to the really inclusive cause we can all serve, the future of life in all its forms, human, subhuman, and (if we can conceive this) superhuman.

4. The radical abstractness of mere self-identity is obscured if one takes the view that by a certain individual, say John Smith, one means the John Smith career, a certain sequence of bodily and mental states from birth to death (or perhaps beyond), as forming in some fashion a unitary whole. Actual bodily or mental states are concrete; but until an individual is dead his career is, to common sense—and, process philosophers hold, in truth—only partly concrete or actual. What has occurred in a person's life constitutes an actual or definite career; but the future is a matter of more or less abstract or indefinite potentialities and probabilities. Only a doctrine of the absolute predetermination of the future can equate what makes a man himself with what actually happens to him. Shall I not be myself tomorrow whether I do just this or that, and whether just this or that is done to me? To deny

this (and Leibniz for one denied it) is to burden one's thought with a radical paradox. For then, the moment John Smith exists at all his entire future history is already real fact. A man's notion that he, and not someone else, could have done otherwise than he has done and that he faces real options for the future, not foreclosed by his character as already formed plus circumstances, must then be taken as illusion. Process philosophers think it more sensible to take the Leibnizian view as the illusion. But then self-identity is indeed incurably abstract; for (like every abstraction) it is neutral as between concrete alternatives.

5. Another illusory basis of egoism is found in a certain view about the relations of God to the temporal process. One of the commonest ways of conceptualizing the difference between deity and other forms of being is to say that, while nondivine beings undergo change and are affected by what has happened around them, God is immutable and immune to influence of any kind. It then follows that the good we can hope to contribute to the future cannot be a value we would thereby confer upon God. For, on the hypothesis, deity can receive nothing, being timelessly complete or self-sufficient simply in itself. And so the harvest we sow must be reaped, its benefits collected, either by ourselves or by others than deity or the supreme reality. But what reason is there to think that these others will in the end escape final destruction? Also, what reason to think that posterity, so far as there is one, will always continue to benefit from our lives in their concrete actuality? Finally, what does it mean to say that our achievement will have contributed something to the happiness of many lives benefiting from our having lived as we have if these many happinesses are scattered about in innumerable consciousnesses? The sum of many pleasures, many happinesses, each in a different state of consciousness, is not itself a greater pleasure or happiness, for it is not a happiness at all. Many apples are not one very large apple—though they are a large quantum of apple flesh and much more useful than just one apple for several people wanting to eat apples. But of what use is happiness, after it has occurred, except to contribute to further happiness? Our achievements "add up" to something only if there is an inclusive consciousness which enjoys them, which values their having taken place. A merely timeless and wholly self-sufficient deity cannot meet this require-

ment. In many writings I, and other authors, have defended a different conception of deity.

Orthodox Hinduism (if there is such a thing) meets the problem of motivation by denying that it exists. It holds that, finally, there are no human selves or careers, but only the one infinitely blissful immutable Brahman. The rest is, to the seer, in some sense mere appearance, or like a forgotten dream. This solves the problem by dynamite, as it were. And why is the problem worth solving if there never was such a problem? What does it really matter whether we accept or reject Hinduism, since in either case nothing has really happened? Verbally one can talk in this way, but the mere fact of continuing to talk contradicts what is said, or at least fails to express it. I hold, with James and Peirce, that a doctrine is merely verbal unless our living can show that we believe it. But how can there be a way to show by living that we believe we are not living, that is, not changing, not reacting to influences from the past in partly determining the future?

Buddhism has never quite committed itself to the doctrine of Maya; or, at least, Buddhism in what I regard as its best forms has not done so. We are to find the permanent and the all-inclusive in the midst of change. Reality is not merely impermanent and localized; but still it is really so. There are these two aspects in a mysterious unity. But the distinction real-unreal is not the key to this unity. The key is rather this: that the actual, concrete self is much less permanent and self-sufficient than Hinduism took it to be, so that all regard for the future transcends self as concrete actuality. The Bodhisattva works for the salvation "of all beings."

Charles Peirce spoke of the "Buddhisto-Christian religion." I believe that the "meeting of East and West" must be chiefly on the Buddhist side of the heritage of India, together with those forms of Hinduism which are not orthodox, taking Sankara as the classic of Orthodoxy. The Gita, fortunately, is somewhat ambiguous and can be taken either way.

Egoism is an illusory doctrine, although the real plurality of careers is an ultimate truth. It is, however, an incomplete truth, the other side of which is that, as the identity of a career is abstract, so is the nonidentity of the diverse careers. Concretely, the momentary states or selves are the realities; but, to have a rational aim beyond the present, they must regard themselves as contributory to future selves generally, no matter to what careers these may belong, in the faith that all lives whatever are embraced in or contribute to a mysterious but real and abiding unity. This unity some Buddhists perhaps, and more easily Christians, Jews, or Mohammedans, may wish to characterize as the life of God. Others prefer a vaguer description. The essential is that the aim of the individual should in principle transcend its own future advantage and take the whole of life into account.

II. Ethics and Freedom

Many writers have argued that the only freedom needed for ethics is lack of constraint in making and executing choices. If an act is fully voluntary, not done under duress or threat and not while the agent is hopelessly intoxicated or impassioned, it can in the ethical sense be considered free, even though the choice was entirely determined by and in principle predictable from antecedent conditions. Nay, more, it is held that such determination is required for ethical responsibility, since acts not determined by character and conditions would be irrelevant to the judgment of persons as good or bad. It is said, too, that since all events must be caused, and since also we have to consider man as ethically obligated, we must believe that moral freedom and determinism are compatible.

With James and many others I reject the foregoing reasoning as it stands. But the issues are somewhat subtle. I agree heartily that voluntary action demonstrates freedom and that any determinism which could possibly hold of a being making conscious choices is compatible with that freedom. But I deny that unqualified determinism could possibly hold of conscious beings. Indeed, with Peirce and others, I deny that it could hold even of inanimate nature. The proper meaning of "all events are caused" is not "all events are fully determined by causes." The proper meaning of cause is necessary condition, a *sine qua non* of a phenomenon. But, granted that all necessary conditions for an event have been fulfilled, it follows, not that the event will, but only that it *may*, take place—unless by "event" one means not what actually happens in all its concreteness but only some more or less abstract kind of event to which the happening belongs. "Effects" as strictly implied by the sum of necessary conditions are less concrete than actual happenings. Conditions set limits within which the abstractness, that is, the indeterminacy, of the implied effect is resolved into the concreteness of what in fact happens. With this understanding I agree that there are no "uncaused" happenings; yet I reject the notion that there are any antecedently determined yet concrete happenings. The statistical character of most natural laws as now known is relevant here. But I hold, with Wigner and some other physicists, that the quantum uncertainty in inorganic systems is not the only limitation upon determinacy; rather, in organisms, especially the highest ones, there are further limitations to causal predictability or orderliness, though even there the limitations are presumably sufficiently slight to give science plenty of scope in searching for order in phenomena.

Of course character is expressed in acts; but each new act creates a partly new character, and character as already formed implies only a certain range of probabilities and possibilities for action. Each moment we shift, for good or ill, this range. This view does all the real work of the deterministic absolutization of the relation of settled character and other conditions to conduct. Absolutes are needless and worse than needless in most problems, including this one. Often the very people who profess to be skeptical of absolutes also defend absolute determinism.

Freedom in the full sense means more than just voluntariness, and no voluntary animal is free in that sense only. Freedom in the full sense means creativity, resolving antecedent, though mostly slight, indeterminacies. Creativity is not, taken generically, unique to man, or indeed to animals. As Peirce, the mature Bergson, and Whitehead believed, it applies even to atoms and particles. But the animals have higher degrees and vastly more significant forms of creativity. Yet even in them the causal limitations are always real and important. We can, apart perhaps from rare climactic moments, shift the probabilities of future action only a little each fraction of a second. That is why life is "real and earnest." We are forever influencing our probable futures. But we are never simply determining them. The future will determine itself.

The reasons for accepting the qualified determinism just outlined far transcend ethics. They also transcend the specific questions arising from the present state of microphysics. It is not possible to do justice to them here. I am deeply confident that unqualified determinism is false, but my reasons for this confidence must be sought, if anyone is interested, in the many writings, including my recent book *Creative Synthesis and Philosophic Method*, in which I have set them forth.

One consequence of the doctrine of universal creativity is that no conditioning, whatever Skinner may believe, will put an end to conflict and frustration. Where free beings interact, there must always be real risks of more or less painful disagreement and opposition. Apart from God, every free agent is fallible, both in understanding and in ethical goodness. Hence neither destructive folly nor destructive wickedness can be ruled out by any institutional arrangements. True, the degree of freedom can be diminished and hence the scope of risks reduced. But the limit in this direction is to make human beings almost as lacking in intensity of consciousness as the lower animals. Intense consciousness means, as Bergson rightly saw, a higher than usual degree of freedom, a greater scope of options for action. To trivialize risks by reducing freedom means trivializing opportunities also.

Obviously Skinner would think of the foregoing paragraph as a good illustration of the bad effects of the belief in creativity. I see his point. But I think he is missing the very meaning of concrete existence. Here the existentialists are indeed right.

However, while the search for a risk-free utopia seems vain, I heartily support the search for a better system of risk-opportunity, more appropriate to our technology than we have now. For instance, the freedom to own handguns is not at all necessary to intensity of consciousness. More important, the freedom for each national group to be judge in its own cause, with no group really judging for mankind, is clearly obsolescent and needs to be combated with every educational and political device we can find or invent for this purpose. The 100 percent American, or Russian, or what-have-you, is an enemy to all of us. We need an element of world citizenship in each person. There is no other way effectively to counterbalance the major evils and dangers of our day, whether atomic war, pollution, unjust extremes of rich and poor, or the coercion of one group by another. Moreover, I think Skinner has helpful suggestions as to how needed social changes can be made. Positive reinforcement is indeed far better than negative. My chief quarrel with Skinner is that it seems obvious that reinforcement is not an unqualifiedly deterministic concept, since it implies causal probabilities, not necessities. What Skinner is really asking us to do, and we need to try to do it, is to shift the probabilities for the future. Conditioning is a fundamental reality. We all agree on that, even though it is very true that some underestimate its importance. Skinner is merely overstating a good case. In this he has a virtual infinity of precedents.

III. MAN, THE OBLIGATED ANIMAL

Man is a thinking, speaking animal. "Thinking animal" is scarcely sufficient, because it is arguable that some other animals can also think, in their humble fashion. But a speaking animal, in a normal use of the word "speaking," can think to a degree not closely approached by the other terrestrial creatures. Man may not, in any very high degree, be a rational animal, but think he does, throughout his waking and dreaming life after infancy. We have now to show that a thinking animal is either ethical or unethical—it cannot be neutral, or simply nonethical.

All higher animals, indeed, it is arguable, all animals, are in some sense and degree social. An animal is more or less interested in other animals. No one who has kept pets can be in doubt about this. Moreover, the instinctive patterns of behavior divide into those that tend to preserve the health and safety of the individual and those that, though they may somewhat endanger the individual, tend to secure the persistence of the species after the individual is dead. Under special circumstances instinct may even produce actions directed to the benefit of individuals of other species. But the extent of such extraspecific service is narrowly limited. And of course the instinctive provision for future results beneficial to the species is largely outside the animal's awareness. Birds building nests, at least for the first time, presumably do not know the reason for this activity. In sum, though subhuman animals act not simply for their own benefit but also for that of other animals, yet, so far at least as their own awareness is concerned, they do this only within very narrow limits of space, time, and kinds of animals benefited.

Thinking on the scale that goes with language produces a change so drastic that it is only quibbling to argue whether it is a difference of kind or of degree. For some purposes at least it is a difference of kind, or if you prefer, a difference that makes all the difference. If thinking does not extend the scope of other-regarding actions infinitely, it does extend them indefinitely. The moment we decide on a limit, we shall have come in sight of passing beyond that limit. We can, in some sense and degree, care about other human beings, wherever and whenever they may be; we can sympathize with the trodden insect, with characters in fiction, with "all sentient beings." We can also inhibit or not strongly feel sympathy for anything but ourselves and perhaps a few others. Indeed, we can largely confine our sympathy to our present self and its immediate or near future, neglecting the months and years to come. Thus we stand before the option: shall we or shall we not generalize self-regard to take the entire personal future into account, *and* generalize regard for others to include the futures of the entire circle of creatures whose welfare depends upon our actions? To use thinking to effect only a little extension beyond instinctive limitations of interest in the future of self and others is an arbitrary restriction of the thinking process. To speak is to be at home with universals. Not just tomorrow concerns me but my life as a whole, and not just that one human being which I am, or my little circle, but human beings generally, so far as I have dealings with them or can influence them. Indeed, not human life only but life as such is the final referent of thought. Here the Asiatics were right against the Western tendency to limit value to humanity.

In the foregoing, apart from the last remark, I am agreeing with Kant: The ethical will is the rational will, the only form of will appropriate to a thinking animal. Conscience is practical reason.

It is sometimes held that ethical obligations are only to other individuals, not to oneself. With Kant I hold this to be a mistake —except in the sense that, taking God into account, there can be no such thing as a strictly solitary individual. But, however that may be, one's present self has duties to one's future self as truly as it has duties to other human beings. To be enlightened, thoughtful, in one's self-interest is truly an ethical requirement. Mere impulse will repeatedly pull one in directions contrary to this requirement, just as impulse will pull one in directions contrary to the requirement to give heed to the needs of others. To be deliberately careless of one's own needs is unethical for the same reason as carelessness about the needs of others; for such behavior springs from failure to generalize the instinctive sympathy of present experience for potential future experience, whether of self or other.

Ethics is the *generalization of instinctive concern*, which in principle transcends the immediate state of the self and even the long-run career of the self, and embraces the ongoing communal process of life as such. The privilege of thought carries with it the sense of a goal that is universal and everlasting, not merely individual and temporary. It makes the individual trustee for nature at large, in the sense in which nature includes humanity. Anything short of this is not quite ethics in the clearheaded sense but mere expediency, or failure to think the ethical business through.

Of course we cannot design the lives of others in the sense and to the degree possible in determining our own actions and careers. This is especially true when we are young, with the largest portion of our careers still to be decided. It is much less true in the prime of life and thereafter, for then our own destinies are more fully determined, and our power over others is increased. But at all times it is irrational to set a higher value upon oneself than upon others collectively, for the others are many and we are but one. Adler may possibly be right in saying that "do gooders" do less good than harm to others. Even so this is relevant only to questions of strategy or tactics, of *how* to promote the cause we serve, not of what cause nor why we should serve it. The ultimate principle remains: we care about life, above all life on the conscious personal level, and especially, for the reasons and to the extent just indicated, our own lives. There is also truth in Maeterlinck's saying, "It is necessary to live naively." Too pedantic an insistence upon altruistic considerations may, by destroying spontaneity and zest, make one a less valuable person, both to oneself and to others. Nevertheless the aim is one's total contribution, taking what one is and what one does into account.

IV. THE AESTHETIC BASIS OF ETHICS

Granted that the ethical or rational motivation is toward the inclusive good, the question remains, how, by what rules of action, can the inclusive good be promoted? What indeed is "good," whether mine or someone else's? Here ethics must lean upon aesthetics. For the only good that is intrinsically good, good in itself, is good experience, and the criteria for this are aesthetic. Harmony and intensity come close to summing it up. Being bored, finding life insipid, lacking in zest or intensity, is not good; however, discord, conflict between intensive but mutually frustrating elements in experience, also is not good. Intensity and beauty of experience, arising not only from visual or auditory stimuli as in painting or music, but in experience of whatever sort, are what give life its value. *To be ethical is to seek aesthetic optimization of experience for the community.*

Emerson was wont to speak of "moral beauty," or the majesty of goodness, and he could follow eloquent praise of the beauty of nature by saying that it paled before the beauty of a right act. An ethically good act is good in two senses: it contributes to harmony and intensity of experience both in agent and in spectators. A good will enjoys a sense of harmony between self and others (insofar, virtue is indeed its own reward); and its consequences, if it is wise and fortunate as well as good, will be to enhance the possibilities in the community for intense and harmonious experiences. Obviously cruelty produces ugliness in the experiences of many; genuine kindness produces beauty, directly in itself, and indirectly in many ways. Parents who fail to inspire in children a sense of the direct and indirect contributions of good actions to beautiful, satisfying experiences fail indeed. Moral exhortations and disciplines which make life seem ugly or boring for self and others are counterproductive.

The insane are those who unwittingly invent an unreal world that gives them more intense and harmonious—or less inharmonious—experiences than the real one as they are able to see it. All basic problems are aesthetic. The "beauty of holiness" is one of the finest of biblical phrases. And one has only to read Emerson's *Journals* to see that moral beauty was for him a reality. His attitude toward slavery, toward the emancipation of women, and in many other matters earned him the right to emphasize the phrase. He saw the ugliness of male chauvinism when not so many did, and no one saw more vividly the ugliness of slavery. He saw, too, the ugliness of war and aggressive nationalism, though perhaps not the necessity of world government as the only feasible alternative. He saw, though inadequately, the beauty of the scientific vision of nature.

It is an aesthetic principle that intensity of experience depends upon contrast. Since memory is central in high-level experiences, an important mode of contrast is between the new elements and the remembered old ones in experience. Put otherwise, for experience to have much aesthetic value there must be significant aspects of creativity. Now that science and technology have so greatly increased the pace of change in the conditions of living there is bound to be a good deal of novelty in life. But the problem is to achieve intense harmony, beauty, in this novelty, rather than intense ugliness. This requires a new measure of creativity, especially social creativity, and the reform of institutions. Here the young are more or less in the right. We cannot simply go on as we are politically and socially. Somehow we have to make ourselves, our whole citizenry, more courageously aware of the possibilities of altering the really hideous disproportion between rich and poor, both within our nation and between nations. We cannot much longer effectively pretend to practice democracy while elections can be bought by oligarchically controlled wealth, and while millions, especially blacks and Latin Americans, are given little chance of participating in social and political life in a self-respecting way. We cannot much longer effectively work for peace while failing to take any steps toward the world government without which there cannot be anything but cold or hot war. We have to inculcate the sense of world citizenship and of membership in all humanity, not just in some part of humanity. Pollution problems have similar implications.

V. ETHICS AND REFORM

Berdyaev's ethical imperative was, "Be creative and foster creativity in others." Today, social and political creativity have a new degree of importance. I agree, too, with Marxists and some contemporary theologians that the driving force for needed reforms must come in substantial measure from the less fortunate. As has been said, the ones to change the system are "those who dislike it." But the fortunate, those who are lucky and successful in providing for themselves and their families, need to learn to dislike the present arrangements vicariously, because of their injustice. History shows that this is difficult and uncommon. Nevertheless, it is an ethical imperative. For those with bitter personal grievances are dangerous reformers if given no help or guidance by those who are more disinterested. This is a central ethical problem. The successful middle class needs to consider carefully how far, if at all, it ought to side with the rich rather than the poor. And the rich, including the richer nations, need to realize their ethically perilous position. The New Testament judgment on wealth has, I believe, more validity than we Americans have ever been willing to grant. Emerson observed that the wealthy systematically voted for the wrong things and against every needed reform. We have to resist the natural tendency of those who have "succeeded" to attribute their success to ethical superiority alone or essentially (as though anyone ever achieved anything without a liberal portion of good luck) or to view those who, by the crude standard of wealth, have succeeded as most worthy, and the economic failures as least worthy, of respect or trust. Complex as these matters are, and granted various qualifications, the basic principle holds that the fortunate tend to overrate the rules of the game (including the tolerated violations) and resist their revision to meet new conditions, while the unfortunate are more willing to attempt this.

Technology has finally destroyed the possibility of an easy conservatism such as worked well enough among primitive tribes and fairly well even in early modern times. Now we must change our ways, and it seems foolish to expect those (including myself) whose personal position pleases them to furnish the chief impetus for change. Yet even they are under obligation, I suggest, to try to understand that their own needs are not the measure of the common good and that some discontent of a vicarious sort would become them. So long as no real end to cold warfare—always threatening hot warfare and to some extent already involving it— and no end to race conflict or to bitter poverty, even in this nation, is in sight (and no end is in sight), we have no right to be content with our procedures. We have to look for better ways.

One further point. I agree both with some of the young and with many Asiatics that we Americans need to revise our shamefully materialistic concept of the "standard of living" so that it is no longer so nearly neutral or worse than neutral ethically (and indeed aesthetically), consisting in large part of preferring conspicuous waste and minor comforts to essential values of health (of which the automobile has in some ways been the enemy), natural beauty, friendship, good feeling among citizens, creative activity, and intellectual and spiritual progress—all of which beyond reasonable argument are more important to achieving that beauty in life which is genuine success.

A Frenchman has coined the phrase "voluntary austerity" to express the idea that there is now a new ethical value upon not demanding for oneself and family all the luxuries at once, a demand which intensifies all our dangers and evils, including the evils of inflation and pollution and the danger of war. The old ascetic and monastic ideals are not necessarily irrelevant, nor is the notion that the really good person is modest in his or her claims to share in the products of human labor and the creativity of nature. In this regard Americans in general are far indeed from the model the world needs to copy. It is in some ways our very selves that we need to recreate.

NOTES

1. A. N. Whitehead, *Adventures of Ideas* (New York: Macmillan Co., 1929), chap. 20, secs. 1-8; *Process and Reality* (New York: Macmillan Co., 1929), chap. 2, sec. 2; also Charles Hartshorne, Paul Weiss, and Arthur W. Burks, eds., *The Collected Papers of Charles Sanders Peirce* (Cambridge, Mass.: Harvard University Press, 1931, 1958), 1:673, 8:82.

2. M. J. Adler, *The Time of Our Lives: The Ethics of Common Sense* (New York: Holt, Rinehart & Winston, 1970).

3. Michael Scriven, *Primary Philosophy* (New York: McGraw-Hill Book Co., 1966), pp. 229-301, esp. 250-72. For Adler's qualifications to the self-interest thesis see *The Time of Our Lives*, pp. 4, 6, 13, 15, 173-74.

4. George Santayana, *The Life of Reason*, one-volume edition (New York: Charles Scribner's Sons, 1953), 5, chap. 8, pp. 462-63.

SUGGESTED READINGS

Hartshorne, Charles. *Creative Synthesis and Philosophic Method*. La Salle: Open Court, 1970.

——— *The Logic of Perfection and other Essays in Neoclassical Metaphysics*. LaSalle: Open Court, 1962.

19 *Dimensions of Freedom*

BERNARD M. LOOMER

A very deep sense of the interplay between rela-
tionality and solitariness undergirds Professor
Loomer's discussion of freedom. The reason that it
is so difficult to account fully for our decisions is
that we *are* our decisions; we do not simply make
them. Our selves are the creations that emerge from
decision. Professor Loomer feels that Judas Iscariot
and Paul of Tarsus were psychological and spiritual
twin brothers, wrestling with the question of whether
God's will could transcend the established great vision of a people. The free decision made all the difference: Paul "said yes, and became the incredible
mind and spirit of the early Church. . . . This is the
mystery of freedom, the transcendence of the emergent self whose mystery is finally opaque to analysis."

Freedom is a composite notion. Its ingre-
dients consist of several contrasting, interdependent, and overlapping dimensions of meaning. Its unitary
meaning is complex and synthetic rather than simple, where simplicity is understood in the classical sense of being without parts.
The unity of freedom is complex because of its close relationship
to the concreteness of actuality wherein unity is always complex
and never simple.[1]

No one dimension of the composite meaning of freedom either exists or appears by itself. Each has its being only in the context of others. Each is what it is in part because of its relatedness
to other dimensions. These elements are distinguishable even
though they are not separable within the life of an individual.

The meanings of these dimensions of freedom are not reducible to each other. In order to be most fruitful, discussions of

323

freedom should identify the specific facets of freedom under consideration. Otherwise confusion, unnecessary contradictions, or apparently irresolvable conflicts may emerge.

If the following analysis of freedom is more rather than less adequate it perhaps would find application in any large perspective, but it should find its most likely home in process modes of thought. At any rate this latter orientation is both presupposed and exemplified in the following discussion. More specifically the social nature of man is assumed but not fully elaborated in this analysis. The focus is on the subjectivity of experience where freedom has its primary center. Also the discussion is limited to the nature of freedom in man.

Freedom as Self-Creation

An individual is largely created and determined by its past contextual world of objectified and efficacious causes. Efficient causes function so as to reproduce themselves. Their creations largely resemble themselves. (In Whitehead's language, the initial stage of a process of synthetic unification is basically conformal in nature.) Yet the individual is an emergent from these causal relations. What emerges is in part determined by the self that emerges. This is the freedom of the individual as self-caused, as *causa sui*, as self-determination, as subjective self-creation. This dimension of freedom is an emergent that is coterminous with the evolution of the individual as a synthetic unification of its prior determining causes.

Freedom is not the absence of cause, in contrast to the determining causes that have initiated the process leading to the birth, development, and final fulfillment of the individual. The notion of the total absence of cause is quite meaningless as a definition of freedom. Nor is freedom at this level to be understood as indeterminacy. Freedom refers to that capacity of the individual to be its own cause in shaping itself. It is its self-causative response to its prior initiating causes. Consequently the individual may be described in terms of *what* it makes of what it has been given. In more existential language the individual may be understood in terms of *how* (Whitehead's subjective form) it responds to its environing world.

This dimension of freedom can be looked at from another perspective. Freedom refers to the individual in his self-centeredness, in his wholistic unity. Freedom in this sense is not a quality of one aspect of the self, for example its will. Freedom is a characteristic of the unity of the total self, a unity that is reflected in all the parts of the self. Self-centeredness has reference to the capacity of the self to act out of its integrity in contrast to its fragmentation. It is the self in its unity where it acts out of itself as a unity and where the actions of the parts reflect this unity. It is the ability of the self to act as a unified whole that permits each of its parts to play its proper role, in contrast to a self that is psychotically or even neurotically dominated by one of its basic impulses. In the latter case the unity of the self is distorted by the usurping power of the rebellious impulse.[2]

The presence of self-centeredness is the basis for a moral and legal sense of responsibility. The relative absence of self-centeredness (or its presence to an insufficient degree) results in the diminution or, in extreme psychological states, the loss of freedom, and the consequent withholding of approbation or culpability in terms of responsibility. But except in cases of serious brain damage or crippling emotional injury the individual is looked upon as free and therefore responsible as a self-creating and centered agent.

This dimension of freedom is not incompatible with the predictability of behavior, insofar at least as this involves the integrity of the self. One may predict, in general even if not in detail, how a free man will act in a certain situation, not because he is externally determined but because he is internally determined in accordance with his own principles or his integrity. In this respect freedom means that "he is his own man."

Freedom as self-creation can be stated in yet other terms. Freedom refers to the self's decision. The self *is* its decision. The self as its decision is what it makes of what it has been given to work with (Whitehead's "givenness"). The self as its decision is its stance in a world into which it has been arbitrarily placed (Heidegger's "throwness"). It is how it responds to its possibilities. The self has been largely determined by its past. In its freedom it cannot move much beyond the limitations (which are also possibilities) inherent within the causes that brought it into being. But the small advance it can make at any point is very important. Freedom is a moment-by-moment affair. The self's decision is its freedom and the basis for the conscience of its responsibility.

The self in its freedom, in its self-creation, is its uniqueness and its mystery. The self in its freedom cannot be reduced to its conditioning causes. Its decision is not simply a function of its motives, however vital they are in the constitution of the self. The choice of the self cannot be explained. The decision cannot be rationalized. The individual cannot tell another, finally, why he made the decision he did because he *is* that choice, that decision. In answer to the question as to why he made the choice that he did the individual can only reply that he is the person who made that choice. If he could "explain" his decision, he would be a function of his explanation or his motives. He would thereby have lost his freedom, his self-creativity. He would also have lost his selfhood and his own mysteriousness.

Freedom cannot be explained—except by itself, and that is no explanation. Explanation in this instance would involve analyzing freedom (or decision or choice) into elements more fundamental than itself. (Or as the tradition would have it: freedom presupposes itself.) As self-creation it is an emergent, but as an emergent it is not reducible to or an epiphenomenon of its antecedent conditions.

The extension of this point leads to the generalization that the course of history cannot be rationalized by any logic, except the "logic" of arbitrary decision whose source lies within the unfathomable depths of the individual who cannot explain his decision even to himself.

Freedom as self-causation means that the individual is free whether he opts for good or evil. Judas Iscariot wrestled with the question whether God's will could transcend the established great vision of a people. In this conflict Judas said no, and entered into our history as a paradigmatic example of a man whose decision led to his self-destruction. Paul of Tarsus, Judas's psychological and spiritual twin brother, said yes, and became that incredible mind and spirit of the early Church. Why these decisions? The answer is silence, unbreakable and unfathomable silence. This is the mystery of freedom, the transcendence of the emergent self whose mystery is finally opaque to analysis.

This dimension of freedom roots in the notion of individuality as a surd that is not simply a collection or synthesis or universals. A pattern of forms (such as Whitehead's "abstractive hierarchy") is not exhaustive of the content of a concrete and formed individual. But actuality is not just the realization of the possible. There is no possible individual because individuality is not a possibility. The actual individual cannot be envisaged. Individuality is a concrete emergent from the process of actualization that utilizes possibilities as factors of formation.

The individual is not a mode of God's being or his action. Within the relational context upon which he is dependent and from which he is an emergent, the concrete individual is independent. God may act, but so does the individual. And when the individual acts it is really he who is acting in that moment and not God, even though in the larger context God may also be acting at the same moment and his action may include and be entwined with that of man's. Each individual begins his momentary existence by an impulse from beyond himself, but in the process of actualization the impulse becomes his. The enabling grace of God, in its action, stops short of usurping the self-creative activity of the individual.

The price of freedom is solitariness. The individual has his being in social relations that are constitutive parts of his concrete actuality. Yet as a communal individual his actuality is unique and solitary. His solitariness in the midst of social relations at the human level is a reflection of his ontological solitariness. This condition is almost unbearable for some people and they apparently are willing to sacrifice their freedom by trying to lose themselves in others. (This effort is one step in the movement away from authentic existence in Heidegger's thought.) The solitariness of freedom is different from loneliness. Loneliness can be overcome by concrete relations with other people. Solitariness cannot.

This ontological solitariness that is a quality of freedom as self-creation is also the basis for the sense of privacy. It is also the foundation for the various freedoms enumerated in the democratic Bill of Rights which is designed to protect the value and the privacy of the individual.

Self-creation is the basic mode of freedom. It is foundational for all the other dimensions. Without freedom as self-creative decision, self-centeredness, and self-determining choice, the other dimensions or modes would have only the appearance and not the concrete substance of freedom. Self-creation comes the closest to being the all-inclusive meaning of freedom. The other modes are dependent on this primary and most concrete manifestation.

FREEDOM AS SELF-TRANSCENDENCE

The second dimension of freedom could be said to be an extension of self-creation. This is freedom as involving the sense of alternatives to what has been achieved. It is a going beyond, a reaching for the more, a transcending. Perhaps most generally and most abstractly it is freedom as a movement toward otherness, a desiring or at times even a yearning for something other than what has been or is now the case. It is freedom as a restlessness, an urge to become or to create something different. In these respects freedom is a transcending of the past or present self, thus a self-transcendence. When the idea of self-transcendence is united with the notion of the unity of the self we have the concept of "spirit." Spirit is the freedom of the self in its unity.

This dimension of freedom, in contrast to freedom as self-creation, is not always present to an appreciable or significant degree. Some individuals have a sense of "other" but only to the extent that they apparently are content to be "another" instance of what they have been. They are free in the sense of making a decision about the quality of their lives, but the urge toward self-transcendence is quite attenuated (Whitehead's valuation "down").

Even in those individuals whose appetitive drive is stronger there is a plenum of possibilities (Whitehead's valuation "up"). This extensiveness ranges all the way from an impulse for a relatively slight modification to a passionate ambition that is unbounded, including a reach that exceeds one's grasp (or what's a heaven for?).

Freedom as self-transcendence, or the movement toward "other," is present in many aspects of our experience. We experience the injustices and inadequacies of our society and devise utopias in which the evils of life will be overcome and all people will realize the largest degree of human fulfillment. We conceive of non-Euclidean geometries and multivalued logical systems and thereby create new worlds of space and thought.

Children play their fascinating games of make-believe in which they act out the roles of various personalities they have known or spontaneously create. In this way they enlarge their understanding of the social world in which they live out their lives.

Adults as well as children daydream, and in their imaginatively created worlds they march, Walter Mitty-like, triumphantly through life, serene, unafraid, possessors of all needed resources, and masters of all situations. There are artists of the imagination who have given us the world of literature, as there are writers of science-fiction who project pictures of universes beyond our knowing, and who help us to reconceive man's place in the entire scheme of things.

Of all the creatures of his acquaintance perhaps only man is self-conscious. With this gift or achievement man is able to abstract himself from himself, as it were, to regard himself as an object, to look upon himself as though he were another self. This is possibly an individual's most intimate experience of self-transcendence and freedom (where freedom is defined as the sense of alternative otherness).

The capacity for self-transcendence is related organically to man's awareness of himself as a creature with intellect. With this kind of mind he is not only able to apprehend the structural aspects of his existence and to conceive of forms; he can also abstract, in thought, these forms from their concrete embeddedness and embodiment. By virtue of this abstractive capacity (which is correlative with the ability of many organisms to objectify themselves into the future through one or more of their perspectives relative to various standpoints) man is released from the heavy and efficacious concretenesses of life. He is freed, to a degree, from the compulsion to repeat endlessly the past in its fullness.

This dimension of freedom finds striking exemplification in Whitehead's thought. In that system the subjective forms (the "hows") of physical feelings are conformed, whereas the subjective forms of conceptual feelings are autonomous. Stated in other terms, how the individual reacts physically to his environing world is conformal to what (the object) he physically feels. How he responds conceptually is determined by his self-creative activity. This bit of autonomy is part of the elbow-room of self-transcending freedom. This free act is the ground for the emergence of conceptual novelty whereby we are enabled to progress from an old idea to a new idea without any intervening physical experience. In Whitehead's perspective this conceptual novelty is the means for the re-creation of physical energy without which we would sink to lower levels of creative activity.

This dimension of freedom is of course illustrated in larger social contexts. One of the dominant characteristics of American life has been the economic, political, and social mobility of its citizens. They have not been confined to the limitations of the conditions of their birth. They have been able to rise to educational and financial levels beyond those of their origins. Despite discriminations against minority groups and contemporary abuses of this mode of life, mobility is still an important facet of our freedom of action. It has enhanced our sense of human dignity.

Freedom as alternative otherness is the core of our concern with the media of communication, the freedoms of speech, press, and assembly. This concern is allied with the conviction that truth as well as justice are better served in the context of alternative viewpoints that are expressed. The habit of being open to divergent understandings or even opinions is a vital ingredient in the art of living better. The competition in the marketplace of ideas is still an essential quality of our democratic way of life. Without this dimension of freedom one of the foundations of democracy would be undermined.

But freedom has qualities of heights and depths that reach far beyond the levels of the discussion to this point. We owe a contemporary awareness of these magnitudes primarily to the sustained brilliance of Reinhold Niebuhr. Freedom is a self-transcending, a movement toward the more, the beyond. But for many or some individuals freedom is also a soaring expansion of the self, a movement toward the unbounded, the unlimited, the other as an indefinite other, or what the tradition refers to as the infinite. Man's spirit contains the quality of insatiableness. Some thinkers within the Christian tradition define the image of God in man in terms of his freedom, his self-transcendence, his aspirations to become God-like. Man's freedom is at once his greatness and the source of his sin.

This insight involves the recognition that no predetermined limits can be placed on modern man's development. There are limits, but these cannot be ascertained in advance. Many previously accepted limitations have been transcended. Once the communal order and bonds of medieval life were broken, an energy was released in Western history that transformed, at first gradually and then more radically, the entire life of Western man. There are natural, historical, and ontological conditions that man is apparently powerless to alter radically or overcome completely, conditions that modern man is reluctant to acknowledge and to accept existentially. (The reiterated Niebuhrian emphasis that every advance in goodness or creativity brings with it the possibilities of greater evil, and understood in the full sweep of its implications, is a case in point.) His refusal or inability to accept these limitations is itself one kind of evidence of the expansive quality of his spirit. Even his illusions portray not only his naiveté (and stupidity) but also the restless surge of his outreach.

Man's freedom is not a capacity of one aspect of himself. It is an outreach or a restiveness that belongs to the unity of his being. Therefore the quality of insatiableness that is characteristic of the freedom of his spirit is exemplified in every aspect of himself. Freedom that is a movement toward the indefinite infects every impulse and need and gives to each the quality of having no point of satiety. The desire for knowledge, power, sex, prestige, wealth, security, and love may have no determinable level of unsurpassable satisfaction. These desires may quickly become inordinate in their claims and not easily subservient to rational control. This quality of freedom complicates the already baffling problems of human relations and fulfillment.

Man is a communal creature, interdependent and partly autonomous. He has a deep need for a creatively ordered society. He lives in the context of relationships. Yet in the outreach of his freedom he may imagine himself as independent of relations and quite self-sufficient. The inordinancy of his impulses and drives may lead to the disruption of necessary societal connections. It can result in the creation of massive inertial destructive forces. In the expansiveness of his freedom he often fails to recognize the limitations of his strength, and thereby his virtues become vices.

Interestingly enough freedom is related to the competitive aspects of our communal existence. In his movement toward the indefinite more, the individual may strive for excellence, even perfection. He may desire to be the best, the first, the champion, the conqueror. In this ambition he enters into competition with his fellows, for he must determine his place in the hierarchy of those who share his goal. The ensuing ambiguities are not adequately amenable to persuasive resolutions.

Ideally, freedom may be conceived as functioning so as to enhance the relational aspects of life. It can and sometimes does lead to a finer sensitivity and a less-defensive openness to others. In our greater freedom we may enable others to acquire the courage to become more free. In our deeper relational respon- siveness we may become more loving agents in the transformation of the stature of our neighbors (as well as ourselves). All this and much more is possible, and desirable. But freedom may and often does become the servant of quite different ends. This is part of the fascinating and bedeviling character of the self-transcendence of freedom.

FREEDOM AS POWER

Freedom as power is the capacity to actualize. It is the abili- ty to effect, to bring possibilities to concrete realization. It refers to factors both internal and external to the individual that deter- mine the level and degree of his fulfillment. The conditions of lim- itation are also the conditions of possibility. Enabling factors leading to actualization contain their own circumscription.

An individual is not free to become anything he theoretically chooses to be. The fantasy world of a Walter Mitty is a long galactic mile from the rude overwhelming life of his concrete ev- eryday existence. A man (or a community of men) may dream of a world at peace where justice flows like a mighty river and where all men are brothers, and may labor to bring it to pass. But the concrete fulfillment of the dream, if it comes at all, lies in a future beyond our present power to effect. This limitation of our power is one point of difference between freedom as power and freedom as self-transcendence. It is also a mark of distinction between freedom as actualization and freedom as self-creation. A person may be free in his self-centeredness to create himself, but he may not be free to the same degree to choose or alter the conditions that set limits to the fullness of his concrete life.

People differ in their capacities in every dimension of life. Yet each of us lives out his days and nights under limitations of energy, strength, intelligence, sensitivity, openness, and the cre- ative power to establish, sustain, and transform relationships. Our lives are at once solitary and societal and therefore relational in character. Our aloneness is experienced within the perimeters of a necessary social context. Thus each of us finds part of his identity by locating himself within the hierarchy of power inherent in each major dimension of life as this functions in the local and wider societies in which we live. (Within my local community I may be known as an outstanding violinist. In the national and international world of musicians I may be judged as quite average or even mediocre.) The question whether we find these limitations and their concomitant relational evaluations endurable or not is itself a matter of freedom.

In predemocratic forms of society the order of life was to a large extent derived from the basic inequalities of power, and therefore of freedom, found among its members. Democratic societies, in the interests of obtaining greater justice and of enhancing the power and fulfillment of all their citizens, have increasingly established conditions and laws to offset the kind of social order derived solely from these inevitable inequalities.

The determination of the inescapable limits of our freedom as power is itself an indeterminate affair. It is an ancient wisdom which tells us that we will not know until we try, that no man knows what he can endure until he is faced with a situation he must endure if he is to survive. This is wisdom and not simply the bland suggestions of an untested and unscarred optimist trying to counsel a person who may be confronted by some rather grim realities. Persistence toward a goal in the face of formidable obstacles and against the tide of opinion that says it can't be done, especially by the one trying it, sometimes results in success. Sometimes it does not. The running of the four-minute mile was always a theoretical possibility—that is, it wasn't an intrinsic impossibility. But it became a real possibility only after Roger Bannister actually accomplished the feat.

It is a widely shared knowledge that most of us most of the time utilize only a fraction of our available powers. In terms of traditional forms of thought we could say that challenging situations do not call out of us resources we did not have. Rather these relational demands free us to actualize what we potentially are. In terms of process modes of expression we might say that an individual is a different person in different relations and contexts. The office, as we say, creates the man.

Our freedom is restricted by inadequate or wrong-headed understandings. It is often reduced in range by our refusal or seeming inability to adopt different standpoints and thereby achieve different perspectives. But our freedom as power is perhaps crippled more because of our psychological blocks and hang-ups. In our fear or anxiety or weakness in the face of concrete relational reality with its threats and promises we shrink the range and level of our openness to experience. We adopt compensatory neurotic or psychotic defenses to protect us from the full blast of the storms and glories of life. Perhaps these protective crutches are necessary. Perhaps none of us is able to encounter life directly or meet it head-on. These devices may enable us to endure, to survive. But they block us from living better and from enlarging our freedom.

Possibly no one of us is able by himself to weaken the power of the shaping and restricting influences of our neurotic contrivances. Perhaps most of us at bottom are divided selves with respect to our organic willingness to endure the suffering involved in our evolution toward greater freedom. Even if we are partially so desirous, we may need the enabling presence of those kinds of relations with others that give us the courage to relinquish our tenacious grip on our self-created security.

Freedom as power, in partial contrast to freedom as self-transcendence, entails the commonsense notion that we should take care to actualize those real possibilities close at hand even while we dream of distant things to come. The point is not trivial. Freedom as transcendence is enhanced by our envisagement of glories that beckon us from the horizon of our ideals. But extended concentration on the distant future may dilute our freedom as power. Part of the politics of freedom consists in the realization of proximate goals. This process may appear to some to be nothing but a series of compromises. But apart from the empowering actualization of what our hands and minds find to do in the creative present, the distinction between theoretical and real possibilities becomes somewhat academic.

Furthermore, apart from the consideration that the present will inevitably more closely resemble the immediate past than the remote future, we should not attempt to shape the present too much in terms of a more ideal future. The future is unclear and indefinite. Ideals are projections from the present. They appear to be clear because they are abstractions. As projected abstractions they cannot possibly take account of concrete novelties that emerge in the variegated processes of history. The future is the complex set of anticipations, hopes, and expectancies of the present. It is a direction and not a content. The present needs to be shaped up to a point by final causes. But this influence must be counterbalanced by the emerging power of the free present. By nature final causes are permissive of alternative modes of fulfillment. They are also subject to transformation by the emergent goals and values derived from the freedom of concrete achievements.

Freedom may be limited or furthered by the unforeseen consequences of our own actions and those of others. These consequences are unforeseen and unforeseeable because actions are subject to emergent developments beyond our intentions. Actions once undertaken may alter whole contexts and sets of relations, giving rise to unpredicted conditions that may pleasantly surprise or devastatingly confound us. Niebuhr's delight in pointing out the baffling ironies of history is a case in point.

We are communal individuals. This means not only that we exist in society. The society exists in us. The basic structures of our society both enlarge and circumscribe our freedom. We feed upon others in all aspects of our existence. To generalize the connotation of popular health advertisements, we are what we eat. We mostly conform to our relational and constitutive contexts. These contexts in which we live, move, and have our being include the virtues, vices, injustices, and estrangements of our common life. An individual may transcend his society to a degree (and this distance is important and decisive) but he does not have the power to be completely untouched or untainted by all the ambiguities and estrangements in which he necessarily participates.

The theological implication of this dimension of freedom is that sinlessness cannot be claimed for any Christological figure. The goodness of life does not come to us through completely pure agents or unambiguous arks of the covenant. The insistence that we may eat only when the food is totally refined and is served by one whose hands are antiseptically clean is moralism of the most destructive kind. It condemns us to a thin diet. It also lessens our capacity to appreciate the good and do battle with evil.

The growth of freedom as power involves the grateful and deep acceptance of our individual and collective pasts with all their limitations. Acceptance does not mean either acquiescence or the conformal compulsion to repeat the past. But unqualified hatred of the past or rebellion against it usurps energy that could be used to actualize positive goals that transcend the limitations of the past. The key to the enhancement of freedom with respect both to the preservation of the best and to the transcendence of the best and the worst of the past is gratitude. It is also the spiritual and humanizing mechanism that helps us to release and redirect the enormous amount of energy normally given over to our self-preoccupation.

The relation between freedom and gratitude leads us to one of the deepest topics in Christian Western history. This is symbolized by St. Paul's confession: That which I would not I do, and that which I would I do not. The simultaneous affirmation and denial of man's freedom recurs throughout our theological tradition. This proposition is a contradiction only if freedom is understood univocally. Luther's doctrine of the "bondage of the will" is finely illustrative. This interpretation of man's predicament did not mean for Luther (as again Niebuhr pointed out) that the self is not centered in itself or that the self is not free over its impulses. It meant that the self is free in the sense of being its own cause, but the self is in bondage to itself. The self is concerned with itself in the form of selfishness. The self is the center of its world and of its commitment rather than God. Consequently the impulses of the self (its drives and desires) reflect the unity of the self in its basic denial of God.

This doctrine meant that man is free to choose evil but not the good. As a centered self, man is free in the sense of being internally determined, but he is not free to choose and actualize the good because he chooses to serve himself. He lacks the power to move toward the other in love, in this instance God and the neighbor. This is the condition of sin. In being internally free the sinner can move toward the other, but the other exists simply as a means to the sinner's selfish end. He does not truly love the other, and consequently his movement toward the other does not establish a true relationship that involves the good of the other, including one's service to God.

The overcoming of sin requires, in Luther's doctrine, the grace of God in Christ. The enabling grace of God does not destroy man's freedom as self-centeredness or as self-creation. But it does break the self's preoccupation with itself. In this snapping of the chains of self-concern the sinner is enabled to move toward the other in the spirit of a more genuine concern for the other. Here, again, the key to this release is gratitude to God for doing for us what we are unable to do for ourselves. The gift of grace must be accepted in true thankfulness.

FREEDOM AS COMMITMENT

This dimension of freedom is a material extension of freedom as power, especially the power to actualize the good. It has to do with what one is bound to, or the object of one's commitment, or the direction of one's trust. Here freedom is correlative with the good or the true or, better, the true good (whatever the authentic good is understood to be). Freedom as commitment can be understood to mean freedom as true fulfillment of the self, or as true selfhood or true self-identity.

St. Paul speaks of freedom as slavery to God's will. Slavery in this connection may be understood not as a forced and powerless subservience to a master or tyrant. It can mean a self-chosen devotion or a grateful trust or a loving obedience. The good to which one is enslaved may be God's will as seen in Jesus Christ. It may be the true self, where this is defined as the image of God in man or as the mind and heart of Christ. The true self may be thought of as the essential self (Tillich) or as the self in its own freedom (Sartre).

In any case the good, in service to which one finds his authentic freedom, usually, or perhaps always, refers to some enfleshed goodness or to some reality actively at work in our midst. The true self or true good is usually not an ideal arrived at theoretically. It is a reflection of some historically embodied goodness that becomes a norm for our thoughts and actions.

Freedom as commitment does not mean that one's choice is free if he chooses either good or evil, or if one chooses to accept or reject God's grace. Freedom as commitment means that one is free only to the degree to which he is "enslaved" to the true good. In this respect freedom as commitment stands in contrast to freedom as self-creation in which one is free in choosing either good or evil.

This distinction is important and not trivial or academic. Sartre, among others, has argued that Christian obedience to God is a denial of man's freedom because it involves a subjection of the individual to the arbitrary will of another. Consequently one must give himself to his own freedom if he is to be and remain free (and truly human). This consideration would have force if

God in his actions toward man did not respect man's freedom as *causa sui*. But in the theological tradition even God's enabling grace stopped short of usurpation. In process thought God's activity is one of the efficacious realities from which the individual is a free self-actualizing emergent. This need not mean that God is indefinitely patient with respect to man's decisions. God's purposes may transcend man's. And in his freedom to actualize these purposes God may by-pass an individual and leave him destroyed as a consequence of his own decision to serve only himself.

It is decisive for man's humanity that he be free to create himself by his own decisions. But freedom as internal determination is neither an absolute good nor the whole of freedom. The fulfillment of man's humanity involves more than his freedom to be his own man and to make mistakes. Man as a self-determining agent can destroy himself and make his planetary home unlivable. Man's true humanity requires for its realization the power to choose and actualize what is truly good for him and his environing world. This process requires all the dimensions of freedom.

It is true that man could not be free in the full sense, and thereby fulfilled, if the God whom he serves were totally alien to man or wholly other. The doctrine of the image of God in man implies, if in fact it does not overtly state, that in some sense there is a continuity between God and man. God is the final end and cause, and yet he is not at all times an enemy to his creatures, even though his appearance as such is a real experience in the lives of many who try to serve him.

The theological tradition has usually defined the image of God in man in terms of freedom, to be sure. Unfortunately the quality of freedom involved in the image has too often been confined to freedom as transcendence. It has not included freedom as an openness to participate more fully in the relational aspects of our common life. In short, the image has not been seen as love. Love is the substance of life, the beginning and the final end. Freedom is its willing and unwilling handmaiden. We are not to love in order to be free. We are to be free, fully free, in order to love more completely. The free gift is a greater enlargement of love than a contribution that is forced and leaves us bitter and empty.

In the evolution of man and his world, the dialogue between God and man continues and deepens. God in his freedom wrestles with man in order that man may actualize himself in all the dimensions of his freedom. The story of this relentless wrestling match cannot be completely written as yet. Surely the outcome is uncertain. The price of liberty may be eternal vigilance. The cost of freedom for both God and man is the joy and suffering inherent in that kind of love which creates and transforms those relationships in which freedom finds its true service and good its fulfillment. The symbol of the cost of freedom is the cross.

NOTES

1. If freedom as a concept has an overarching or undergirding simple unity that manifests itself in seemingly diverse guises, I find that I am unable to define this simplicity to my own satisfaction.

2. In this dimension of freedom self-centeredness does not mean egotism or selfishness. Egotism refers to the object of concern. Self-centeredness is a way of speaking of the organization or the ordering of the self.

SUGGESTED READINGS

Niebuhr, Reinhold. *Nature and Destiny of Man* (2 vols.). New York: Chas. Scribner's Sons, 1949.

Whitehead, Alfred North. *Process and Reality*. New York: Macmillan, 1929.

20 The Price of Greatness ("Ford to Nixon")

BERNARD M. LOOMER

This reflection, even though historically dated, is included both because the memories of Watergate are still close, and because the experience is still being digested. But the more important reason is that it illustrates the need for religious experience to nourish political experience. "Confession" and "absolution" are not merely personal affairs—they have a proper place in the affairs of state where reconciliation is equally a condition of unity and of greatness. Professor Loomer has a long-standing interest in the American experience, in what it and Christianity have to say to each other that is of significance. Here Christianity speaks to contemporary American experience.

We the American people stand at a decisive moment in our history. As a nation made up of representatives from most of the countries of the world, and as a community of people who are the inheritors of the original American dream, we have arrived at a major crossroad in our odyssey as the people of a covenant. We can either achieve a greatness beyond what we have realized before in our history, or we can continue our present downward path toward mediocrity. The decision as to which direction we take rests to a considerable degree on one man.

Our situation may be set forth in terms of a proposed encounter between President Ford and President Nixon in which President Ford makes the following proposal to President Nixon:

Mr. President, I have requested this audience with you because I desperately need your help. I am unable to function adequately as the President of the people. My hands are tied and I

341

am not able to loosen the ropes that bind me. Only you can free me.

But I am not speaking only for myself, Mr. President. The people are not free. And they cannot undo their bonds. Only you can release them from the chains that were forged out of the Watergate affair and its repercussions. Only you can unite them. Only you can overcome the divisiveness that exists within each one of us and among us. Only you can heal the wounds of the spirit of the people that are crippling us and draining us of our national strength. These wounds are running sores, Mr. President. The infection of the poison of evil is still rampant in the body politic. The poison must be removed and the wounds cleaned so they may heal. And only you can do this.

In order to fulfill my constitutional obligation as President to restore tranquility to a troubled people, and in order to ease your own anxious spirit, I extended to you an absolute pardon for any wrongdoing that you committed or may have committed. I did this in the absence of any confession of guilt for evil acts on your part. But my presidential act of pardon did not bring either tranquility or unity. I had hoped by this act of pardon to put our dark immediate past behind us so we could tackle the awesome problems facing us with a renewed energy of creative good will. But this renewal has not occurred, Mr. President. We are a divided and frustrated people. The darkness in our past is still in our midst. Only you can remove it.

I stated to the American people, Mr. President, that only I have the power and the opportunity to restore tranquility to our people, that only I through an act of presidential pardon could overcome the bitterness and the corrosive cynicism. I see now more clearly that my act, however constitutional, was not sufficient. I attempted to do what only you can accomplish.

My act of forgiveness was not effective. It was not efficient in that it did not and could not bring the desired result. I acted from a clean conscience and, I hope, a good heart. But my action was mostly futile because forgiveness without an adequate confession of guilt is like attempted therapy without the acknowledgment of sickness by the patient. The willingness to forgive should not be contingent on the wrongdoer's confession of guilt. Hopefully a willingness to forgive may enable the guilty to confess. But the fruitfulness of forgiveness is absolutely dependent upon the confession of guilt. Without confession there is no health or peace or reconciliation either for the guilty or for those sinned against.

Mr. President, I need, the people need, and I believe you need your public confession of guilt for evil deeds committed.

You have, of course, my continued assurance of a full and complete pardon.

I think I am aware of what I am asking of you. I think I appreciate what your public confession would cost you. It would bring you a suffering greater than any you have ever known or dreamed of undergoing. Its range and intensity would far exceed even the agony of your resignation of the presidency, the brokenness of your dreams and ambitions, and the despair and emptiness of your present exile. You will experience it as the ultimate in shame. In your mind it will mean utter disgrace and complete loss of face. It will appear to you to take away the standing you hope your name will bear in the history of the American presidency. To you it will symbolize the final defeat of all you cherish and all you have worked to achieve. In short, to you it will mean total ruin.

Believe me, Mr. President, if there were any other alternative open to me I would not make this seemingly impossible request of you. I can only guess at the courage required to respond in the affirmative. Yet the needs of our people enable me to summon up enough courage to dare to ask you to do what you may think is the one thing you must not and cannot do.

I am concerned about the future of this great country you love, as I am concerned about the future of your name in history. We have been and we are a great people. I hope that the American dream is still alive. But our greatness is being radically reduced in size. We need to become again a united and free people. But to restore our greatness we need great leadership.

It was President Lincoln who taught us the cost of the unity of a people, the price of greatness in the face of great wrongdoing. He showed us in an unforgettable way that the struggle to actualize a towering vision involves the supreme sacrifice, the giving of one's life. No lesser cost can purchase the needed health and sanity of a people. Through the life and death of this one man the needed reconciliation of a divided nation became possible.

Mr. President, I am asking you to reconcile us as a people by an act of confession. It will seem like death to you, but I assure you it will be a fuller life for all of us, including yourself. This better life, if it is to come at all, can come only through you.

The price of unity is enormous. But the gains will be commensurate to the cost, I assure you. You will have the deep gratitude of myself and the American people. You will also have the forgiveness of the people who are not demanding blood but who do require a catharsis of the spirit.

You will be able to walk the streets of this country with dignity and honor and security. You will be free to leave the exile of your own imprisonment.

Mr. President, if you accede to my request I deeply believe that future generations of Americans will accord you a place in the history of the American presidency that will exceed your fondest dreams. It will go far beyond the position you have earned through your efforts to establish peace between ourselves and the Russian and Chinese people. Through this act you will become in truth more the president of this nation than you ever were when you occupied the office. In contrast to your present experience of defeat and despair, this act will enable you to grow in stature in the hearts of the people. You will not need to fight to defend and preserve your place in history. It will be given to you freely and gladly. To paraphrase Mr. Churchill, this act would become your finest hour.

When, in the history of man, has a great and powerful nation ever confessed to its own sin? Through your act of confession and contrition this nation would be able to do so to the world of our fellow-men. Your act would be your act, but not just yours alone. We as a people are bound together in our common situation. Your act would be our act of confession. Through you a new tradition of human political leadership would be established. It has been said that to err is human and to forgive divine. It needs to be added that to confess and to forgive are also deeply human. They are in fact essential requirements of the human spirit. They need to become elemental characteristics of adequate and humane political leadership. We do not ask for perfection. We do ask for and need sizeable stature in our leaders. Without this we will surely perish as in fact we are now doing.

But beyond all this that I have said, those who will experience the greatest gain will be the people. We will be cleansed and renewed and given a new spirit. At one stroke we will be restored to our honored place of leadership in the family of man. We will be freed to tackle our staggering problems. Beyond this we will be freed from our self-preoccupation. All our basic problems are global and not merely national. All our answers must be global in scope. To play our role in global affairs we must be released more fully from our own imperialistic impulses. We need to confess as a nation to all the peoples of the earth. In this act creative energies beyond what we have known can be unleashed.

If you respond affirmatively to my request I propose a general amnesty for all those involved in the Watergate affair and for all those alienated by the Vietnam war.

Mr. President, for your sake, for my sake, for the sake of the American people and on behalf of all men everywhere, I ask for your confession.

SPIRITUALITY

John B. Cobb, Jr.
Bernard Lee

21 *Spiritual Discernment in a Whiteheadian Perspective*

JOHN B. COBB, JR.

It is commonplace, if not trite—because it is so obvious—to observe that religious understanding and religious experience have undergone drastic alteration in our recent generation. Nor are we out of transition. Yet it is increasingly the task to sort out what has been going on, to identify patterns and movements, and above all to discern the spirits that move us. To some extent, Professor Cobb offers "prophecy" in this chapter, not in the sense of foretelling a future, but discerning how we`should live now so as to be open to the future. He is interested in seeing what "death of God" theology, liberation theology, human potential theology, etc., have to say to us with the help of discerning critique.

John B. Cobb, Jr. was born in Japan of Methodist missionary parents. He was educated at Emory University, the University of Michigan, and the University of Chicago where he received the Ph.D. from the Divinity School in constructive theology. He has taught at Young Harris College, Emory University, and since 1958 at the School of Theology at Claremont and the Claremont Graduate School. He is an ordained minister in the Southern California-Arizona Conference of the United Methodist Church. His publications include A Christian Natural Theology, God and the World, *and* The Structure of Christian Existence. *He coedited with James M. Robinson the "New Frontiers in Theology" series and is coeditor with Lewis S. Ford of* Process Studies. *Professor Cobb is also Director of the Center for Process Studies.*

The thesis of this essay is that in the situation that is now emerging, the Whiteheadian understanding of God's action in us and in our world can give helpful direction to new forms of spiritual discipline. This situation is arising out of the confusion of the decade of the sixties and can best be viewed against that background. Hence, Section I surveys the theological events of the sixties in the effort to find pointers toward a new religious synthesis; and Section II offers reflections on the possible Whiteheadian contribution to the spiritual formation in the context of such a synthesis.

I

During the sixties, paralleling the decline of interest in the churches, there was a dramatic growth of interest in topics with which the churches have traditionally dealt. For example, while Church-initiated programs for college students declined drastically, courses in religion boomed. Similarly, while prayer meetings and other pious exercises disappeared from the life of many a conventional congregation, young people engaged in an intensive and often disciplined quest to learn methods of meditation and to gain religious experience.

There were many ironies in the situation. As our churches became secular, our culture grew religious. As our churches sought relevance through social action, our culture withdrew into individual experience of consciousness-expansion and deepening. As ministers learned techniques and even goals of counseling from secular psychologists, whole segments of secular psychology were merging into the religious quest abandoned by the Church.

The churches' failure to meet religious needs is in part the result of our general theological failure. In times when the Church knew what it had to say about man and God, the implications of this message for personal life and worship were fairly clear. But when the Church has no definite idea of its distinctive shared convictions, its criteria become effectiveness and relevance. Since the leaders of a congregation have no consensus as to what the mission of the Church may be, the common point of reference is found in the congregation's growth and vitality—or at least survival. With those criteria, churches engage in whatever activities people find sufficiently interesting and beneficial to bring them to church and to support the program.

The central theological question in the sixties, as in every age of Christian thought, was the question of God. In much of the literature this fact was obscured, since many theologians found it easier and more relevant to write about man rather than God and even to avoid what was called "God-language." But the theologians of the death-of-God saw clearly how important for Christian faith this reticence was. When theologians speak the name of God with embarrassment or avoid it altogether, then indeed God as experienced and believed reality is, in Martin Buber's language, "eclipsed," if not dead. With this eclipse it is understandable that the churches lost their bearings and failed to give guidance to the spiritual quest.

The conservative response to those who proclaimed the death-of-God was that what had died was one image of God. That response was too facile. It implied that another image of God, usually that of the speaker, was alive and vital, whereas in fact that was not true. For example, those of us who had earlier learned to think of God in the way process philosophy and theology have taught, under the influence of John Dewey, Henry Nelson Wieman, and especially Alfred North Whitehead, felt that we had already taken adequate account of the problematic posed by the death-of-God theologians and could even be glad that they were helping to overcome the neo-orthodox image of God against which in particular they were reacting. But it was not true that we had learned to speak of God in an effective and persuasive way, even if intellectually we could defend what we had to say. We had had little impact on the actual meaning of "God" as that word functioned in the Church or in the wider culture. The death-of-God theologians were correct in asserting that what was actually meant by God by the majority of Christians had been emptied of conviction and reality. Defenders of belief in God can reply that there is some other reality that a few people name as God, but the critique exposed their position—in this case I should say *our* position too.

Hence, even those of us who felt that we had conceptually dealt with the problematic of "God-language" found ourselves caught in the same bind as the Church as a whole. If God was to become real again for thoughtful Christians, conscious of the cultural currents of our time, other changes in outlook would be required.

Several lines of development seem to be converging toward a new possibility of speaking authentically of God, even though none of them stresses that word. These are first the future orientation of what is sometimes called the hope movement; second, the continuing interest in the human potential movement and in altered states of consciousness; and third, the various liberation movements. I will deal with them briefly in that order.

Christianity was originally a strongly eschatological movement. That is, Christians lived in vivid expectation of the new age. They associated the God whom they worshiped chiefly with the future. They saw the past and the present in light of what they anticipated. But, without abandoning belief in a coming End, the Church gradually subordinated this future orientation in thought about God to a past and present orientation. God was thought of primarily as the one who is above and who, from above, has acted in the past in creation and redemption. This does not mean that at one stage Christians doubted that God was above or had acted in the past and then came to doubt that he would act in the future. The point is that the dominant image of God changed.

In the period between the two world wars this change was heightened. Especially under the influence of existentialist thought, the present moment became the all-important time. Interest in the past and future was regarded as distracting from the decision that could be made only in the Now. The imagery with respect to God's action was "perpendicular from above." That is, God was thought to be known in every moment as the one who *now* gives and demands while remaining radically transcendent. It was above all the image of height whose collapse was rightly announced in the sixties.

Alongside the images of height had been images of depth. Tillich especially had given new life to these images from the mystical tradition. But depth like height was bound to the present moment. Bishop Robinson in his famous *Honest to God* opted for God in the depths against the God who is up there and out there, but in the course of the decade energy flowed in another direction.

In Catholic circles the figure who dominated the sixties was Teilhard de Chardin. Teilhard's vision locates the present inside a vast movement of cosmic history toward a final consummation. He does not talk much of God, but his vision locates the divine in the energy that draws all things into a final redemptive communion-union. Sometimes that final outcome is itself spoken of as God.

In Germany, there was a marked resurgence of interest in Marxism, especially the imaginative and humanistic form of Marxism represented by Ernst Bloch. Marxism, too, locates the present in terms of its relation to the anticipated outcome. In Bloch's humanistic form it eschews a narrow preoccupation with economics and recognizes the relative autonomy of other dimensions of human existence. It points us to the power of the not-yet as a call and claim upon the present, always freeing us to go beyond what is established toward the genuinely new possibilities of the future.

The sixties witnessed also a marked revival of Hegelianism. Like Teilhard and Bloch, Hegel located humanity within a vast movement toward a fulfilling End. Although Hegel associated the End with the reality of his own time and place, twentieth-century Hegelians have viewed it as yet to be realized.

This climate has been congenial to the reappropriation of the original imagery of Christianity. The theologians who have done so have not always stressed language about God. The idea of the Kingdom of God often seems to them less likely to misrepresent their meaning. But they are telling us that as Christians what we confront as decisive for our lives is not an eternal and never-changing being but a future that judges the present but also beckons and promises and gives us creative freedom and new possibility. This future cannot be conceived as a purely indeterminate openness or as passively there waiting for our decisions. To function as the contemporary sensibility sees it, it must have an ever-changing but definite character in relation to which our decisions are to be made. To function as ultimate ground of reassurance it must have its own mysterious actuality. In describing that actuality it is natural once again to speak of God.

The human potential movement is the matrix in which the second line of development can be found. This movement developed against a strong scientistic tendency in psychology to suppose that readjustment to equilibrium was the grounds of human activity. Psychology seemed unable to talk of any genuine creativity or novelty or growth and even to rule these out. Academic psychologists undertook to explain man reductionistically. Clinical psychologists helped people adjust to social expectations. Humanistic psychology emerged as a third force to proclaim that man can aim at more than adjustment. The human potential movement developed methods whereby this "more than" can be experienced and actualized. Hardly had it begun to do so before religious techniques, images, and ideas came into play. In the burgeoning variety of contemporary movements clear lines can no longer be drawn between psychological and religiously oriented movements.

These movements rarely speak of God. In this way they too witness to the death-of-God in our culture. But they nevertheless may be paving the way for the renewal of authentic affirmation of God. At the very least they are overcoming the major obstacles to such affirmation in the past. They are breaking out of the limited sense of reality that identifies it with the objects of sense experience and supposes it to be exhaustively grasped in the categories of the natural sciences. If they do not speak of God, it is because the image of God in our culture is so bound up with moral obligation and metaphysical transcendence, and perhaps also with the inhibiting and restricting culture from which people are rightly breaking free.

Still what they are finding has a positive relation to God. In many different ways the human potential movement assumes and witnesses to a force for growth and creative novelty that operates in and through people when they allow it to do so. It calls for trust toward the bodily wisdom, the unfettered imagination, and spontaneous feelings, in confidence that when these are allowed to develop the results will be a greater good. This implies that there is a principle of growth working in all things and that to open and adapt oneself to that principle is the means of fulfilling potentialities. In describing this principle, too, it becomes appropriate once again to speak of God.

A third family of movements have in common the idea of liberation. They are closely related to both the future orientation of recent theology and the human potential movement, but they take their stand more concretely in particular historical situations. There are ethnic liberation movements among which the blacks have led the way. There are class and national liberation movements, which have received their fullest articulation in Latin America. And there is the women's liberation movement, which has brought the issues home, quite literally, to all of us.

The direct impact of any movement of liberation upon theology is to bring to consciousness the extent to which our ordinary images of the divine are perverse. We see now that we have worshiped, and still worship, a white God, an imperialist God, and a male God. For some this recognition supports the rejection of any belief in God at all. But for others it has heightened the awareness of the importance of the religious dimension of our existence and of how we conceive reality in an ultimate sense. To acknowledge the ideological taint in our thought of God can lead to rejection of the whole question, but it can also give rise to a fresh chance to think realistically about who or what God really is.

These three movements have in common a refusal to interpret the future as simply the projection of the past. As against the dominant scientistic mentality of the past two centuries, they deny that time is the unfolding of a necessity that is given with the pattern of extant forces. They imply that there is another influence at work in addition to the efficient causation of the past. Human experience is acted upon by possibility as well as by settled actuality, and people are called to act responsibly and freely in relation to that possibility. To name as God that which gives power and relevance to possibility and thus frees us to transcend mere repetition of the past is to speak in continuity with our Christian past and in harmony with our present need.

If this is understood merely to mean that we are now able once again to believe in God without recasting our existential relation to him, it has been misunderstood. When Dietrich Bonhoeffer spoke of man come of age and of God allowing himself to be edged out of the world, he did not mean that God as he exists in himself has changed his spatial or temporal location or his essential nature. But he did very much mean that the appropriate and Christian mode of human relation to God changes, and that the way the Church has often presented the meaning of God's reality in the past is now harmful rather than redemptive.

This is a complex topic, but one central element in it can be lifted up. In too much of the Church's actual effective teaching God has been presented as the sanction for established morality. To sanction and transmit received values and customs is a function that religion has had in almost all societies, and it is not a vicious or evil one. No society can survive without accepted patterns of doing things that restrict individuals in favor of the communal need and welfare. Such a pattern almost necessarily is spelled out in taboos or laws. Because of their importance and the urgent need of gaining their acceptance by each new generation, they are treated as sacred, and whatever images of the sacred exist are associated with them.

This means that individuals experience God chiefly in terms of demand and guilt. God requires obedience to the law and when people fail to obey, they experience condemnation as from God. Furthermore, the law with which they associate God is the inherited law. Obedience to God and obedience to the elders, especially the parents, are very much intertwined. To worship God in this context is to renew the childish experience of impotence and of acceptance of authority. To that extent it is a renunciation of adult responsibility and of the new ideas and possibilities that conflict with the inherited law and the God who sanctions it. That means that to believe in God and worship him is, for many people, a reaffirmation of the past against the present and the future.

When God is known chiefly in this way, then piety consists in a repeated renewal of one's commitment to the inherited values. When this piety is vital, it entails a deepening and maturing of these principles. People can examine their lives in illuminating ways in light of these received norms and thus learn more about themselves. They can become richly sensitive to the needs of others. Since the values inherited through the Christian community are noble and lofty ones, we should not despise the piety that celebrates them and seeks a personal and loving relation to the God who is their author. But such piety becomes the enemy of growth when that growth entails questioning and transforming of the traditional norms themselves.

Fortunately, this conservative element of the Church's teaching has never stood alone. Jesus and the prophets have been the central Christian heroes, and their direction was to challenge rules and ideas that were established in the name, and with the sanction, of God. They experienced God as the one who stood beyond and before the achievements of the past, even the religious and ethical norms of the past, and who called people into a new reality. In the most radical way Jesus invited people to live from the reality of the Kingdom of God that was the Not-yet rather than in terms of the given.

If God is now again viewed by us as the call forward into a new reality rather than as sanction for the old, that will entail for most Christians a deep inner alteration of piety. But we will at the same time be surprised at how strongly the language of the Bible and much of our traditional liturgy support this shift. We will learn to name God not in relation to our guilt but in relation to our willingness to act daringly in spite of guilt. We will give ourselves to God not as a way of giving up the struggle but precisely as a response to the one who calls us into the thick of things without advance instructions and guidelines.

Neither the theologians of hope nor the leaders of the human potential movement intend to celebrate change for the sake of change. Simple rejection of the past is usually not growth but petty rebellion. The call is to build upon the past, to take advantage of its achievements, but not to be limited by it. That means that the call is to novelty in a fuller sense—to that newness that is able both to encompass what is given by the past and to transcend it.

There is a difference in the imagery of the theology of Hope and the human potential movement that makes their synthesis difficult. The theologians of hope locate the principle of hope in the temporal beyond. The leaders of the human potential movement locate the principle of growth in the present within. A piety directed to the future would seem different from a piety directed to an inner principle. But the movements of liberation manage to combine and integrate these two dimensions.

II

At this point Whitehead's understanding of God is peculiarly illuminating, and in the remainder of this essay I want to sketch relevant aspects of his thought and to discuss the further specificity that this can give to the shaping of a new Christian piety.

Whitehead directs our attention to the individual momentary human experience. In this respect he resembles the existentialists. But for Whitehead this momentary experience is the point at which the full richness of its particular past comes to bear, and he encourages us to appraise this inclusion of the past positively. The more of my personal past and of the past of the entire world I can incorporate into my new experience the richer it will be. But the new experience is not simply a product of the interaction of those past experiences. It involves a decision that selects elements from the past for inclusion and emphasis at the expense of others. That decision is the creative act of the new experience and not simply the necessary outworking of the forces from the past.

The decision by which a momentary experience constitutes its own definiteness is made in relation to some aim. Otherwise there would be random chaos, and there would be no meaning. We decide to some end. But when that is recognized it is all too easy to suppose that the end is determined by the past, so that the vaunted freedom of the experience is again threatened. Whitehead, however, does not see it this way. The end in terms of which the new experience actualizes itself in its decision cannot be a repetition of any former end. It must be an end that is relevant to just the past that this experience has, and that past is not identical with that of any other experience. It must be an end that is novel in its particularity. It may even contain elements that were not present in earlier experience, although this is not always the case. The end comes as a lure or call or opportunity from the realm of possibility rather than as an imposition of patterns from the settled past. Furthermore, the end is settled not simply in terms of what will enable that momentary experience to actualize itself and enjoy an optimum of experience but also in terms of how it can contribute to future experiences. In human terms we do not simply seek to squeeze what joy we can from the moment, for we are concerned also with how our present enjoyment will contribute to the future. Much of our present joy involves anticipation of that future, just as much of our present misery comes from dread of that future.

How does this aim enter into the experience if it is not simply derived from past experiences? The answer might seem to be that it is chosen by the new experience itself. But then we would be in a confusing circle. We sought the end to guide the decision. We cannot now affirm that the end is chosen in the decision. No, the end is given by the future, we might say. It is the lure of a specific relevant possibility for the immediate future as that relates to a more distant future. At this point Whitehead does not hesitate to speak of God. It is God who so orders possibility as to render it into a relevant lure for each new experience. In experiencing the ideal possibility for realization we are experiencing God.

This account is still not sufficient. If the decision about how to incorporate the settled past is made in terms of God's purpose for the occasion, then the decision seems no longer free and there appears to be no moral responsibility. But we know that we are responsible. How can that be?

The answer is that God does not compel us to do what he calls us to do. Apart from God's ordering of possibility so as to lure or persuade us to move forward creatively into the future, there would be no principle of decision. Decision would be either determined by the past or random. There is more order and direction and novelty in life than could be explained in that way. But if the decision were determined by God, then we could not explain the disorder, confusion, and evil in the world. Whitehead teaches that the decision is made in relation to the aim derived from God, but it is influenced by all the other factors in experience as well, and finally it is free and responsible.

Whitehead sees that human experience witnesses to a universal "intuition of immediate occasions as failing or succeeding in reference to the ideal relevant for them. There is a rightness attained or missed, with more or less completeness of attainment or omission" (*Religion in the Making*, 60-61). People are finally responsible for the extent to which they embody the normative possibilities given them by God.

Now let us suppose that this Whiteheadian understanding of God could be brought into convincing relationship with the contemporary sensibility. That would have important implications for the development of new forms of piety, for Christian piety is the expression in life of the implications for life of what is believed about God in his relation to humanity.

The primary aim of piety on this view is to conform one's decisions to the possibilities offered by God. That is, of course, in full continuity with the aim of Christian piety generally, which has been "to do God's will." The question is always what God's "will" is and how it is to be known. At this point Christians have differed, and this contemporary account has its own distinctive, if difficult, implications.

The variety of the past can be suggested by abrupt schematization. In much of traditional Roman Catholicism, God's will was known through the received teaching of the Church. If no specific relevant teaching existed, the implication of existing teaching was worked out through casuistry. In much of traditional Protestantism, God's will was known through the Bible. The individual believer was supposed to have an unmediated relation to this Word, although in fact his reading was shaped by the community in which he lived. In much of traditional rationalism, the individual conscience or reason was supposed to contain the intuitions or principles that guide right action in each instance.

Obviously the implications of contemporary thought about God lead away from these legalistic systems. In the past, also, there have been other approaches to understanding God's will, sometimes mixed with these objective ones. For example, the view that God is all powerful and all wise has led to attempts to be passive in relation to God. One might "let go and let God." That sometimes meant that by relinquishing decision to chance, as in the casting of lots, or in closing one's eyes and opening the Bible at random, God was supposed to determine the outcome. Or it might mean that when one emptied one's mind and went limp, God was thought to determine what happened.

Another approach to ascertaining God's will has been an active one. People have used prayer as an occasion for insistently requesting God's guidance. Despite Jesus' explicit statement that we are not heard for our much speaking, Christians have often thought that the intensity of their prayers would result in God's making known his will.

All these practices suppose that God is external to us and that the knowledge we need must therefore be imparted to us from without. There are, however, other traditions that recognize the immanence of the needed knowledge. Historically the Quakers have stood for the confidence that there is an inner light and that guidance comes from within. Situation ethicists expect that one can immediately perceive what love requires in the concrete particularity of a situation. This is not different from Augustine's famous: Love God, and do as you please. Other Christians have felt themselves guided through hunches and impulses and even visions and dreams.

The ultimate implications of Whitehead's understanding of God for piety belong more to this latter family of practices. Whitehead teaches that in fact God's aim is effectively present in every experience. In every moment a decision is being made with respect to it. Of course, this process is most of the time below the level of consciousness or at its fringes. Clear conscious decision in relation to clear conscious knowledge of ideal possibilities is a rare phenomenon. The concern of piety is not primarily directed to this but rather to the continual little decisions by which we are constantly constituting ourselves. Hence the goal of piety cannot be to achieve clear consciousness with respect to the divine aim. What we want is actually to align ourselves with God's purposes rather than to achieve a propositional knowledge of what those purposes are.

But how is this to be done? Conforming action to social expectations and established rules of conduct is generally a good idea and will protect one from egregious error in many instances. To this extent it may be a useful propaedeutic to aligning oneself with God. But any tendency to absolutize these rules must be resisted. Our task is to be sensitive to the particular new possibilities of the fresh moment, and these cannot be derived from anything in the settled past.

On the other hand, passivity will not do either. If one decides not to decide, to whatever extent one succeeds, the results will be shaped by the strongest forces impinging upon one. There is no reason to suppose that the aim derived from God will be stronger than the clamorous demands of the other factors that form the experience. To conform oneself to the changing call of God is not passively to be shaped by him but actively to overcome the forces that block such conformation.

From this we can derive clues as to more positive answers. Our task is to free ourselves from the power of those forces that inhibit our alignment of ourselves with the divine aim which is toward growth in ourselves and others. Each of us knows what some of these inhibiting forces are. For example, we incline to self-justification. We want to be able to approve of ourselves and to that end we need the approval of others. Hence our tendency to bold and creative action is often stymied by our anxiety as to what others will think of us. Likewise when others withhold the approval we seek, we expend our psychic energy in self-pity and rage, refusing to heed the call to let the past be the past and to enter into the new possibilities of the future. In this and many other ways we turn the past into a limitation upon our freedom rather than into a resource for effective action and richer experience.

If we believe that God is in fact present in us as the ground of the deepest sense of rightness, then we will need to trust that sense of rightness, while recognizing that in its conscious form it by no means purely expresses God's aim. If we trust it and act upon it, much as the ethical situationists advocate, we will gradually develop the capacity to distinguish the rightness more clearly. The old advice holds. Act upon the little light you have, and more will be given. Resist such action because the light is so dim and because you want more certainty in advance, and the light will grow still dimmer.

For most of us at relatively advanced stages of moral maturity the primary enemy of alignment with the divine aim is the projection of our own past purposes. We are not opposing to the divine aim strong tendencies toward violent antisocial acts or extreme self-indulgence. Instead, our very moral strength becomes restrictive. We determine to respond in the future as we have responded in the past, that is, to live by rules that have worked for us and to carry out established purposes. This good becomes the enemy of the better. The achievements of one day hinder growth the next day if one tries to repeat them in changed circumstances. Hence one needs constantly to check oneself to see whether one is allowing the actual situations to direct one's fresh response rather than imposing upon that response the patterns of the past.

Although God's aim in every situation is unique and we must avoid trying to deduce it from general principles, there is nevertheless one generalization supported both by the New Testament and by Whitehead. God's aim is always toward inclusiveness both in relation to the past that is taken account of and in relation to the future in anticipation of which one acts. That is to say that empathetic love and agape describe the direction of growth. Both apply first to one's relation to one's own past and future. The more one empathizes with one's own past and has agape toward one's own future, the better. But they apply also to others. The more of the experience of others, human and nonhuman alike, one can empathetically incorporate, and the more of the future of others one can hold in view in love, the better. This love is not a legal requirement, but it is a corrollary of all conformation to God's purpose. One cannot deduce from love what it is that needs to be done, but to whatever extent one sees and feels the situation in terms of empathy and agape, one will be open to what that situation requires. One's purpose will blend with that of God. One can act beyond one's own understanding.

We begin by noting the avid interest in our society in special techniques for self-improvement and for gaining religious experience. The foregoing account of the implications for piety of a Whiteheadian understanding of God has dealt more broadly with a stance toward life. What does this account have to offer those who are seeking to deepen their experience?

The first thing we must say about special disciplines is that the Christian does not have to practice them. They are not means to salvation. God's gifts are not contingent upon them. We are saved as we are and do not earn God's favors.

But the second thing to be said is that we are free to practice special disciplines and to experiment with techniques. It is un-Christian to engage in such activities as a way of freeing or saving ourselves. But when we recognize that liberation or salvation has been freely given to us, then it is fully appropriate to exercise our freedom in disciplined ways. One appropriate way is to pray. The major specific contribution that Christianity can make to the current quest for deeper religious experience is authentic prayer.

The greatest problem with prayer today is the image of that to which it is directed. The reason Oriental religious techniques are so much more acceptable is that they do not presuppose personal communication. The image of God as a person has been closely identified with the God "up there" and "out there," and for the present it is too uncertain and confused to give reality to prayer. Perhaps in time the principle of growth and the call of the not-yet can be imaged more personally. Whitehead can help in that direction as well. Meanwhile prayer need not be dependent on personalistic imagery.

Prayer can be understood broadly to include the whole stance of openness to God and responsiveness to the divine call. This is of primary importance. But in order that any life orientation be strengthened, most people need and want to isolate and intensify it at particular times and places. Patriotism does not consist in singing the national anthem and pledging allegiance. Still, in occasional observances a pervasive stance of loyalty is highlighted and reinforced. Similarly, prayer has its place as a specific practice of intensification of the Christian stance toward God.

The essence of prayer is attention to something one believes to be real and supremely important, and the exercise of the appropriate response. When such belief is lacking, there can be meditation and consciousness-changing techniques, but no prayer. When there is a convincing image of God, there will be prayer in this specific sense. The content and character of prayer vary according to the image.

The exposition I have given of the nature of God's call confirms the ancient association of prayer to God with love of neighbor. In the past, love of neighbor has been expressed in prayer chiefly through intercession. Intercession has thus been the most generous, and perhaps the most Christian, aspect of prayer. Yet of all forms of prayer many find intercession the least acceptable. It is at the farthest remove from the meditation practices that are gaining a wide hold in our culture.

Perhaps we can develop a contemporary form of intercession as a step toward disciplined sensitization to God's call. In the context in prayer we can practice loving our neighbors. This would not consist in overt actions or verbal professions of love, but we would spend time empathetically entering into the life, the feelings, the needs, and the hopes of other persons and consciously willing their good. This is particularly valuable in relation to persons who are experienced as unattractive or as threats.

In order to engage in this activity it is not necessary to ask specific goods for those with whom we empathize, if such intercession seems unreal. But the practice of a loving attitude so strengthens the sense of our interdependence that intercession is a natural outcome. If we do, as I believe, affect one another by what we are and feel as well as by our overt actions and words, then we can help one another to be open and receptive, loving and free, and for these ends at least we can "intercede." Thus the exercise of love, undertaken in order to open ourselves, can become a help to others too, and of course in many instances our behavior toward those for whom we pray will be changed.

But even for those who do not believe that we can help one another in this way, the exercise of love can be meaningful. It can counteract the major obstacle to responsiveness to God's call which is the tension between our narrow interests and perceptions and God's aim at a more inclusive realization contributing to a more inclusive future. It can reduce the contrast between what we want to do and what we believe we ought to do. It can so broaden our concerns as to reduce the debilitating effects of anxiety about our individual futures without reducing a constructive concern about the future in general.

Sensitization to God's call can also be helped by relaxation. Techniques of relaxation are now well developed. Sometimes they are used as a step toward passivity, and that is not the Christian goal, but they can also be used as a means of achieving openness —openness to the present environment, openness to the unconscious, and openness to the body. Instead of subordinating these to our established interests and purposes and projecting meanings upon them, relaxation can enable us to see and hear and feel what is there. Often we discover that what we have repressed is finer than what we have imposed, but the Christian goal is not simply to free all this. It is rather to gain a synthesis on the basis of including what we too easily exclude.

Openness to *what is* heightens our experience of wonder and awakens gratitude in place of resentment and fear. It increases our sense that life in general and in its concreteness is a gift. It expresses itself naturally in prayers of praise and thanksgiving. The recognition of how little we appropriate and appreciate our gifts and of how we have impoverished ourselves and hurt others by our closure expresses itself in confession. But such confession is not a grovelling in guilt. It becomes immediately a joyful acceptance of the more that we have denied ourselves.

None of this should be done if it does not in itself seem to correspond to that rightness in things of which Whitehead wrote. Such correspondence does not insure that prayer will be easy and comfortable, but it does insure that it will not be felt as artificial or inauthentic. Prayer that is forced against the deepest urge within the soul will not lead to the heightened sensitivity and responsiveness to that urge, which is the final goal. This whole procedure is based on the conviction that there is in all experience a trustworthy lure to self-transformation through realization of new possibilities. The purpose of the practice of love and openness is, first, to do what our preliminary understanding of God's purpose asks of us, but finally to become more open to the unpredictable call of God. This suggests that we will take more seriously, although still critically, the impulses, inclinations, images, and hunches that we experience in an attitude of love and receptive openness.

Here arises the next great element in prayer—self-examination. Wherever Christian movements are vital, along with the Spirit of God, other spirits make their claims. Discerning the spirits is itself a spiritual gift. Today in our efforts to understand the sources of our impulses we can be aided by the vast storehouse of wisdom in clinical and humanistic psychology as well as in traditional religious experience. In addition, we need one another in order to test the directions that suggest themselves to us. But finally each stands alone listening for what she or he is called to do.

However, the major way in which we can learn to conform more fully with the highest possibility for our life is not through consciously received impulses. The directive agency of God as the principle of growth and the lure of the future is subtler than that. That it has been effective is sometimes more apparent in retrospect and even to others than in the anguish of decision and action. There is no guarantee of overt success, certainly not of escape from suffering. Yet at some deep level of the soul there is a wholeness or unity that is the measure of spiritual strength.

My favorite religious novel is Bernanos's *Diary of a Country Priest*. Especially because the picture I have drawn is so simplified and even romantic in its depiction of what God calls us to be, I strongly recommend that book. The young priest is sick, and without medical attention he is dying of cancer. He has no special gifts of appearance, personality, and intellect. We would probably not like him. He has few successes visible to him, and some of the consequences of his actions even appear destructive. He prays intensely, but he sees himself as a failure even in his spiritual life.

Yet it is clear to the reader that the priest's heart is pure in Kierkegaard's sense. He wants only to serve his people and thereby to serve God, and because of his single-mindedness he has a redemptive effect on others that he himself does not understand or recognize. He acts beyond his own understanding and intention.

This portrait is exaggerated, of course. God does not call most of us to live in such pain, loneliness, and misery as this priest. But only in that exaggeration does the essential thing about prayer become manifest. The one thing, utterly simple and utterly difficult, the supreme task that is attained only as pure gift, is purity of heart. "Thy will, not mine, be done."

This language of will, however, today misleadingly suggests externality, overagainstness, and even laws. We can better express the point by using another kind of biblical imagery. What we are to cultivate in prayer is an attitude of willingness to be crucified repeatedly to the old self and to rise repeatedly to the new. The continual letting go of every self-image and self-justification by which we live in order to become a new creation is to be enacted in prayer in order that it may be less consciously renewed throughout daily life.

The forms of prayer I have suggested do not presuppose that God is personal in the usual sense of that word. The practice of loving attention to others, openness to one's world, self-examination, and willingness to be repeatedly transformed can even be conducted authentically without any God-language at all. Those who find talk of God disturbing are encouraged to make the experiment. But it is my conviction that, in the process, biblical language about God, and Christ, and the Spirit, and grace will take on new meaning. Despite all changes in world view that separate us from the New Testament, the reality to which it testifies and even much of its language have a remarkable capacity to renew themselves today.

SUGGESTED READINGS

Lee, Bernard. *The Becoming of the Church: A Process Theology of the Structures of Christian Experience.* New York: Paulist Press, 1974.

Williams, Daniel Day. *The Minister and the Care of Souls.* New York: Harper and Row, 1961.

22 *The Appetite of God*

BERNARD LEE

Following the clues of the biblical experience of God, and the understandings of God in Whitehead and Hartshorne, Professor Lee holds that God has an appetite of imposing size—not merely after a manner of speaking, but in *deed* so. It is difficult to see how history can matter really to God if he does not have an appetite for the goodness of its outcome. Human passion and human appetite have not been approached in Christian tradition as a fundamental resource for spirituality, for there wasn't much about eros that was also about God, at least as God was understood. In this chapter, Professor Lee presents process understandings of God that point to his large appetite. And then he deals with three areas of human experience: intimacy, the coercive outreachings of sexuality, and eating food, indicating each as a possible source of religious experience.

One of the most important differences between the interpretation of our experience of God in classical theology and in process theology is that in the latter case God has an appetite of imposing size, whereas in the first case his actuality is all at once and forever complete and fulfilled. God is not really hungry. In that tradition God's intrinsic glory is absolutely complete—it is full. Human goodness adds to his extrinsic glory, of which he has no need. At best, God takes dessert to be polite.

The important thing concerning the process conviction about the appetite of God is that (to the extent that this perception is indeed adequate) the whole appetitive dimension of human experience expresses something real about God and has, therefore, a yield in religious experience not too much explored in Christian tradition. (The courtly and love imagery of some of the mystics, such as John of the Cross, is a scattered exception.) Eros as well

369

as agape is in the love of God. The analogy of divine eros with human eros does not include the essential bodiliness of the human experience. But it is not far afield to process modes of thought (à la Whitehead, Hartshorne, and Teilhard) to liken the cosmos to the body of God. There is not time to dwell upon that here—but such a position does not carry in process thought the problematic of pantheism that is involved in substance modes of thought.

I would like to indicate first that a divine appetite accords with biblical experience. Then I would like to indicate some aspects of the dominant theological reflection in Christianity upon the possibility of God having something added to him (without which it makes no sense to speak of an appetite). Thirdly, using the natural theology of both Charles Hartshorne and Alfred North Whitehead, I would like to characterize the appetite of God. And lastly, I would like to consider three experiences of human eros for the power of those realities to unveil the character of God's love for us: (a) intimacy; (b) the compulsiveness of sexual attraction; and (c) the experience of eating.

THE BIBLICAL EXPERIENCE

The biblical account of God is dipolar. And it was not the character of the Old Testament mind that it felt a philosophical urgency to reconcile the two. Both were "true" experiences, so they stood side by side.

There is the experience of God who does not change—like a rock, which was the metaphor of the unchanging thousands of years before evolution turned even the rocks loose. This God knows all that will transpire long before it becomes historical fact.

There is equally the God who can change and be changed. He can be persuaded by the plaintive voices of Abraham and Moses. "Please spare your children." He can be bargained with. "What if I find ten just men instead of twenty?" He can be embarrassed into lenience. "You made a Covenant with us and the pagans know it. What will they think of you if you do not care for us well?" He can clearly change his mind:

Yes, as the clay is in the potter's hand, so you are in mine, House of Israel. On occasion I decree for some nation, for some kingdom, that I will tear up, knock down, destroy; but if this nation, against which I have pronounced sentence, abandons its wickedness, I then change my mind about the evil which I had intended to inflict on it. On another occasion, I decree for some nation, for some kingdom, that I will build up and plant; but if that nation does what displeases me, refusing to listen to my voice, I then change my mind about the good which I had intended to confer on it. (Jeremiah 18:6b-10)

The mainstream of Christian tradition has tended strongly to get consistency in the picture of God by opting for the immutability of God, and presuming that the other references are anthropomorphisms.

THE MAINSTREAM THEOLOGICAL REFLECTION

Classical theology, molded by the presuppositional conviction that unchangeableness is normative of the perfection of being, selected images of God's immutability and omniscience (which also embraced the future) as the truer metaphors. And the metaphors of God receiving history *really* into his experience and *really* interacting with it could only be man's projections.

In Scholastic theology the distinction is made between a real relation and a logical relation. Real relation implies that someone or something has itself been changed in some way as a result of the relation. Logical relation refers to a member of a relationship which is not changed by the relation. If I read an inscription on a tombstone I receive new information, and I am different after the reading from what I was before the reading. I sustain a real relationship. The tombstone is no different because I read it. It sustains only a logical relation. The inscription makes a difference to me, or better, in me. That's a real relation. But I make no difference to or in the stone. It is unaffected by me. I matter not in its regard.

Since God was held to be absolutely immutable, he could only cause effects. He could in no *real* way be himself affected. He could only give, he could not *really* receive anything into himself. He could make a difference to and in everything. Nothing could make a difference to and in him. And so agape became the picture of God's love. All his giving was with no vested interest, for his actuality could not really receive anything into it. Under this persuasion, agape alone had real sacramental value, and eros was left largely (though not entirely) without sacramental content. I say "largely"—theologically this was so; but at the same time asceticism made certain options for eros, e.g., in some spirituality of marriage (including Paul's), and, as I mentioned before, in some of the mystics.

Process theology offers some possibilities for introducing greater coherence into the human experience of God. It is not a panacea. Not a final word. Later generations will smile, I am sure, at some of the naivetés of our process mythology. But for the moment I am convinced that it is one of the better available interpretive lights to use in the theatre of human experience, and that includes the human experience of God. And after all, the show must go on.

PROCESS APPROACHES

It is not within the scope of this presentation to try to persuade toward the process conviction that "becoming" and not "unchangeableness" is normative of being. I will be working with an acceptance of that presupposition: the process IS the reality, as true of God's reality as of any reality. I want to develop, rather, the implications of that conviction. John Cobb's *A Christian Natural Theology Based on the Thought of Alfred North Whitehead* is an excellent presentation of the philosophical bases of a process natural theology.

It is at first startling (at least it startled me) to hear the statement that the *concretely actual* God is finite. But that would be only half the dipolarity of God as Charles Hartshorne understands it. The other half of the statement is that the *abstract character* of God is infinite, absolutely unbounded. And these two— the abstract character of God and the concrete actuality of God— must be understood in their organic, interrelated and interdefining dynamics.

We have long talked about "rationality" as one of the characteristics of human experience. If you tell me that there is a normal human being named George who lives in your neighborhood, I can conclude that George, because he has the rational character of normal human beings, knows things. That is real information which I have, but it is abstract. For I cannot tell you concretely what he actually knows. But his concrete actuality knows particular individual things. To be real it is not enough to have an abstract character. That abstract character must express itself in concrete, definite, particular ways—actuality is definitely this and not that. Actuality is always individualized, it is de-fined, that is, de-finite. Finiteness is a condition of actuality.

But that is not enough yet. I can go on to say that the character of human rationality is limited and finite. No man can know the whole of reality. Only some small portion. Human knowing, in its character, is necessarily fragmentary. No man can love all people. Only some limited number of persons. Human loving, in its character, is necessarily fragmentary. In other words, not only is human actuality finite, but its abstract character is finite. In this God differs decisively with the rest of reality. It is the character of God to know *all* reality and to love it *all*. His knowing and loving are unlimited—they embrace all that is real. But the "all" which his character as God commits him to know and love is finite. The universe is finite. His actuality is defined (partly but really) by the individual (i.e., particular) finite realities to which he relates with knowledge and love. We—created history—have the incomparable privilege of contributing to the actuality of God in being the real objects of his knowing and loving. The concrete actuality of God is a finite expression of his infinite character—and finite in this context bears no divine shams, for definition and individuality are the condition of being actual. God's concrete actuality is the real historical expression of his infinite character of knowing all and loving all.

We matter deeply, therefore, to and in the actuality of God. There is no way not to have a hankering, be he God or be he man, for that which matters deeply. God has an appetite for us. Given the infinite character of God, his appetite is bound to be immense!

Now to Whitehead, and I must again apologize for the summariness of the presentation. There is some strong resemblance between the Whiteheadian and Hartshornian dipolar conceptions of God, but there are significant (though compatible) differences. Whitehead understands God to have a primordial nature and a consequent nature. And he is careful at one point to insist that we are making a rational distinction and not positing two natures.

In his primordial nature God offers the world the whole of its possibilities, some of which will be actualized and some not. It is a process as well as a Christian presupposition that the movement of history is a creative *advance*. God, in his creative contribution to historical process, does not simply offer possibilities at random—he offers those possibilities that call history to be more, to be self-transcending. These offerings of God, Whitehead insists, are persuasive, and never coercive. The possibilities to be more are offered. It is up to the caprice of the will of creation to be in fact more rather than less. Sometimes indeed there is a less rather than a more. But the overall configuration, as elusive as that may seem in the face of a scarred and bloody history, is that of a more and not a less. The Christian symbols of pleroma and parousia affirm that faith. God offers us the possibility of more. And more than anything he wants that more to happen. But he does not force, or human freedom would not be real. In Bernard Loomer's fine phrase, "The moment of decision-making is ours alone in its fullness. God awaits that moment. He stands behind us, just off our shoulder, and holds his breath."

The consequent nature of God has to do with his standing breathlessly over man's shoulder. The consequent nature is God's immediate and total response to each individual's response to him, that is, to the possibilities he offers each individual for each's self-creation. Here again, because God seriously persuades creation toward its own betterment, he has a desire and a will for it: he has a vested interest in its outcome. The outcome is the real object of his experience, his consequent nature. His consequent actuality is shaped by the decisions with which we shape our own actuality. His interaction with us respects the definite shape that we have decided. He knows and loves the particular, finite outcome of our decision, taking deeper delight in those finite outcomes which mean that some "more" has accrued. Satisfaction rewards the achievement of desires for more, again, be he God or be he man. The appetite of God for the "more" of man is not inconsiderable!

What is common to the dipolar models of Hartshorne and Whitehead is that history really matters to and in the actuality of God. Hartshorne develops especially the unlimited, unfragmented character of God's knowing and loving, and the concrete, finite ways in which the histories that we create are the finite "food" for the infinite "appetite" of the God who knows and loves (food and appetite are not Hartshorne's images). Whitehead pays particular attention to the "more" which is God's design and desire for the world, and to the persuasiveness of God in facilitating the world's achievement of its more. Whitehead uses the word "lure" to express how he persuades. God sets out to be alluring! He entices. In *Adventures of Ideas* Whitehead speaks even of the Divine Eros.

HUMAN EROS AND THE APPETITE OF GOD

Against this background I want to explore three areas of human experience for their yield in religious experience. All three have to do with human eros (only one in the more limited sexual sense). By eros I mean the life instinct, the large sense of the passionate drive for life and growth, and the power of those passionate instincts that derives from their satisfaction. Sexuality is of course the most obvious and immediate, the closest and most assertive expression of eros, but it is certainly not exhaustive of eros.

Anytime there is "something about" human experience that is in some real way "something about" God or how God comports himself with man, there is the stuff of religious experience. But for the experience to become religious experience, the Christian community must bring interpretation to bear upon the human experience. It has been the business of this presentation so far to suggest that process natural theology can generate a hermeneutic that deepens the appetitive life of man as a resource for religious experience.

In what follows I merely want to suggest three such resources, the first of which is intimacy.

INTIMACY

Covenant is the principal metaphor of biblical experience, to the extent even that we have named that written collection of experience Old Covenant (Testament) and New Covenant (Testament). Quantitatively, it is without end. Covenant endures forever. Qualitatively, it bears the marks of tenderness and intimacy: sometimes like that of a man and woman; sometimes like that of a parent for a child; sometimes like that of one for a chosen friend.

There is the remarkable allegorical history of Yahweh's love for Israel in the sixteenth chapter of Ezekiel:

I said to you . . . Live, and grow like the grass of the fields.

You developed, you grew, you reached marriageable age. Your breasts and your hair both grew, but you were quite naked. Then I saw you as I was passing. Your time had come, the time for love. I spread part of my cloak over you and covered your nakedness; I bound myself by oath, I made a covenant with you—it is the Lord Yahweh who speaks— and you became mine. I bathed you in water, I washed the blood off you, I anointed you with oil.

In Hosea, chapter eleven, there is the classic parent-child metaphor:

When Israel was a child I loved him . . .
I myself taught Ephraim to walk,
I took them in my arms;
Yet they have not understood that I was the one looking
     after them.
I led them with reins of kindness,
with leading strings of love.
I was like someone who lifts an infant close against his
     cheeks;
Stooping down to him I gave him his food.

Jesus also addresses Jerusalem in parent image in Matthew 23:37:

Jerusalem, Jerusalem, you that kill the prophets and stone those who are sent to you! How often have I longed to gather your children, as a hen gathers her chicks under her wings, and you refused!

In a single verse in Jeremiah 31:3 quantity and quality of Covenant are together:

I have loved you with an everlasting love,
So I am constant in my affection for you.

In a recent book, *The New Agenda* (Doubleday, 1973), Andrew Greeley recommends that both theologically and pastorally it would be far more fruitful to shift the focus in marriage "From Indissolubility to Intimacy" (that is the title of the chapter on marriage, only one of the topics he treats in the book). He does not in any way demean permanence in marriage as a sacrament of God's Covenant with man, but feels it would best be served by working at those dynamics of Covenant that foster our will to make it never, never end:

> I take it [Greeley says] that it is self-evident that the psycho-dynamics of intimacy are such that there is a strain toward permanency in any important relationship. We simply do not want good things to end. The more intimate the rela-tionship, the greater the strain toward permanency (p. 143).

Greeley develops this insight particularly in relation to marriage. But the experience of intimacy is far broader, of course, than marriage. And in its multifarious appearances it is a possible resource of religious experience.

> In an intimate relationship [Greeley continues] we are chal-lenged to break out of ourselves, to put aside our fears, our anxieties, our uncertainties, our insecurities, and to let others see us as who and what we are so that we may see our essen-tial selves as reflected in the eyes of the other. By permitting the other to challenge us, to call us forth, to strip away our protections, our defenses, our disguises, we run the risk of surprise, surprise that he seems to like what he sees and surprise at that marvelously attractive stranger we see re-flected in his eyes. Being called forth and being surprised are essentially part of the same life experience (pp. 147-148).

It should be part of the function of Christian community to encourage and sustain the experience of intimacy in human life. And equally important, the Christian community is called to proffer that interpretative intuition of faith which can make of human intimacy a religious experience. It does that (among many other ways) by pointing out that the interhuman posture that best facilitates a life of self-transcendence is likewise the posture that opens us most radically to the life of God, that is, the commit-ment to entertain a relationship of intimacy with him.

The religious significance of intimacy, then, is at least two-fold. The God who calls us to be more, to engage always in acts of self-transcendence, can most easily draw us to those acts of growth in him when our intimacy with him exposes us to the deepest levels of his caring. Perhaps for modern man intimacy ought to be a more frontal sacramental metaphor than justice even, or righteousness. Clearly though, and for the sake of realism, sacramental metaphors like justice and righteousness are critical symbols when "homework" must be done in an unjust world as a propadeutic to loving intimacy. But intimacy with God is what we are finally about.

The second kind of religious significance of intimacy is that it is *really* something about God as well as something about human experience. As human intimacy grows and becomes more perfect, we are in an increasingly better position to understand the quality of the appetite of God for us, and the caring which that appetite elicits in our regard. And knowing that, the quality of our response to God is apt to be a larger and more enduring YES. And hopefully, a permanent YES.

THE COERCIVE OUTREACHING OF SEXUALITY

In my book *The Becoming of the Church*, I suggested that availability was too weak a word to speak of God's relation to history. And I suggested the French word *disponibilité* as better. Whereas availability means sitting in your chair waiting for someone to come in, *disponibilité* means sitting with obviousness on the edge of your chair, inviting someone by your very stance to come in and bring you to your feet. I also used the image of a Beckoner who is constantly out front urging us to "Come on," and doing it in a tone of voice or with a gesture that holds the promise of adventure. Whitehead speaks of God as a "lure" to the events of history. And he also insists repeatedly that the action of God is persuasive and not coercive. But it seems to me that the biblical testimony of God's relation to history is far stronger, more assertive, more aggressive, more receptive than words like *disponibilité*, Beckoner, lure, or persuasion are able to convey. I think those images are not askew; they are just insufficient.

It was a few pages on sexuality in Henry Nelson Wieman's *The Source of Human Good* (Carbondale, Ill., Southern Ill. Univ. Press, 1967) that suggested to me some powerful elements of sacrament in the universal human experience of being sexually aroused. It is from that book that I took the title of this section.

Since I have spoken several times of sacramentality, I would like to digress for a very brief moment about the sense of that. When "something about" human experience is also in some genuine way "something about God" (as best as we can fathom him), we can use that element of human experience to put us in touch with the something about God. What I am suggesting in this section is that there is something about how a human being is in a state of sexual arousal that corresponds to something about how God is. This is surely an unaccustomed way to speak of God in Christian tradition. It strains the imagination to use sexual imagery where there is no appetite, and the classical conceptualization of God was quite consistently agapistic. But the reconceptualization of God as one with an immense appetite (and as I have said already, this fits much better the biblical experience) opens the way to touching real things about God in the appetitive and erotic dimensions of human experience. That seems important because it can enlarge our understanding of God. But more than that (and one needs to say over and over again that these conclusions depend upon the adequacy and validity of the process presuppositions), these things seem important because they open the way for developing the sacramentality of the erotic dimensions of human sexuality.

There are three further marginalia scribblings that I want to move into the text of this presentation. First: yes, I am aware of the daimonic character of sexual urgency; there's great danger wherever there's great power. Second: in view of the virtual absence of sexual language in the description of God, I am keenly aware of the boldness of the sacramentality of aroused sexuality (what a student in one of my classes referred to as "holy horniness"). And third: as with all metaphors, just because some elements of a comparison are valid, one must not look for parallel resemblances in each element of the analogate. Carrots are like beets in that both are edible roots; but one mustn't be offended if carrots are not red.

Wieman speaks of human sexuality as the (1) "bio-psychological condition" that (2) "breaks down the egoism which otherwise confines the individual," (3) "and makes him profoundly responsive not only to one other person but to all persons and interests concerned with the loved one" (*op. cit.*, p. 238). The first two elements do not apply to God; it is in the third element that there is something erotic to explore in God's regard. It would belabor the obvious to try to demonstrate that human responsiveness is greatly heightened in moments of sexual arousal, or that the *compulsion* to relate is added into the desire to relate in moments of sexual arousal. Think, for example, of Molly's Yes in James Joyce's *Ulysses*:

> . . . and then I asked him with my eyes to ask again yes
> and then he asked me would I yes . . . and first I put my
> arms around him yes and drew him down to me so he could
> feel my breasts all perfume yes and his heart was going like
> mad and yes I said yes I will Yes.

I am suggesting that Christian faith posits a God who loves the world with such power and such will-to-relate and be-related-to, that in the additional and compulsive power which sexual arousal adds into human desire there is something real about the character of God's love.

In his characterization of sexuality Wieman points to its role in breaking down protective resistances to responsiveness, and speaks of this as the "coercive outreaches of sexuality." Again, it is the latter element of this description that seems to say something about God's relationship with humanity, which is not a mere readiness to take man in, but a coercive outreaching on the part of a Cosmic Lover (to steal a favorite expression of Norman Pittenger) aroused to make love with human history. And it is that aspect of divine comportment that the student I referred to previously called "holy horniness."

I cannot claim to know exactly what Leonard Cohen intended by the imagery of his song, "Suzanne." But the middle stanza, being about Jesus, at least suggests that it might not be amiss to explore the sometimes erotic images of the first and third stanzas for what they say about religious experience. In any event, the song has been used frequently in Catholic liturgies by young people (it was banned specifically by title at one time in the Oakland diocese), some kind of testimony, therefore, to its susceptibility to religious metaphor. For example:

> And just when you mean to tell her that you have
> no love to give her, she gets you on her wavelength
> and lets the river answer that you've always been her lover,
>
> And you want to travel with her,
> and you want to travel blind,
> And you know that you can trust her,
> For you've touched her perfect body with your mind.

As soon as Suzanne gets you on her wavelength there is no forgetting; whereas before you had no love to give her, you are ready to travel with her, ready to travel blind. In the second stanza, about Jesus and mankind, the chorus is almost identical:

> And you want to travel with Him
> And you want to travel blind,
> And you think you maybe trust him,
> For He's touched your perfect body with his mind.

The third stanza returns again to Suzanne:

> Suzanne takes you down
> To her place by the river,
> You can hear the boats go by,
> You can spend the night forever,
> And the sun pours down like honey
> On our lady of the harbour;
> And she shows you where to look
> Amid the garbage and the flowers. . .

It would demean the song to make it subject to this kind of exegesis all along the line (perhaps it has already!). But it is not an unfamiliar story—the things that being in love can do by way of transformation. Who better than our God knows to look among the garbage of our histories to find the flowers and to cherish them enough to discount the garbage. If garbage abounds, flowers superabound (Romans 5:20). Lovers know that sort of thing best.

EATING FOOD

There is a sense in which we have no closer and more intimate relationship with anything in the world than with the food we eat. To be sure, it is not an interpersonal relationship and in terms of important kinds of values for human life (especially in those experiences that are distinctly human), our relationship with food is of course a lower-level relationship. Yet the eating of food remains a unique kind of experience in how we make food part of ourselves. Food is other than we are before we eat it. We take it in (ingestion), we assimilate parts of it so thoroughly that those parts lose their otherness to us, and lose it completely (digestion); then finally, and with no apologies, we discard what is of no use (elimination). So basic, so daily, so inescapable is that experience that the symbolic power of eating food is hardly a surprise. "Identification, introjection, incorporation, is eating. The oldest and truest language is that of the mouth" (Norman O. Brown, *Love's Body*, New York, Random House, 1966, p. 165).

In Freud's psychology the oral stage is the first movement in the development of personality. The eating experience provides the "oral basis of the ego" (Brown, *ibid*.). Although process thought has not dwelt upon the eating experience as a philosophical model, I think the model could be extended beyond Freud's psychological usage to one of metaphysical import. There is an easy transition from "process *is* reality" to the German proverb, "*man ist was man isst*" (a man *is* what he eats). The categories of identification, introjection, and incorporation are easily adaptable to Whitehead's description of an actual entity. An actual entity is the sum total of its experiences. An actual entity does not first exist and then have experiences. Its experiencing is its reality.

The world, for Whitehead, is an interlocked community of events. All actual entities are interrelated. But the world is so vast that most of those "other" actual entities are negligible in their impact. An actual entity constitutes an effective world that is much smaller than the entire world. It does that by identifying what is potentially relevant to its own becoming, of then introjecting those parts of the world that are of value, and of giving them a role in one's own reality—which is, finally, incorporation. "Incorporation" is of course very close to the food model—it means emBodyment.

In a short and unfortunately neglected little essay that appears in *Science and Christ* (New York, Harper, 1968) Teilhard de Chardin extends the sense of "body" in a way that is faithful to process instincts, congenial to Christian thought, and in support of the proverb, "*man ist was man isst*":

> The prevailing view has been that the body . . . is a *fragment* of the universe, a piece completely detached from the rest [of the universe] and handed over to a spirit that informs it.

> In the future we shall have to say that the Body is the very Universality of things, in as much as they are centered on an animating Spirit, in as much as they influence that spirit, and are themselves influenced and sustained by it. . . .

My own body is not these cells or those cells that belong *exclusively* to me: it is *what*, in these cells *and* in the rest of the world feels my influence and reacts against me. *My* matter is not a *part* of the universe that I possess *totaliter*: it is the *totality* of the Universe possessed by me *partialiter* (pp. 12-13).

It is the aim of Hindu asceticism and mysticism to achieve an experience of the real unity of self and universe. The sense of the otherness of things is illusory, and the illusion must be surrendered. One of the Upanishads uses the image of eating the universe (which is done through contemplation). Piece by piece I eat it till there is no otherness left. *"Tat tuam assi"* ("Thou are that.")

Whoever meditates on the universal self as the measure of the span from earth to heaven, and as the same as the self, eats all the world as food, all beings, all selves (Chandogya Upanishad, Bk. V).

All this talk about eating may seem a circuitous route to the Pauline concept of Mystical Body, and to the Christian experience of the Lord's Supper. But I think, first of all, that "that oldest and truest language of the mouth" helps show the intimate connection between the Lord's Supper and the Mystical Body; and secondly, I think that in both regards our understandings are often impoverished (and therefore our experiences) because we are at such remove in those experiences from the delightful sensuality, sociality, and downright earthy pleasure in good meal experiences. Nor is this a defense for gourmandise. McDonald's hamburgers and Howard Johnson's ubiquity are clues to the increasingly purely pragmatic approach to food; it might behoove us to get closer to the far-ranging potential of the meal as a deeply human experience, with much to tell us about who and how we are.

The basic eucharistic symbolism of breaking bread and sharing the Covenant cup is rooted, for its meaning, in the Old Testament paschal meal. But I am suggesting that it is fitting to appropriate these others senses of eating into that context as well. The Christian experience in its totality is one of inCorporating and being inCorporated. We eat the Jesus-event. We identify it, introject it, digest it, and hope that we may be justified in saying: "I live, now not I, but Christ lives in me."

And the reverse is equally true: the Jesus-event eats us at the Lord's table, for we become the Body of Christ. *"Man ist was man isst."* The Body of Christ is what the Jesus-event eats. And need it be pointed out that the appetite of the Jesus-event is by no means anemic. It is the business of the Jesus-event to make sure that God, with that appetite of his for us, is not undernourished.

SUGGESTED READINGS

Fenton, John Y., ed. *Theology and Body.* Philadelphia: Westminster, 1974.

Greeley, Andrew. *The New Agenda.* Garden City: Doubleday, 1973. (Especially ch. 3, "From Indissolubility to Intimacy.")

——— *Sexual Intimacy.* Chicago: Thomas More, 1973.

Marcuse, Herbert. *Eros and Civilization.* New York: Vintage, 1962.

Wieman, Henry N. *The Source of Human Good.* Carbondale: Southern Illinois University Press, 1946. (Especially ch. 9, "Morals.")

COMMITMENT

Robert E. Doud

23 Identity and Commitment

ROBERT E. DOUD

In many areas (e.g., marriage, life in religious communities) the psychological possibility of permanent commitment has been questioned. Part of the problem is that legal, contractual reasons for commitment are not sufficiently persuasive for large segments of modern folks. With the help of process modes of thought, Professor Doud works with the notions of trajectory and Covenant to forge out some other-than-juridical reasons for the possibility and advisability of commitment.

Robert E. Doud is presently Professor of Systematic Theology at the Washington Theological Coalition in Washington, D.C. He is completing his doctorate at the Claremont Graduate School where he is working at "A Whiteheadian Catholic Christology." He received his M.A. in theology from De Paul University, and also spent a year of research in philosophy at Loyola University in Chicago. He has worked in campus ministry and seminary formation.

This article is an attempt to show the relation of identity and commitment in categories mostly derived from process thought. Process thought is growing on the contemporary American Catholic scene. It is fraught with its own internal set of problems, both philosophical and theological, but it also shows promise of adding a fresh approach to our understanding of ourselves and to our own spirituality. This article will try to present what the process approach to identity is, staying close, for the most part, to the insights of Alfred North Whitehead. It will hopefully show the close rela-

387

tionship of identity and commitment in process thought. It shall only hint at directions for this approach within Christian spirituality.

EVENTS AND THE PERSON

Our identity is a series of microscopic events. We are only one of these events at any given time, but any one of the events we are can only be understood in relation to the events preceding it and succeeding it. There are many things that happen to us along life's way to make us the person we are. There are many decisions that we ourselves make in becoming the person we are. Every miniscule event is in some way a matter of things that happen to us, and a matter of things that we decide for ourselves. Our identity is not a static thing, determined once and for all at some moment of our life. Today we accept the view that life is growth. Our identity is modified from moment to moment, from influence to influence, from decision to decision. Our identity has to do with the series of events that makes us us. This is the view of identity taken by process thought.

Our identity, as we usually speak of it, is a series of events that we take to be our own personal history. Each event is responsible to be faithful in some way to the events that precede it. This fidelity includes and presupposes change. Fidelity is concern for preserving continuity with one's past, and aiming at a future, more developed selfhood. Identity presumes change, but it values continuity and stability. Fidelity is identity's respect for its own trajectory. The continuance of this respect is commitment. Strictly speaking, an event is only identical with itself, but our usual sense of "identity" is of a series of mutually interpreting events. The trajectory influences the coming events, and each new event affirms the trajectory.

MULTIPLE EVENTS AND IMMANENCE

Speaking in terms of a trajectory implies a social constitution, insofar as it implies a single direction covering a sequence of multiple events. Such a sequence of episodes has a single direction or meaning, and is thus in some sense an intelligible unity. An intelligible unity, usually a natural coherence in space-time, is what classical metaphysics meant by a substance. In classical metaphysics, the substance remained the same through many accidental changes. In process metaphysics, there is no underlying substrate that remains the same through a succession of changes. This is not to say that no intelligible unity may be discerned among diverse events. There is such identity, but this identity is not substantial; it is momentary and provisional. Identity is processive and sequential, a matter of common direction; it is a trajectory, historically and socially constituted, not statically enduring.

This kind of identity implies immanence. The events on the trajectory are not simply juxtaposed. Their relation to one another is not merely external. A later event on the trajectory includes in its constitution the earlier events on the trajectory. The earlier event is immanent in the later event. Every event has a past in which earlier events that have affected it are included. Thus, a past event on a trajectory includes all the earlier events on the span. A past event has meaning only insofar as it is immanent in a present event. Not all earlier events are of equal meaning and importance in a present event. Some past events are immanent in a trivial way, some in a significant way. Just how much importance they will have is due to how important they were when they were present, and to how important they are now interpreted to be in the present event, and to how important they might have been in intervening events. Some past events may be so contained in a present event that the present is almost a duplicate of them. Other past events may be present as totally anesthetized, as completely denied, by the actual constitution of the present. Thus a cherished memory of a wedding day on one's fiftieth anniversary may be a very close copy of the wedding day itself. In a conversion experience, one may remember and bitterly reject some portion of one's past. Thus two past events may be present by immanence, but they are present in vastly different ways.

ATOMIC DECISION AND COMMITMENT

Each atom of experience is constituted by a decision. The present unit of identity on the trajectory orchestrates all the influences bearing upon itself into an arrangement in an originally self-determined moment of identity. This "actual entity," as Whitehead calls it, decides how its own past will affect it. It selects the past events which will have a positive effect, and which, a negative effect. It is important to stress that each moment has its own decision which interprets the whole span of its past. It is here that we reach the question of commitment, that is, the question of continuity from atomic decision to atomic decision.

A commitment is a concern on the part of a person to preserve a certain direction in the trajectory that he is. Every instant will be a novel integration of all that he already is, plus new factors assimilated from the environment. Every instant will involve some kind of a decision as to how to be himself, how to integrate novelty with continuity. A commitment is not static. It has a certain quality of continuity, but it also constantly absorbs novelty. To live is to change, but to live a committed life is to live with an inner directedness, which is in every instant modified, reinforced, or reinterpreted. In a trajectory that is committed, each actual entity has the concern to authentically interpret its past and to decisively influence its future. Commitment thus requires a high degree of consciousness and a certain deliberate transcendence of the present into the past and into the future.

In a radical process view, we are different persons in every moment of our lives. We know that a person is capable of great changes from instant to instant; yet what gives us our personal character is not so much instantaneous uniqueness, but the uniqueness of our whole trajectory. The accumulation and the selection of influences over a lifetime give a personal style in which novelty is disciplined into a selfhood and harnessed as energy for an expression which bears the mark of the whole personal trajectory. Maturity is the acquiring of this style of life. We are different in every instant, but this singleness achieves continuity in style.

Every trajectory is unique, but in achieving style, trajectories may make themselves parallel. Every trajectory is social in that it is a span on which there are many personal moments. There is a heightened sense of socialness, our usual sense of the social, when we begin to speak of a plurality of trajectories. What gives a span its social character is its deliberate patterning itself in some ways on other spans, near or far, to which he chooses to be related. To some extent, all persons freely pattern themselves on one another, and thus we have the phenomenon of community. Imitation or fellowship or discipleship is a part of every personality. Thus community is a part of personality. Community is a result of the mutual patterning of personal trajectories on one another.

COMMITMENT AND RENEWED DECISION

In order for there to be a commitment, it has to be renewed in every decision along the trajectory. Part of that commitment may be the decision to stay parallel to the other trajectories in the process of mutual patterning. On any one span there is a line of inheritance between the successive persons (personal moments) which comprise the trajectory. The word "inheritance" is used by Whitehead, and it points out the social (plural) character of the identity of any one of us. We are many selves related by inheritance and mutual immanence through time. This is just another way of defining "trajectory," which is a handier and more picturesque term, but which is not a term used by Whitehead. Inheritance is traceable. It is the quality a trajectory has, whereby one decision can be seen to unfold from its predecessors and to unwind into its successors.

No commitment may be said to last a lifetime, until that life is over, and the whole trajectory may be traced. The commitment is revisable and revised in every decisional moment on the trajectory. There is novelty in every instant. Sometimes the novelty is very great; sometimes it is trivial. The commitment is changed somewhat in each atomic decision. No decision is forced to respect the trajectory. The trajectory can be broken at any point. There can be a massive incursion of novelty, which we may judge to be for the better or for the worse. Thus a conversion experience is a sudden and massive change for the better. There can also be a sin experience which is a great and quick change for the worse. Such decisions radically alter a person's basic commitment. Later decisions may try to get him back on the old trajectory, or they may rebuild into a new trajectory, which then also draws from some of the values of the old one, which it always keeps as its past.

THE FREEDOM OF THE ACTUAL MOMENT

We see how freedom, novelty, spontaneity are maximized on the process perspective, and how this may work for well or for ill in particular cases. Commitment is less stringent than in views more on the "substantive" line. In a particular case, a commitment may seem to have one smooth trajectory through a whole lifetime. This smoothness is not due to a "substantial" decision at any one moment in the span. The smoothness is "accidental." It is a function of a trajectory of decisions, any one of which may have reversed the original one. The statement that any commitment is only provisional is only an affirmation that a decision may reverse the decisions that precede it. The beauty of a smooth trajectory is in the style with which it is achieved, always in the face of a barrage of alternatives not taken. Saints reflect to us their acute awareness of the possibility of their falling into sin, even in their advanced stages of spirituality. Sinners happily report their changes of heart, even from the depths of decadence and malice.

A process perspective gives a maximum of importance to the freedom of the individual moment, and it allows a maximum of external influence through its view of universal relativity, reflected in the very constitution of the actual entity, which we cannot fully develop here. It thus allows great room for the influence of grace, in the constant mutual conditioning of persons and trajectories. The controversial point is that in no moment on the trajectory is it possible to make a decision which will finally determine all other decisions. The vocational decisions we make are treated as provisional. This still leaves a wide range in which to discern well-made and poorly made decisions, decisions made at mature moments, and decisions made at phases of a person's life where they could only border on the trivial. It also allows for more dramatic shifts from one well-made decision to a very different well-made decision within one lifetime, on the basis of novelty in a person's life, and of creativity in arranging possibilities already present.

A term of Whitehead's that is again almost synonymous with our own "trajectory" is that of "historic route." It means that a person ("living person," in Whitehead's terms) is a history of microcosmic personal events. The direction of the route is not given once and for all in any one event, but each occasion contributes something to what is an accumulated directionality. Thus the making of the direction is itself historical. No event is completely bound by the direction of its past, but neither is any event free of the influence of its past. Every occasion must contribute something to the direction-making process. This it does in such a way as to leave future occasions free to make their own personal contribution.

PROCESS AND COVENANT

A reflection on the Biblical covenants may be helpful here. The uttered word in which the covenant was struck could not be annulled or retracted. It created a moral force which was not retractable. The moral force gave stability to the physical course of events, even though, in fact, the covenant was always being violated. Such changes in the covenant were looked upon as evil. It was also true that the covenant did undergo changes that were looked upon as acceptable. Thus, the covenant was a theme covering a fairly wide variety of circumstances, all of which were of great religious moment. The sacredness of the covenant is reflected in the creation events, the protoevangelium, the rainbow in the clouds, the walking through the divided parts of sacrificial victims, the eating of salt, circumcision, the Sinai lawgiving. Joshua's renewal at Schechem, the Nathan oracle to David, the dedication of Solomon's temple, the renewals of Josiah, Hezechiah, and Ezra. The covenant gave stability to all the events of the sacred history. The covenant lived in its renewals, not in its relics. It was a developing reality, always being restruck in a new event, which intended to be faithful to the past and creative of the future. There was no static once-and-for-all covenant. There was only a pluriformity of successive covenants. There is a trajectory of covenant commitments. The binding power of the covenants was to a God who led His people through different events, not to its formulations in situations of the past. In the distillation of events over the centuries, it is this binding power which cannot be annulled or retracted. Israel's own interest in her history is more prognosticative and promise-oriented than antiquarian.

COMMITMENT AND HOPE

A commitment is a hope structure. It is made when a person perceives the pattern of his own trajectory, and objectifies in himself the hope for his successors to follow on that trajectory. If a commitment is well made, it should determine the trajectory in a persuasive way for some time to come. To be well made, it involves a true perception of how the trajectory has already developed, and of where it is likely to go as a result of its own inertia and future decisions insofar as they may be tested in present inklings.

A commitment is a highly conscious affirmation of a personal direction insofar as it can be embodied in a single decision. Such a self-summing-up and self-projection is made with the hope of massive influence on subsequent decisions. This influence acts as a liberating influence on later decisions; it frees them to absorb and realign other influences, rather than to agonize over and be preoccupied with the direction of the trajectory itself. On a yearly retreat, one may pour energy into the very direction of the trajectory; but through the working year, one must be able to presume the trajectory in donating attention to other projects.

There may be some later decisions in which the trajectory itself is re-evaluated or rescinded. This is to be accepted as the normal course of events. One decision may reinterpret many earlier decisions in a radical way, but at every point in the trajectory, each authentic decision involves a hope that its own direction will be taken. This hope has a cumulative, but not determinative effect in each new decision.

Great psychic energy may be expended by a series of decisions just to maintain the direction. This would be true when a person is preparing to make a large decision like marriage or entering religious life. It might also take place when stress is threatening to change the direction of a trajectory in a significant way. This expenditure of energy may be helpful or not. It may be the leadership of a great personality which will have an ameliorating effect on the environment and an authenticating effect on a person. It may also be the rigidity of a person who is chronically apprehensive about change and defensive about matters of his own identity. Generally, it is not healthy for a long series of decisions to have to be made just to hold unwaveringly to a trajectory. This is indicative of an unhealthiness, either in the environment which a healthy person is trying to change, or in the person, who is unyielding to the ordinary influence of the world about him.

It is the job of a deciding entity to absorb new influences into itself, sometimes with welcome, sometimes with apathy, sometimes with hesitation. Thus it also orchestrates its environment into a healthier situation for itself. Unless it is in a drift that yields to every influence, however, it will have a healthy experience of stress. It is in stress that the strength of its hope is shown. A commitment in stress must be able to look forward to a victory or a reconciliation in joy. This is the basic condition of hope. There is a basic stress in the very equilibrium that is life itself.

Hope is one moment's optimism for the next moment. The presence of hope is the measure of the health or illness of an organism. Hope is the life-energy of commitment. Without hope, there is only a limpness in the trajectory that ultimately may give up all care about setting its own direction. This is moral death, the giving up of the constant decision that the life trajectory demands. Life is hope and commitment is hope's creative tension.

SUGGESTED READINGS

Brown, Delwin. "Freedom and Faithfulness in Whitehead's God," *Process Studies*, II, 2 (1972).

Cobb, John B. Jr. *A Christian Natural Theology*. Philadelphia: Westminster, 1965.

Hartshorne, Charles. "Personal Identity from A to Z," *Process Studies*, II, 3 (1972).

DEATH AND DYING

Robert B. Mellert

24 *A Pastoral on Death and Immortality*

ROBERT B. MELLERT

Today there is a remarkable pluralism in the interpretation of religious symbols. Yet there is often a great pastoral need to speak, and there is not time or place to sort out meanings. For example, if someone in great desperation asks for prayer, that is probably not the moment to ask: How do you understand God to act in the world? In this chapter, Professor Mellert addresses himself to pastoral counselling with the dying, or with family or friends of someone dying. What consolation and help can be offered that is honest and forthright, and yet acknowledges different understandings of "immortality," "heaven," "eternal happiness"? Professor Mellert makes large use of Whitehead's thought to derive a pastoral approach to death.

Robert B. Mellert received his training at John Carroll University (A.B.), the University of Fribourg (S.T.L.), and Fordham University (Ph.D.). His publications include What Is Process Theology? *(Paulist, 1975), "Models and Metanoia," in* Proceedings *of the American Philosophical Association, and Abstracts for* Process Studies. *At the present time he is a member of the Task Force on Genetics and Human Reproduction at the Yale School of Medicine, New Haven, Connecticut.*

Those who divide their time between the world of academic scholarship and that of the pastoral ministry know that these worlds are very different and often difficult to reconcile. Frequently the person seeking spiritual guidance expects the kind of reassurance ordinarily associated with pastoral counseling. But if the pastor is also an academician in theology or philosophy, he may find it very difficult to satisfy the person because of his unwillingness to repeat the religious myths and doctrines unexamined. How can such a pastor give the consolations of the ministry and still be true to himself and his listener? Unless he is content to divide himself schizophrenically between teacher and consoler and simply perform as expected, he must find an adequate philosophical basis for the spiritual advice he wishes to give.

This type of situation occurs frequently for the theologian/minister, but it is perhaps the most difficult to resolve in cases of death and bereavement. A person who is dying or who has recently suffered the loss of a loved one often wants the consolations of divine mercy, immortality, heaven, and eternal happiness. And it is pointless—indeed it can be cruel—to suggest at such a moment, either by word or silence, that there may be unresolved philosophical questions about some of these conclusions.

If the minister is to be helpful to the dying or the bereaved, there are two requirements he must be able to fulfill. First, he must be able to hear the spiritual needs of the person he is assisting, understand his fears and doubts, and discern to what extent he believes his religious symbols literally. Secondly, in order to dialogue honestly with religious language, the minister must have previously worked out for himself a philosophical position that provides him with an intellectually honest way to meet the needs of his listener, whatever his level of religious sophistication. In this essay, I would like to share a philosophical perspective relevant to this second condition.

For my part, the philosophy of Alfred North Whitehead has been most helpful in dealing with this problem in a way that is logical and coherent in its theoretical synthesis, and rich in the possible imagery available for consoling the dying and the bereaved. For Whitehead dying (or to use his term "perishing") is the antithesis of "emerging," and each is continually occurring in every moment in every bit of reality. Only in the constant ebb and flow of emerging and perishing are change and enrichment possible.

The essential character of reality is that it is constantly becoming. There are literally no permanent actualities, and no underlying essences; there is only the renewal or restructuring of old actualities in a series of interpenetrating events. And yet, there is something that endures through it all, both in the series of actualities we call "persons" and in the complex harmony of all actualities we call our world.

To understand the complex philosophical categories by which Whitehead explains the subtleties of his philosophical system is a formidable task in itself. This cannot be done with any adequacy in a short paper such as this. Rather, I will attempt to make use of only those terms that are essential to my purposes here, and to by-pass almost entirely the intricacies of the Whiteheadian system itself.

In his essay on "Immortality"[1] Whitehead says that there are two abstract worlds, the "World of Value" and the "World of Activity." Neither is explainable except in terms of the other. Value can only be explained in terms of its realization in concrete actualities as they emerge and perish. Thus, "value" is always experienced as "values." Values are concrete, individual, and unique contributions to future actualities. The realization of a particular moment of actuality is likewise the realization of a particular value, and this becomes part of the data for the succeeding moments of actuality. Values derived from the past are thus immanently incorporated into each emerging occasion. This is what Whitehead means by "immortality." Nothing that is of value is ultimately lost. Apart from such immanent incorporation, nothing could be preserved, and "value" itself would have no ultimate meaning.

This understanding of value will be helpful for the next concept we must consider, and that is Whitehead's very original notion of "God." God, like every actuality, is dipolar, reflecting both the mental and the physical, both the World of Value and the World of Activity. These two aspects in the divinity he describes as God's primordial and consequent natures. Taken by itself, the primordial nature is God in abstraction, alone with himself.[2] It is God as a ground of limitation or principle of determination,[3] that is, God as the basis for continued emergence of actuality and the fact of change. This nature of God is immanent in all reality and provides the ultimate reason *how* things become what they are.

The consequent nature of God is the more difficult concept to grasp. Just as the World of Value is pure abstraction unless it is realized in the World of Activity, so also must God, if he is to be actual, be really related to the World of Activity and allow it to be incorporated into himself. Since activity implies fact and change, these also pertain to God. This side of the divine reality is God's consequent nature, and it directly concerns what God has to do with the actual world. God's actuality is constituted by his gathering into himself every bit of temporal actuality that has emerged and perished, so that each is immanent in God and preserved everlastingly by him. This is another way of explaining Whitehead's fundamental notion of immortality. In his primordial nature, God is immanent to us as the foundation and basis for emergence and for the possibility of value in determining what we are. In his consequent nature we are immanent to God in the concrete, unique, and individual values we contribute to the actualization of his abstract nature. So what we become is immortalized in the consequent nature of God.

This may seem like a great deal of idle philosophizing to come up with a product that is just as tenuous as the religious myths and images it is supposed to justify. But I would suggest that Whitehead's insight is not all that removed from our rational experience. Philosophy has always acknowledged that God is in a kind of polar contrast with the world, because, on the one hand, mundane language cannot be literally applied to God, and on the other, that which is inexplicable in human discourse man generally assigns to a deity. Can we not affirm with Whitehead, then, that any explanation of the world requires God, and that any explanation of God requires a world?[4] And further, that insofar as the world is many, God is the one upon which that plurality is based, and insofar as the world is one, God is the reason for the uniqueness of each of its multiple elements?[5] Whitehead is merely confirming our experience that God is somehow both other than and immanent to the world of our reality, and that just as God preserves the reality of that world, so we preserve the reality of God. Or, to put it another way, God adds Value to the world; the world adds Activity to God.

In this context, then, the perishing of an actuality need not be its extinction. Rather, it can be understood as a kind of switching of modes. Whereas in the emerging of an actuality God's immanence is felt in the incorporation of value, in its perishing that actuality is felt immanently in God as a fuller realization of the divinity. In this way that actuality continues to have an impact in God and thus in subsequent actualities where God's immanence continues to be felt in the formation of the future. Death, then, is emphatically not a passing into nothingness. Nor is it a passing to another world in which man continues to experience his self-contained existence as an independent soul with noncorporeal empirical powers. Instead, it is immanent incorporation into God, in whom each actuality is experienced everlastingly for its own uniqueness and individuality. In dying one "gets out of the way" of the present in order to be available in a new way to the future.

Does this doctrine of immortality, which Whitehead calls "objective immortality," correspond to the faith expectations of those who seek the reassurance of an afterlife, a place of eternal happiness, or a heaven? At its most fundamental level, I think that it does. The basis for this belief, I would suggest, is the impossibility of man's conceiving of himself as not being. The one absolute and certain experience that endures throughout his entire life is the experience of being in the present, recalling the past, and anticipating a future. One experiences a profound continuity with oneself in space and time.

Everyone has moments of unconsciousness where his experience of the world around him is temporarily interrupted. The most common example is sleep. But one always awakes to find himself the same person he was when he slumbered. There is an experience of the continuity of the self as far back as the memory permits. To think of this continuity as being abruptly and completely terminated is almost impossible to imagine or accept. This is the reason why man so often seeks to find a place and a time for himself after his death. That place can be a mythical paradise free from the evils and insecurities of earthly existence, or it may simply be a place in the records of history or in the lives of one's offspring. However he imagines it, it gives him some grounds for time in which to maintain the continuity of self into the future.

This problem is acute in Western culture where one must reconcile death and immortality with lineal time. For lineal time, unlike cyclical time, implies an ending, termination or death, or at least a state of permanence, where time (and therefore change) is no more. Hence, the common Western belief that once the final state of man has been reached, the world of activity is effectively excluded from his existence. This is just as true for the agnostic, who believes that his personal extinction is permanent, as it is for the believer, who anticipates personal salvation in a heaven where suffering and sin are no more. In both cases, death is a permanent thing, and the forces of change are no longer relevant. The alternative to total annihilation is bare existence in a perfectly static state!

The belief of permanency after death has always been one of the difficulties of the Christian doctrine of heaven. On the one hand, Christian faith holds that at the moment of death the eternal fate of the person is irretrievably sealed. Heaven is eternal happiness and hell is eternal punishment. In a sense, this is necessary, because if the happiness is to be perfect, it cannot be threatened by change. Since the possibility of change is itself the cause of insecurity, perfect happiness is realizable only in the state of total security and stability. So, the Christian believes in the permanence of his final state.

But what possible meaning can be assigned to experience if it does not involve change? To experience is to take account of things outside the self and to allow them to affect the self, and this implies undergoing some change in the self. What we experience becomes a part of us. This necessarily alters the reality of the continuity that is the self and implies an absence of certitude about the future. Consequently, when personal experiences are admitted as part of the belief in heaven, the belief in the absolute changelessness of the afterlife is put into serious question. Thus, the dilemma. Either personal experience is retained, in which case the series of actualities constituting the self continues, and change is still possible; or personal experience is abandoned in favor of permanency, in which case immortality can only consist in the completed self experienced by another as an objectively immortal actuality.

The advantage of Whitehead's thought is that it permits an explanation of the religious hereafter according to either possibility. My own preference is for the latter, but I can still be philosophically consistent in using the former when the needs of the person seeking consolation indicate that the former would be more helpful.

Let me begin with an explanation of the latter possibility, since this is a more direct application of Whitehead's own doctrine of "objective immortality." Here the emphasis is on permanency. What one was during life, especially during the final moments in life, determines what one is eternally. In this interpretation, the series of actualities that constitute the continuity of the self throughout one's personal history culminate in one final actuality in which that history is synthesized. The entire continuity, but especially this final synthetic actuality in the continuity, is experienced by God and becomes a part of the data of God's own actuality. In this way each person is immortalized everlastingly in God, retaining permanently his own uniqueness and individuality, and contributing that uniqueness as data to a fuller appreciation of value and possibility for the future. However, this interpretation does not allow for any further subjective experience or subjective change.

One can also argue for the possibility of "subjective immortality" using the thought of Whitehead.[6] In this interpretation the series of actualities that constitutes the continuity of self is not interrupted or terminated by death; it only changes the environment in which it does its experiencing. The ordinary environment for the experiencing self is the body. However, there is no necessary reason why the series of actualities that constitutes the self cannot continue in some other nonmaterial environment. Hence, death can be understood as the detachment of that dominant series of actualities we recognize as the self from the many supportive material series that constitute the material body. The new environment is the consequent nature of God, where the serial reality of the self continues to experience and to change, but without any direct attachment to the material world.

Given the Whiteheadian frame of reference, both of these interpretations are philosophically consistent within themselves, even though they may not be reconcilable with each other. Therefore, the decision regarding which to choose can depend upon the need of the person being counseled. If the minister sees that the person he is counseling does not want a reaffirmation of traditional symbols about life after death and is fairly comfortable with the thought of accepting death in this particular circumstance (whether it be his own death or the death of a beloved), the minister can generally find his basic orientation for the counseling session in Whitehead's "objective immortality." Ordinarily such a person is more concerned with articulating a meaning and value for the past than with anxieties about the future. Hence, appropriate statements might suggest that goodness is never lost, that the world is permanently enriched by the past, and that God himself is magnified because of the goodness of a human person. In this way the minister can affirm and support the one who is grieving, not only with the assurance of endurance in human memory, but with comforting religious thoughts about permanent endurance in the mind of God and a lasting efficacy upon the future of the world.

If, however, the person who comes for help is apparently committed to a literal belief in the myths of the afterlife, or if he has not been able to come to grips with the finality of death, the minister may find that the major concern is anxiety about the future. His ministry may then demand that he offer some assurances about a personal continuity and perhaps the possibility to repent and convert from the mistakes of this life. This is possible within the framework of "subjective immortality." Here the minister may—with an underlying philosophical consistency—suggest that when a person dies he is taken up into God for an evaluation of his life, that he will be able to experience the effect that his life had on the world, and that he will have the opportunity to repent of its evils and focus on the good. Then he will be able to experience through God's power the good and evil in all of reality. Essentially, what this orientation does is to offer philosophical justification for the traditional ideas of divine mercy and leave ultimate judgment to God.

The most difficult case is the person who comes with a series of questions beginning with "Why?" Frequently such a person has tried to avoid confronting death until suddenly he finds himself helpless, having neither resolved for himself the meaning of life nor constructed a credible afterlife. Finding a way to comfort such a person is the most difficult task of all. Perhaps it may be impossible, and the minister may ultimately have to acknowledge that to the person himself. But if consolation is possible, it can come about only if the minister carefully listens to the complaints being made. Often a clue as to the kind of consolation that may be acceptable, and the kind that will only aggravate the anger, comes from what the person is saying. Allowing such a person to freely vent his feelings, even though they may be hostile and even blasphemous, gives the minister time to listen. Then, perhaps, he may be able to help the person construct a temporary myth to deal with the situation, at least to the point of being able to cope with the present moment. If it is a case of bereavement rather than dying, another encounter may be important weeks later after the emotions of the situation have subsided, in order to help the person resolve the question more fully for himself.

In the above cases, the approaches offered are merely suggestions that might apply in particular cases. They are, obviously, only appropriate when they are genuinely helpful to the particular person being consoled. The point I wish to stress is more fundamental. On the basis of a Whiteheadian orientation, the minister is in a position to go beyond nondirective counseling and honestly assist the person in deepening that person's own beliefs and consolations without the minister ever having to impose his own.

The richness of Whitehead's thought is such that it provides a solid philosophical framework for a great diversity of human experience and a means of synthesizing that experience in interesting new ways. It can account for, and indeed deepen, the thinking of traditionalist and liberal alike, and it can also be an effective instrument of translating between their different interpretations of their experiences of reality. And this is the fundamental task of ministering to the sorrowing and the dying: to understand, to support, and to deepen. For this task I have found the thought of Alfred North Whitehead eminently valuable.

NOTES

1. Published in Schilpp, Paul Arthur, ed., *The Philosophy of Alfred North Whitehead* (New York: Tudor Publishing Co., 1951), pp. 682-700.

2. Whitehead, Alfred North, *Process and Reality* (New York: Macmillan, 1929), Free Press Paperback edition, 1969, p. 39.

3. Whitehead, Alfred North, *Science and the Modern World* (New York: Macmillan, 1925). Free Press Paperback edition, 1967, pp. 178-79.

4. Whitehead, *Process and Reality*, pp. 409-11.

5. *Ibid.*, p. 410.

6. Cf. Griffin, David, "The Possibility of Subjective Immortality in Whitehead's Philosophy," *University of Dayton Review*, VIII, 3, pp. 43-56.

SUGGESTED READINGS

Kubler-Ross, Elisabeth. *On Death and Dying.* New York: Macmillan, 1969.

Mellert, Robert B. *What Is Process Theology?* New York: Paulist Press, 1975.

PRAYER

Robert M. Cooper
Lewis S. Ford

25 God as Poet and Persons at Prayer

ROBERT M. COOPER

It is possible that the Death of God movement marked the final stage of the long, tedious, and necessary religious purification demanded by the modern age. In the sixties it was hardly fashionable for a public figure to be caught at prayer. But once again (and it came upon us somewhat by surprise) it is O.K. for congressmen to go to weekly meetings with their colleagues to pray. And one can call upon God publicly for reasons more personally real than mere protocol or rhetoric. So it becomes necessary again to theologize about persons at prayer in a way that is congenial to our post-death-of-God, contemporary sensitivities. And that is what Professor Cooper is about in this chapter, with the help of Whitehead's natural theology.

Robert M. Cooper received his training at Catawba College (B.A.), Berkeley Divinity School (S.T.B.), University of the South (S.T.M.), Louisiana State (M.A.), and Louisiana State University (D.Div. in the History of Religions). An Episcopal priest, he is currently Professor of Ethics and Moral Theology at Nashotah House, Episcopal Seminary, and he is also priest-in-charge of St. Simon the Fisherman Church in Port Washington, Wisconsin. Professor Cooper is Associate Editor of the Anglican Theological Review *and Editor of the* Nashotah Review. *He has published a number of articles in theology, philosophy, and literature, and has published poetry in several journals and magazines.*

Alfred North Whitehead has remarked that God "is the poet of the world, with tender patience leading it by his vision of truth, beauty, and goodness."[1]

411

One knows, coming as it does in the concluding chapter of *Process and Reality*, that this is not mere cant, but rather that it is supported by some of the most careful and elegant thinking in the history of Western philosophy. The comment is obviously an assertion about God, and craves to be balanced by another from the person-ward end (or in Whitehead's formulation, from the "worldly" end). Such a balancing statement may be found in *Religion in the Making*: ". . . God in the world is the perpetual vision of the road which leads to the deeper realities."[2]

This essay will deal with Whitehead's doctrine of God, but that will not be the primary concern. The principal direction is toward the establishment of a philosophy of prayer.[3] An attempt will be made to carry this out in accordance with the principles of Whitehead's philosophy, particularly as they may be discovered in *Process and Reality*. The ramifications of such a generalized effort cannot be carried on here into exhaustive applications to specific major religions of the world, but is, rather, to be confined to only one of them. The writer, being most familiar with the Christian tradition, will concentrate his efforts at application in that area. I must, first, however, state the scope of the inquiry as I see it.

We may not, in the beginning, be content with a definition—albeit only a provisional one—of "prayer." I hope that from a discussion of Whitehead's conception of God and his role (both in his primordial and in his consequent natures) in creativity, we will find an implicit and operational definition of prayer; to be sure, it will be highly general. I will begin, then, with a discussion of Whitehead's conception of God and move from that to a consideration of the relationship of the individual to God. It is my thesis that persons recapitulate, in prayer, but to a lesser degree, God's role as "the poet of the world." Some other background is necessary, however, as preliminary to a discussion of Whitehead's conception of God, viz., we must see what Whitehead intends by his use of the word, "vision," which we have seen in both of the quotations with which this essay began.

A glance at the index of subjects in *Process and Reality* will soon indicate that there are few[4] references in that work to "vision." The connection of vision, or seeing, and knowledge (knowing) in the Bible is commonplace.[5] It has been used in book titles to indicate certain modes of understanding or perceiving the world, e.g., *The Tragic Vision and the Christian Faith*,[6] and *The Vision of Tragedy*,[7] to mention but two. Our ordinary daily idiom, "I see," is understood by all to mean, "I understand." (Cf. the Greek, οἶδα, εἴδω .) We are familiar too with the fact that it is frequently, although not altogether, more meaningful to point to—to show, or to demonstrate visually—something, than it is to speak of it. Though Whitehead notes that language is the distinguishing feature of man, the poverty and inadequacy of man's language is a leitmotif of *Process and Reality*. He says, for example, that

> Language is thoroughly indeterminate, by reason of the fact that every occurrence presupposes some systematic type of environment. . . . A precise language must await a completed metaphysical knowledge.[8]

Indeed, every statement is a compromise with the nature of things.

In writing of the eucharistic mystery, John Calvin said of it: "I experience more than I understand." That is, experience is not utterly (without remainder) reducible to understanding. If that be the case, and if we may use the phrase of Kierkegaard's Johannes de Silentio, viz., that language is "the broker of the finite," then no human utterance captures experience without remainder. Our experience is greater (other) than our language, because it is greater (other) than our understanding. Although, in this sense, every statement is a compromise with the nature of things, Whitehead is able to say, and we too agree with him, that "Expression is the one fundamental sacrament."[9] Vision may be propositional, but it need not be. Let us examine, therefore, Whitehead's elaboration of the notion and then we shall turn to deal with his conception of God. In doing so, we will be following in a general way the course of treatment in *Process and Reality*.

Whitehead states in his first chapter, significantly entitled "Speculative Philosophy," that

> the first requisite is to proceed by the method of generalization so that certainly there is some application; and the test of some success is application beyond the immediate origin. In other words, *some synoptic vision* has been gained.[10]

In a more dramatic way this same goal is expressed in the final section of that work when Whitehead writes that "Philosophy may not neglect the multifariousness of the world—the fairies dance, and Christ is nailed to the cross."[11] His desire is for "some synoptic vision" of "the multifariousness of the world." It may be merely trivial to indicate that such a purpose places Whitehead in the company of all of those creative people—religious visionaries, artists, musicians, mathematicians, poets—who have sought a vision of wholeness and have attempted to express it: and who could perhaps have asserted that their very diverse efforts were manifestations of "the one fundamental sacrament." For Whitehead, the quest is endless, the process interminable; and this lends a feeling of pathos to the closing section of *Process and Reality*, entitled—somewhat ironically—"Final Interpretation."

Whitehead is not altogether happy with the term "vision," however; and suggests that "envisagement" is perhaps a better one; a judgment expressed in his discussion of "Some Derivative Notions," apropos particularly of treating "conceptual prehensions." The "conceptual prehensions" are, as he says, "entirely neutral, devoid of all suggestiveness."[12] An alternative way of speaking of "conceptual prehensions" is to speak of "appetitions" —or, of what Bergson called "intuitions." For Whitehead, "A conceptual prehension is a direct vision of some possibility of good or evil—of some possibility as to how actualities may be definite."[13] Here we are dealing with a *purely* mental operation, free-floating as it were with no connection to any specific actuality, or indeed, to any world. An example[14] (the example will, I believe, become more coherent to the reader as he continues) of what is meant by "free-floating" can be given, though not without peril of enervating the view of Whitehead. Something broadly in use is the Lord's Prayer. One can pray that familiar prayer *as if* one were someone else. That is, imaginatively I am another: a friend, an enemy, a child, spouse. I begin, "Our Father," and allow that phrase to lead me, to lure me, where it will, to see my commonality with the other, to see my distinctiveness. Lines or phrases of poems can be similarly utilized. I may allow them to invite me to novelty, to possibilities which could be actualized. One might say that, in traditional religious (ascetical theological) terminology, he is dealing with "contemplation."[15] Strictly speaking, on Whitehead's own terms, there is no untrammeled "vision," even by God in his primordial nature. There is, rather, *im-*

pure prehension inasmuch as the, or at least one (in order to accord with Whitehead's own principle of relativity) physical prehension must be accounted for in the process.[16] He sums up this portion of his discussion, saying that

> God's "primordial nature" is abstracted from his commerce with "particulars," and is therefore devoid of those "impure" intellectual cogitations which involve propositions. It is God in abstraction alone with himself. As such it is a mere factor in God, deficient in actuality.[17]

Whitehead has said, minimally, that a feeling, in his terms, is "a positive prehension."[18] More elaborately, he states that "A feeling is the appropriation of some elements in the universe to be components in the real internal constitution of its subject. The elements are the initial data; they are what the feeling feels."[19] How crucial this is for his entire "Essay in Cosmology" which relies so heavily upon becoming, upon process, may be seen in his assertion that "This doctrine of 'feeling' is the central doctrine respecting the becoming of an actual entity."[20] Among the actual entities of the world are individual persons. Among the most deeply feeling of these are likely to be poets, but every actual entity feels through both, or either, as the case may be, the physical pole and the mental pole of itself.

God, likewise, along with the eternal objects and the world of actual entities, is a feeling occasion. It is God who sees the best configuration of things both in the world of the actual entities and in the realm of the eternal objects. Indeed, "Apart from the intervention of God, there could be nothing new in the world, and no order in the world."[21] From the person-ward end of things, by virtue of our "conscious imagination," "we are feeling the actual world with the conscious imputation of imagined predicates be they true or false."[22] This is a philosophy which preserves the reality of our experience, inasmuch as it accounts for "the incurable 'particularity' of a feeling"[23]—the feeling of the individual person.

Specifically, the "three stages in the process of feeling are (1) the responsive phase, (2) the supplemental stage, and (3) the satisfaction."[24] "Satisfaction" is the conclusion of a concrescing, prehending, experiencing, entity; all indetermination is eliminated. There are two phases in the achieving of satisfaction. The actual occasion, initially, is "the phase of pure reception of the actual world in its guise of objective datum for aesthetic synthesis."[25] The feelings of other actual entities in this stage are not felt as feelings for the particular actual occasion concerned, but are seen rather in "a nexus of mutual presupposition." The second stage involves the objectification of certain of these hitherto merely received from the actual world in the particular actual occasion. Some of them, hitherto indeterminate, are positively prehended and become ingredient in the concrescing experience. They "are transformed into a unity of aesthetic appreciation immediately felt as private." The feelings of these objective actual occasions are felt as the feelings of the subject itself. As Whitehead says, "This is the incoming of 'appetition,' which in its higher exemplifications we term 'vision'."[26] There is more to be said.

In the supplemental stage (in aesthetic supplement) "there is an emotional appreciation of the contrasts and rhythms inherent in the unification of the objective content in the concrescence of one actual occasion." It is in this phase that "perception is heightened by its assumption of pain and pleasure, beauty and distaste."[27] These pure physical feelings require "an influx of conceptual feelings," and the two groups must be integrated, lest there be mere blind feeling on the part of the particular actual occasion. At this juncture, "intellectual 'sight' " is required, in the form of the negative prehension in which the potentially ingredient actual occasion or eternal object is dismissed from that particular concrescence as trivial. Therefore, "there is always mentality in the form of 'vision,' but not always mentality in the form of conscious 'intellectuality'."[28]

Again, some examples—offered with the same caveat as before, viz., that they may tend to enervate the tightly reasoned views of Whitehead—may clarify what I intend by speaking of God and persons at prayer as "poets." I have already suggested that phrases or lines of poems can be used as lures. They can show me how I *might* feel, and in showing me possible feelings they show me possible *beings*, possible actions. The reader is invited to let the following lines of poetry have their way with him. The first is the incantatory opening lines of Gerard Manley Hopkins' "The Windhover: To Christ our Lord."

> I caught this morning morning's minion, king-
>   dom of daylight's dauphin, dapple-dawn-drawn Falcon,
>   in his riding

Of the rolling level underneath him steady air, . . .[29]

or the lilt of this lyric stanza from e. e. cummings:

Sweet spring is your
time is my time is our
time for springtime is lovetime
and viva sweet love[30]

and finally this exquisite short poem by the Welsh priest-poet,
R. S. Thomas, "Pisces":

Who said to the trout,
You shall die on Good Friday
To be food for a man
And his pretty lady?

It was I, said God,
Who formed the roses
In the delicate flesh
And the tooth that bruises.[31]

These lines, and this poem, in my present vulgar sense, are "lures
for feeling"; they can be prayers, or they can lead me to (the edge
of) prayer. They are for me, in either case, occasions for novelty;
and as such they make the world.

The quotations at the beginning of the essay have indicated
that there is, in Whitehead's own thought, a connection between
the conceptions of "vision" and "God"; and we have reached the
point of transition from a summary of Whitehead's notion of
"vision" to a discussion of his conception of God.

For Whitehead, God is not the source of the metaphysical
principles set forth in *Process and Reality*, but is subject to them
as is any other actual entity in the process of creativity. For
Whitehead, God is, as we have seen, "the poet of the world, with
tender patience leading it by his vision of truth, beauty, and
goodness." God is, for Whitehead, the valuator of potential concrescence of the eternal objects in actual occasions. God did not
bring the world into being out of nothing, for, according to Whitehead's ontological principle,[32] nothing comes from nothing—
"the rest is silence." God is necessary to the philosophical system
which Whitehead is adumbrating. Whitehead has pointed out[33]
that not since Aristotle has God found his way into metaphysics

necessarily, i.e., by the force and thrust of the argument itself; but that since Aristotle he had been metaphysically defended for his usefulness, or necessity, on religious or other partisan grounds. God has, according to Whitehead, all too often been the object of senseless "metaphysical compliments." Why is God necessary for Whitehead's cosmology?

God does not create the world from nothing, as we have seen, nor does he create the eternal objects. God, in his primordial nature, satisfies both the requirement of the ontological principle and that of the principle of relativity. There has to be at least one entity so that there may be anything in the world at all; and there must be at least one entity so that any other things in the world may be oriented in terms of it, and thus with respect to one another (order).[34] One may say further, that a third Whiteheadian principle requires God's existence also, viz., the reformed subjectivist principle. All experience is had in terms of some *object* by a subject. This is not the familiar cul-de-sac of solipsism for it is not pure subjectivism. There are real actual occasions which are objectively ingredient in a subjective actual occasion. God is necessary, in his primordial nature, and as an actual entity in Whitehead's system—not, be it well noted, *ab initio*, and exhaustively defined (by "metaphysical compliments"), but as the concept which lends not only coherence, but possibility itself, to the system. God is required in Whitehead's cosmology on at least three counts: (1) by the ontological principle; (2) by the principle of relativity; and (3) by the reformed subjectivist principle. Like Aristotle's God, Whitehead's is required by the direction and logic of the argument. What does God do?

If one may assume that there are the eternal objects, potentially ingredient in experience, one must then have the means whereby they are prehended in actual occasions. God is the means whereby this happens. Whitehead says that "The primordial nature of God is the acquirement by creativity of a primordial character"; and further that

> His conceptual actuality at once exemplifies and establishes the categoreal conditions. The conceptual feelings, which compose his primordial nature, exemplify in their subjective forms their mutual sensitivity and their subjective unity of subjective aim. These subjective forms are valuations determining the relative relevance of eternal objects for each occasion of actuality.[35]

God, not unlike a proposition in Whitehead's understanding, "is a lure for feeling, the eternal urge of desire."[36] There is more to be said about Whitehead's conception of God, for in addition to his primordial nature, God has what our philosopher speaks of as his consequent nature.

God is involved in creativity. He is the valuator of the potential ingression of the eternal objects in actual occasions. He is subject to the same metaphysical principles which govern all actual entities. His prehension, "vision," of the eternal objects is not exhaustive. His *appetition* for their ingression in actual occasions is immensely extensive, but not exhaustive. His *perception* of the good in any given occasion is profound by virtue of the role which he has played as "the acquirement by creativity of a primordial character." He too is involved in life, and we have had several occasions already to note this: he is "the poet of the world, with tender patience leading it by his vision of truth, beauty, and goodness." God is, by virtue of his consequent nature, involved in life; his "satisfaction" is not yet; it is yet to be. It is in this sense that Whitehead is able to say that God is "the great companion— the fellow-sufferer who understands."[37] Before leaving this discussion of Whitehead's conception of God, and moving on to the person-ward aspect of this essay, let us note three final comments by him which relate the notions of "vision" and "God" in his system. First, "God and the World stand over against each other, expressing the final metaphysical truth that appetitive vision and physical enjoyment have equal claim to priority in creation." Secondly, "God is the infinite ground of all mentality, the unity of vision seeking physical multiplicity." And finally,

> The theme of Cosmology, which is the basis of all religions, is the story of the dynamic effort of the World passing into everlasting unity, and of the static majesty of God's vision, accomplishing its purpose of completion by absorption of the World's multiplicity of effort.[38]

God is the visionary poet and the ground of all mentality.

The poet's, to be sure, is not the only variety of creative activity that is to be seen active about us, though it is doubtful that there is a greater or more significant kind, lest perhaps it be the philosopher's or the religious visionary's. The "poet of the world" is largely fabricator, or inventor, of the world. Other languages, in their words for "poet," stand us in better stead for understanding the weight of the term than does our own English. Mention may be made here of three: viz., Italian's *il fabbro*; German's *der Dichter*; and Greek's ὁ ποιητής. The poet in these languages is understood in the racial, linguistic history of their respective speakers as a "maker," a "fashioner." I have already indicated the way in which Whitehead understands God to be a fashioner of the world. As one learns to expect from extensive reading of this philosopher, his words are carefully and aptly chosen. It is not, therefore, mere dramatic convenience that God is spoken of by him as "the poet of the world."

The poet, in our experience, is not a creator out of nothing. He has material given him with which he works. His effort may not always be at a vision of the whole, but he seeks to juxtapose, to relate, to account for, "the multifariousness of the world" where "the fairies dance, and Christ is nailed to the cross." "The one fundamental sacrament" of the philosopher and of the poet is, to be sure, expression, but it takes different shapes. God, in Whitehead's terms, is "the lure for feeling, the eternal urge of desire." He is the valuator of the potential ingression of eternal objects in actual occasions. He is this by virtue of his "vision" which is necessarily more extensive than that of any other actual entity, by virtue of his being creativity's acquirement of a primordial character. When a given actual occasion is dismissing as trivial a potential prehension which God *sees* will result in evil, then God is our fellow sufferer; but not fellow sufferer merely, for he values the potential ingression otherwise and his own continually concrescing self is thereby altered. God's desire may be frustrated. The poet's vision may lack wholeness.

Conceptually, the poet's vision may be defective, for, though it strives for wholeness, not unlike God's it cannot be final or exhaustive. "Each task of creation is a social effort, employing the whole universe."[39] There is another level on which it may be defective, viz., on the level of articulation. A sacrament does not exhaust the reality of the thing which it would celebrate; and though expression be "the one fundamental sacrament," it too is defective in that it does not exhaust the whole. (Cf. again Calvin's "I experience more than I understand.") Language is never adequate to the occasion. In *The Concept of Nature*, Whitehead had observed, almost trivially (but the observation is illuminated by the insight of genius), that "something is going on." Before anyone, however, can grasp it in articulation the entire configuration of the universe is altered. This is not, of course, to say that science is trivial. Language is simply not able to catch all of that which is going on ("the incurable poverty of language"), and neither, of course, does any effort at symbolization, whether it be scientific, artistic, mathematical, or logical.

The poet attempts to communicate his vision, to articulate his way of seeing the world, but the test is always in the poetry itself. One does not ask of a poem: Is it true? One may ask, Is it beautiful? or, as John Ciardi puts it, "How does a poem mean?"[40] And by that question he may, on Whitehead's grounds, be endeavoring to feel the feeling of the actual occasion of the making of the poem. "Satisfaction" results for the reader conformally with feeling the poem and what it has so caught of the nexus of mutual presuppositions. In Whitehead's terminology, it is proper also to say that poetry is *propositional* inasmuch as it makes assertions about process; and simultaneously, of course, it participates in creativity by becoming potentially an object for another subjective actual entity. What others have thought or said, or might have thought or said (see the examples of verse quoted above, and the suggested use of the Lord's Prayer), can become for me the occasions of novelty, occasions of self- and world-creation; and, of course for Whitehead, the creation of God.[41]

For Whitehead, a proposition is "a lure for feeling." It operates "between" the eternal objects and the realm of actual entities (or occasions). It is free-floating in terms of both.[42] The eternal objects are the potential predicates, the subjects of which are the actual occasions. The possibility of novelty is in the potential ingression of an eternal object in an actual occasion, and a proposition is one of the means whereby this may happen. "Vision" may be said to be enhanced potentially, suggestively, and creatively by a pure proposition. It can only be judged once it has been positively prehended by a concrescing actual occasion. The proposition is "a lure for feeling," for objectification by a subjective actual occasion in conformal feeling. God too is "a lure for feeling" in a not altogether dissimilar sense. We must attempt now to draw the connection of this lengthy line of talk about the analogous roles of God and the poet to what has been asserted earlier, viz., that man recapitulates in prayer, but to a lesser degree, God's role as "the poet of the world."

It was stated at the beginning that a definition of prayer would emerge from the discussion. It does seem that there is an implicit definition of "prayer" in our speaking of the roles of God and of the poet. Prayer, on the one hand, may be purely contemplative and may be said to correspond to God's primordial nature in his envisagement of the realm of eternal objects. Prayer may, on the other hand, be seen to have as it were a "consequent nature," viz., that of the involvement of the actual occasion in which it is ingredient in the process of the world. This is a philosophy of prayer in which it (prayer) is ingredient in the process of the world. This is a philosophy of prayer in which prayer actually does change things. The idea of the propositional feeling, of the proposition as a lure for feeling, can be quite pertinent to those who would pray in a highly liturgical tradition. The fixed liturgical prayers, be they ancient or modern, can be such lures for feeling; and we remember the emphasis upon the *particularity* of the feeling. It presupposes one's being ingredient in the world, and need not be merely a benign bemusement with regard to the state of the world. The person who prays, not unlike the poet, may have a vision of the world; he has his way of seeing the world and this is rooted deeply in the nature and character of experience. The poet and the person who prays may determine from their visions of the potentialities of objectification in a given (or more generally) actual occasion valuations of the ingression in that particular subject of the object purely prehended. The range of this vision is not as wide as God's nor is it as profound.[43] It is, however, possible for the person who prays to contemplate possibilities for himself and for other actual entities, and to the extent to which he is able to do so, he is potentially able to alter some situations. In many others, he must lament, and in others he may exult, for like God, he is—although not to the same degree—companion and fellow sufferer to the world.

Like God, the person who prays (prays in the poetic sense which I have been suggesting) does not control what happens except only in a very few instances in a lifetime and in those instances to a very limited extent. There is, then, a degree, to which a pragmatic criterion has been fulfilled. One may say, further, that prayer—in a sense—justifies itself as an activity even when it is not concretely a fabricator. To the extent to which poetry is the only achievement of satisfaction possible, so prayer. They each may be seen as occasions of the *celebration* of life (process, experience), and not in the sense that all celebrations are joyful or gay. They may be occasions of celebration simply because life is whatever it happens to be. The vision of the person who prays has seen that there is freedom as long as there is creativity; and in this vision he has seen good and evil, beauty and distaste, change and everlastingness. This much of the discussion has been on the more general level. In the beginning of this essay I suggested that some more specific comments might be made about a particular religion, and that the one with which the present writer is most familiar is Christianity.

Primitive Christianity attempted to take account of a new experience in the lives of various peoples, who otherwise had little in common—or nothing at all, apart from their common humanity. That experience was of a new understanding of life, life in which Jesus Christ figured prominently as the key to its coherence. These various peoples—subjects—had had this man as object in their own lives directly, or by the preaching and living demonstration of him by others. He had, in either case, been impurely prehended by them. He was ingredient in their lives both by physical prehension and by conceptual prehension. He was not exhausted in any actual occasion or by any actual entity. He himself prehended God, and was the means of God's being prehended by others; he was himself "a lure for feeling." This brief paragraph can hope to be no more than merely suggestive, for what is involved here is the necessity for a thorough Christology were one to pursue this further.[44]

Not only for primitive and contemporary Christians, but for all men, life has been forever qualified uniquely by the actual occasion of Jesus Christ (as, of course, by Buddha, Mohammed, etc.); and this may be said as well for those who never suppose that they should worship him, as well as for those who do so devoutly. All of their experience must include his objectification—objectification in multifold occasions. Prayer, then, for the Christian will not be moving altogether on the conceptual, or contemplative, level, in the sense formerly indicated, but will be taking account, in its vision of the whole, of Jesus Christ's having become object for the praying subject.

Application to a particular religion or tradition, other than Christianity, would be made in other ways by a person within that religion or tradition. The present effort has been to suggest, albeit most briefly, what shape prayer may take when attempting to account for Jesus Christ in human experience, within the generalizations previously offered about prayer. Finally, this essay has been an attempt to offer some speculative thinking concerning prayer (largely in terms of the enterprise of poetry) on Whiteheadian grounds. It has attempted merely to be suggestive, and therefore, has raised not a few problems. Outstanding among the problems raised is that of the fact that there is considerable departure implied here from the usual Christian doctrines of prayer, and this is largely due to the fact that Whitehead's doctrine of God is unlike any other in the history of thought. If this essay, however, has offered a philosophy of prayer, it may be amenable to the formulation of a ground for secular[45] "prayer"; and thus afford further a context for discussion between religionists and secularists. In any case, prayer, as it has been outlined in this essay, is prayer in which man is not only praying *to* God, but *with*, and indeed *beyond* God. The significance of such a view for the study of the history of religions, or for the theology of the history of religions, seems to be very promising, but the development of such possible views is beyond the purpose of this particular piece of writing.[46]

NOTES

1. *Process and Reality: An Essay in Cosmology*, Harper Torchbooks Edition (New York: Harper & Brothers, 1960), p. 526. Hereafter cited as *PR*.

2. *Religion in the Making*, Living Age Books Edition (New York: Meridian Books, Inc., 1960), p. 151, cf. pp. 147, 149. Hereafter cited as *RM*.

3. What prayer is, and how it may be understood, have frequently been subjects of religious discussion. The recent discussion of "the death of God" demonstrated that one of the first things to fall in that "new theology" was prayer, both as a concept and as a practice. Bishop Robinson's chapter, "Worldly Holiness," in his *Honest to God* (London: SCM, 1963) was a first very firm step in that direction, though he owed most of what he said there to Bonhoeffer. He set forth a view of prayer which was by no means new, viz., one in which the Christian, by virtue of his relationship to Jesus, attempts to sanctify all that he touches. Here one might compare my "Leitourgos Iesou Christou: Toward a Christian Theology of Prayer," *Anglican Theological Review*, Vol. XLVII, No. 3 (July, 1965) 263-275. From Robinson it was not very far, if one took a few quick steps to this side and then to that, to the position of Paul M. van Buren.

In the first part of his three-part essay on "The New Theologians" in *The New Yorker* (Nov. 13, 1865) Ved Mehta reported van Buren as having said that he does not pray and that he avoids exercising his ministry as an Episcopalian priest if he can do so. If God is dead, then, presumably it is at least merely ill-advised to pray to him, if in fact it is not downright stupid. Van Buren's view has since changed, as witness his recent article, "Theology Now?" *The Christian Century* (May 29, 1974), 585-89.

4. That paucity may, however, be misleading. The index is not exhaustive of the instances in which the term is importantly used in the work, though most of the significant ones are recorded.

5. Cf. John 1:47ff, I Corinthians 13:12, Ephesians 3:9-10, I John 3:1ff; and see John 20:27-29, Acts 17:22ff; II Corinthians 3:18, 5:11, and Hebrews 4:13. The truly classical passage in John 9.

6. *The Tragic Vision and the Christian Faith*, ed. by Nathan A. Scott, Jr. (New York: Association Press, 1957).

7. Richard B. Sewell, *The Vision of Tragedy* (New Haven: Yale University Press, 1959).

8. *PR*, p. 18.

9. *RM*, p. 127.

10. *PR*, p. 8, my emphasis.

11. *PR*, p. 513.

12. *PR*, p. 49.

13. *PR*, p. 50.

14. I have attempted to elaborate this material in a popular manner in an unpublished paper, "Something About Praying," written during a fellowship at the College of Preachers, Washington Cathedral, February, 1969. I am also indebted to Alice Greenwald for her unpublished paper, "'Where Prayer Has Been Valid': An Analysis of the *Four Quartets*."

15. See Lionel S. Thornton, *The Incarnate Lord: An Essay Concerning the Doctrine of the Incarnation in its Relation to Organic Conceptions* (London: Longmans, Green, 1928); cf., for example, pp. 244, 373, and *passim*. See also Thomas Aquinas, *S.T.* 2a 2ae, q. 180, a 3, ad 1m concerning *theoria*, or contemplation as *simplex intuitus veritatis*.

16. In at least one place, *PR*, Part III, Whitehead does admit the possibility of a novel eternal object given in a pure conceptual prehension being integrated into a physical prehension without passing through the conceptual phase; this may suggest a sacramental doctrine for those inclined to find such a concept valuable.

17. *PR*, p. 50.

18. *PR*, p. 337.

19. *PR*, p. 353.

20. *PR*, p. 356.

21. *PR*, p. 377.

22. *PR*, p. 419.

23. *PR*, p. 420.

24. *PR*, p. 323.

25. *Idem.*

26. *Idem.*

27. *PR*, p. 325.

28. *PR*, p. 326.

29. *Gerard Manley Hopkins: A Selection of His Poems and Prose* by W. H. Gardner, The Penguin Poets Series (Baltimore, Md.: Penguin Books, 1953), p. 30.

30. e. e. cummings, *Poems 1923-1954* (New York: Harcourt, Brace, 1954), p. 420.

31. R. S. Thomas, *Song at the Year's Turning* (London: Rupert Hart-Davis, 1959), p. 110.

32. See, regarding the "ontological principal": Plato, *Theaetetus* 160 BD; and the battle of the giants and the gods, *Sophist* 246.

33. *Science and the Modern World*, Mentor Books (New York: New American Library, 1960), p. 156f.

34. Cf. *PR*, p. 344.

35. *PR*, p. 522.

36. *Idem.* The reader is asked to recall what has been said above about poetry as "lures."

37. *PR*, p. 532.

38. *PR*, pp. 539-530.

39. *PR*, p. 340.

40. John Ciardi, *How Does A Poem Mean?* (Boston: Houghton Mifflin, 1959).

41. Again, I am indebted for insight to the unpublished paper by Alice Greenwald. " 'Where Prayer Has Been Valid': An Analysis of the *Four Quartets*."

42. "Between physical purposes and the conscious purposes introduced by the intellectual feelings there lie the propositional feelings which have not acquired consciousness in their subjective forms by association with intellectual feelings. Such propositional feelings mark a stage of existence intermediate between the purely physical stage and the stage of conscious intellectual operations. The propositions are lures for feelings, and give to feelings a definiteness of enjoyment and purpose which is absent in the blank evaluation of physical feeling into physical purpose. In the blank evaluation we have merely the determination of the comparative creative efficacies of the component feelings of actual entities. In a propositional feeling there is the 'holdup'—or, in its original sense, the epoch—of the valuation of the predicative pattern in its relevance to the definite logical subjects which are otherwise felt as definite elements in experience." *PR*, p. 427.

43. This can be said, I believe, without one's having to assert that God's nature is personal. It is not required in Whitehead's systematic treatise that God be invested with human attributes. God may, however, be seen to serve as a model for the way in which men are capable of being understood as self-transcending entities. I am not holding, however, that this is Whitehead's own view.

44. Cf. Lionel S. Thornton, *op. cit.* Thornton speaks of the Bible as "a literature of experience," saying that the common New Testament experience, though it is variously stated, is that of Jesus as Redeemer. More recently, Reginald H. Fuller has written: "The basic datum of NT Christology is not the concept of Jesus as eschatological prophet, but his proclamation and activity which confront men and women with the presence and saving act of God breaking into history and his utter commitment and entire obedience to the will of God which made him the channel of that saving activity. To interpret this datum in terms of explicit Christology was the task of the post-Easter church, in whose *kerygma* the Proclaimer became the Proclaimed" (*The Foundations of New Testament Christology*, New York: Charles Scribner's Sons, 1965), pp. 130-131; cf. pp. 106, 142f.).

45. "Secular" is not to be taken as a negative term here, but ought rather to be understood along the lines developed by Raimundo Panikkar in his *Worship and Secular Man* (Maryknoll, New York: Orbis Books, 1973).

46. Although the context is different than the present one of prayer and poetry, the following short paragraph points in the direction in which I would go: "I admit that I myself feel most impressed by [Gerardus] Van der Leeuw's words. *The world can suddenly reveal itself as Revelation.* This is one of the most remarkable thoughts Van der Leeuw left to us, and if I am honest, I should say that it corresponds exactly to my own experience. It is the experience I like to call the experience of I-should-have-known. You read a hymn to Visnu and you suddenly realize: "If I had only known, I might have addressed God like that." No, more precisely still: "I should have known all along that that is how I should have addressed God" (Kees W. Bolle, "The History of Religions and Christian Theology," *Anglican Theological Review*, Vol. LII, No. 4, October, 1971, 263).

26 Our Prayers as God's Passions

LEWIS S. FORD

"Prayer is a persuasive and fundamental dimension of religious life," Professor Ford begins, "from the elaborate liturgies of perfected ritual to the anguished cry of the heart in need." And then he states the modern question: "If God orders and controls all things in accordance with his eternal purposes, what difference can our prayers make?" It is a characteristic of process theology to understand that God is really affected by the world, by human decisions (theology, under the impact of Greek philosophy, could not allow any *real* affect of creation on God—notwithstanding biblical intuitions to the contrary). In this chapter, Professor Ford offers a model for understanding how human prayer affects God's affection for the world.

Prayer is a pervasive and fundamental dimension of religious life, from the elaborate liturgies of perfected ritual to the anguished cry of the heart in need. Theological reflection on prayer, in comparison, is rather scarce. It is something of an embarrassment to classical theism. If God orders and controls all things in accordance with his eternal purpose, what difference can our prayers make? How can we presume to beg God to alter that which he in his infinite wisdom has proposed to do? And if our prayers of intercession are not designed to petition a change in God's will, why are they addressed to God rather than being simple expressions of our wishes? Perhaps they are disguised expressions of what we intend or hope to do under God's guidance, on the assumption that though he could control all things, God voluntarily relinquishes some of that control for us for a time so that we might have freedom of will. But what can our prayers tell God if he already knows the future as if it were actual? Or, if we exclude intercessory prayer as presumptuous and unnecessary, restricting ourselves to adoration and praise, what need has God for our praises? How can our praises enrich what is already perfect bliss? How can they even affect an eternally unchanging and impassible being? We know by being contingently affected by that which we know; if this is unsuitable for God and he knows rather by creating that which he knows, then he knows the very praises we make to him by creating them. Is not this just an elaborate form of self-praise in which we are used as its instrumentalities, the very thing we condemn as the height of egotism in human conduct?

The biblical tradition, insofar as it was uninfluenced by these nagging doubts of classical theism, has a very robust feeling for prayer. Men could protest their ill-treatment at the hands of God and challenge the justice of his actions. God's will could be altered: the repentance of the Ninevites spared their city from divine destruction to Jonah's dismay and anger (which he did not hesitate to express to God in prayer, Jonah 4:2f), and King Hezekiah's prayer granted him a reprieve of fifteen years of life (2 Kings 20). Abraham and Moses became past masters at bargaining with God, finding all sorts of reasons to deter God from proceeding according to his declared intention (Genesis 18, Exodus 32).

Process theism, offering a viable alternative to the changeless, omnipotent, absolute sovereign of classical theism, may provide us with a theory of prayer adequate to its contemporary practice and able to help us reappropriate these oft-suppressed elements in the biblical witness. Process theism, as expounded by Alfred North Whitehead and Charles Hartshorne, denies that God controls things by determining what they shall be; the course of the world is the conjoint ouctome of creaturely decisions made in response to divine persuasion. As omniscient, God knows everything actual as actual and everything possible as possible, but the future, the not-yet-actual, is radically indeterminate and cannot by nature be known as if it were already actualized. God's experience of the world is contingent upon what in fact happens as a result of creaturely decision, and grows with the course of the creative advance. Since God always wills what is good, what actually happens is not always in accordance with his will. Insofar as there is evil, his will has been thwarted. But as the creative source of all values, he is ultimately responsible for the evolutionary advance of the universe and for the highest aspirations we strive to achieve.

In this brief sketch of a theory of prayer, we do not intend to reargue the case for process theism, but merely to mention some of the assumptions governing our construction. One further idea needs to be introduced: the bold conjecture proposed by Ramanuja and Fechner, and reaffirmed by Hartshorne, that the world is God's body, or that God should be conceived as the self or mind of the universe. This suggestion is often summarily dismissed as pantheistic, but a doctrine of pure immanence would be better expressed by saying that God is the life-force of the universe, analogous to the life coursing through all the cells of the body. Mind is immanent within the body, influencing and directing its activities, but it is also transcendent, seeking meanings and goals beyond the capacity of the mind to grasp. Classical theism will also reject the analogy on the grounds that God is the external creator of the world who, having once existed in solitary splendor, decided one day to create the world *ex nihilo*. For process theism, however, this absolute dependence of the world on the creative will of God is replaced by a symbiotic relationship in which God supplies the values and creative possibilities for the creative advance of the world, in turn for which the world provides God with actualities to enrich his experience. The hierarchy of dominance is replaced by an eco-system of mutual interaction. To be sure, insofar as the creative advance must be likened to the growth of the body, the analogy breaks down, for our minds cannot foster the growth of the body (cf. Matthew 6:27), but if we concentrate on God's sustaining and directing activity, it may well prove helpful. Paul used this analogy to describe the relationship between the living, risen Christ and the Christian believers in his discourses on the Body of Christ (I Corinthians 12; Ephesians 4:11-16; Colossians 1:15-20), and we may generalize it to express the relation between God and all his creatures.

The analogy also depends upon our understanding of the relation between mind and body. A Cartesian dualism, whereby the mind/body relation is pictured as a "ghost in the machine," to use Gilbert Ryle's phrase, will not do. Whitehead eschews any absolute dichotomy here. Actualities are conceived in terms of events, not things or minds. Every actuality is the subject of its own present process of coming into being, and an object for subsequent acts of becoming. While only very special actualities are conscious, every actuality enjoys some degree of mentality insofar as it achieves some novelty in its response to the world, but is physical insofar as it habitually repeats established patterns. Plants are vast societies of such actualities acting in interrelation to one another. "A tree is a democracy of cells," Whitehead once wrote. In animals one strand or series of such actual occasions stands out as a directing agency for the activities of the organism as a whole. While all the cells of the body have their own feelings and enjoy some measure of mentality in their living responses to their surroundings, that one strand of occasions is properly called the organism's mind because it specializes in novel behavior. It is the function of the mind to adjust to the novelties arising in the environment, to contemplate the possible alternatives of action, and to coordinate the activities of the body insofar as this is needed. The cells in my finger are perfectly capable of handling all their own homeostatic processes of oxygen-intake and tissue repair, whether my mind is awake and active or asleep, but my fingers cannot type these words without the directing agency of the mind.

Since all the cells of my body are living and feeling in interaction with my mind, political analogies may be in order. Where a tree may be a democracy, an animal is more like a constitutional monarchy. The mind is fitted by nature to reign over the body, but this political order ought not degenerate into either tyranny or anarchy. The Freudian analysis of repression, whereby the superego dimension of the mind in its rigidity suppresses all expression of bodily feeling, only to suffer abrupt and often violent emotional outbursts, follows the pattern of tyranny and revolt. The utterly uninhibited, spontaneous, aimless life of those seeking to let all their feelings express themselves illustrates the opposite danger of anarchy. The mind is meant to direct the body, but in a way which is truly responsive to the bodily feeling, i.e., to the feelings of all those actualities of the body that collectively constitute the mind's unconscious.

According to Whitehead, every sensation or perception or thought or imagining, in short, every feeling is tinged with some affective or emotional tone (technically, the subjective form of a prehension). We do not merely feel *what* we feel, but *how* we feel what we feel makes a difference: sadly or joyously, tenderly or contemptuously, calmly or angrily, boredly or excitedly, matter-of-factly or dazedly, etc. Moreover, we also feel the feelings of others in terms of the affective tones with which they were felt—so much so, that in many contexts, the words "feelings" and "emotions" are interchangeable.

Thus the emotional tones accompanying the mind's sensations or thought have at least two possible origins, and we shall distinguish them accordingly. We shall use the term "affections" in a somewhat old-fashioned sense to refer to those emotional tones originating out of the mind's own response to that which it is perceiving and contemplating, and "passions" to refer to those emotional tones the mind derives from feeling the feelings of its bodily members. Without the body we may have affections, but no passions. Passions require the mind to be passive, receptive to the feelings of others, and on those occasions when our passions are aroused the feelings of our body are insistent, incessant, clamoring for our attention. This is most dramatically evident in hunger and sex. We can eat anytime, but it is more pleasurable when we are moderately hungry, while severe hunger can seriously interfere with our intended activities by its insistent demands. Sex without love points to a dislocation or dissociation between the passions and the affections of the mind, which function best in harmony, while the sexual act cannot even be performed, let alone enjoyed, dispassionately, without arousing bodily feeling.

This may seem a long introduction for a theory of prayer, if not a downright digression, but it will be seen to be necessary in terms of our definition of prayer. *Prayer, as the feelings of creatures addressed to God, form the passions of God.* Without the feelings of his creatures, God could rule the world justly, dispassionately, as Aquinas and Spinoza suppose he does. His decisions could even be tinged with his affections: the appetitions or valuations with which God clothes his thoughts. But without creaturely feeling, God could never experience passion. The God of the philosophers may be dispassionate, but not the God of Abraham, Isaac, and Jacob. Is this merely a crude anthropomorphism of our forefathers, or does it express a deep truth our enlightened rationalism has been blind to? Depth psychology has recovered for us the importance and significance of the passions of the body for human well-being, and perhaps it is time to appreciate their role for divine well-being as well.

Dispassionate thinking is often our ideal, for our passions can interfere to distort the cool processes of reason. Moreover, for many decisions our bodily feelings are irrelevant, since they concern abstract ideas, business affairs, other people with no direct bearing upon our physical bodies. Finally, God's decisions must above all be just, and we demand of our human judges that they be totally impartial as the only way of insuring their fairness. As Hartshorne has pointed out, however, we require impartiality because we are so imperfectly partial. We tend to take sides in conflicts, denigrating the claims of the one in order to more fully empathize with the claims of the other. But God is perfectly partial to all, completely loving each of his creatures. God loves the sinner, fully empathizing with his concerns and grievances, as well as the one sinned against. God's justice is not strict adherence to abstract ideals that must be modified or ignored in the operation of his love; it is the social dimension of his love. God adjudicates among his creatures by the way in which he unifies together in a single complex harmonious feeling his feelings of total empathy with each of his creatures.

Our passions adversely affect our judgments primarily for two reasons: because of the sort of beings we are and because of the fragmentary nature of finite self-interest. Our mentality is a derivative by-product of our physical existence. Most creatures in this world have only a modicum of mentality, dominated by feelings of blind emotion. Even the human mind, the most advanced organ of novelty in the entire evolutionary process of the world so far as we know it, exists in large measure for the survival and well-being of the body, a fact we may hide from ourselves from time to time until our bodily well-being is seriously threatened. We cannot easily escape from our biological heritage, and have only recently extricated ourselves from the level of blind instinct. God, by contrast, originates out of pure conceptual thinking, as Whitehead has put it, from a primordial envisagement of all pure possibilities. Since his relation to physical actualities and the passions they engender is derivative and secondary, there is no danger for him to become the slave of passions. Our bodies also symbolize the locus of our self-interest, since we prize them above all, as Satan well knew (Job 2:4-5). As Langdon Gilkey has so ably and dramatically documented in the *Shantung Compound* (Harper & Row, 1966), our ability to judge and deliberate fairly and justly is seriously undermined whenever our basic self-interests are threatened. The more we are able to reason, the more we are able to deceive ourselves through devious and artful rationalization. "For even saintly folk will act like sinners / Unless they have their customary dinners," Bertolt Brecht reminds us in *The Threepenny Opera*. Our judgments are distorted by the fragmentary character of our self-interest, since we lavish attention and concern upon that small bit of the world which immediately affects us, often at the expense and disregard of the rest. Such distortion cannot affect God, however, if his body embraces the whole world, for then there can be no contrast between that which is his and that which remains. Divine self-interest as concern for the well-being of his body, the world, excludes nothing.

As we have mentioned, God originates out of pure conceptuality, creating himself by creating the entire realm of pure possibilities that, when integrated with his experience of the world, can serve as lures for actualization in furthering the creative advance. The formation of such pure possibilities is completely independent of what actually happens, being made "from the foundations of the world." For those decisions the feelings of his creatures are quite irrelevant, except in a very general and abstract way, just as our bodily feelings are irrelevant to many of our decisions. But all the other decisions God makes concern the specific course of the history of the world. They directly concern and involve his creatures, and hence our feelings are pertinent to God's decisions as forming the context of bodily feeling out of which he decides.

Leibniz oversimplified the relations between possibility and actuality when he supposed God simply decides between different sets of compossibilities. This would be sufficient if the transition between possibility and actuality simply requires a divine fiat calling worlds into being *ex nihilo*. But if every actuality grows out of prior actualities, the real possibilities (i.e., those possibilities capable of being actualized) must be dependent on such prior actualities. Leibniz's God can choose dispassionately among abstract possibilities, for no actual creatures are as yet involved. The God of process theism ought not to decide dispassionately concerning real possibilities, but consult the feelings of those involved.

Without the world God lacks companionship; without a body

he lacks passion, for as we have understood it, passion requires the feeling of the feelings belonging to one's bodily members. God *could* make all of his decisions dispassionately, just as he could exist in solitary splendor; but such decisions would betray a certain avoidable thinness of feeling, a lack of the multidimensionality that rationality imbued with a coordinated and integrated passion could provide.

Prayer, we have said, consists in these feelings of creatures as addressed to God. Such a definition, obviously, is much broader than what we ordinarily mean by prayer. Explicit prayer is an intentional act directed toward superior beings, usually divine, though one may pray to the emperor, and it might make sense to say that dogs may "pray" to their masters. Ordinarily, prayer is an occasional conscious undertaking, but we mean it to apply to all of our feelings, as these are felt by God. Nor do we restrict ourselves to human feelings, but include the feelings of all subhuman creatures as well. If God depended upon our conscious, explicit prayers for his passionate experience, it would be quite impoverished indeed. That experience has all the richness of feeling felt by all his creatures, everywhere and at all times.

What, then, is the function of explicit prayer? If by our very feeling we are praying to God, why should we set aside special occasions when we consciously seek to make our feelings "known" to God? These should be times for eliciting and focusing our feelings and needs in the context of the divine. Often it is only in such times that we "realize" our thankfulness and gratitude toward God, both in the sense of recognizing that we are indeed grateful and in the sense of allowing that feeling of gratitude to come to expression, to become fully formed within us. Vague, adumbrated, indefinite substrata of feeling may become articulate and full-bodied through their verbal expression in prayer. "Let Israel be glad in his Maker, let the sons of Zion rejoice in their King! . . . For the Lord takes pleasure in his people" (Psalms 149:2,4). Prayer, in focusing and expressing our joy in God, directly contributes to his pleasure, just as the direct sense of the health of our bodily members contributes to our sense of well-being.

In petitionary prayer we are reminded of our wants and needs before God. Those wants and needs are always with us, but ordinarily we do not place them within the context of divine concern and response. This all-embracing context often enables us to grasp our wants and needs in a truer perspective, while at the same time helping us to realize that these are not merely our concerns but God's as well. If our theory of prayer is correct, however, the intellectual content of our prayers has no intrinsic significance. He that searches the heart has no need to be informed of our wants and needs, but he does seek to experience our emotional response to those wants and needs. The intellectual content of prayer is instrumentally significant as a vehicle for eliciting such response. Since we are so deeply involved in our immediately felt needs, their verbal expression is frequently the most effective means for eliciting our feelings. They are more effective than the articulation of the world's problems, which may objectively be far more important and pressing than our petty concerns, but which are felt *by us* more remotely. They may on occasion be more effective than prayers of praise which, while they verbally articulate the feelings we deem are suitably addressed to God, may not elicit such feeling, or elicit it only partially. Explicit prayer, in fact, has no essential need of intellectual content provided it is capable of eliciting feeling. "Speaking in tongues" may be an effective way of praying, particularly as a way of by-passing our self-conscious inhibitions and allowing our unconscious depths of feeling to come to expression (cf. Romans 8:26).

Should God answer prayer? Clearly not in all cases, as when both sides at war pray for total victory, or when the requests made presuppose a faulty understanding of divine power. In general, however, we may say that God's response to prayer would be analogous to our response to our own passions. We do not ignore our bodily feelings lightly, for any attempt to repress them summarily is not only psychologically damaging but denies them their right to be heard. On the other hand, we do not simply yield to every passion. In responding to our bodily members we should be guided by their feelings, but not dominated by them. For the outlook of the mind is considerably more far-reaching than bodily feeling, able to foresee and reckon with consequences and alternatives in ways blind emotion is unequipped to handle. Likewise God seeks our welfare by making his decisions in terms of the widest context of relevance appropriate, but those decisions include taking into account and being receptive to the feelings of his creatures affected thereby. God's decisions are rationally made, but this intellectual aridity is fleshed out by a deep undercurrent of passionate feeling.

SUGGESTED READINGS

Brown, Delwin, James, Ralph E., Jr., Reeves, Gene, editors. *Process Philosophy and Christian Thought.* Indianapolis and New York: Bobbs-Merrill Co., Inc., 1971.

Cobb, John B. Jr. *God and the World.* Philadelphia: Westminster, 1969.

Cousins, Ewert H., editor. *Process Theology.* New York: Newman, 1971.

Hartshorne, Charles. *The Divine Relativity.* New Haven: Yale University Press, 1948.

Leclerc, Ivor. *Whitehead's Metaphysics: An Introductory Exposition.* New York: Macmillan, 1958. (Indiana Univ. Press, Midland Books, paperback, announced for spring, 1975.)